Women and their Money 1700

This book examines women's financial activity from the early days of the stock market in eighteenth-century England and the South Sea Bubble to the mid twentieth century. The essays demonstrate how many women managed their own finances despite legal and social restrictions and show that women were neither helpless, incompetent and risk-averse, nor were they unduly cautious and conservative. Rather, many women learnt about money and made themselves effective and engaged managers of the funds at their disposal.

The essays focus on Britain, from eighteenth-century London to the expansion of British financial markets of the nineteenth century, with comparative essays dealing with the United States, Italy, Sweden and Japan. Hitherto, writing about women and money has been restricted to their management of household finances or their activities as small business women. This book examines the clear evidence of women's active engagement in financial matters, much neglected in historical literature, especially women's management of capital.

This book charts the sheer extent of women's financial management and provides for economic, social, cultural and gender historians material grounded in empirical research essential for understanding women's place in capitalist societies.

Anne Laurence is Professor of History at the Open University and author of *Women in England 1500–1760: A Social History*. **Josephine Maltby** is Professor of Accounting and Finance, University of York. **Janette Rutterford** is Professor of Finance at the Open University and author of *Introduction to Stock Exchange Investment*.

Routledge international studies in business history
Series Editors: Ray Stokes and Matthias Kipping

Women and their Money 1700–1950

Essays on women and finance

**Edited by Anne Laurence,
Josephine Maltby and
Janette Rutterford**

Routledge
Taylor & Francis Group

LONDON AND NEW YORK

First published 2009
by Routledge
2 Park Square, Milton Park, Abingdon, Oxon OX14 4RN

Simultaneously published in the USA and Canada
by Routledge
711 Third Ave, New York, NY 10017

Routledge is an imprint of the Taylor & Francis Group, an informa business

First issued in paperback 2012

© 2009 Selection and editorial matter, Anne Laurence, Josephine Maltby
and Janette Rutterford; individual chapters, the contributors.

Typeset in Times by Wearset Ltd, Boldon, Tyne and Wear

British Library Cataloguing in Publication Data
A catalogue record for this book is available from the British Library

Library of Congress Cataloging in Publication Data
Women and their money 1700–1950: essays on women and finance/edited
by Anne Laurence, Josephine Maltby and Janette Rutterford.
p. cm.
Includes bibliographical references and index.
1. Women–Finance, Personal–History. 2. Finance–History. I. Laurence,
Anne. II. Maltby, Josephine. III. Rutterford, Janette.
HG179.W5765 2008
332.0240082'0903–dc22   2008025174

ISBN13: 978-0-415-41976-5 (hbk)
ISBN13: 978-0-415-54255-5 (pbk)
ISBN13: 978-0-203-88599-4 (ebk)

Contents

Figures

Tables

Contributors

John Black is a part-time Research Associate at the School of Accounting and Finance, Bristol Business School, University of the West of England. He entered academic life late, having previously served in the Regular Army (Royal Army Medical Corps and Royal Army Pay Corps) for 15 years. This was followed by a further 15 years as a secondary-school teacher in Bristol where he taught economics and business studies. John Black is conducting further research into the role of the War Office Finance Branch and army pay services during the First World War for future publication.

Ann M. Carlos is Professor of Economics at the University of Colorado and at University College, Dublin. Her current research with Professor Larry Neal focuses on the microfoundations of the London stock market in the late seventeenth and early eighteenth century. Her other research project, in collaboration with Professor Frank Lewis, analyses various aspects of the Native American economy in the Canadian sub-Arctic in the eighteenth century.

Philip L. Cottrell is Professor of Financial History at the University of Leicester and has published studies of the London capital market's mid-nineteenth-century development; Victorian industrial finance; the finance of transport improvement – railways and shipping; British overseas investment; the growth of joint-stock banking from the local level to being nationwide; and the interaction of business, politics and finance in the 'West's' involvement with east-central Europe during the inter-war period.

Mark Freeman is Lecturer in Economic and Social History at the University of Glasgow. He was educated at the Universities of Oxford and Glasgow, and has also worked at the Institute of Historical Research and the Universities of York and Hull. He has published widely on many aspects of modern British social and economic history, and is now working on a study of corporate governance in British business before 1844, co-authored with Robin Pearson and James Taylor, and to be published by the University of Chicago Press.

David R. Green teaches in the Geography Department at King's College, London. His research interests focus on a range of topics relating to the provision of welfare from the Poor Law through to various aspects of inheritance. He is currently working on an ESRC-funded collaborative project relating to wealth and shareholding in England and Wales between 1870 and 1930. His latest book, *Pauper Capital: London and the Poor Law 1790–1870* was published by Ashgate in 2008.

Naoko Komori is Lecturer in Accounting at Sheffield University Management School where she completed her PhD. Previously, she has worked in the Faculty of Economics at the University of Wakayama, Japan and at Manchester Business School. Her major research interests are in the areas of gender and accounting; the development of accounting and auditing in non-Anglo-Saxon social contexts; the changing status of auditing in Japan and its effects on corporate governance and accountability processes. Her research has recently received funding from the Japan Foundation.

Anne Laurence is Professor of History at the Open University and works on early modern women in Britain and Ireland. She has a particular interest in women and patronage and in how women paid for the objects of their patronage: clergymen, sermons, schools, houses, almshouses and churches. She also works on the development of the early stock market and, in particular, how women participated in it.

Stefania Licini is Associate Professor of Economic History at the University of Bergamo, Italy. She graduated in Economics in 1981 and completed her PhD in Economic and Social History in 1998. Her research interests focus on the economic and social history of nineteenth-century Italy. Author of a number of books, she has presented papers at several international conferences and has written articles published in Italian and English academic journals.

Karen Maguire is a PhD candidate at the University of Colorado at Boulder, with an expected graduation date of May 2010. Her previous work includes 'Financial Acumen, Women Speculators, and the Royal African Company during the South Sea Bubble' with Professors Ann Carlos and Larry Neal. She is writing her dissertation, under the direction of Professor Lee Alston, on the political economy of regulating oil and natural gas development in several Western states.

Josephine Maltby is Professor of Accounting and Finance at the York Management School, University of York. She was previously Professor of Financial Accounting at the University of Sheffield. In addition to her work on the history of women as investors, she researches the history of accounting and corporate governance and accounting within the British Empire.

Larry Neal is Professor Emeritus of Economics, University of Illinois at Urbana-Champaign, Visiting Professor, London School of Economics and Research Associate at the National Bureau of Economic Research. His research interests include monetary and financial history, European economic history and the economics of the European Union. He is past president of the

Economic History Association and the Business History Conference. From 1981 to 1998, he was editor of *Explorations in Economic History*. He is author of *The Rise of Financial Capitalism: International Capital Markets in the Age of Reason*, Cambridge University Press, 1990; *The Economics of the European Union and the Economies of Europe*, Oxford University Press, 1998; co-author (with Rondo Cameron) of *A Concise Economic History of the World*, 4th edn, Oxford University Press, 2002; and *The Economics of Europe and the European Union*, Cambridge University Press, 2007, as well as numerous articles on American and European economic and financial history. His current research, funded by two NSF grants, deals with development of microstructure in securities markets and risk management in the first emerging markets.

Lucy A. Newton, BA, PhD, is a Lecturer in the Department of Management, University of Reading. She previously held positions at the University of Leicester and the University of East Anglia. She was a Council member of the Association of Business Historians 1997–2000 and was elected as a Trustee of the Business History Conference, serving from 2004 to 2007. Lucy has published on a variety of areas of British financial history including the development of early joint-stock banks; trust and banking in the nineteenth century; banking and industrial finance in the inter-war period; female investment in the early nineteenth century; and capital networks in industrial regions. She is currently researching bank marketing and public relations in the twentieth century.

Robin Pearson is Professor of Economic History at the University of Hull. He was educated at the universities of Edinburgh and Leeds. He has published widely on various aspects of British and international economic and business history, with a particular focus on the insurance industry. In 2002 he won the Harvard-Newcomen Prize for best article in business history. His most recent book, *Insuring the Industrial Revolution*, won the 2004 Wadsworth Prize for Business History. He is currently working on a study of corporate governance in British business before 1844, co-authored with Mark Freeman and James Taylor, and to be published by the University of Chicago Press.

Tom Petersson is Associate Professor at the Department of Economic History, Uppsala University. One of his research areas is the development of the Swedish financial system. He is currently involved in research projects concerning the Swedish financial revolution in the late nineteenth and early twentieth centuries and the development of Stockholm as a financial centre for the Swedish economy.

Nancy Marie Robertson, BA, MA, PhD, is Associate Professor of History and the Director of Women's Studies at Indiana University, Purdue University Indianapolis. She holds an appointment in the Philanthropic Studies Program and is a Fellow with the Center for the Study of Religion and American Culture. She has had a variety of public history positions, including as

Assistant Director of the Margaret Sanger Papers Project and Consulting Historian for the JP Morgan Chase Archives. Her research interests include women; voluntary associations; and social change. She is the author of *Christian Sisterhood, Race, Relations, and the YWCA, 1906–46*, University of Illinois Press, 2007.

Eve Rosenhaft is Professor of German Historical Studies at the University of Liverpool. She studied at McGill University and the University of Cambridge, and has held fellowships in Britain, Germany and the United States. She has published widely on aspects of German social history since the eighteenth century, including labour, gender, urban culture and issues of race and ethnicity, as well as on financial culture and early life insurance.

Janette Rutterford is Professor of Financial Management at the Open University Business School. Her research interests include both modern finance issues, such as pension-fund investment strategies and equity valuation, as well as the history of investment, in particular that of women investors. She is currently working on an ESRC-funded collaborative project relating to wealth and shareholding in England and Wales between 1870 and 1930, as well as the history of new issues.

Claire Swan, MA (Hons) MPhil, is a PhD student in History at the University of Dundee. Her doctoral thesis on the Scottish investment trust industry is funded by the Carnegie Trust and is expected to be completed in 2008. She has worked as a research assistant at Queen Mary College, University of London, and has published her undergraduate dissertation as *Scottish Cowboys and the Dundee Investors*, Abertay Historical Society, 2004. A version of her Master's thesis was published in *Scottish Archives* 13, 2007. She has presented her research both nationally and internationally.

James Taylor is Lecturer in History at Lancaster University. He was educated at the University of Kent. His book, *Creating Capitalism: Joint-Stock Enterprise in British Politics and Culture, 1800–1870*, was published in 2006, and he is the author of several articles exploring aspects of British economic and cultural history. He is currently working on a study of corporate governance in British business before 1844, co-authored with Mark Freeman and Robin Pearson, and to be published by the University of Chicago Press.

Stephen P. Walker, BA, PhD, CA, is Professor in Accounting at Cardiff University and was previously Professor of Accounting History at Edinburgh University. He has held visiting positions in Australia and New Zealand. He was President of the Academy of Accounting Historians in 2007 and editor of *Accounting Historians Journal*, 2001–2005. He is a former Convenor of the Accounting History Committee of ICAS and Academic Fellow of the ICAEW. He has published widely on the history of accounting and gender, social identity and the accountancy profession. In 2005 he received the Hourglass Award of the Academy of Accounting Historians. He is a member of the editorial boards of a number of journals in accounting and accounting history.

Christine Wiskin worked in industry, the civil service and the law before becoming a mature student. She studied for an ESRC-funded doctorate in History at the University of Warwick where she taught modern British and world history. She also taught women's studies and history at the University of Gloucestershire, as well as lecturing and publishing on eighteenth-century English businesswomen. She is now an independent scholar, researching aspects of business history in eighteenth- and nineteenth-century provincial England.

Susan M. Yohn is a Professor of History at Hofstra University in Hempstead, New York. Her work has focused on women religious reformers, their organisations, and more recently on women and money. She is the author of *A Contest of Faiths: Missionary Women and Pluralism in the American South-west*, Cornell University Press, 1995 and 'Crippled Capitalists: The Inscription of Economic Dependence and the Challenge of Female Entrepreneurship in Nineteenth-Century America', *Feminist Economics* 12 (1–2), January–April 2006, pp. 85–109.

1 Introduction

*Anne Laurence, Josephine Maltby and
Janette Rutterford*

Historians working in social and economic history and in women's and gender history usually discuss the economics of women's lives in terms of poverty, powerlessness and absence of money and of waged and unwaged work. Women's financial affairs have made little impact on accounting history, business history or financial history. Where moneyed women have attracted notice, historians' views have been highly gendered. W.D. Rubinstein's study of the very wealthy in Britain since the industrial revolution excludes women 'because of the haphazard nature of inheritance of large fortunes by women in England and the difficulties of tracing biographical details of their lives'.[1] The very small number of women who were wealthier than their husbands or fathers, he argues, probably owed their funds either to tax-avoidance schemes or to 'shrewd investment and cautious spending by the heiress or her advisors'.[2] He notes the small number of women who made business fortunes, and also the small number of inherited industrial fortunes by comparison with fortunes derived from commerce or land.[3] His views are not surprising in view of the kind of attention given to the wealthy in the nineteenth-century press. In 1872, the *Spectator* published a list naming the 124 individuals who had left £250,000 or more at death between 1861 and 1871; this included five women, of whom one was a noted heiress and political hostess, two appeared in lists of charitable donors from time to time, and the other two made virtually no public impact.[4]

In contrast to the work of economists and economic historians, who consider the market to be gender neutral, has been that of literary scholars and cultural historians who have discussed whether the market itself was gendered. Following J.G.A. Pocock, many scholars have commented on the representation of credit as a woman and the feminisation of the market. Catherine Ingrassia's work has explored the representation of women as sexually and financially rapacious in their participation in the South Sea Bubble, while E.J. Clery has shown how women featured disproportionately in the backlash that followed the Bubble.[5]

Introducing the concept of gender challenges ideas about the nature of rationality and whether women can reasonably be conceptualised as 'emotional' economic actors in contrast to 'rational' economic men. If the market is 'rational' can it really be gender neutral? The work of feminist economists and philosophers considers women's capabilities, repudiating the notion common to both Western and non-Western societies, that women are emotional and that emotions are feminine and the enemies of reason.[6] Martha Nussbaum has convincingly demonstrated that emotions do not arise from women's nature, rather from the circumstances of many women's lives.[7] Furthermore, what might seem rational in the twenty-first century often did not seem so in the eighteenth or nineteenth centuries: considerations that might be important to us may have been insignificant in past times. For example, we are increasingly concerned with the consequences of longevity for our own financial futures; before the twentieth century there was the likelihood of death at a relatively young age often occurring speedily and unexpectedly, though whether 'the brevity and uncertainty' of life, as Richard Dale suggests, increased the attraction of get-rich-quick commercial ventures is debatable.[8]

At the same time, assumptions about women's incapacity have inclined both historians and present-day commentators to treat women's financial management as conservative and averse to undue risk, directed at providing income rather than trading gains or capital growth. As Laurence and Carlos and Neal have shown for the eighteenth century and Rutterford and Maltby for the nineteenth century, women were present and active in financial markets, and, while many of them did require an income, they were also active traders.[9]

The women who make up the subject matter of this book include a few who were numbered among the very rich of their time, but the majority were prosperous upper-class women living on incomes provided by their families, or middle-class women engaged in managing their own finances or running businesses. Many of the women who appear on these pages had to take an active interest in their own finances because they did not have much money. Within the household, married and unmarried women were concerned with income and expenditure. The development of banks, the stock market, government debt and a host of financial 'products' such as bonds and lottery tickets required middle-class as well as wealthier women to make judgements and decisions about how to dispose of their funds. The growing numbers of women in waged work required women further down the social scale to take an active interest in pensions and savings.

Common to the women who people these pages was the experience of possessing or acquiring money and looking after it themselves, and of gathering knowledge and experience in doing so, frequently in the face of legal disabilities and social disapprobation. So this book seeks to chart, in a variety of settings, the extent of women's financial activity, and to explore how they acquired their knowledge and used it to manage their financial affairs. While we do not explicitly consider arguments about emotion, women's nature and economic rationality, many of the chapters look at how women's financial actions made sense in the particular circumstances in which they found themselves. Perhaps the most important story told by the studies in this book is that, despite the different legal regimes under which women lived, women took control of their affairs within existing constraints which usually permitted little financial independence for married women and limited independence for unmarried or widowed women. So a significant theme of this book is women's agency.

The chapters in this book are concerned with two broad themes: one is women's command of financial and investment knowledge and the other is investment behaviour. They identify key features of women's financial and investment behaviour for the various periods and territories with which they are concerned, the significant factors influencing it, and the implications for our understanding of women's role as investors. Many of the chapters deal with Britain, which, after the Netherlands, had the earliest financial markets. Chapters on other countries show how differences in legal systems, in marriage practices and in financial institutions could have an impact upon women's experience.

So this book is concerned with some of the many ways in which women engaged with understanding and managing their own finances in the period covering the start of the stock market in England, the enactment of Married Women's Property Acts in the nineteenth century, the integration of women into the waged workforce as factory, service and office workers, and the impact of the First World War, with comparative studies from Sweden, Japan, Germany, Italy and the United States. It offers the view that women were active in the stock market and in other forms of financial management, that it is possible to quantify this activity, and that they were competent economic actors. This introduction is concerned with the context for women and finance in Britain and with some of the general issues raised by a discussion of these subjects over such a long period. Separate introductions to the sections provide historical context.

Gender

We know a good deal about men's financial affairs, their attitudes to risk, their participation in the market, and the professionalisation of banking, stockbroking and accounting. Men are generally assumed to outnumber women so overwhelmingly that women's financial behaviour scarcely signifies or is merely supplementary to men's. When women are considered, they are taken to be conservative both in choice of investments and in their management, and women making business decisions are considered not to be risk-takers. Women played little part in the emergence of the financial professions; they were, for example, excluded from membership of the professional organisation of chartered accountants in England and Wales until 1919 and from the floor of the London stock exchange until 1973.[10] But set against this is the 'law', enunciated by the economic historian Joan Thirsk, that:

> whenever new openings have appeared in the English scene, whether in crafts, or in trade, and, in the modern world, in new academic endeavours, or in the setting up of new organisations in the cultural field, women have usually been prominent alongside men, sometimes even out-numbering them.... But that situation has only lasted until the venture has been satisfactorily and firmly established ... when [it] fall[s] under the control of men.[11]

This might prompt us to look at women's participation in the financial revolution of the early eighteenth century in a different light. It might, too, suggest that subsequent developments in financial markets, in the professionalisation of investment and accounting, in the concept of the portfolio, the development of savings schemes and in attitudes to risk, deserve examination to see whether women and men acted and reacted in the same way. Attitudes to investment and speculation influence the definition of sensible financial management by men and women: the great growth in the share-owning population of Britain after 1870 required that putting money into the stock market be conceptualised in some way that emphasised its prudence rather than its risk; investment for income was acceptable, and, as Itzkowitz puts it, speculation was domesticated.[12]

But the purpose of the chapters in this volume is not merely to fill in a missing piece of history, it is also to draw attention to the fact that financial behaviour takes many different forms. Women are one of the sub-sets of investors that are easiest to identify. Gender, apart from its intrinsic significance, offers a way of identifying a group of financial actors who might be supposed to have common interests or characteristics that influence their financial behaviour. Certainly it is easier, in a list of customers, shareholders or employees, to distinguish men from women, in a way that is extremely difficult and time-consuming to do with such characteristics as age, wealth or marital status.[13]

In the early days of trading in stock, the press identified women as being foolish and short-sighted gamblers, primarily on the basis of women's supposed nature rather than their actual behaviour.[14] Newspapers such as the *London Journal* reported at the time of the South Sea Bubble in 1720 that 'The ladies have mortgaged their pin money', had stopped buying clothing and ornaments and that such was the frenzy that 'there is not a pawnbroker in London of any figure that has any money left'.[15] At the same time, journalists noted the names of women who had made fortunes in trading stock. Historians have not necessarily done much to dispel this reputation for irresponsibility. Malcolm Balen, for example, writes of women throwing themselves at John Law for shares in the early-eighteenth-century Mississippi scheme.[16] But what startled commentators at the time of the South Sea Bubble was the visibility of women's participation.

In reality, women had been significant investors as early as 1685 and were able legally to deal in the market because, being a new phenomenon, no one had thought to exclude them.[17] P.G.M. Dickson, writing on the eighteenth-century financial revolution in England before the impact of second-wave feminism, identified women as one of the groups worthy of attention (though they do not qualify for an entry in his index) – around one-fifth of the investors in a variety of different forms of stock and government debt were women.[18] Alice Clare Carter noted that 'women investors [in the eighteenth century] seem to have been much more capable than is generally believed'.[19] Alongside the idea of women as emotional and irrational speculators, as the use of the market spread, they were conceptualised as cautious, risk-averse investors interested in income rather than trading gains.

Under English common law, single women (whether spinsters or widows) had virtually the same rights over property as men; the position was very different for married women.[20] So a woman's capacity to operate independently in affairs of property and finance was much affected by her marital status. In considering gender, finance and property, gender is not a single category of analysis. Married Women's Property Acts, passed at different times in the various common-law jurisdictions during the nineteenth century, gave married women rights over property they brought to the marriage and property they acquired during it, but few of them at first pass gave married women rights comparable to those of women without husbands.[21]

Gender also provides an interesting, if sometimes difficult, basis for comparison between countries. The difficulties arise from differences in legal rights, especially in relation to women's capacity to own and freely to dispose of property, to dowries and to dower, and also from uneven economic development between countries.

Class

The chapters in this volume covering earlier periods deal with upper- and middle-class women, since these were the women who had money to dispose of. They extend the work started by Peter Earle on the middle classes in late-seventeenth- and early-eighteenth-century London that alerted historians to the idea that women not only ran businesses, but also owned capital.[22] He demonstrates that middle-class London citizens between 1660 and 1720 increased their investment in government debt by 400 per cent, while their ownership of stocks and bonds rose by a mere 30 per cent, but he also notes that the greatest exposure to stock was among the richest citizens. Poorer people put their money into leases, loans and government debt.[23] He does not break down these figures by gender, but he does suggest that women were as much a part of this financial transformation as men. Most landed families until well into the nineteenth century used non-land assets for limited and temporary purposes, to lodge money for short periods or to provide an assured income.[24]

Women and credit in early modern England have been the subject of historians' attention for some time.[25] Judith Spicksley notes that their ownership of credit was characterised by dispersing the risk by making numerous small short-term loans to relatives and neighbours and that by 1700 lending by single women had become a more formal business, and was increasingly likely to be secured by a formal credit instrument.[26] Earlier strictures against usury had been abandoned and the most objectionable feature of money-lending was to charge *excessive* interest.[27] Indeed, it was almost a Christian duty to ensure that the money of those who were incapable (orphans, widows, the physically or mentally incapacitated) was carefully managed.[28] Margaret Hunt, looking at middle-class finances, suggests that families continued to be a vital source of capital for business throughout the eighteenth century and that lending institutions did not become significant until the nineteenth century.[29]

The work by Leonore Davidoff and Catherine Hall on men and women of the English middle class has been immensely influential. They subscribe to the view that middle-class women in the nineteenth century were increasingly defined by their inactivity, providing 'hidden investment' in family businesses as business and family affairs were increasingly differentiated.[30] They describe a world in which marriage structured the meaning of property for both men and women.[31] They also see the development of separate spheres – one public and male, the other private and female – as coincident with the development of industrial capitalism. All this was dependent upon a general increase in wealth that 'enabled dependent women to be supported while keeping their capital in circulation'.[32] The implication of the development of the domestic ideology was that women would work for wages or run a business only when forced to do so by the absence of male support.

The rare women who owned and managed substantial and successful businesses, such as Sarah Child, who ran Child's Bank after her husband's death in 1782, or Lady Charlotte Guest, who ran the Dowlais ironworks from 1852 to 1855, have been the subject of occasional studies, but are commonly viewed as dogs walking on their hind legs. There were a few large-scale and unsuccessful women's enterprises such as those of Lady Mary Herbert who, having ventured and lost a large sum of money in John Law's Mississippi scheme in the 1720s, lost a further fortune in a silver mine speculation, and Sarah Clayton who, having successfully turned round her brother-in-law's failing colliery in the 1740s and 1750s, overstretched herself with her own colliery and was declared bankrupt shortly before her death in 1779.[33]

Recently, several studies of women who ran smaller businesses have appeared and have challenged the stereotype of women's businesses as small-scale, temporary and undercapitalised.[34] Christine Wiskin's chapter discusses three businesswomen: Eleanor Coade, the manufacturer of architectural ceramics; Charlotte Matthews, banker and bill-broker; and Jane Tait, dress-maker and milliner. Women have traditionally operated businesses in spaces unoccupied by men and, especially in pre-industrial economies, primarily in the textiles and clothing trades, the second-hand trades and pawnbroking, victualling and service industries.[35] Peter Earle notes that women were more likely to be creditors than debtors in London bankruptcy cases in late-seventeenth- and early-eighteenth-century London.[36] Women were essential to the development of the new eighteenth-century trades serving the growing population of consumers and exploiting opportunities offered by urban sociability, and they continued to work in these trades in the nineteenth century.[37] The conclusion of these studies is that women were active in more trades, were often operating at a higher financial level and in a wider variety of different kinds of partnership, and continued to be active further into the era of separate spheres in the nineteenth century than is suggested by Davidoff and Hall.[38]

The volume of writing on middle-class and propertied women is small by comparison with writing on women's place in the workforce – whether waged or unwaged – which has dominated studies of the economic position of women.

The development of capitalism has been seen primarily in terms of industrial capitalism, the force that created the industrial revolution and restructured the working lives of lower-class men and women, imposed time discipline, wage dependence, urbanisation and new attitudes to skills, as well as changes in social and family relationships. Following Alice Clark's book of 1919 and Ivy Pinchbeck's of 1930, historians of women in Britain have divided into pessimists who see the industrial revolution as having caused a deterioration in women's position, and optimists, who see it as having created the conditions for women's emancipation.[39] Works of gender history primarily treat women as participants in household economies or as subjects of capitalist employers.[40] The labour history background of many historians of post-industrial-revolution women's work, and the wider influence of socialist feminism, has focused their attention on women as employees, and their relations with employers and with men in the workplace. There is a consensus that women were essential to the process of industrialisation and that its effects had different consequences for men and for women.[41]

But there is little in the literature that touches upon women who put their money into capitalist enterprises, whether as large-scale investors or as working women looking for a return on their savings. Studies of savings have tended to concentrate on friendly societies and the cooperative movement and such small-scale schemes as Christmas clubs.[42]

Coverture and women's real and personal property

Married women under English common law were prevented by the legal doctrine of *feme coverte* (coverture) from owning land (real property), but widows and spinsters (as *feme sole*) owned it on exactly the same terms as men.[43] Personal property (rents, mortgage income, stocks and shares, jewellery, etc.) were also subject to the husband's control. Only pin money was the wife's own, though in practice household goods and linen were treated as the wife's property (paraphernalia). There were, as we shall see, a variety of ways in which coverture could be circumvented and by the time of the Married Women's Property Act in 1870 which abolished coverture in England and Wales, these were very widely used. It was not, however, until the Married Women's Property Act of 1882 that married women acquired over their property the same rights as women without husbands.[44] The effects of the Acts have been much debated but it seems that the disposition of married women's wealth was significantly affected by them. Until the first Act, women were more likely to hold real property than personal property; although neither they nor their husbands had free disposal of the real property. Women who married after 1870 (the first to whom the Act applied) held much more of their property as personal property – savings and investments – over which they now had a suitable degree of control.[45] A further effect was that many more women had to make wills. A subject for future research must be a comparative study of the investment decisions of women before and after the Married Women's Property Act.

At the beginning of the period to be studied in this book, dowries or marriage contracts were usual. Under these, property passed from the bride and/or her family to the husband in return for legally enforceable provision for widowhood. Amy Louise Erickson has demonstrated convincingly that marriage settlements were widely used, and not solely by the rich and landed, to reserve part of the estate to wives personally (separate estate) or to provide a jointure (maintenance for widowhood beyond the custom of dower which gave a widow a life interest in one-third of her late husband's real property).[46] Separate estate developed as a way of preserving the wife's family's interest in property and was often used on remarriage by widows with children.[47] Although married women's separate estate was not recognised under English *common* law it was recognised by Chancery which did not acknowledge the existence of coverture.[48]

Provision for widowhood was not necessarily provision for old age; in eighteenth- and nineteenth-century Britain there were many young widows: the single-parent family was as common as it is today but for the reason that marriages were abbreviated by the early death of one of the parents (divorce was virtually impossible). And single-parent families were more likely to have female than male heads not least because widowers showed a more marked preference for remarriage.[49]

In 1833 the custom of dower, intended to provide for widows, was abolished. In practice it had already been superseded by many varieties of trust and by various Acts of Parliament that allowed men to dispose of their personal estates by their wills, notwithstanding the custom of setting aside certain portions for widows and children.[50] Of particular concern, given that many widows had to bring up young children, was an assured income. By the nineteenth century separate estate had to be managed by trustees and was for the sole use of the wife.[51] The trust, including the marriage settlement, continued in popularity throughout the nineteenth century, even to the point, as Chantal Stebbings suggests, of being an integral part of Victorian society, used by 'gentlemen, clerks in holy orders, butchers, printers, merchants and yeomen [who] were typical of the range of middle-class settlors', as well as by landed aristocrats.[52] Morris has concluded that trusts 'took women out of active participation in the economy' because they were made dependent on income from capital which was managed by trustees.[53] But the terms of trusts varied: the life tenant's ability to influence the trustees' behaviour might be 'imperative' rather than merely 'discretionary'; Morris himself quotes the example of a widowed Leeds woman in the mid nineteenth century writing regularly to her trustees about her investment and loans and the quality of the latest railway share issues.[54]

The Victorian trust, which might be testamentary or *inter vivos*, was a continuation of the forms of marriage settlement and jointure developed to circumvent the terms of dower. Testamentary settlements often took the form of a fund with income to the widow, and the remainder to the children. The *inter vivos* trust was often a marriage settlement, typically a capital sum of between £2,000 and £10,000 invested in, for example, consolidated bank annuities with the income devolving on the survivor, then to the issue of marriage as appointed, or vesting when they reached the age of 21 or married.[55] There was the continuing risk that the widow might find herself in financial distress as her growing off-spring made increasing demands on her, and she might need to change her investment behaviour accordingly. *Blackwood's* magazine in 1876, for instance, described the plight of the widow left 'with £5,000 and a rising family' compelled to move the money from government or railway loans in the hope of a higher return from 'more highly priced loan stocks which are the refuge of the widow, the clergyman and the reckless'.[56]

Real property (land) was not subject to coverture, but a wife could not alter, rent or dispose of land or buildings without her husband's consent. Until 1898 no real property was included in English probate valuations, which means that it is almost impossible to estimate how much land women owned or how much income they derived from it.[57] In the 1870s and 1880s John Bateman published lists of the 2,500 landowners with 3,000 acres and an income of more than £3,000 a year: of these, women made up about 5 per cent.[58] The social cachet that attached to landownership was of less significance for women than for men; for many the possession of land was merely an interlude in its transmission from one man to another. During the period of this study the price of land rose but its yield fell. In 1700 the usual price of land was 20 years' purchase, i.e. 20 times its annual yield of 5 per cent. Despite the increase in other investment opportunities in the eighteenth century, demand for land remained high but, with less land available to buy, the price rose to 30 years' purchase, giving a yield of less than 3 per cent.[59] By the late nineteenth century the instability of the estate market, as a result of war and the introduction of Death Duties in 1894, made land a much less attractive option unless it had potential for mineral extraction or industrial development or was in a neighbourhood where urban development was possible.

The significance of landownership also changed over the period. The wealth of eighteenth-century peers was held primarily in land rather than stock or government debt.[60] With the greater safety of mortgages and loans on personal bonds, the development of the capital market and the fall in the interest rate, landowners borrowed on the security of land. So women's income derived from land (normally from settlements made to landowners' daughters and widows) was increasingly commuted into securities bought on loans secured on land.[61] For the longer term, such people more commonly put money into mortgages that were secure and yielded a higher return than land.[62] The decline in the amount of government stock available in the mid nineteenth century (a consequence of the country not being at war) meant that there was a greater interest in equities: in the 1820s chiefly insurance, gas, water and canal companies; in the 1830s and 1840s in railways.[63] An expanding range of homes for money included government funds, bonds of foreign and colonial governments and foreign railways.[64] Alongside the wealthy landowners was a growing class of well-off people whose estates were made up primarily of personal property. From 1714 the usury rate in England – the rate of return on mortgages, bonds and private debts – was limited to 5 per cent. Government debt, however, was not constrained by this regulation, nor were rent charges or interest on land.[65] Government debt generally provided a lower rate of return but it was more secure and more liquid than private debt and lacked the disadvantages of landowning.

Charting women's presence in finance

Women generally constitute between 5 and 15 per cent of the total population of businesspeople, investors, bank customers or financial decision-makers discussed in this volume.[66] However, a common finding is that although the value of women's participation in different kinds of economic life tends to be lower per capita than that of men, there seem to be few, if any, economic spheres from which women were completely absent. The authors see women as agents in financial affairs despite the legal and social disabilities under which they found themselves.

To manage their finances women needed knowledge, and the processes by which they acquired and applied it form one of the themes of the volume. In England, share prices were published in the newspapers from the late seventeenth century; more specialist services were provided by the development of a business press.[67] Although there have been studies of how business professionals learned to use emerging institutions – the stock market and banking – none has addressed the question of how non-professionals in general and women in particular acquired and applied knowledge of these new vehicles.[68] The extent and range of women's financial presence makes it quite clear that they had this knowledge, though how far they exercised it themselves, rather than through bankers, brokers and trustees is hard to estimate. During the nineteenth century the amount of financial information available in the press expanded to match the increase in investment opportunities – by 1824 there were 624 joint-stock companies – and by the 1840s a new kind of financial journalism aimed at middle-class family readers joined the specialist press.[69] While newspapers for the general reader included money columns, specialist newspapers such as *The Railway Bell and London Family Newspaper*, 3 January 1846, included a 'Column for the Fair Sex' with 'Fashions for the Week'.[70] Prospectuses for new financial products started to mention women, and their presence at investment company meetings was noted as, for example, at the annual meeting of the Fourth City Mutual Investment and Building Society in 1869 and the Oxford Building and Investment Company in 1883.[71]

While knowledge was available to women, they were nevertheless regarded as at risk of making terrible mistakes in financial matters. The early stock market was presented as an alternative form of work for middle-class women, but as an extension of gaming for upper-class women.[72] It was taken for granted that men speculated, though few took the risks described by Anthony Trollope's character Auguste Melmotte. Melmotte was supposedly based on the company promoter Baron Grant (1830–99) who exploited the gullibility of clergy, widows and other 'small yet hopeful investors', and with the proceeds built the largest private mansion for its time in London which was demolished by his creditors in 1883.[73]

There are a number of methodological problems arising from the fact that it is usually very much harder to obtain detailed information about women's finances than men's, especially for earlier periods. Married women's money was commonly inseparable from their husbands' and, while there are a good many women's account books and wills, it is often difficult to reconstruct from them either the whole amount or the constitution of the entire portfolio of money and property owned by the account-keeper. Many women's finances were conducted through trusts or male agents, which makes it even harder to detect the composition and value of their holdings. Nevertheless, it will be apparent that the authors of the chapters in this volume have used a wide variety of different kinds of source, and both quantitative and qualitative methods, to explore women's financial activities.

The majority of the women who form the subject of these chapters were unmarried or widowed. As some of the chapters show, married women could evade some of the restrictions placed on their ownership of property and their management of wealth, but for most of the period covered by this book it is difficult to recover much detail about their financial activities. Both spinsters and widows were likely to be poorer than their male counterparts. Many widows had only a life interest in property which at their death would return to the late husband's family. Since the property usually went to the widow's children this was not necessarily an exceptionable arrangement, but it certainly limited widows' freedom of action and can be seen as an extension of the convention of *feme coverte*.

Women and account-keeping

A connection between women's ability to run their own businesses and to make or at least understand their own investments is provided by their understanding of accounting. It is clear that women from the Middle Ages onwards were accustomed to keep records of household expenditure and were assisted in doing so by advice books. Christine de Pisan wrote in the fifteenth century of the need for women to supervise their revenues and expenses, not hesitating to enquire for details of their agents and paymasters, and reviewing their records.

> Wives should be wise and sound administrators and manage their affairs well.... They should have all the responsibility of the administration and know how to make use of their revenues and possessions.... [A wife] ought to know how much her annual income is and how much the revenue from her land is worth ... and try to keep to such a standard of living as their income can provide and not so far above it that at the year end they find themselves in debt.[74]

Advice books, manuals of husbandry and housekeeping all preached the virtues of thrift and keeping accounts. The themes remain similar from the seventeenth to the twentieth centuries. The Marquis of Halifax, after offering lengthy guidance about religion and husbands, remarked in his advice to his daughter that

The art of laying out money widely, is not attained without a great deal of thought; and it is yet more difficult in the case of a wife, who is accountable to her husband for her mistakes in it: it is not only his money, his credit too is at stake.[75]

More or less contemporary with him, Hannah Wolley emphasised the importance of writing, arithmetic and accounting in girls' education.[76] A 'banker's daughter' in 1863 published *A Guide to the Unprotected* exhorting women to keep accounts and likening those who did not do so to someone at sea without a chart.[77] The author of works on jam-making and housecraft also published in 1903 a manual of financial advice for women containing instructions on how to read a company prospectus and the difference between 'safe' and 'speculative' investments.[78]

In the household economies of the sixteenth and seventeenth centuries women were close to the world of work and to the finances of business. Ingrained habits of accounting owed their origins not only to a belief in prudent financial management but also to the exercises in spiritual accounting and self-examination that were such an important part of the worlds of godly men and women in the seventeenth century. Amanda Vickery, writing about middle-class women in the eighteenth century, devotes a chapter to their 'Prudent economy'. They had to be active as managers, needing to keep extensive written records about purchases, stores and wages; in a genteel household, with a staff of up to ten the norm, these were important expenses to control.[79] Such account-keeping was part of what Vickery calls 'the exercise of power', and played a major social and economic role for women who were not in the world of waged work. Finn points out the extent in the eighteenth and nineteenth centuries to which diaries and autobiographies dealt with exchanges of goods and money – purchases, loans and gifts: 'Like novels, diaries and autobiographies trace their genealogy to the account book, and share that genre's preoccupation with calculations of the individual's fluctuating balance of personal debits and credits.'[80] The separation between household and money-making activities that took place with industrialisation for men was much less sharp for women.

Women's lives: expectations and work *c.*1700–*c.*1950

This volume covers a period not normally considered as a whole by historical demographers of England, who divide it at 1851 with the appearance of the first reliable national census data. Until that year, population history relies primarily upon baptism, marriage and burial registers for the Church of England, supplemented after 1837 by civil registration of births, marriages and deaths. Although we present below a brief account of the population changes over the period 1700–1950, it is important to remember that it was only from the middle of the nineteenth century that knowledge of these figures had an impact upon either human behaviour or policy-making.

There is a complicated connection between demographic trends and human behaviour. We all, for example, recognise that there is a greater likelihood that we will survive to the age of 90 than our grandparents. But for at least half the period covered by this book there were no national statistics for births, deaths or life expectancy. People's behaviour was influenced by the life events that overtook those around them. It was observable that many children did not survive to adulthood, that many parents died leaving young families. Time-honoured custom, reinforced by the law, made provision for widows. (A widower, by virtue of the marriage taking place, already had the right to his deceased wife's property unless there was a settlement.) Families recognised the unpredictability of life events but there is little evidence that families planned for particular contingencies. Life insurance companies began operations in the late seventeenth century but taking out a life insurance policy was regarded as a kind of gambling and relied upon very rough and ready estimates of risk.[81] However, by the middle of the nineteenth century, Victorian social statistics derived from the census began to influence policy-makers and thus people's behaviour.

Throughout the period covered by the book women's life expectancy was greater than men's by a couple of years. Overall life expectancy at birth for men and women together rose from mid-30s in 1701 to early 40s in 1871 (Wrigley and Schofield's figures do not distinguish between men and women).[82] Figures compiled later show that for those born in 1841, male life expectancy at birth was 39 years, female 42 years; for those born in 1901 it had risen to 51 and 58 years of age respectively; and from age 58 in 1901 female life expectancy rose to age 72 in 1931.[83]

The chances of death in childhood or young adulthood were very much greater before the early twentieth century; generally it is reasonable to say that if a woman survived tuberculosis in her teens or 20s, her first pregnancy and late pregnancy she had a reasonable expectation of living to at least 60.[84] It is worth dwelling on these statistics because many of the women who are the subjects of chapters in this book were unmarried or widowed; with life-expectancy figures such as these there were many young widows. However, it is wrong to assume, because the average life expectancy at birth was low, that people's lives were somehow accelerated and that they acquired the qualities of old age faster than people do nowadays.

Marriages in England in 1700 conformed to a pattern common to north-western Europe: plebeian women frequently left home in their early or mid-teens and worked in farms or households, usually in some form of domestic service, saving money until they married in their mid-20s. Higher-status women brought money or property from their family to the marriage. Men were normally about 18 months older than the women they married. The mean age of marriage for both men and women fell during the eighteenth century from late 20s and by the early nineteenth century it was down to the early 20s with a significant number of marriages taking place between people in their teens.[85] In the second half of the nineteenth century the age rose to 25–26 and it continued to rise until the 1920s.[86] A high age of marriage means that even a poor woman is likely to have some property when she marries, savings from her paid work rather than a dowry from her family. A lower age of marriage tends to mean that poverty is a much greater problem in early married life when children are being born and the wife cannot undertake paid work.

Demographers note that a high age of marriage is often accompanied by a high proportion of people never marrying.[87] In the 1690s, 16–18 per cent of people of marriageable age did not marry, by comparison with 5–7 per cent in the late eighteenth century. Around 10 per cent of the population in the early nineteenth century never married, a figure that rose to 20 per cent in the second half of the century when the age of marriage began to rise.[88] The 1851 census and subsequent censuses drew attention to fact that unmarried women were more numerous than unmarried men and that their numbers were rising.[89] The low rate of nuptiality between 1871 and 1911 meant that the proportion of never-married women increased relative to the proportion of widows.[90] There were marked regional variations: in Hampstead, a prosperous middle-class London suburb, in 1861 less than 28 per cent of women were married, compared with 64 per cent in the working-class district of Poplar.[91] The number of 'surplus' women continued to rise during the twentieth century, from 1.3 million in 1911 to 1.7 million in 1931. Between 1914 and 1950 the incidence of marriage rose continuously, the shortage of husbands for women of the generation to marry during or soon after the First World War making surprisingly little difference.[92]

Though the Victorians wrote as if the 'surplus women' question was an entirely new social problem, spinsters were not a novelty; the census merely made the numbers visible, creating something of a moral panic, which perhaps says more about male attitudes to unattached women than about demographic realities.[93] Politicians, policy-makers and commentators, working on the assumption that a 'natural' gender balance in the population was parity of numbers of men and women, and comparing England with settler societies in the United States and the British colonies where men greatly exceeded women in number, sought 'solutions' to the 'problem'. Unmarried lower-class women were assumed to have gainful employment in factories and domestic service, so it was believed that the 'surplus' of women was predominantly middle-class.[94] The lack of employment for middle-class women created concern about how the 'thousands and thousands of destitute educated women [who] have to earn their daily bread' could survive.[95] But, though single women were seen by their contemporaries as 'doomed to an unhappily penniless and lonely existence', the 1881 census report showed that the numbers of unmarried woman were highest in towns which had substantial middle-class and leisured population.[96] These middle-class women without husbands had necessarily to take an interest in financial matters.

For radicals, such as Anna Jameson, Barbara Leigh-Smith and Harriet Martineau, the answer to the 'surplus women' problem was to improve female education, extend the range of occupations open to women, and raise the wages paid to women (since routinely they received less than men for the same work), thus enlarging the very restricted opportunities open to middle-class women to take gainful employment and lead satisfying lives outside marriage. Conservatives, widely represented in the press, looked to ways of increasing marriage opportunities and emigration to reduce the numbers of unmarried women and retain the culture of domesticity. They treated women who had no husbands as having 'failed'.[97]

Until around 1870, married women might expect to have between six and seven live births; from 1870 a dramatic decline began so that the average number of births to a woman by 1940 was just over two.[98] Teenage pregnancies were very uncommon, as were illegitimate births for much of the period, though children could not necessarily be expected to grow up in a two-parent family as death and desertion took their tolls. Levels of infant mortality were at their highest in the first half of the eighteenth century, remaining pretty constant until the end of the eighteenth century. Infant mortality did not diminish substantially until about 1900, after which it declined precipitously.[99] A decline in family size has considerable implications for the role that women may play in the workforce.

Most women who had an occupation in the eighteenth century engaged in unwaged work, as members of a household that, certainly until the later years of the century, was a significant economic unit as a farm or workshop in which the members of the household played different roles according to their sex, age and capabilities. The most significant form of independent economic activity open to women was to run a business. The process of industrialisation from the late eighteenth century is seen as separating home and workplace and cutting off women from the world of waged work except for a period between childhood and marriage. However, until well into the twentieth century the most significant form of waged work for women was domestic service, an occupation that in many ways replicated the working relationships of the family or household business. Most women working in such conditions had little money to dispose of beyond their immediate needs; younger women saved in anticipation of marriage, but the sums involved rarely gave rise to the need for any special kind of financial services.

Before the inclusion of occupational categories in the census, it is almost impossible to estimate the numbers of women engaged in waged work and even after that it is probable that there was considerable under-recording of *married* women's paid work. However, it is possible to chart a general decline in women's participation in the paid workforce from the early nineteenth century, though this was not uniform by region, occupation or across time.[100] Women did not work on equal terms with men and wages and benefits were virtually never equal. Changes in the Poor Law, in nuptiality and family size, in migration and employment patterns may well have played their part. But what contributed to a further decline in the number of women in paid work from roughly 1880 to 1930 is much harder to estimate.[101]

The earliest pensions for women were paid by charities, by parishes under the old Poor Law and by friendly societies, and were for the relief of poverty. During the nineteenth century large organisations such as the railways, utilities companies and banks introduced superannuation schemes for men (men in public employment had had pensions since the seventeenth century), but few women were entitled to occupational or contributory pensions in their own right as employers assumed that they would spend only a limited period of their lives in paid employment.[102] The universal provision of benefits for workers is a feature of the twentieth century: state pensions were introduced in 1909, but they were means-tested, for the over-70s, and were conceived of as a supplement to other funds rather than income to live on. Even after the 1925 Pensions Act widened the scope of provision with a statutory contributory scheme, and lowered the pensionable age to 65, women often found it difficult to keep in employment until they were eligible for a pension.[103] Women's exclusion meant that in an era when men's needs were met by pension schemes, there was a considerable population of women who needed to concern themselves with financial matters and with the management of their funds for income if they were unable to work.

An article published in 1930 in the *Financial Review of Reviews*, an influential investment periodical, considered that there was a need for investment products aimed specifically at women investors.

> There are few women workers, beyond the period of youth, who are not haunted with the spectre of a time when infirmity and old age will overtake them … unfortunately, there are many [women] who are either careless or constitutionally incapable of control of money, and to this class a permanent investment of a safe kind would be a boon.[104]

Opportunities for building up funds included insurance, savings funds and investment. Lucy Yates, writing in 1908, recognised that women 'do not insure as they should do, that is, they are more chary of doing so than men' because of the obstacles set by insurance companies – rates calculated on large sums (£1,000); quarterly or annual premiums unsuitable for women with fluctuating incomes; a medical examination; and other formalities.[105] By the 1920s, however, some insurance companies were offering insurance products specifically for women, such as the Prudential Assurance Company's 'Everywoman' policy, aimed at single working women, which paid out on marriage or at term if the holder remained single.[106]

Two women writing during the First World War commented that women had been impelled into financial responsibility by the absence of male relatives to advise them and that War Loan promotion had made its impression on them:

> The War Loans have brought to the individual notice of women sound schemes for the investment of their money, the prospectuses of which … were simply and clearly written, with the particular aim of interesting and attracting the embryo investor. Indeed, many women received their first lesson in investment from these prospectuses, which patriotism compelled them to study, and the interest thus aroused will not entirely disappear after the War.[107]

The link with War Loan and War Savings Certificates, which were issued between 1916 and 1918, was perpetuated in Post Office Savings Certificates that were deliberately targeted at less affluent savers through War Savings Associations located in 'churches, shops, social groups, clubs, [and] men's and women's organizations'.[108] By June 1929, 918 million certificates had been sold, representing a cash investment of £720 million. Allowing for conversions and withdrawals, the balance outstanding at that date was still £483 million. During the early twentieth century, Post Office and savings banks accounts multiplied. The Post Office Savings Bank had 9,818,000 active accounts and the balance due to depositors at the end of 1928 was £288,690,000, and there were 119 different trustee savings banks with total amounts due to depositors at 28 November 1928 of £159 million plus £5 million surplus funds.[109]

It appears that in the early twentieth century the number of women investing in financial securities increased. *The Economist* study of 1938, which examined investment in unit trusts, found that among savers, 'nearly one-quarter were described as spinsters, rather more than a sixth as married women ... while one out of every nine was a widow'.[110] Hartley Withers, a prolific financial journalist and commentator in the inter-war years, described 'a new class of savers and investors' who were responding to a new market, with rapid ups and downs in the level of company formations and a vogue for fixed interest securities.[111] For Withers, women brought to this new market 'that wide-eyed sceptical curiosity that makes women so formidable' in their interventions.[112] Sargant Florence, 20 years later, quoted a *Financial Times* study published in 1949 which found that the proportion of women shareholders in 40 British companies of all sizes varied between 61 per cent and 20 per cent, averaging 40 per cent of all single accounts and 8 per cent of joint accounts.[113]

The development of women's financial activity in the twentieth century – the interaction of new educational and employment opportunities, state support and savings schemes and investment products – is a story that largely remains to be told. What is evident, however, is the continuity over the period covered by this book – the extent to which women needed to deal with the same preoccupations of low income and widowhood, and the uncharted willingness of many of them to do so through investment.

Interdisciplinary work

Feminist economics has developed out of a belief that 'Economics has been more impervious and more resistant to women's realities and women's concerns and more resistant to change than other social sciences'.[114] Feminist economists have turned to such disciplines as anthropology, psychology and sociology to understand how beliefs and 'sense of need' may be formed outside the confines of the rational economic man of neo-classical economics.[115] In particular, they have looked to history to show how institutions and beliefs may change over time and, more particularly, to social history and to women's history as models for how women and gender relations may be integrated into the discipline.

Authors of the chapters in this volume come from departments of history, geography and economics and schools of business, management and accounting, drawing on approaches from these disciplines and from women's and gender history. The chapters range across a variety of historical sub-disciplines from the econometric and cliometric to the social and cultural and draw on both quantitative and qualitative data. It has been a feature of work on this subject that there has been a remarkable convergence of interest from so diverse a range of subject areas.

The contributions here demonstrate how gender offers a different point of view from which to study the world of finance, business and accounting. The doyenne of gender history, Joan Scott, warns historians not to perpetuate the exclusion of women by establishing a separate women's business history.[116] As she points out, gender is present in business but is not part of the dominant narratives. Supposedly dealing with the neutral world of markets, they portray an overwhelmingly male world. Business history is concerned with progressive development rather than with the messy and temporary arrangements which characterise so much of women's business. These points are just as applicable to finance and accounting. The aim of this volume, then, is not simply to insert women into these histories and to document their agency in business, finance and accounting, but to use gender to explore economic practices and relationships in the world of money.

The chapters demonstrate how resourceful women were, in a variety of places and at different times, despite legal, economic and social disabilities. English women seem to have had greater freedom than their German counterparts in the eighteenth century; the effects of the Married Women's Property Acts in England, Scotland and the United States seem to have been different. A subtext in many of the chapters is the development of business life from the household (in which women might readily play a part, though the extent of their activity is unmeasurable) to the separate workplace/workshop/business premises in which they made and sold goods and conducted business. This change seems to have coincided with the development of more formal credit instruments, of banks and of joint-stock companies and government debt. Women, who had been an important source of personal credit in pre-industrial societies, making individual arrangements with debtors for the payment of interest and the repayment of capital, became 'customers' for 'financial products'. Differences in economic development between the nations and territories examined here also tell a story, as do variations in the use of dowries and formal financial arrangements made by families on behalf of their female members.

Perhaps the one universal feature of all the women's financial and economic activity reviewed in this volume is that it was smaller than comparable activity for men. Their per capita ownership of stock, businesses and land was normally less in value than men's per capita ownership and the constraints under which they practised were greater. But what also comes over very clearly is those areas where the record is silent about women's economic activity – sometimes it is silent about men's activity as well. Nevertheless, the chapters tell their own stories of women's activity and engagement with the economic worlds of which they were a part.

The chapters are arranged broadly chronologically and we have added introductions to the legal background of women's financial activity in England in the eighteenth and nineteenth centuries and in the United States in the nineteenth century. Many of the chapters originate from the special issue on women, accounting and investment of *Accounting, Business and Financial History* 16 (2006), and from the sessions on *Women's Financial Decisions: their Wealth, their Decisions, their Activity 1700–1930*, held at the International Economic History Association meeting in Helsinki in 2006. The editors and authors are grateful for permission from Routledge (Taylor & Francis) to reproduce material first published in the journal.

Notes

1 W.D. Rubinstein, *Men of Property: The Very Wealthy in Britain since the Industrial Revolution*, 2nd edn, London: The Social Affairs Unit, 2006, p. 38.
2 Rubinstein, *Men of Property*, p. 319.
3 Rubinstein, *Men of Property*, p. 320.
4 *Spectator*, 16 November 1872, pp. 1454–6.
5 J.G.A. Pocock, 'The mobility of property and the rise of eighteenth century sociology', in J.G.A. Pocock, *Virtue, Commerce and History: Essays on Political Thought and History, Chiefly in the Eighteenth Century*, Cambridge: Cambridge University Press, 1985, p. 114; Catherine Ingrassia, 'The pleasures of business and the business of pleasure', *Studies in Eighteenth Century Culture* 24, 1995, reprinted in Ross B. Emmett (ed.), *Great Bubbles: vol. 3 The South Sea Bubble*, London: Pickering and Chatto, 2000, pp. 324–30; Catherine Ingrassia, *Authorship, Commerce and Gender in Early Eighteenth-Century England*, Cambridge: Cambridge University Press, 1998, p. 2; E.J. Clery, *The Feminization Debate in Eighteenth-Century England: Literature, Commerce and Luxury*, Basingstoke: Palgrave, 2004, p. 56.
6 Martha C. Nussbaum, 'Emotions and women's capabilities', in Martha C. Nussbaum and Jonathan Glover (eds), *Women, Culture and Development: A Study in Human Capabilities*, Oxford: Clarendon Press, 1995, pp. 360–1.
7 Nussbaum, 'Emotions', p. 306.
8 Richard Dale, *The First Crash: Lessons from the South Sea Bubble*, Princeton, NJ: Princeton University Press, 2004, p. 3.
9 Anne Laurence, 'Women investors, "that nasty South Sea affair" and the rage to speculate in early eighteenth-century England', *Accounting, Business and Financial History* 16 (2), 2006, pp. 245–64; Ann Carlos and Larry Neal, 'Women investors in early capital markets 1720–1725', *Financial History Review* 11, 2004, pp. 197–224; Janette Rutterford and Josephine Maltby, '"The widow, the clergyman and the reckless": women investors in England 1830–1914', *Feminist Economics* 12, 2006, pp. 111–38.
10 England and Wales was the first territory to admit women as chartered accountants. In 1967 the New York Stock Exchange admitted its first woman member.
11 Joan Thirsk, 'The history women', in M. O'Dowd and S. Wichert (eds), *Chattel, Servant or Citizen: Women's Status in Church, State and Society*, Irish Historical Studies 19, Belfast: Institute of Irish Studies, Queen's University, 1995, pp. 1–2.
12 David Itzkowitz, 'Fair enterprise or extravagant speculation: investment, speculation and gambling in Victorian England', *Victorian Studies* 45 (1), 2002, pp. 121, 126;

Mary Poovey, 'Writing about finance in Victorian England: disclosure and secrecy in the culture of investment', *Victorian Studies* 45 (1), 2002, p. 18.

13 Until well into the nineteenth century, single women were not reliably distinguished from married women by title: 'Mrs' could be used of unmarried as well as married women. It is still difficult to establish the marital status of women with the title 'Lady'.

14 Ingrassia, 'The pleasure of business and the business of pleasure', p. 318.

15 *The London Journal*, 30 April–7 May 1720, p. 2.

16 Malcolm Balen, *A Very English Deceit: The Secret History of the First Great Financial Scandal*, London: Fourth Estate, 2002, pp. 72–3.

17 John Carswell, *The South Sea Bubble*, rev. edn, Stroud: Alan Sutton, 1993, pp. 8, 119.

18 P.G.M. Dickson, *The Financial Revolution in England: A Study in the Development of Public Credit 1688–1756*, London: Macmillan, 1967, pp. 267, 282.

19 Alice Clare Carter, 'English public debt in the eighteenth century', 1968, reprinted in Alice Clare Carter, *Getting, Spending and Investing in Early Modern Times*, Assen, Netherlands: Van Goram, 1975, p. 139.

20 Amy Louise Erickson, 'Coverture and capitalism', *History Workshop Journal* 59, 2005, pp. 1–16. English common law was in force in Wales, Ireland and in many British colonial possessions. Scotland used Roman (civil) law but was influenced by common law.

21 Married Women's Property Acts were passed in 1848 in New York; 1870 and 1882 in England and Wales; 1879 in New South Wales; 1881 in Scotland; 1872 and 1884 in Canada, for example. In states of the United States influenced by Spanish civil law, married couples had property in common.

22 Peter Earle, *The Making of the English Middle Class: Business, Society and Family Life in London 1660–1730*, London: Methuen, 1989.

23 Earle, *Making of the English Middle Class*, pp. 146–7.

24 John Habakkuk, *Marriage, Debt and the Estates System: English Landownership 1650–1950*, Oxford: Clarendon Press, 1994, p. 489.

25 B.A. Holderness, 'Credit in a rural community 1660–1800', *Midland History* 3, 1975, pp. 94–116; B.A. Holderness, 'Credit in English rural society before the nineteenth century', *Agricultural History Review* 24, 1976. R.G. Griffiths, 'Joyce Jeffreys of Ham Castle: a seventeenth-century business gentlewoman', *Transactions of the Worcestershire Archaeological Society* new series 10, 1933, pp. 1–32; B.A. Holderness, 'Elizabeth Parkin and her investments 1733–66: aspects of the Sheffield money market in the eighteenth century', *Transactions of the Hunter Archaeological Society* 10, 1973, pp. 81–7; Bernard Elliott, 'An eighteenth-century Leicestershire business woman: the Countess Mary Migliorucci of Nevill Holt', *Leicestershire Archaeological and Historical Society Transactions* 61, 1987, pp. 79–82; W.C. Jordan, *Women and Credit in Pre-Industrial and Developing Societies*, Philadelphia, PA: University of Pennsylvania, 1993; R. Tittler, 'Money lending in the West Midlands: the activities of Joyce Jeffries 1638–1649', *Historical Research* 67, 1994, pp. 249–63.

26 Judith Spicksley, '"Fly with a duck in thy mouth": single women as sources of credit in seventeenth-century England', *Social History* 32, 2007, pp. 187, 195.

27 James Steven Rogers, *The Early History of the Law of Bills and Notes: A Study of the Development of Anglo-American Commercial Law*, Cambridge: Cambridge University Press, 1995, p. 99.

28 Spicksley, 'Single women as sources of credit', p. 201.

29 Margaret Hunt, *The Middling Sort: Commerce, Gender and the Family in England, 1680–1780*, Berkeley, CA: University of California Press, 1996, p. 22.

30 Leonore Davidoff and Catherine Hall, *Family Fortunes: Men and Women of the English Middle Class 1780–1850*, rev. edn, London: Routledge, 2002, pp. 277–9.

31 Davidoff and Hall, *Family Fortunes*, p. xxvii.

32 Davidoff and Hall, *Family Fortunes*, p. 195.

33 Details of these women may be found in the *Oxford Dictionary of National Biography*. Women could be declared bankrupt if they were either widows or spinsters, or if they were married women with separate estate arrangements.

34 Christine Wiskin, 'Urban businesswomen in eighteenth-century England', in Rosemary Sweet and Penny Lane (eds), *Women and Urban Life in Eighteenth-Century England: 'On the Town'*, Aldershot: Ashgate, 2003, pp. 87–110; Hannah Barker and Karen Harvey, 'Women entrepreneurs and urban expansion: Manchester 1760–1820', in idem pp. 111–30; Alison Kay, 'Small businesses, self-employment and women's work-life choices in nineteenth-century London', in D. Mitch, John Brown and Marco H.D. Van Leeuwen (eds), *Origins of the Modern Career*, Aldershot: Ashgate, 2004, pp. 191–206; Nicola Phillips, *Women in Business 1700–1850*, Woodbridge: Boydell Press, 2006; Hannah Barker, *The Business of Women: Female Enterprise and Urban Development in Northern England 1760–1830*, Oxford: Oxford University Press, 2006.

35 Beverly Lemire, 'Peddling fashion: salesmen, pawnbrokers, tailors, thieves and the second-hand clothes trade in England, c.1700–1800', *Textile History* 22, 1991, pp. 67–82; Beverly Lemire, 'Petty pawns and informal lending: gender and the transformation of small-scale credit in England, c.1600–1800', in Kristine Bruland and P.K. O'Brien (eds), *From Family Firms to Corporate Capitalism: Essays in Business and Industrial History in Honour of Peter Mathias*, Oxford: Clarendon Press, 1998, pp. 112–38.

36 Earle, *Making of the English Middle Class*, p. 168.

37 Margot Finn, 'Women, consumption and coverture in England, *c.*1760–1860', *Historical Journal*, 39, 1996, p. 704; Wiskin, 'Urban businesswomen in eighteenth-century England', p. 89; Barker and Harvey, 'Women entrepreneurs and urban expansion', p. 114.

38 For a discussion about the relative merits of fire insurance records, trade directories and census data for providing information about businesses owned and run by women see Barker, *The Business of Women*, pp. 42–54. For critique of Davidoff and Hall, see Simon Morgan, *A Victorian Woman's Place: Public Culture in the Nineteenth Century*, London and New York: I.B. Tauris, 2007, pp. 2–3.

39 Alice Clark, *Working Life of Women in the Seventeenth Century*, with an introduction by Amy Erickson, London: Routledge, 1992; Ivy Pinchbeck, *Women Workers and the Industrial Revolution 1750–1850*, London: Frank Cass, 1969. The literature on women's work in England from the seventeenth century onwards is enormous, but almost all of it refers back to Clark and Pinchbeck.

40 See, for example, Merry E. Wiesner-Hanks, *Gender in History*, Oxford: Blackwell, 2001, pp. 65–77. The extensive further reading considers gender and class, gender and work, notes that there has been little work on other aspects of gender and economic life, and ignores the idea of women as owners of capital. Katrina Honeyman's exemplary *Women, Gender and Industrialisation in England 1700–1870*, Basingstoke: Macmillan, 2000, considers women as workers and employees rather than as employers or mobilisers of capital.

41 Honeyman, *Women, Gender and Industrialisation*, p. 15.

42 Nicola Reader, 'Female friendly societies in industrialising England 1780 1850', University of Leeds PhD thesis, 2005.

43 Erickson, 'Coverture and capitalism', pp. 1–16.

44 Lee Holcombe, *Wives and Property: Reform of the Married Women's Property Law in Nineteenth-Century England*, Toronto: University of Toronto Press, 1983, p. 201.

45 Mary Beth Combs, 'Wives and household wealth: the impact of the 1870 Married Women's Property Act on wealth-holding and share of household resources', *Continuity and Change* 19, 2004, p. 148.

46 Amy Louise Erickson, *Women and Property in Early Modern England*, London: Routledge, 1993, p. 226.

47 Amy Louise Erickson, 'Property and widowhood in England 1660–1840', in Sandra Cavallo and Lyndan Warner (eds), *Widowhood in Medieval and Early Modern Europe*, Harlow: Longman, 1999, p. 147.

48 Susan Staves, *Married Women's Separate Property in England 1660–1833*, Cambridge, MA: Harvard University Press, 1990, pp. 18–24.

49 Margaret Pelling, 'Finding widowers: men without women in English towns before 1700', in Sandra Cavallo and Lyndan Warner (eds), *Widowhood in Medieval and Early Modern Europe*, Harlow: Longman, 1999, p. 46.

50 The Act of Parliament of 1692 allowed inhabitants of the province of York to dispose of their personal estates by their wills, and similar Acts were passed in 1696 for Wales, and in 1725 for the City of London. Davidoff and Hall, *Family Fortunes*, p. 209; Statutes at Large, 4 Gulielmi & Mariæ, c.2; Statutes at Large, 7 & 8 Gulielmi III, c.38; Statutes at Large, 11 George I, c.18.

51 Phillips, *Women in Business*, p. 41.

52 Chantal Stebbings, *The Private Trustee in Victorian England*, Cambridge: Cambridge University Press, 2002, pp. 5, 6.

53 R.J. Morris, *Men, Women and Property in England 1780–1870: A Social and Economic History of Family Strategies amongst the Leeds Middle Classes*, Cambridge: Cambridge University Press, 2005, p. 372.

54 Stebbings, *Private Trustee*, p. 80; Morris, *Men, Women and Property*, p. 314.

55 Stebbings, *Private Trustee*, p. 10.

56 Quoted in George Robb, *White-Collar Crime in Modern England*, Cambridge: Cambridge University Press, 1992, pp. 29–30.

57 Rubinstein, *Men of Property*, p. 238. Only since 1926 has *all* real property been included in the valuation.

58 John Bateman, *The Great Landowners of Great Britain and Ireland*, 4th edn, London: Harrison, 1883. Bateman's lists published in 1876, 1878, 1879 and 1883 were compiled from statistics collected by the government from parish valuation lists. (David Spring, introduction to Bateman, reprinted by Leicester University Press, 1971, p. 10.) Some 43,000 owners of more than 100 acres of land were identified, which would suggest that there were in the region of 2,000 women who owned more than 100 acres.

59 G.E. Mingay, *English Landed Society in the Eighteenth Century*, London: Routledge and Kegan Paul, 1963, pp. 38–9.

60 Dickson, *Financial Revolution*, pp. 258, 281.

61 Mingay, *English Landed Society*, pp. 36–8.

62 Habakkuk, *Marriage, Debt and the Estates System*, p. 490.

63 Morris, *Men, Women and Property*, p. 362.

64 Habakkuk, *Marriage, Debt and the Estates System*, p. 492.

65 Gregory Clark, 'Debts, deficits and crowding out: England 1727–1840', *European Review of Economic History* 5, 2001, p. 406.

66 They were about 5 per cent of the owners of businesses in eighteenth-century provincial towns (Wiskin, 'Urban businesswomen in eighteenth-century England', p. 91); about 5 per cent of those who owned more than 3,000 acres of land and had incomes of £3,000 (Bateman, *The Great Landowners*); around 10 per cent of the customers of Hoare's Bank (Laurence, 'Women investors', p. 250).

67 Larry Neal, *The Rise of Financial Capitalism: International Capital Markets in the Age of Reason*, Cambridge: Cambridge University Press, 1990, pp. 17–18; Natasha Glaisyer, *The Culture of Commerce in England 1660–1720*, Woodbridge: Royal Historical Society Studies in History, new series, 2006, p. 5.

68 Ann Carlos, Jennifer Key and Jill Dupree, 'Learning and the creation of stock market institutions: evidence from the Royal African and Hudson's Bay Companies,

1670–1700', *Journal of Economic History* 58, 1998, pp. 318–44; Peter Temin and Hans-Joachim Voth, 'Banking as an emerging technology: Hoare's Bank 1702–1742', *Financial History Review* 13, 2006, pp. 149–78.

69 Poovey, 'Writing about finance', p. 18.

70 Sarah J. Hudson, 'Attitudes to investment risk amongst West Midland canal and railway company investors, 1760–1850', University of Warwick PhD thesis, 2001, p. 180.

71 *Daily News*, London, 19 November 1869; *Jackson's Oxford Journal*, 21 April 1883.

72 Ingrassia, *Authorship, Commerce and Gender*, p. 35.

73 William Amos, *The Originals: Who's Really Who in Fiction*, London: Jonathan Cape, 1985, p. 350; *Oxford Dictionary of National Biography*, Michael Reed, 'Baron Grant'.

74 Christine de Pisan, *The Treasure of the City of Ladies*, translated and with an introduction by Sarah Lawson, Harmondsworth: Penguin, 1985, p. 130.

75 George Savile, Marquis of Halifax, *The Ladies New-Years Gift, or Advice to a Daughter*, 2nd edn, London, 1688, pp. 86–7.

76 Hannah Wolley, *The Compleat Servant-Maid*, London, 1677, cited in Amy Louise Erickson, 'Possession – and the other one-tenth of the law: assessing women's ownership and economic roles in early modern England', *Women's History Review* 16, 2007, p. 377.

77 A Banker's Daughter, *A Guide to the Unprotected in Everyday Matters Relating to Property and Income*, London: Macmillan, 1863, p. 18.

78 Lucy H. Yates, *The Management of Money: A Handbook of Finance for Women*, London: Horace Cox, 1903.

79 Amanda Vickery, *The Gentleman's Daughter*, New Haven, CT and London: Yale University Press, 1998, pp. 127, 134.

80 Margot Finn, *The Character of Credit: Personal Debt in English Culture 1740–1914*, Cambridge: Cambridge University Press, 2003, p. 64.

81 Geoffrey Clark, *Betting on Lives: The Culture of Life Insurance in England 1695–1775*, Manchester: Manchester University Press, 1999, p. 7.

82 E.A. Wrigley and R.S. Schofield, *The Population History of England 1541–1871: A Reconstruction*, London: Edward Arnold, republished Cambridge: Cambridge University Press, 1989, p. 529.

83 Pat Thane, 'Old women in twentieth-century Britain', in Lynn Botelho and Pat Thane (eds), *Women and Ageing in British Society since 1500*, Harlow: Longman, 2001, pp. 208, 479.

84 David Coleman and John Salt, *The British Population: Patterns, Trends and Processes*, Oxford: Oxford University Press, 1992, pp. 52–3; Anne Laurence, *Women in England 1500–1760: A Social History*, London: Weidenfeld and Nicolson, 1994, p. 28.

85 Wrigley and Schofield, *Population History*, p. 255; Andrew Hinde, *England's Population: A History since the Domesday Survey*, London: Hodder Arnold, 2003, p. 188; E.A. Wrigley, R.S. Davies, J.E. Oeppen and R.S. Schofield, *English Population History from Family Reconstitution 1580–1837*, Cambridge: Cambridge University Press, 1997, p. 140.

86 Michael S. Teitelbaum, *The British Fertility Decline: Demographic Transition in the Crucible of the Industrial Revolution*, Princeton, NJ: Princeton University Press, 1984, p. 98; Martin Pugh, *Women and the Women's Movement in Britain, 1914–1999*, 2nd edn, Basingstoke: Macmillan, 2000, p. 223.

87 Wrigley and Schofield, *Population History*, p. 265.

88 Wrigley *et al.*, *English Population History*, p. 195; Hinde, *England's Population*, p. 188.

89 Judith Worsnop, 'A re-evaluation of the "problem of surplus women" in nineteenth-century England', *Women's Studies International Forum* 13, 1990, p. 22.

90 N. Tranter, *Population since the Industrial Revolution; The Case of England and Wales*, London: Croom Helm, 1973, p. 105, quoted in Robb, *White-Collar Crime*, pp. 29–30.

91 R. Woods, *The Population of Britain in the Nineteenth Century*, London: Economic History Society, 1992, p. 42.

92 Pugh, *Women and the Women's Movement*, p. 222.

93 Pat Jalland, 'Victorian spinsters: dutiful daughters, desperate rebels and the transition to the new women', in Patricia Crawford (ed.), *Exploring Women's Past*, Sydney and London: George Allen and Unwin, 1984, p. 130.

94 Worsnop, 'A re-evaluation', p. 23.

95 Bessie Rayner Parks, *Essays on Women's Work*, London: Alexander Strahan, 1865, p. 79.

96 Philippa Levine, ' "So few prizes and so many blanks": marriage and feminism in later nineteenth-century England', *Journal of British Studies* 28, 1989, p. 151.

97 Worsnop, 'A re-evaluation', pp. 24–6.

98 The rise in the population in the eighteenth century was the result of more people marrying and having children rather than families becoming larger. Wrigley and Schofield, *Population History*, p. 254; Simon Szreter, *Fertility, Class and Gender in Britain 1860–1940*, Cambridge: Cambridge University Press, 1996, p. 1.

99 Robert Woods, *The Demography of Victorian England and Wales*, Cambridge: Cambridge University Press, 2000, p. 247; see also Kate Fisher, *Birth Control, Sex and Marriage in Britain 1918–1960*, Oxford: Oxford University Press, 2006.

100 Sarah Horrell and Jane Humphries, 'Women's labour force participation and the transition to the male breadwinner family 1790–1865', *Economic History Review* n.s. 48, 1995, p. 105.

101 Jane Humphries, 'Women and paid work', in June Purvis (ed.), *Women's History in Britain 1850–1945: An Introduction*, London: UCL Press, 1995, pp. 93, 100.

102 Deborah Simonton, *A History of European Women's Work: 1700 to the Present*, London: Routledge, 1998, p. 251; Pat Thane, *Old Age in English History: Past Experiences, Present Issues*, Oxford: Oxford University Press, 2000, pp. 85, 194, 236–7, 243–5, 326.

103 *Treasury Committee on Pensions for Unmarried Women: Minutes of Evidence on the Complaints which are made as to the Position of Unmarried Women under the Contributory Pensions*, London: HMSO, 1938, para 434.

104 A. Wright, 'The State and the small investor', *Financial Review of Reviews*, January 1930, p. 35.

105 Lucy H. Yates, *A Handbook of Finance for Women*, London: Horace Cox, 1908, p. 62.

106 London: The Prudential Archive.

107 J. Greig and M. Gibson, 'Women and investment', *Financial Review of Reviews*, June 1917, p. 175.

108 Helen Fraser, *Women and War Work*, New York: G. Arnold Shaw, 1918. Available online: www.gutenberg.org/files/14676/14676–8.txt (accessed 11 June 2007).

109 R.K. Bacon, *The Small Investor's Handbook*, York: The Yorkshire Post, 1934, p. 33; Wright, 'The State and the small investor', p. 33.

110 Quoted in Barnard Ellinger, *The City: The London Financial Markets*, London: P.S. King and Son Ltd, 1940, p. 278.

111 Hartley Withers, *The Quicksands of the City and a Way through for Investors*, London: Jonathan Cape, 1930, p. 18; A. Essex-Crosby, 'Joint-stock companies in England 1890–1930', University of London M.Comm. thesis, 1938, p. 137.

112 Withers, *The Quicksands of the City*, p. 28.

113 P. Sargant Florence, *Ownership, Control and Success of Large Companies*, London: Sweet and Maxwell, 1961, p. 179.

114 Michèle A. Pujol, *Feminism and Anti-Feminism in Early Economic Thought*, Cheltenham: Edward Elgar, 1992, p. 2.

115 Rebecca M. Blank and Cordelia M. Reimers, 'Economics, policy analysis and feminism', in Marianne A. Ferber and Julie A. Nelson (eds), *Feminist Economics Today: Beyond Economic Man*, Chicago, IL: University of Chicago Press, 2003, p. 16.
116 Joan Scott, 'Comment: conceptualising gender in American business history', *The Business History Review* 72, 1998, p. 248.

Bibliography

A Banker's Daughter, *A Guide to the Unprotected in Everyday Matters Relating to Property and Income*, London: Macmillan, 1863.

Amos, William, *The Originals: Who's Really Who in Fiction*, London: Jonathan Cape, 1985.

Bacon, R.K., *The Small Investor's Handbook*, York: The Yorkshire Post, 1934.

Balen, Malcolm, *A Very English Deceit: The Secret History of the First Great Financial Scandal*, London: Fourth Estate, 2002.

Barker, Hannah, *The Business of Women: Female Enterprise and Urban Development in Northern England 1760–1830*, Oxford: Oxford University Press, 2006.

Barker, Hannah and Harvey, Karen, 'Women entrepreneurs and urban expansion: Manchester 1760–1820', in Sweet, Rosemary and Lane, Penny (eds), *Women and Urban Life in Eighteenth-Century England: 'On the Town'*, Aldershot: Ashgate, 2003, pp. 111–30.

Bateman, John, *The Great Landowners of Great Britain and Ireland*, 4th edn, London: Harrison, 1883, reprinted with an introduction by David Spring, Leicester: Leicester University Press, 1971.

Blank, Rebecca M. and Reimers, Cordelia M., 'Economics, policy analysis and feminism', in Ferber, Marianne A. and Nelson, Julie A. (eds), *Feminist Economics Today: Beyond Economic Man*, Chicago, IL: University of Chicago Press, 2003, pp. 157–74.

Carlos, Ann and Neal, Larry, 'Women investors in early capital markets 1720–1725', *Financial History Review* 11, 2004, pp. 197–224.

Carlos, Ann, Key, Jennifer and Dupree, Jill, 'Learning and the creation of stock market institutions: evidence from the Royal African and Hudson's Bay Companies, 1670–1700', *Journal of Economic History* 58, 1998, pp. 318–44.

Carswell, John, *The South Sea Bubble*, rev. edn, Stroud: Alan Sutton, 1993.

Carter, Alice Clare, 'English public debt in the eighteenth century', 1968, reprinted in Carter, Alice Clare, *Getting, Spending and Investing in Early Modern Times*, Assen, Netherlands: Van Goram, 1975.

Clark, Alice, *Working Life of Women in the Seventeenth Century*, with an introduction by Amy Erickson, London: Routledge, 1992.

Clark, Geoffrey, *Betting on Lives: The Culture of Life Insurance in England 1695–1775*, Manchester: Manchester University Press, 1999.

Clark, Gregory, 'Debts, deficits and crowding out: England 1727–1840', *European Review of Economic History* 5, 2001, pp. 403–36.

Clery, E.J., *The Feminization Debate in Eighteenth Century England. Literature, Commerce and Luxury*, Basingstoke: Palgrave, 2004.

Coleman, David and Salt, John, *The British Population: Patterns, Trends and Processes*, Oxford: Oxford University Press, 1992.

Combs, Mary Beth, 'Wives and household wealth: the impact of the 1870 Married Women's Property Act on wealth-holding and share of household resources', *Continuity and Change* 19, 2004, pp. 141–63.

Dale, Richard, *The First Crash: Lessons from the South Sea Bubble*, Princeton, NJ: Princeton University Press, 2004.

Davidoff, Leonore and Hall, Catherine, *Family Fortunes: Men and Women of the English Middle Class 1780–1850*, rev. edn, London: Routledge, 2002.

Dickson, P.G.M., *The Financial Revolution in England: A Study in the Development of Public Credit 1688–1756*, London: Macmillan, 1967.

Earle, Peter, *The Making of the English Middle Class: Business, Society and Family Life in London 1660–1730*, London: Methuen, 1989.

Ellinger, Barnard, *The City: The London Financial Markets*, London: P.S. King and Son Ltd, 1940.

Elliott, Bernard, 'An eighteenth-century Leicestershire business woman: the Countess Mary Migliorucci of Nevill Holt', *Leicestershire Archaeological and Historical Society Transactions* 61, 1987, pp. 79–82.

Erickson, Amy Louise, 'Possession – and the other one-tenth of the law: assessing women's ownership and economic roles in early modern England', *Women's History Review* 16, 2007, pp. 369–86.

Erickson, Amy Louise, 'Coverture and capitalism', *History Workshop Journal* 59, 2005, pp. 1–16.

Erickson, Amy Louise, 'Property and widowhood in England 1660–1840', in Cavallo, Sandra and Warner, Lyndan (eds), *Widowhood in Medieval and Early Modern Europe*, Harlow: Longman, 1999, pp. 145–63.

Erickson, Amy Louise, *Women and Property in Early Modern England*, London: Routledge, 1993.

Essex-Crosby, A. 'Joint-stock companies in England 1890–1930', University of London M.Comm. thesis, 1938.

Finn, Margot, *The Character of Credit: Personal Debt in English Culture 1740–1914*, Cambridge: Cambridge University Press, 2003.

Finn, Margot, 'Women, consumption and coverture in England, *c*.1760–1860', *Historical Journal* 39, 1996, pp. 703–22.

Fisher, Kate, *Birth Control, Sex and Marriage in Britain 1918–1960*, Oxford: Oxford University Press, 2006.

Florence, P. Sargant, *Ownership, Control and Success of Large Companies*, London: Sweet and Maxwell 1961.

Fraser, Helen, *Women and War Work*, New York: G. Arnold Shaw, 1918.

Glaisyer, Natasha, *The Culture of Commerce in England 1660–1720*, Woodbridge: Royal Historical Society Studies in History, new series, 2006.

Greig, J. and Gibson, M., 'Women and investment', *Financial Review of Reviews*, June 1917.

Griffiths, R.G. 'Joyce Jeffreys of Ham Castle: a seventeenth-century business gentlewoman', *Transactions of the Worcestershire Archaeological Society* new series 10, 1933, pp. 1–32.

Habakkuk, John, *Marriage, Debt and the Estates System: English Landownership 1650–1950*, Oxford: Clarendon Press, 1994.

Holcombe, Lee, *Wives and Property: Reform of the Married Women's Property Law in Nineteenth-Century England*, Toronto: University of Toronto Press, 1983.

Holderness, B.A. 'Credit in English rural society before the nineteenth century', *Agricultural History Review* 24, 1976.

Holderness, B.A., 'Credit in a rural community 1660–1800', *Midland History* 3, 1975, pp. 94–116.

Holderness, B.A., 'Elizabeth Parkin and her investments 1733–66: aspects of the Sheffield money market in the eighteenth century', *Transactions of the Hunter Archaeological Society* 10, 1973, pp. 81–7.

Honeyman, Katrina, *Women, Gender and Industrialisation in England 1700–1870*, Basingstoke: Macmillan, 2000.

Horrell, Sarah and Humphries, Jane, 'Women's labour force participation and the transition to the male breadwinner family 1790–1865', *Economic History Review* n.s. 48, 1995, pp. 89–117.

Hudson, Sarah J., 'Attitudes to investment risk amongst West Midland canal and railway company investors, 1760–1850', University of Warwick PhD thesis, 2001.

Humphries, Jane, 'Women and paid work', in Purvis, June (ed.), *Women's History in Britain 1850–1945: An Introduction*, London: UCL Press, 1995, pp. 85–105.

Hunt, Margaret, *The Middling Sort: Commerce, Gender and the Family in England, 1680–1780*, Berkeley, CA: University of California Press, 1996.

Ingrassia, Catherine, 'The pleasures of business and the business of pleasure', *Studies in Eighteenth Century Culture* 24, 1995, reprinted in Emmett, Ross B. (ed.), *Great Bubbles: vol. 3 The South Sea Bubble*, London: Pickering and Chatto, 2000, pp. 324–30.

Ingrassia, Catherine, *Authorship, Commerce and Gender in Early Eighteenth-Century England*, Cambridge: Cambridge University Press, 1998.

Itzkowitz, David, 'Fair enterprise or extravagant speculation: investment, speculation and gambling in Victorian England', *Victorian Studies* 45 (1), 2002, pp. 121–47.

Jalland, Pat, 'Victorian spinsters: dutiful daughters, desperate rebels and the transition to the new women', in Crawford, Patricia (ed.), *Exploring Women's Past*, Sydney and London: George Allen and Unwin, 1984, pp. 129–70.

Jordan, W.C., *Women and Credit in Pre-Industrial and Developing Societies*, Philadelphia, PA: University of Pennsylvania, 1993.

Kay, Alison, 'Small businesses, self-employment and women's work-life choices in nineteenth-century London', in Mitch, D., Brown, John and Van Leeuwen, Marco H.D. (eds), *Origins of the Modern Career*, Aldershot: Ashgate, 2004, pp. 191–206.

Laurence, Anne, 'Women investors, "that nasty South Sea affair" and the rage to speculate in early eighteenth-century England', *Accounting, Business and Financial History* 16 (2), 2006, pp. 245–64.

Laurence, Anne, *Women in England 1500–1760: A Social History*, London: Weidenfeld and Nicolson, 1994.

Lemire, Beverly, 'Petty pawns and informal lending: gender and the transformation of small-scale credit in England, c.1600–1800', in Bruland, Kristine and O'Brien, P.K. (eds), *From Family Firms to Corporate Capitalism: Essays in Business and Industrial History in Honour of Peter Mathias*, Oxford: Clarendon Press, 1998, pp. 112–38.

Lemire, Beverly, 'Peddling fashion: salesmen, pawnbrokers, tailors, thieves and the second-hand clothes trade in England, c.1700–1800', *Textile History* 22, 1991, pp. 67–82.

Levine, Philippa, ' "So few prizes and so many blanks": marriage and feminism in later nineteenth-century England', *Journal of British Studies* 28, 1989, pp. 150–74.

Mingay, G.E., *English Landed Society in the Eighteenth Century*, London: Routledge and Kegan Paul, 1963.

Morgan, Simon, *A Victorian Woman's Place: Public Culture in the Nineteenth Century*, London and New York: I.B. Tauris, 2007.

Morris, R.J., *Men, Women and Property in England 1780–1870: A Social and Economic History of Family Strategies amongst the Leeds Middle Classes*, Cambridge: Cambridge University Press, 2005.

Neal, Larry, *The Rise of Financial Capitalism: International Capital Markets in the Age of Reason*, Cambridge: Cambridge University Press, 1990.

Nussbaum, Martha C., 'Emotions and women's capabilities', in Nussbaum, Martha C. and Glover, Jonathan (eds), *Women, Culture and Development: A Study in Human Capabilities*, Oxford: Clarendon Press, 1995.

Parks, Bessie Rayner, *Essays on Women's Work*, London: Alexander Strahan, 1865.

Pelling, Margaret, 'Finding widowers: men without women in English towns before 1700', in Cavallo, Sandra and Warner, Lyndan (eds), *Widowhood in Medieval and Early Modern Europe*, Harlow: Longman, 1999, pp. 37–54.

Phillips, Nicola, *Women in Business 1700–1850*, Woodbridge: Boydell Press, 2006.

Pinchbeck, Ivy, *Women Workers and the Industrial Revolution 1750–1850*, London: Frank Cass, 1969.

Pisan, Christine de, *The Treasure of the City of Ladies*, translated and with an introduction by Sarah Lawson, Harmondsworth: Penguin, 1985.

Pocock, J.G.A., 'The mobility of property and the rise of eighteenth century sociology', in Pocock, J.G.A., *Virtue, Commerce and History: Essays on Political Thought and History, Chiefly in the Eighteenth Century*, Cambridge: Cambridge University Press, 1985, pp. 103–25.

Poovey, Mary, 'Writing about finance in Victorian England: disclosure and secrecy in the culture of investment', *Victorian Studies* 45 (1), 2002, pp. 17–41.

Pugh, Martin, *Women and the Women's Movement in Britain, 1914–1999*, 2nd edn, Basingstoke: Macmillan, 2000.

Pujol, Michèle A., *Feminism and Anti-Feminism in Early Economic Thought*, Cheltenham: Edward Elgar, 1992.

Reader, Nicola 'Female friendly societies in industrialising England 1780–1850', University of Leeds PhD thesis, 2005.

Robb, George, *White-Collar Crime in Modern England*, Cambridge: Cambridge University Press, 1992.

Rogers, James Steven, *The Early History of the Law of Bills and Notes: A Study of the Development of Anglo-American Commercial Law*, Cambridge: Cambridge University Press, 1995.

Rubinstein, W.D., *Men of Property: the Very Wealthy in Britain since the Industrial Revolution*, 2nd edn, London: the Social Affairs Unit, 2006.

Rutterford, Janette and Josephine Maltby, '"The widow, the clergyman and the reckless": women investors in England 1830–1914', *Feminist Economics* 12, 2006, 111–38.

Savile, George, Marquis of Halifax, *The Ladies New-Years Gift, or Advice to a Daughter*, 2nd edn, London, 1688.

Scott, Joan, 'Comment: conceptualising gender in American business history', *The Business History Review* 72, 1998, pp. 242–9.

Simonton, Deborah, *A History of European Women's Work: 1700 to the Present*, London: Routledge, 1998.

Spicksley, Judith, '"Fly with a duck in thy mouth": single women as sources of credit in seventeenth-century England', *Social History* 32, 2007, pp. 187–207.

Staves, Susan, *Married Women's Separate Property in England 1660–1833*, Cambridge, MA: Harvard University Press, 1990.

Stebbings, Chantal, *The Private Trustee in Victorian England*, Cambridge: Cambridge University Press, 2002.

Szreter, Simon, *Fertility, Class and Gender in Britain 1860–1940*, Cambridge: Cambridge University Press, 1996.

Teitelbaum, Michael S., *The British Fertility Decline: Demographic Transition in the Crucible of the Industrial Revolution*, Princeton, NJ: Princeton University Press, 1984.

Temin, Peter and Voth, Hans-Joachim, 'Banking as an emerging technology: Hoare's Bank 1702–1742', *Financial History Review* 13, 2006, pp. 149–78.

Thane, Pat, 'Old women in twentieth-century Britain', in Botelho, Lynn and Thane, Pat (eds), *Women and Ageing in British Society since 1500*, Harlow: Longman, 2001, pp. 207–31.

Thane, Pat, *Old Age in English History: Past Experiences, Present Issues*, Oxford: Oxford University Press, 2000.

Thirsk, Joan, 'The history women', in O'Dowd, M. and Wichert, S. (eds), *Chattel, Servant or Citizen: Women's Status in Church, State and Society*, Irish Historical Studies 19, Belfast: Institute of Irish Studies, Queen's University, 1995, pp. 1–11.

Tittler, R., 'Money lending in the West Midlands: the activities of Joyce Jeffries 1638–1649', *Historical Research* 67, 1994, pp. 249–63.

Tranter, N., *Population since the Industrial Revolution: The Case of England and Wales*, London: Croom Helm, 1973.

Vickery, Amanda, *The Gentleman's Daughter*, New Haven, CT and London: Yale University Press, 1998.

Wiesner-Hanks, Merry E., *Gender in History*, Oxford: Blackwell, 2001.

Wiskin, Christine, 'Urban businesswomen in eighteenth-century England', in Sweet, Rosemary and Lane, Penny (eds), *Women and Urban Life in Eighteenth-Century England: 'On the Town'*, Aldershot: Ashgate, 2003, pp. 87–110.

Withers, Hartley, *The Quicksands of the City and a Way through for Investors*, London: Jonathan Cape, 1930.

Woods, R., *The Population of Britain in the Nineteenth Century*, London: Economic History Society, 1992.

Woods, Robert, *The Demography of Victorian England and Wales*, Cambridge: Cambridge University Press, 2000.

Worsnop, Judith, 'A re-evaluation of the "problem of surplus women" in nineteenth-century England', *Women's Studies International Forum* 13, 1990, pp. 21–31.

Wright, A., 'The State and the small investor', *Financial Review of Reviews*, January 1930.

Wrigley, E.A. and Schofield, R.S., *The Population History of England 1541–1871: A Reconstruction*, London: Edward Arnold, republished Cambridge: Cambridge University Press, 1989.

Wrigley, E.A., Davies, R.S., Oeppen, J.E. and Schofield, R.S., *English Population History from Family Reconstitution 1580–1837*, Cambridge: Cambridge University Press, 1997.

Yates, Lucy H., *A Handbook of Finance for Women*, London: Horace Cox, 1908.

Yates, Lucy H., *The Management of Money: A Handbook of Finance for Women*, London: Horace Cox, 1903.

2 Women and finance in eighteenth-century England

Anne Laurence

This brief section gives some of the common financial and legislative background to the chapters on the eighteenth century. At this time by far the most important occasions for the transmission of wealth for women were marriage and inheritance. Dowries or marriage contracts accompanied marriages of people of quite modest means with the intention of providing for widowhood. In England, unlike many other European countries, there was no direct relationship between dowry (the property a woman brought with her at marriage) and dower (the provision made for a widow), though a marriage contract made either before or after the marriage might establish such a connection. One of the most important characteristics of the period was the growing importance of wealth in forms other than land, which meant that women were increasingly likely to bring money or securities as a dowry or as part of a marriage contract, and were increasingly likely to inherit money and securities and to have to manage them for survival.

The early part of the period in England is often described as 'the financial revolution' and is taken to be synonymous with the creation of the National Debt in 1693 and the foundation of the Bank of England in 1694. To manage the debt, the government experimented with a variety of different mechanisms such as Exchequer Bills, annuities, lottery tickets and debt for equity swaps. By 1718 the high cost of the public debt, especially of long-term annuities paying 7 per cent interest, led the South Sea Company, a chartered trading company, to suggest that it undertake another debt-for-equity swap; a mechanism used with the Bank of England in 1694 and the East India Company in 1708 when annuities were exchanged for stock in the company. In addition to swapping public debt for South Sea company equity (which it did in three tranches), the South Sea company issued four new share subscriptions. During the spring and early summer of 1720 not only did South Sea company prices soar (though they started to fall in mid-August and ended the year at a price similar to that in January 1720), but so also did all other equity prices.

Although the South Sea Bubble is identified as the moment when a wider public became involved in the stock market, in truth, wealthy non-landed people had already been buying and selling stock for some years. The difference that the South Sea scheme seems to have made is that it increased activity in the secondary market, allowing some investors to make money on the trading of shares. Government use of the burgeoning secondary market for equity points to the importance of the characteristics of that market. Transparent pricing made securities that were more readily negotiable than government debt. In addition, the process of selling government annuities was extremely laborious by comparison with transferring stock. Beyond the market, the growth of deposit banking for private customers made it easier for out-of-town customers to take part in the market. This growth had come about because of the greater legal security of bills of exchange and promissory notes given by Acts of 1698 and 1704.

In addition to a spot market, the stock market by 1720 had developed many of the characteristics associated with modern markets: a complex system of loans and a market in options and futures. These developments, as well, perhaps, as the anonymity of the market – as much as the ramping up of prices in 1720 – brought much market trading into disrepute. Barnard's Act of 1734 attempted to prohibit dealing in options and futures.

Apart from the whole question of coverture (discussed in the Introduction to this volume), two particular aspects of the law affected women's capacity to be active in the market. In theory, the disposition of personal property (rents, mortgages, income from loans, dividends) became a husband's at the moment that a woman married. Marriage contracts and women's separate estate were mechanisms for denying husbands control over married women's property, but the law failed to keep up with the development of new financial instruments. Income from rents or mortgages paid to married women became the husband's, as did the income from securities. But, unlike rents and mortgages, which were secured on land that belonged to someone else, the stock itself belonged to the woman. Until the early nineteenth century it was believed that stock could be reduced into the husband's possession only if it were actually redeemed.[1] Latterly it was believed to be his if it were transferred into his name. It is not clear what actual effect this had on married women's capacity to operate independently, but it took several test cases to clarify the matter in the nineteenth century.

A second feature of the law was the existence of the right of *feme sole merchant* (or *feme sole trader*) in London and some provincial cities. This was intended to allow a woman to run a business in her own right without her husband incurring liability for her trading debts. By the nineteenth century, for this to be enforced, a female trader had to prove that her husband played no part in the business at all, but the provision had the advantage that the woman was liable for debts only to the extent of her separate assets.[2] In general, even in the earlier period, this right seems to have been used more as a mechanism to protect against possible bankruptcy than as a means to allow married women commercial freedom.

Notes

1 W.S. Holdsworth, *A History of English Law*, 9 vols, London: Methuen, 1925, vol. 7, p. 542. Securities carried the added advantage that, until the Napoleonic wars, dividends

were not taxed (P.G.M. Dickson, *The Financial Revolution in England: A Study in the Development of Public Credit 1688–1756*, London: Macmillan, 1967, p. 253).

2 Nicola Phillips, *Women in Business 1700–1850*, Woodbridge: Boydell Press, 2006; pp. 41, 44.

Bibliography

Dickson, P.G.M., *The Financial Revolution in England: A Study in the Development of Public Credit 1688–1756*, London: Macmillan, 1967.

Holdsworth, W.S., *A History of English Law*, 9 vols, London: Methuen, 1925.

Phillips, Nicola, *Women in Business 1700–1850*, Woodbridge: Boydell Press, 2006.

3 Women in the city

Financial acumen during the South Sea Bubble

Ann M. Carlos, Karen Maguire and Larry Neal

Gone are the days when a woman was dependent on a man for a financially secure future. They are single handedly creating their own money-wise ways. Women in all positions of life – single, married, divorced, full-time workers, stay-at-home moms – are playing a bigger role in managing their (and their family's) finances – and they're winning.[1]

Introduction

A quick online search on the term 'women investor' will provide a list of resources specifically directed at women. This includes sites with advice for women and even firms with financial advisers marketing themselves specifically towards women. The quotation above comes from one such site. Northwest Mutual takes a particularly historical perspective, arguing that, unlike in the past, women now can be the arbitrators of their own financial destiny and furthermore, they argue that women today are financially able and astute in their financial operations. The view that women securing their own financial destiny is something new is, in part, what this chapter seeks to dispel. We show that not only were women involved in capital markets from their inception but that women showed considerable financial acumen and profited from such investments, even to the point of making money while men as a group lost money.

The view that women were financially able and active in their own financial matters is one that runs counter to the perception of women's financial dependency on men, whether father, husband, brother or uncle. Running in tandem is a perception of early stock markets as gambling devices complete with moments of speculative frenzy and hysteria. The behaviour and actions of those involved in such markets has important consequences not only for how we view the development of early stock markets but also, and perhaps even more importantly, how we understand women's historical financial dependence or independence. This chapter examines women's participation in the London stock market during a period of heightened activity, that of the South Sea Bubble in 1720, and explores the extent of financial acumen shown by those women in their trading activity. We focus on two specific stocks: shares in the Bank of England which can be considered a blue-chip or safe investment, and shares in the Royal African Company which was a very risky stock.

Using actual stock transfer records for both of these companies, we explore market activity by all women who bought or sold shares in these two companies across the year 1720. We find that as a result of their speculations in the market, women as a group enjoyed capital gains. The distribution of such gains, however, was highly unequal. Some women made money and some lost. Some even made a considerable amount of money. When we compare men and women's trading activity in the relatively more stable Bank of England stock, again we find that some men made money and some lost but, in contrast to women, men as a group lost money. Thus the market not only provided an avenue for financial gain and independence for some women but also women's conduct in the market speaks more generally to the financial acumen of women as a group.

With the emergence of joint-stock companies in seventeenth-century Europe, secondary markets for their securities slowly came into being. These stock markets, then as now, provided a mechanism by which original purchasers of company stock could resell their claims to other savers. Knowing that they can acquire liquidity whenever they require it, the original lenders are more willing to lend in the first place. Secondary buyers are also more willing to buy, knowing they too can resell these claims if necessary. Secondary markets, however, cannot play these roles unless there are a variety of individuals in the market with different savings objectives or time horizons.[2] If everyone wants only to buy or if everyone just wants to sell, there is no market. Disparate timing of purchases and sales is a necessary condition for a secondary market, but timing is not the whole picture.

Capital markets create opportunities for investors in a number of different, though interrelated, ways. These assets provide the possibility of financial gains that may come from selling shares for more than the purchase price. Also, shares purchased on these secondary markets provide a potential income stream through the payment of dividends. Because they are transparently priced and liquid, these shares can also be used as collateral for investment or business. Of course, if everyone in the stock market simply wants to receive regular dividends indefinitely, there is little incentive to trade and therefore less opportunity for capital gains. As mentioned above, diversity in the market is important.

Despite what would appear to be beneficial attributes of a stock market, in many of the contemporary writings from the end of the seventeenth through the eighteenth century, the stock market is portrayed as a gambling facility. A contemporary poem from 1700 captures these sentiments, not merely equating the buying of shares with that of 'childish' toys, but financial activity itself with madness.

> The Coffee-man leaves Chocolate, Tea, Coffee,
> To know what price for Bank-Stock and East-Indie
> The Lady pawns her Plate and Jewels

To buy some shares in Bank, or Old or New.
The young Heir mortgages his House and Lands,
To purchase Childish Toys at Jonathan's.

That for the prospect of uncertain Gain
Loses his Time and Substance in the main.
If these Men be not mad, pray tell me whence
Is Madness; these have lost both Wit and Sence.[3]

This view of the market appeared to have been confirmed with what many saw as the speculative excesses of the South Sea Bubble in 1720. We believe that secondary markets in securities should not be dismissed as mere gambling devices, even at the outset of the eighteenth century, but rather represent a major financial innovation. Here we investigate market activity by one set of actors, women, and use their actions to speak to women's financial acumen across 1720.

Women's financial independence

As was noted in the first section, discussions of women's financial activity in the early modern period have to be embedded in women's economic, social and legal position in a society. A woman's primary role was to take care of the household and children, so women were generally described in terms of marital status: wife, widow or spinster. Discussion of women's capital-market activity, therefore, takes place in the context of ownership of assets. Because English law did not differentiate between men and single women, whether spinster or widow, any single woman could legally own property, sue or be sued, and have an independent legal identity. Although circumscribed in their options, some women could and did have income.

With the advent of the capital market, there was now another financial avenue open to women. By the beginning of the eighteenth century the emerging stock market in London had become increasingly available for individual use.[4] At least to some degree, and perhaps even to a very large degree, the stock market was anonymous. Although some contemporaries viewed the emerging capital market as a gambling device whereby inexperienced women (though not exclusively women), having lost their common sense, would sell their 'plate and jewels' in a fruitless quest, dissipating their inheritance, dower or other lump sum, Ingrassia, in her portrayal of commerce and gender, argues that 'stock-jobbing allows the women to transcend, however, briefly, constraints on their activities and increase their knowledge, discretionary income, and power'.[5] Ingrassia has questioned the implications of such speculative behaviour in cultural and social terms.[6] Here we question the specific activities of women in the capital market. How did women stockholders, as a group, manage their assets? The newly emerging capital market added to the array of financial instruments now available for women to use on their own behalf. Instead of lending money to small businesses, women could buy stock in publicly traded companies. The passive receipt of dividends that was possible with shareownership could have provided women with a stream of income. At the same time, shareownership allowed women the potential for active management of their money and for capital gains from such investment activity.

The Royal African Company and the Bank of England

The Royal African Company received a royal charter in 1672 giving it a legal monopoly of English trade along the coast of Africa from modern-day Senegal to Angola and between Africa and the West Indies. As a joint-stock company, it raised its capital through the sale of shares. At the time the Royal African Company received its charter, it was the second largest of the English joint-stock companies after the East India Company. But by the time of the South Sea Bubble in 1720, the Royal African Company was a shell of its former self. The wars of the 1690s severely disrupted its trade which, in conjunction with the opening of the African coast to licensed traders, led to a loss of profitability.[7]

The charter called for a paid-up capital of £100,000 sold in £100 denominations, where £100 was the book value of a single share.[8] In 1697, the Company had a book value of the capital stock of £1,101,050.[9] However, by 1712, it was essentially bankrupt with a share priced at £2 on a book value of £100. As a result, it underwent a major financial reorganization, dramatically writing down the existing capital stock and exchanging all bonds outstanding for shares.[10] As a result of the reorganization, the book value of the capital stock of the Company was written down to £451,350. The share price rebounded to £60 but then stabilized in the £20 range from 1715 to 1720, standing at £24 at the beginning of 1720.[11]

The pattern of dividends mirrors the pattern of stock prices and the Company's financial circumstances. Although small dividends were paid between 1702 and 1707, thereafter no further dividends were paid and there was little expectation of any future dividends being paid.[12] Then, in April 1720, perhaps hoping to benefit from a rising market, the Royal African Company offered a large new stock issue to the value of £1,569,600; almost four times the value of the existing stock. In order to obtain agreement for a new issue, the senior shareholders were promised a dividend of 10 per cent in April 1721. No dividend was promised on the newly issued stock. To differentiate between the existing shares and the new issue, we label the existing shares 'senior' and the new issue 'engrafted'.[13] The difference in dividend payments between the senior and engrafted stock led to different market prices for these shares once the two shares' prices were recorded in the financial press (see Figure 3.1). Thus, on the eve of the South Sea Bubble, the Royal African Company was a trading company whose shares basically carried only the possibility of speculative gains or losses. The issue of the engrafted stock in May 1720 did nothing to change the fundamental structure of the company. It is this purely speculative nature of an investment in this company that makes it an interesting case study for an analysis of the financial acumen of women investors.

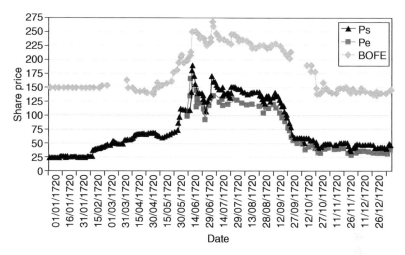

Figure 3.1 Prices of Royal African Company senior shares, Ps, and engrafted shares, Pe and Bank of England shares (BOFE) (source: John Castaing, *The Course of the Exchange*, London: 1720).

In contrast to the Royal African Company, the Bank of England must, especially by 1720, be considered the blue-chip stock of the period. The Bank of England came into existence in 1694 as a joint-stock company. It had an initial capital stock of £1.2 million. By 1710 the book value of the capital stock was £5,559,995, which remained unchanged during the next decade. By 1700, the market price of a share already above 100 rose from 123 in 1701 to roughly 150 at the beginning of January 1720. Again in contrast to the Royal African Company, the Bank of England paid regular dividends twice yearly.

We analyse the financial acumen of those women who invested in shares in each of these two very distinct companies over the year of the South Sea Bubble period of 1720. This period is differentiated from other years by the sharp rise and fall of share prices. This fluctuation in pricing, initially driven by the financial needs of the post-war British government, provides a dynamic period to study market participation among all groups, including women. The price of Bank of England shares listed in the financial press show that it started the year at 150, rose to 180 in May and 250 in June, falling back to 147 on the last day of the year. The market price of Royal African Company senior stock was 24 in January, rising to 50 in March and 60 in April. It then hit a high of 195 in early June. By September, the price had fallen back to 60 and ended the year at 45. The first listing in the financial press for the engrafted stock does not occur until the end of May when the price was 95. It rose to a high of 163 and ended the year at 35. As is still the case today, the timing of transactions matters; buying high and selling low will result in financial loss and the converse financial gain. We now explore the extent of women's market activity in each of these companies during this Bubble year and ask to what extent women as a group showed financial acumen with regard to the market?

Women in the stock market

All joint-stock companies kept careful record of who owned their stock.[14] The data used here come from the transfer books of the Bank of England and of the Royal African Company for 1720 and from John Castaing's *Course of the Exchange*. The transfer ledgers document the date of transfer, the name of seller and of buyer, and the book value of shares transferred. In the Bank of England ledgers, the clerks also noted occupation and address. As the transfer ledgers provide both first and family name, for most people this gives a unique identifier.[15] Any discussion of financial acumen by individuals or of capital gains or losses must begin with an analysis of the pattern of transactions. We begin with the Bank of England and then describe the pattern for the Royal African Company.

Bank of England stock

Over 1720, there were roughly 6,844 transactions with an average book value of £871.30.[16] Narrowing our focus to those cases in which a woman was a seller or a buyer, we find there were 623 transactions in which a woman was listed as seller and 537 listed as buyer. The book value of their transactions comprised 13 per cent of the total value of transactions. Of course, any individual could have multiple transactions. Thus in these 6,844 transactions, there were only 2,233 unique sellers and 2,304 unique buyers of Bank stock, of which women made up 18 per cent (406) of unique sellers and 16.3 per cent (366) of unique buyers. In sum, there were 577 unique women as either buyers, sellers or both. We cannot say if this is large or small, but it shows that women were represented in the market. Women shareholders sold £417,120 book value of shares and purchased £371,480 book value; with an average sale of £658 and an average purchase of £675. As might be expected, value per transaction is lower than the average including men. Yet despite the inequality in income distribution and women's poorer access to land and other forms of credit, some women did hold large portfolios of this financial asset and had access to capital.

Using information on social or marital status from the Bank of England ledgers, we categorize women as nobility, spinster, widow or wife. We might expect that access to capital would be different for members of the nobility. Women's transactions by value and number and social and marital status is shown in Table 3.1. Given legal restrictions, the majority of women were unmarried, either spinsters or widows. Of the wives listed, four sellers were Dutch and five buyers were foreign. Thus, spinsters and widows were the main actors in the market but two-thirds were in the market only once, as shown in Table 3.2, as was also the case for men. While the other third was more active, there does not seem to be any evidence here of what the literature called 'speculative excess'. There were six women with more than six sales and two with more than six purchases. One of these was Johanna Cock who had 29 sales. Johanna Cock was, in fact, a broker or market maker in Bank of England stock and the thirteenth largest buyer of Bank stock in 1720. The size of individual transactions is shown in Table 3.3. The most common book values of shares transferred were £500 and £1,000 block. What is important to note from this table is that the market was capable of subdividing a single share and transactions did take place at less than a £100 book value. The smallest transaction was a sale of £6 book value by Prudence Thorold to Thomas Westley, another major broker.

Women were involved in the market for Bank stock. But how did these women fare? Were they indulging in speculative excesses and dissipating their capital or were they able to use the market for financial gain? While we cannot say that each woman was making her own decision to buy or sell, there is no reason to believe that women were not buying and selling on their own behalf. In order to measure women's financial performance during the Bubble, we categorize women by their level of activity. Thus, we have five groups of women: women who only sold; only bought; were net buyers; net sellers; or whose book value of sales and purchases were equal. For each, we have the book value of shares involved, date of transfer and the market price of Bank stock on that date. Bank share price is given in Figure 3.1. While the price rises and falls over the

Table 3.1 Women's transactions by value and number by social and marital status in Bank of England stock

	Book value of shares		Number of transactions	
	Sellers	*Buyers*	*Sellers*	*Buyers*
Nobility	38,532	20,830	34	21
Spinster	145,264	132,430	231	245
Widow	217,969	203,388	323	259
Wife	15,355	7,000	35	12
Total	417,120	363,648	623	537

Source: Bank of England transfer books, 1720, AC28/1545–1554.

Table 3.2 Number of unique women sellers and buyers by number of transactions in Bank of England stock

Number of transactions	Sellers	Buyers
1	276	264
2	88	69
3	19	21
4	11	8
5	6	2
6+	6	2
Total	406	366

Source: Bank of England transfer books, 1720, AC28/1545–1554.

Table 3.3 Number of transactions by women sellers and buyers by block size transferred in Bank of England stock

Book value of shares (£)	Sellers	Buyers
<100	21	12
100	59	71
101–199	16	10
200	64	58
201–399	49	33
400–499	36	19
500	185	185
501–999	38	32
1,000	127	155
1,001–1,999	21	10
2,000	27	22
2,000+	15	17

Source: Bank of England transfer books, 1720, AC28/1545–1554.

course of 1720, there are occasions when the price falls during a rise and rallies during a fall. Thus gains or losses will depend on the price on the date of purchase and on the date of sale.[17]

Aggregating across the experiences of each individual woman, we find that women made money. With the market price of Bank shares starting the year at 150 and ending at 147, women traders on aggregate did better than those who passively held their shares. As a trading group, their net position was £24,264 across 576 women.[18] Men as a group lost –£44,971.[19] There were, however, gainers and losers. Within each category of women, whether sellers only or buyers only, or those with multiple net trades, some made money and some lost. If we focus only on those women who sold and bought the same book value of shares, their within-year net position is the difference between the market price on the purchase and the market price of the sale. The 65 women in this group were net gainers to the amount of £14,759. But there were some losers: 20 of these women lost money.

The transfer ledgers, as detailed above, clearly show that women were active in the market for Bank of England shares during the Bubble and we estimate that these women as a group had financial gains from their actions. Given that most women were in the market only once, there does not appear to be any great speculative frenzy. At the same time, Bank of England stock was the least risky of the shares in the market. We now explore women's activities in the market for Royal African Company stock, which essentially in today's terms had junk-stock status or was below investment grade.

Royal African Company stock

In estimating financial gains and losses for women in the market for Royal African Company (RAC) stock, we begin with activity in the senior stock and then in the engrafted stock, and treat these as two separate stocks.[20] In January 1720, there were 4,500 senior stocks potentially available for trade. Across the year, there were 1,100 transactions with an average book value of £600. In total there were 603 buyers and 583 sellers. When we focus on women, there were 59 buyers and 44 sellers with 103 transactions. Women constituted 8.46 per cent of buyers and 7.37 per cent of sellers with an average purchase of £417 and an average sale of £437. Although we again find a female presence in this market, it is at a level lower than in the Bank of England market. This might speak of a greater level of risk aversion by women or greater conservatism.

Using the same methodology as in our estimates of financial gains and losses in Bank stock, we determine the financial position of each woman and aggregate over the group. For those who only sold or only purchased, we take their position relative to the beginning or end of the year. The remarkable rise and fall in the share price created an opportunity for net gains. But as in Bank stock, neither the rise nor decline was uniform. Again see Figure 3.1, where we show the market price for the senior stock and for the newly engrafted stock discussed in the next paragraph. Timing was everything. Those who only sold had financial gains of £179 per person, or £5,910 in total. The 29 women who only purchased this senior stock lost money as did five of the six women with multiple purchases. Their aggregate net loss totalled –£8,225, or –£205 per women. The five women who were net sellers had gains of £326 per head. What we find in summary is that aggregating over all women who were in the market for senior Royal African Company shares, women as a group essentially broke even trading in these shares.

In April 1720, the directors authorized an offering of £1.59 million book value of stock, or 15,696 new shares. There was a total of 4,336 transactions from April to December for this engrafted stock. In contrast to the more senior stock, more women were involved. There were 223 buyers involved in 483 transactions, or 11 per cent of total transactions. Of those who bought stock in this offering, only 83 sold. Overall there were 309 purchases and 174 sales. The average book value of purchases, £654, was larger than the senior stock. The records suggest that there were at least 29 women belonging to the nobility representing 13 per cent of the group, whereas they comprised 11 per cent for the senior stock. Of these women, 20 still held at least some of their stock at the end of the year. Table 3.4 gives the pattern of transactions.

Estimating financial gains and losses for the women shareholders of engrafted stock is more complicated than for either the Bank stock or the senior stock. The Company minutes note that purchasers paid for these shares by instalment, which was common. Ignoring the time discount that lowered the present value of the cost of a share, the price was either £17 or £22 per £100 book value.[21] The Company sold shares from the beginning of May; however, the first published price came only on 28 May. Because so many transactions occurred in May, the pricing of stock for May is crucial. We use two pricing rules. The first assigns the 28 May price to all transactions in May. The second takes the initial offered price and increases that incrementally to the £95

Table 3.4 Transactions by women in senior and engrafted stock by month for Royal African Company

		Senior (#)			Engrafted (#)		
		Purchase	Sale	Total	Purchase	Sale	Total
1719		1	2	3	0	0	0
1720	January	0	3	3	0	0	0
	February	1	4	5	0	0	0
	March	16	9	25	0	0	0
	April	8	4	12	0	0	0
	May	3	2	5	89	7	96
	June	18	8	26	48	51	99
	July	6	4	10	53	33	86
	August	2	5	7	36	18	54
	September	4	5	9	27	11	38
	October	0	0	0	28	19	47
	November	1	0	1	18	28	46
	December	0	0	0	10	7	17
1721		7	6	13	1	1	2
Total		67	52	119	310	175	485

Source: Royal African Company, The National Archives, Kew, England, Transfer Books T70/198, 199, 200, 201, 202.

recorded at the end of May. Overall gains or losses for women (and indeed also for men) depend critically on which of these two pricing rules is used. Considering that the engrafted stock ended the year at £35, using the first pricing rule dramatically reduces the number of dates when the market price is above £95. Using the second rule, we increase the number of such dates. So a woman who purchased on 2 May and held her shares would end the year with paper losses under the first rule and paper gains under the second.

Again, within nearly every categorization of women, some women made money and some lost. Under the first pricing scenario where all transactions in May are valued at the 28 May market price, over the seven months from May to December, women had market losses of –£66,135, or –£318 per woman. However, this pricing scenario should be considered the absolute upper bound on the level of capital losses. Not only have we excluded women who were recorded only as selling (because we do not have a listing of the purchase), but this pricing rule definitely overstates the actual transaction price of many May transactions. Under what we consider to be the more realistic pricing rule, we again have women who gain and lose, but the number of women who lose declines. When we aggregate over all women, we now find that as a group they experienced financial gains of £4,030, or £19.10 per head. So even in this market for a highly volatile share, women as a group, under what must be considered the more reasonable pricing rules, make money.

Conclusion

Widows, especially, were a source of capital for small investors in that they lent out their money. Such activities also left them open to default by their borrowers. The emergence of a secondary market for shares created another avenue to financial security for women with assets. The purchase of relatively risk-free securities meant that women could now live off the dividend stream. But it equally meant that they could participate more actively in the market in a quest for capital gains. The South Sea Bubble was a period of heightened financial activity measured by the value of capital stock that changed hands or by the number of people involved in the market. Given these metrics, it is not difficult to understand contemporary descriptions of the market as frenzied or the period as a time when the world went mad. Madness, frenzy, gambling or even hysteria all suggest a lack of control and an environment in which one's assets would be lost or dissipated. Our analysis of women's financial performance in this market goes some way to attenuating these views.

Women were active participants in the stock market over the course of the Bubble. At least some women were taking advantage of this new financial innovation. Research on the role of gender in the tech bubble of the 1990s notes not only that women made financial gains but that they did better than men.[22] From our evaluation of women's financial acumen in Bank of England stock, women investors as a group gained financially from their trading activities in this stock. Indeed, as in the tech bubble, they did better than their male counterparts. It has been argued that for the tech bubble these gains came about because women were more conservative than men. While we cannot speak of a difference between female and male strategies in Bank stock per se, women's activity in Bank of England stock was considerably higher than in Royal African Company stock. Yet even in the more risky Royal African Company stock, women as a group again showed financial acumen.

Notes

1 Northwest Mutual website: www.nmfn.com/tn/learnctr-articles-page_wi_conquer_finance (accessed 4 April 2007).
2 Secondary markets in securities, as in any resale market, obviously need formal institutions to enforce contracts and property rights and informal institutions that enable participants to trust each other without elaborate contracts or constant litigation. The formal institutions were already in place in England by 1689 and the informal institutions were in place by 1720.
3 Edward Ward, *The Picture of a Coffee-House, or, the Humour of the Stock-Jobbers*, London, 1700, p. 14.
4 Ann M. Carlos, Jennifer Key and Jill Dupree, 'Learning and the creation of stock-market institutions: evidence from the Hudson's Bay and Royal African Companies, 1670–1700,' *Journal of Economic History* 58 (3), 1998, pp. 318–44.
5 Catherine Ingrassia, *Authorship, Commerce and Gender in Early Eighteenth-Century England: A Culture of Paper Credit*, Cambridge: Cambridge University Press, 1998, p. 34.
6 Ingrassia, *Authorship, Commerce and Gender*, p. 34.

7   Ann M. Carlos and Jamie Brown Kruse, 'The decline of the Royal African Company: fringe firms and the role of the charter', *Economic History Review* 49 (2), 1996, pp. 295–317.

8   The book value of £100 provides an index against which to measure the market price.

9   William R. Scott, *The Constitution and Finance of English, Scottish and Irish Joint-Stock Companies to 1720*, 3 vols, Cambridge: Cambridge University Press, vol. 2, 1910, p. 32.

10 In fact, because there was at this time no legally defined mechanism for doing so, it was very difficult to wind up a chartered joint-stock company.

11 Scott, *Constitution and Finance*, vol. 2, pp. 28–35.

12 Scott, *Constitution and Finance*, vol. 2, pp. 33–35.

13 In an agreement dated 7 April 1720, one Joseph Taylor paid £75,696 for the whole issue. Thus, Joseph Taylor bought the issue at 4.82 per cent of its book value, or he paid £4.8 per £100 book value and the Company received £75,696 as a new cash infusion. As stock was sold in units of £100 book value, there were now 15,690 new or 'engrafted' shares available for sale in the market.

14 This was needed for dividends and for voting at the annual general meetings.

15 Common names such as Mary Cooke or John Smith are the exception. However, given that most people were in the market only once, this is not a serious problem.

16 In other words, the book value of the capital stock turned over completely.

17 For a more complete discussion see Ann M. Carlos and Larry Neal, 'Women investors in early capital markets, 1720–1725', *Financial History Review* 11 (2), 2004, pp. 197–224.

18 We did not include Johanna Cock or a widow who received a large block on the death of her husband in July and continued to hold.

19 See Ann M. Carlos and Larry Neal, 'The micro-foundations of the early London capital market: Bank of England shareholders during and after the South Sea Bubble, 1720–1725', *Economic History Review* 59 (3), 2006, Table 6, p. 517.

20 For a more complete discussion see Ann M. Carlos, Karen Maguire and Larry Neal, 'Financial acumen, women speculators, and the Royal African Company during the South Sea Bubble', *Accounting, Business and Financial History* 16 (2), 2006, pp. 219–43.

21 The minutes give the instalments as 5 per cent payable on 1 June, 5 per cent payable on 1 September and 7 per cent payable on 1 December. Included in the Minute Book of the General Court on an undated loose sheet was a statement of an up-front payment of 5 per cent.

22 See Brad M. Barber and Terrance Odean, 'Boys will boys: gender, overconfidence, and common stock investment', *Quarterly Journal of Economics*, 116 (1), 2001, pp. 261–92.

Bibliography

Barber, B.M. and Odean, T., 'Boys will be boys: gender, overconfidence, and common stock investment', *Quarterly Journal of Economics* 116 (1), 2001, pp. 261–92.

Carlos, Ann M. and Kruse, Jamie Brown, 'The decline of the Royal African Company: fringe firms and the role of the charter', *Economic History Review* 49 (2), 1996, pp. 295–317.

Carlos, Ann M. and Neal, Larry, 'The micro-foundations of the early London capital market: Bank of England shareholders during and after the South Sea Bubble, 1720–1725', *Economic History Review* 59 (3), 2006, pp. 498–538.

Carlos, Ann M. and Neal, Larry, 'Women investors in early capital markets, 1720–1725', *Financial History Review* 11 (2), 2004, pp. 197–224.

Carlos, Ann M., Key, Jennifer and Dupree, Jill, 'Learning and the creation of stock-market institutions: evidence from the Hudson's Bay and Royal African Companies, 1670–1700', *Journal of Economic History* 58 (3), 1998, pp. 318–44.

Carlos, Ann M., Maguire, Karen and Neal, Larry, 'Financial acumen, women speculators, and the Royal African Company during the South Sea Bubble', *Accounting, Business and Financial History* 16 (2), 2006, pp. 219–43.

Castaing, John, *The Course of the Exchange*, London: n.p.: 26 March 1697–30 June 1720.

Ingrassia, Catherine, *Authorship, Commerce and Gender in Early Eighteenth-Century England: A Culture of Paper Credit*, Cambridge: Cambridge University Press, 1998.

Scott, William R., *The Constitution and Finance of English, Scottish and Irish Joint-Stock Companies to 1720*, 3 vols, Cambridge: Cambridge University Press, 1910–12.

Ward, Edward, *The Picture of a Coffee-House, or, the Humour of the Stock-Jobbers*, London: n.p., 1700.

Bank of England Archives, London

Transfer Books 1720 AC28/1545–1554.

National Archives, Kew, London

Royal African Company: Minute Book of the Court of Assistant T70/90; Minute Book of the General Court T70/101; Transfer Books T70/198, 199, 200, 201, 202.

4 Women, banks and the securities market in early eighteenth-century England[1]

Anne Laurence

This chapter is, above all, about women's agency, about their participation in the stock market, their increasing use of banks and the implied political choices in those activities. The understanding of women's political action, as a result of 20 years of research into both women and the relations between men and women, has led to an extension of our understanding of the political world beyond that of the male 'political nation' to include women's influence, patronage and the informal politics of locality, church and corporate bodies.[2] This chapter explores a further manifestation of women's participation in the politicised world of early-eighteenth-century England, especially during the period of the South Sea Bubble.

This chapter is concerned with women investors in the South Sea Bubble of 1720 and the role that one particular bank played in facilitating their participation. The daring swap of government debt for equity in the South Sea Company and the share issues that accompanied this, the rapid inflation in share prices in the first half of 1720 and the ensuing collapse have become a byword for a stock-market boom and bust. Historians of the Bubble have been much hampered by the destruction of the South Sea Company's share registers, so the customer ledgers of Hoare's Bank that record its customers' purchases and sales of stock, lottery tickets and government debt, dividend and interest payments on stock, and prizes from the lottery are a valuable source for the investment activities of private individuals at the time of the South Sea Bubble. The use of a bank was itself a novel activity – banks had until the late seventeenth century largely taken mercantile customers and dealt in loans and money transfers rather than serve as deposit banks. But by no means all banks acted for customers in this way. So this chapter considers the investments made by women customers of Hoare's Bank and the way in which their participation in the market was facilitated by the bank. The investment choices made by the bank's customers give some credence to Bruce Carruthers's arguments about the politicisation of the market, so the chapter concludes with a consideration of the role of politics in the finances of Hoare's Bank customers.

Women and investment

Attitudes to women's investment behaviour have been contradictory: in the eighteenth century, women were taken as the prime example of those affected by the fever that swept up the population during the South Sea Bubble; later commentators have tended to treat them as conservative investors, choosing stock backed by the government for its supposed safety, the Bank of England over the other chartered companies, and annuities and bonds over stock.[3] Stock investment was seen as 'suitable for patriotic and prudent gentlemen, but ill-advised and dangerous for women', though it was patriotic to buy government debt.[4] Women were believed to lack judgement and to be gullible enough to be duped by unscrupulous brokers and jobbers.[5] It has long been assumed, too, that women were primarily interested in investment income rather than in trading gains. However, recent work on women and finance, stimulated by the interest in female agency, has shown that women were not passive participants in the market, but traded for profit and made active, and not always risk-free, investment choices.[6]

It has been clear for some time that women were significant holders of credit in early modern England. In her study of single women in early modern England, Amy Froide shows how 'never-married women served an important economic role as property holders, rentiers and as private and public moneylenders'.[7] She also shows how lending was professionalised with the greater use of formal instruments by both single and widowed women to make interest-bearing loans to a variety of borrowers – acquaintances, kin and urban corporations.[8]

Women were, by the time of the Bubble, a significant proportion of the investing community. In the absence of share registers it is impossible to know for certain whether they invested in disproportionate numbers in the South Sea Company. Hoppit argues that only 6 per cent of the investors of the initial South Sea Company subscription in 1720 were women. However, since a significant proportion of stock was owned by people whose government annuities had been converted into South Sea stock under the debt-for-equity swaps, the proportion of women owners (as opposed to purchasers) may well have been higher since women constituted 20 per cent, for example, of the owners of 1707 government annuities, though the value of their holdings was only 9 per cent of the total.[9] We know that in 1723 women were about 20 per cent of the proprietors of South Sea stock, owning 12 per cent of the company's value.[10] Carlos and Neal have shown that women who traded in Bank stock during the period of the Bubble made positive capital gains. They have also found that women increased as a proportion of the total number of investors in the Bank of England and that the proportion of capital they held grew.[11]

Apart from the stock market, investors could buy government debt which had the advantage of security but the disadvantage that it was not readily liquid.[12] Short-term government debt had expanded greatly during the 1690s, mainly through anticipating revenue from Customs, Excise, Land Tax, Malt Tax and other taxes.[13] There was also a system of raising loans on military and naval supply; Navy Bills paid a good rate of interest but were difficult to assign and therefore not very liquid.[14]

During the early years of the eighteenth century the number of taxes on which short-term loans were raised for the government was considerably reduced in favour of long-term loans. After the conclusion of the war with France in 1713, the government required less money and funds were raised principally on the Land and Malt Taxes. Dickson notes that between one-quarter and one-third of the lenders to the Land Tax loans were women, though their investment amounted to a smaller proportion.[15]

One of the most significant vehicles for government debt from 1694 was the lottery. A succession of lottery issues offered tickets that paid an annuity with prizes of either a larger annuity or a cash sum. The prices of lottery 'blanks' (i.e. lottery tickets without prizes, paying only the basic interest) were quoted in the newspapers alongside the prices of stock on the Bank of England, and the East India, South Sea and Royal African Companies.[16] The attraction of lotteries was not simply the chance of winning, but the assured returns and the fact that lottery tickets could be bought without the intervention of discredited stock-jobbers; women seem to have made up at least one-third of the owners of the earlier state lottery tickets.[17] The secondary market in tickets meant that at least some of the initial sum was recoverable. The disproportionate involvement of women in the lottery gave rise to almost one-third of the owners of 5 per cent government annuities of 1717 being women since this had originated in the lotteries of 1711–12.[18]

The role of land as an investment for women is extremely difficult to estimate and real property was not normally included in financial settlements for women. However, on Lawrence Stone's figures for the increasing number of landowners leaving no son to succeed, one would expect there to be a rising number of women who controlled land.[19] While many women, from widowed aristocrats to aged servants, received incomes for life from land, one of the features of the eighteenth century was the increasing use of mortgages and loans to buy annuities or stock to provide income for dependants, leaving the landowner with greater freedom to manage his property.[20] Judith Spicksley's figures of bequests in the diocese of Lincoln from fathers to eldest or only daughters show that, by the 1690s, cash was far and away the most important inheritance for women.[21]

Hoare's Bank and its customers

From 1708, when an Act of Parliament removed the limit of 100 on the number of registered stockbrokers, brokers' and jobbers' numbers expanded (the distinction between the two roles was rather less clear-cut in the early eighteenth century than it subsequently became, and there were also a good many people dealing in stock on behalf of others who were not registered).[22] The widely held prejudice against brokers and jobbers expressed in 1721 by George Berkeley arose from the view that industry was the only true way to wealth, because 'projects for growing rich by sudden and extraordinary methods, as they operate violently on the passions of men,... must be ruinous to the public'.[23] Not everyone shared his views, for a newspaper reported in 1720 that 'Stock-jobbing is now become so laudable, that many great ladies forsake their tea, cards and chat to go to Change Alley.'[24]

The development of stockbroking, combined with the use of letters of attorney, made it possible for people outside the City of London not only to own securities, but to buy and sell them. Originally, purchases of shares had to be registered in person at the company offices by the new owner. These new devices made it possible for absentees to buy and sell securities, opening up the markets to investors outside the City of London. At the same time, improved negotiability of bills and notes made it possible for private individuals to use banks more easily. The coincidence of these developments meant that Hoare's Bank, in Fleet Street, London, was able to develop a clientele of wealthy and well-connected out-of-town customers. Partners of the bank offered advice on investment, and were involved as jobbers and brokers, buying and selling stock both on their own account and for their customers, of whom about 10–12 per cent were women.[25]

Partners and customers of Hoare's Bank had strongly held high-church and Tory views. Many of the customers were kin and included such well-known Tories as members of the Finch and Hastings families, and high-church activists such as Robert Nelson. The bank acted for the Society for the Propagation of the Gospel, the Society for Promoting Christian Knowledge, and various bodies associated with the charity schools movement. Temin and Voth are inclined to see these connections as the bank's assurance for the solidity of their customers, but given the novelty of private banking, it seems more probable that the presence of a wealthy and well-connected clientele was a selling point to attract new customers and an advertisement of the bank's solvency.[26]

Women customers of Hoare's Bank

Evidence of the investments of Hoare's Bank customers comes from two sources: from the bank's deposit ledgers and from the correspondence of six of its women customers. Plainly, the wealth of customers and their political and religious complexion means they cannot be taken as a proxy for the investing public, but this is unique evidence for relatively large numbers of women.

There are two series of deposit ledgers for the early eighteenth century. One, designated by letters, contains the accounts of customers whose business took up one or more double page spreads in the ledger, often with five or ten transactions a month. An especially active customer might have several double-page spreads in one ledger, but because clerks carried on until the pages were full, the accounts might not be on consecutive pages. As the books were filled up serially, ledgers covered overlapping periods of time. The second series, designated by numbers, contains the accounts of people who did very little business with the bank, often only a single encashment of a bill; some of these may have been people who just had little use for banking services, others must have done their main business with other banks.

The ledgers record customers' purchases and sales of a variety of investments through the bank, chiefly stock, bonds and annuities in the chartered companies; receipts of dividends and interest from stock, bonds and annuities in the chartered companies (in the case of bonds it can be difficult to distinguish between interest paid and maturity; there were few sales as most bonds were very short term); payments of interest from loans on Tonnage, Excise, Navy Bills, survivorships and the like; and occasional purchases, sales and income from smaller companies. What they do not reveal is stock purchases, sales and dividend payments made through an intermediary; land purchases and sales and income from lands (probably because they were dealt with through individuals whose names cannot be identified from the ledgers); purchase and sale of government debt in the form of Navy Bills, Excise, tonnage, etc.; purchase of stock in small companies and in insurance companies; much about personal loans and bonds; sales in options and futures (which were permitted until the Act of 1734 which put an end to much of the secondary speculation in stock); or transfers of government annuities into South Sea stock (the basis for much of the activity in the South Sea Bubble).[27] In addition, there is no trace of foreign-exchange dealings or of investments in foreign companies such as the Mississippi scheme or the Dutch East India Company.

Women, chiefly widows and spinsters, made up around 12 per cent of the bank's customers in the early eighteenth century and over the period the total number of customers rose. A few married women had accounts jointly with their husbands. Table 4.1 shows all the women's accounts and a sample of men's, and illustrates how the number of women making extensive use of the bank (Ledgers F and G) grew over the period 1719–24, but that the number of women making occasional use of the bank (Ledgers 21–4) declined. Almost half the women who did extensive business were active in the stock market and the proportion increased over the period of the South Sea Bubble. The increase in their stock-market participation was by the same percentage as the increase in men's stock-market participation, though from a lower starting point. The proportions of women occasional users who participated in the stock market were lower and increased over the period, though more gradually.[28] What is difficult to explain is why the percentage of occasional men users who participated in the stock market was normally less than half that of the women occasional users. One possible answer is that a substantial number of these men did their main business somewhere else: Sir George Caswall and Sir George Savile were MPs (and Caswall had very considerable financial interests); Jonathan Gurnell was a Quaker financier; Dudley North was the wealthy son of the financier of the same name; Henry Cornelisen was a son-in-law of one of the partners of Hoare's Bank; and Jabez Collier was a lawyer. Savile was heir to the Marquis of Halifax's fortune and must surely have needed more than occasional banking services. Another possible answer is that the bank made a point of providing brokerage services for women customers.

Table 4.1 Proportions of Hoare's Bank customers with stock in chartered companies or lottery tickets

	Dates	Female (%)	Male (%)[a]
Ledger F	1719–24	46 [6/13]	60 [9/15]
Ledger G	1720–4	56 [15/27]	70 [14/20]
Ledger 21	1718–22	22.5 [30/133]	9 [14/155]
Ledger 22	1719–23	25 [31/126]	14 [18/130]
Ledger 23	1720–4	28 [28/100]	10 [11/113]
Ledger 24	1721–5	31 [30/98]	11 [14/129]

Source: Hoare's Bank customer ledgers.

Note
a Sampled by taking every eighth account in the ledgers.

Figures 4.1, 4.2 and 4.3 show for all women customers the numbers of transactions involving the different companies, how significant trading in South Sea Company stock was, how the lottery declined in importance (though after the 1720s there were fewer new lotteries) and how the women customers of Hoare's Bank showed no preference for supposedly safe Bank stock. Purchases of stock in general exceeded sales, especially in the case of the South Sea Company, where the number of interest payments indicates that people held on to the stock. The women with active banking records showed themselves keen to divest

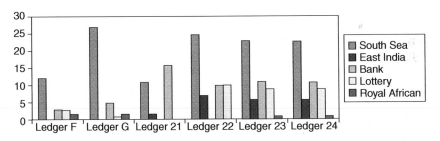

Figure 4.1 Number of women's stock and lottery purchases through Hoare's Bank 1718–25.

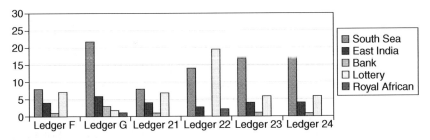

Figure 4.2 Number of women's stock and lottery sales through Hoare's Bank 1718–25.

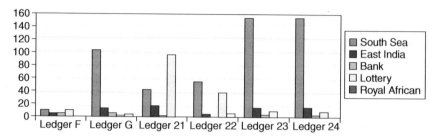

Figure 4.3 Number of women's dividend and interest payments and lottery prizes though Hoare's Bank 1718–25.

themselves of East India stock as numbers of sales exceeded numbers of purchases. If we can equate women who did little business with the bank with having little financial knowledge, we can see how significant the lottery was for them as a source of income and how it seems to have been replaced by the South Sea Company.

The correspondence of the Hastings sisters – Lady Betty Hastings the heiress and her four impoverished half-sisters – with their friend Mrs Bonnell in London reflects very clearly the patterns shown by the ledgers.[29] Lady Betty's account records are in the alphabetical series of ledgers, the other women's in the numbered series. Lady Betty bought and sold stock, holding on to little of it for any length of time, her aim apparently to make a capital sum from the South Sea Company share issues of 1720 rather than to generate income, since she had £3,000 a year from her Yorkshire estates.[30] Her half-sisters, who were taking a much greater risk than she, bought stock in the South Sea Company in 1720, when the price was declining, and despite their losses held on to it, two of them continuing to hold it until the 1750s.[31] One of them, Frances, pondered selling her East India stock in the autumn of 1720, hearing that its price was falling.[32]

But is the same story told by the *value* of the transactions of the bank's women customers? Figures 4.4, 4.5 and 4.6 show the pre-eminence of South Sea stock, especially for the women who were most financially active, and that women were buying more often in amounts of smaller value (as one would expect with the collapse in the value of South Sea stock). The fact that the sales are not greatly below the purchases in value suggests that few of these women made massive losses. The less financially active women seem to have had a greater spread of investments, but seem to have sold most of them when prices were very low. The pattern of dividend payments from the South Sea Company suggests, too, that a good many women, having bought the stock decided to hang on to it for income. Ledger 22 probably contains the largest number of accounts for the period when the South Sea Company was not paying dividends.

The total number of purchases increased but their individual value decreased, as one might expect with the total decline in the stock market after the South Sea Bubble, likewise, there was a rising number of sales but each sale was of a

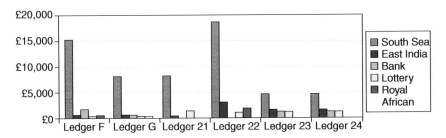

Figure 4.4 Value of women's stock and lottery purchases through Hoare's Bank 1718–25.

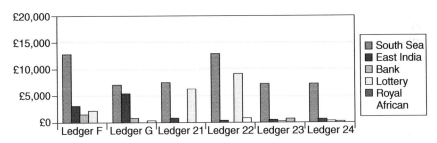

Figure 4.5 Value of women's stock and lottery sales through Hoare's Bank 1718–25.

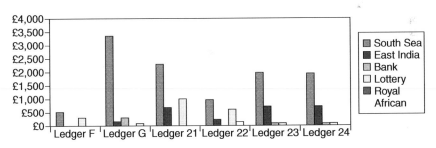

Figure 4.6 Value of women's dividends and interest payments and lottery prizes through Hoare's Bank 1718–25.

declining value. However, the rise in number and value of interest payments from the South Sea Company suggests that customers were right to hold on to their stock. The rising value of payments of East India Company dividends suggests that many already owned East India stock in 1718 and were simply adding to it by their purchases in the early 1720s.

How can we account for the overwhelming preference for South Sea stock when Bank of England stock would seem to have been a safer bet? It is difficult not to conclude that Hoare's Bank was instrumental in encouraging, advising or facilitating the purchase of South Sea stock. The Hoare family had a connection with the company and, unlike the other chartered companies which tended to be dominated by Whig interests, the South Sea Company was a predominantly Tory enterprise. Temin and Voth have demonstrated that personally the partners of Hoare's Bank did very well from the South Sea scheme and that their customers, as measured by the bank's loan books, also did well.[33] It is particularly noteworthy that the women customers who had the greatest predilection for South Sea stock were those who did the greatest amount of business with the bank, who had closest contact with the partners and who shared their political and religious views.

Politics and the market

Bruce Carruthers has argued that parts of the early-eighteenth-century market were politicised, that is to say that investors did not simply judge where to put their money on the basis of safety, the value of returns or ease of access, but according to value judgements related to the affiliations of investor and the perceived politics of the investment. One group of debtors – the government – created a financial constituency with an interest in the government's survival while creditors had a financial interest in the ability of the government to repay its debts. He believes that market transactions were embedded in a highly politicised social context and that political considerations could outweigh financial considerations in people's decisions to buy and sell.[34]

Dickson notes that short-term loans on Land Tax seem to have been relatively unpolitical, while long-term government borrowing – the government annuities that were partly exchanged for equity in the South Sea Company in 1720 – was highly politicised.[35] David Stasavage argues that government creditors after 1688 were chiefly Whigs because Tories tended to be more closely aligned with landed interests, people who generally disliked taxation which was a necessity if government debt was to be repaid.[36] Susan Staves's work on women investors and the possibilities of voting as shareholders has led her to conclude that women holders of stock were 'uninterested in ideology, [preferring] collecting and distributing presents (or bribes), and developing connections for their family interests'.[37]

In a separate literature, Elaine Chalus has demonstrated how women were 'functioning members of the political world', a part of the political life of the nation in a society that was becoming more politicised as the 'rage of party' spread.[38] As 'disenfranchised members of the extra-parliamentary nation' they were, nonetheless, political actors.[39] Parliament met more often and for longer as the eighteenth century progressed, creating a penumbra of friends and relations of parliamentarians whose lives were closely bound up with the politics of the day. Unfortunately, while she looks forward to the nineteenth century, she says little about the period before 1760. Nor does Susan Kingsley Kent in her *Gender and Power in Britain 1640–1990*.[40] But the world of familial contacts and patronage existed in the early eighteenth century and was one in which women played a full part, even if the strength of party divisions was less.

The evidence presented here on the investment patterns of the women customers of Hoare's Bank suggests that women were self-conscious investors, especially those who did a substantial amount of business with the bank. But it also suggests that if we accept Carruthers's thesis of the politicisation of the market, which certainly seems to be borne out by the preferences of Tory customers of a Tory bank for a Tory company, women were not just financial agents but making political choices as well. The disproportionate preference for the South Sea Company's shares over those of the other moneyed companies and the level of purchases and sales does not indicate a population of passive investors waiting for their dividends.

Notes

1 I am grateful to the partners of C. Hoare and Co. for permission to use their archives and to their archivist, Pamela Hunter. This chapter draws on Anne Laurence, 'Women investors, "That nasty South Sea affair" and the rage to speculate in early eighteenth century England', *Accounting, Business and Financial History* 16, 2006, pp. 245–64, and on the paper 'Women, banks and the securities market in early eighteenth century England', given at the International Economic History Association conference held in Helsinki in 2006.
2 For example, Adrian Wilson has shown how politicised was the world of charity hospitals in the eighteenth century in 'Conflict, consensus and charity: politics and provincial charity hospitals in the eighteenth century', *English Historical Review* 111, 1996, p. 604.
3 P.G.M. Dickson, *The Financial Revolution in England: A Study in the Development of Public Credit 1688–1756*, London: Macmillan, 1967, pp. 256, 268–9.
4 S. Staves, 'Investments, votes and "bribes": women as shareholders in the chartered national companies', in H.L. Smith (ed.), *Women Writers and the Early Modern British Political Tradition*, Cambridge: Cambridge University Press, 1998, p. 269.
5 Staves, 'Investments, votes and "bribes"', p. 270.
6 Ann Carlos and Larry Neal, 'Women investors in early capital markets 1720–1725', *Financial History Review* 11, 2004, pp. 197–224; David R. Green and Alastair Owens, 'Gentlewomanly capitalism? Spinsters, widows, and wealth holding in England and Wales, c.1800–1860', *Economic History Review* 56, 2003, pp. 510–36; Josephine Maltby and Janette Rutterford, '"She possessed her own fortune": women investors from the late nineteenth century to the early twentieth century', *Business History* 48, 2006, pp. 220–53 and Janette Rutterford and Josephine Maltby, '"The widow, the clergyman and the reckless" – women investors in England 1830–1914', *Feminist Economics* 12, 2006, pp. 111–38, as well as the special issue of *Accounting, Business and Financial History* 16, 2006, have all considered aspects of women's investment.
7 Amy Froide, *Never Married: Singlewomen in Early Modern England*, Oxford: Oxford University Press, 2005, p. 115.
8 Froide, *Never Married*, pp. 134–6.
9 Dickson, *Financial Revolution*, p. 268.
10 Julian Hoppit, 'The myths of the South Sea Bubble', *Transactions of the Royal Historical Society* 6th series, 12, 2002, p. 150; Dickson, *Financial Revolution*, p. 282.
11 Carlos and Neal, 'Women investors', p. 214.
12 Kenneth J. Weiller and Philip Mirowski, 'Rates of interest in eighteenth century England', *Explorations in Economic History* 27, 1990, p. 6.
13 Gregory Clark, 'Debts, deficits and crowding out: England 1727–1840', *European Review of Economic History* 5, 2001, p. 409.

14 Weiller and Mirowski, 'Rates of interest', p. 6; Dickson, *Financial Revolution*, pp. 399–401.

15 Dickson, *Financial Revolution*, pp. 343, 358, 424.

16 Malcolm Balen, *A Very English Deceit: The Secret History of the South Sea Bubble and the First Great Financial Scandal*, London: Fourth Estate, 2002, pp. 16, 34, 35; C. L'Estrange Ewen, *Lotteries and Sweepstakes: An Historical, Legal and Ethical Survey*, London: Heath Cranton, 1932, p. 163; Anne L. Murphy, 'Lotteries in the 1690s: investment or gamble?', *Financial History Review* 12, 2005, p. 232.

17 Murphy, 'Lotteries in the 1690s', pp. 241, 242; Dickson, *Financial Revolution*, p. 282.

18 Murphy, 'Lotteries in the 1690s', p. 242.

19 In the later sixteenth century, 26 per cent of landowners left no son; by the eighteenth century this figure was 63 per cent. Lawrence Stone and Jeanne C. Fawtier Stone, *An Open Elite? England 1540–1880*, abridged edn, Oxford: Oxford University Press, 1986, p. 63.

20 Ann Carlos, Karen Maguire and Larry Neal, 'Financial acumen, women speculators, and the Royal African Company during the South Sea Bubble', *Accounting, Business and Financial History* 16 (2), 2006, pp. 222–3.

21 Judith Spicksley, 'Usury legislation, cash and credit: the development of the female investor in the late Tudor and Stuart periods', *Economic History Review* 61, 2008, p. 282.

22 S.R. Cope, 'The stock exchange revisited: a new look at the market in securities in the eighteenth century', *Economica* 45, 1978, pp. 2–3.

23 George Berkeley, *An Essay Towards Preventing the Ruine of Great Britain*, London, 1721, pp. 5, 6.

24 *The Weekly Journal or British Gazetteer*, 26 March 1720, p. 1563.

25 Ann Carlos, Jennifer Key and Jill Dupree, 'Learning and the creation of stock market institutions: evidence from the Royal African and Hudson's Bay companies, 1670–1700', *Journal of Economic History* 58, 1998, pp. 320, 340; Frank T. Melton, *Sir Robert Clayton and the Origins of English Deposit Banking*, Cambridge: Cambridge University Press, 1986, p. 216; Peter Temin and Hans-Joachim Voth, 'Riding the South Sea Bubble', *American Economic Review* 95, 2004, p. 1657.

26 Peter Temin and Hans-Joachim Voth, 'Banking as an emerging technology: Hoare's Bank, 1702–42', *Financial History Review* 13, 2006, p. 178.

27 Cope, 'The stock exchange revisited', pp. 8–9.

28 These figures differ from those published in Laurence, 'Women investors', because they disaggregate men and women and the basis of the sample is different, but the general tale they tell is similar.

29 Laurence, 'Women investors', pp. 251–9; Anne Laurence, 'Lady Betty Hastings, her half-sisters and the South Sea Bubble', *Women's History Review* 15, 2006, pp. 534–6.

30 For a detailed analysis of her trading, see Laurence, 'Women investors', pp. 251–5.

31 Laurence, 'Women investors', p. 256.

32 National Library of Ireland, Smythe of Barbavilla Papers, MS 41,580/11, Frances Hastings to Jane Bonnell, 7 September 1720.

33 Temin and Voth, 'Riding the South Sea Bubble', pp. 1658, 1666.

34 B.G. Carruthers, *City of Capital: Politics and Markets in the English Financial Revolution*, Princeton, NJ: Princeton University Press, 1996, pp. 5–6. But see Larry Neal's criticisms that without price data the results are unsatisfactory. *Economic History Review* 50, 1997, pp. 560–1.

35 Dickson, *Financial Revolution*, p. 425.

36 David Stasavage, *Public Debt and the Birth of the Democratic State: France and Great Britain 1688–1789*, Cambridge: Cambridge University Press, 2003, p. 6.

37 Staves, 'Investments, votes and "bribes"', p. 278.

38 Elaine Chalus, 'Elite women, social politics and the political world of late eighteenth

century England', *Historical Journal* 43, 2000, p. 671; eadem, *Elite Women in English Political Life*, c.*1754–1790*, Oxford: Clarendon Press, 2005.
39 Chalus, 'Elite women, social politics', p. 672.
40 Susan Kingsley Kent, *Gender and Power in Britain 1640–1990*, London: Routledge, 1999. Susan Whyman, however, has looked at women of the Verney family and their role in early-eighteenth-century politics. Susan Whyman, *Sociability and Power in Late-Stuart England: The Cultural World of the Verneys 1660–1720*, Oxford: Oxford University Press, 1999, especially chapter 6.

Bibliography

Balen, Malcolm, *A Very English Deceit: The Secret History of the South Sea Bubble and the First Great Financial Scandal*, London: Fourth Estate, 2002.

Berkeley, George, *An Essay Towards Preventing the Ruine of Great Britain*, London, 1721.

Carlos, Ann and Neal, Larry, 'Women investors in early capital markets 1720–1725', *Financial History Review* 11, 2004, pp. 197–224.

Carlos, Ann, Key, Jennifer and Dupree, Jill, 'Learning and the creation of stock market institutions: evidence from the Royal African and Hudson's Bay companies, 1670–1700', *Journal of Economic History* 58, 1998, pp. 318–44.

Carlos, Ann, Maguire, Karen and Neal, Larry, 'Financial acumen, women speculators, and the Royal African Company during the South Sea Bubble', *Accounting, Business and Financial History* 16 (2), 2006, pp. 219–44.

Carruthers, B.G., *City of Capital: Politics and Markets in the English Financial Revolution*, Princeton, NJ: Princeton University Press, 1996.

Chalus, Elaine, *Elite Women in English Political Life*, c.*1754–1790*, Oxford: Clarendon Press, 2005.

Chalus, Elaine, 'Elite women, social politics and the political world of late eighteenth century England', *Historical Journal* 43, 2000, pp. 669–97.

Clark, Gregory, 'Debts, deficits and crowding out: England 1727–1840', *European Review of Economic History* 5, 2001, pp. 403–36.

Cope, S.R., 'The stock exchange revisited: a new look at the market in securities in the eighteenth century', *Economica* 45, 1978, pp. 1–21.

Dickson, P.G.M., *The Financial Revolution in England: A Study in the Development of Public Credit 1688–1756*, London: Macmillan, 1967.

Ewen, C. L'Estrange, *Lotteries and Sweepstakes: An Historical, Legal and Ethical Survey*, London: Heath Cranton, 1932.

Froide, Amy, *Never Married: Singlewomen in Early Modern England*, Oxford: Oxford University Press, 2005.

Green, David R. and Owens, Alastair, 'Gentlewomanly capitalism? Spinsters, widows, and wealth holding in England and Wales, c.1800–1860', *Economic History Review* 56, 2003, pp. 510–36.

Hoppit, Julian, 'The myths of the South Sea Bubble', *Transactions of the Royal Historical Society* 6th series, 12, 2002, pp. 141–65.

Kent, Susan Kingsley, *Gender and Power in Britain 1640–1990*, London: Routledge, 1999.

Laurence, Anne, 'Lady Betty Hastings, her half-sisters and the South Sea Bubble: family fortunes and strategies', *Women's History Review* 15, 2006, pp. 533–40.

Laurence, Anne, 'Women investors, "That nasty South Sea affair" and the rage to speculate in early eighteenth century England', *Accounting, Business and Financial History* 16 (2), 2006, pp. 245–64.

Maltby, Josephine and Rutterford, Janette, '"She possessed her own fortune": women investors from the late nineteenth century to the early twentieth century', *Business History* 48, 2006, pp. 220–53.

Melton, Frank T., *Sir Robert Clayton and the Origins of English Deposit Banking*, Cambridge: Cambridge University Press, 1986.

Murphy, Anne L., 'Lotteries in the 1690s: investment or gamble?', *Financial History Review* 12, 2005, pp. 227–46.

National Library of Ireland, Smythe of Barbavilla Papers.

Neal, Larry, review of Carruthers, *City of Capital*, *Economic History Review* 50, 1997, pp. 560–1.

Rutterford, Janette and Maltby, Josephine, '"The widow, the clergyman and the reckless" – women investors in England 1830–1914', *Feminist Economics* 12, 2006, pp. 111–38.

Spicksley, Judith, 'Usury legislation, cash and credit: the development of the female investor in the late Tudor and Stuart periods', *Economic History Review* 61, 2008, pp. 277–301.

Stasavage, David, *Public Debt and the Birth of the Democratic State: France and Great Britain 1688–1789*, Cambridge: Cambridge University Press, 2003.

Staves, S., 'Investments, votes and "bribes": women as shareholders in the chartered national companies', in Smith, H.L. (ed.), *Women Writers and the Early Modern British Political Tradition*, Cambridge: Cambridge University Press, 1998, pp. 259–78.

Stone, Lawrence and Stone, Jeanne C. Fawtier, *An Open Elite? England 1540–1880*, abridged edn, Oxford: Oxford University Press, 1986.

Temin, Peter and Voth, Hans-Joachim, 'Banking as an emerging technology: Hoare's Bank, 1702–42', *Financial History Review* 13, 2006, pp. 149–78.

Temin, Peter and Voth, Hans-Joachim 'Riding the South Sea Bubble', *American Economic Review* 95, 2004, pp. 1654–68.

Weekly Journal or British Gazetteer, The.

Weiller, Kenneth J. and Mirowski, Philip, 'Rates of interest in eighteenth century England', *Explorations in Economic History* 27, 1990, pp. 1–28.

Whyman, Susan, *Sociability and Power in Late-Stuart England: the Cultural World of the Verneys 1660–1720*, Oxford: Oxford University Press, 1999.

Wilson, Adrian, 'Conflict, consensus and charity: politics and provincial charity hospitals in the eighteenth century', *English Historical Review* 111, 1996, pp. 599–619.

5 Women investors and financial knowledge in eighteenth-century Germany

Eve Rosenhaft

Any attempt to survey the bases for women's financial activity in eighteenth-century Germany faces a serious problem of evidence. This is to some extent a consequence of the relatively limited historiography. Business historians in Germany have been slow to adopt the kinds of cultural analysis that have enabled the dissection of gendered representations and practices and made women's financial activity visible in Britain.[1] Similarly, the vision of the eighteenth century as a key period in the emergence of a consumer society, which has been central to historical understanding of changing attitudes to money, savings and investment, has only recently been taken up in the German historiography – in spite of the pioneering conceptual work done by German social theorists on this very theme earlier in the twentieth century.[2]

To some extent, of course, the silence of the historical literature reflects the relative unimportance of the eighteenth century in German economic development. We have to look hard in the German sources to find the kinds of representations of the world of goods and commerce that permeate English popular culture in the same period, and there are good reasons for this. It was only in the nineteenth century that the effects of political fragmentation were overcome and the kind of dynamic could develop in both the industrial and the financial sectors that would make the notion of the 'popular investor' (of either sex) conceivable.[3] Accordingly, what work there is on women in modern business in Germany has focused on the nineteenth and twentieth centuries and on women's roles as company directors and managers or in family firms.[4]

There is a paradox here, though. If the eighteenth century has been of little interest to 'mainstream' economic history, it has a central place in German feminist historiography. In particular, the decades between 1750 and 1850 have been identified as a watershed in the emergence of modern gender relations, as the discursive construct of a polarity of gender characters established itself and was deployed to underpin an institutionalised concept of separate spheres.[5] In the German context, this has been associated specifically with the emergence of a new administrative and service middle class, whose ethical self-consciousness stamped the culture of the period and carried within it significant potential for social and institutional innovation. It is among these middle-class men and women, who typically defined themselves as without heritable property and reliant on the careful management of money incomes for their survival, that we would (and do) seek the first generations of 'modern' investors. But while the project of elaborating and critiquing the 'separate spheres' thesis has produced some excellent case studies of middle-class family life, these have emphasised affective and domestic relations and made little or no reference to financial practices and strategies.

It could even be argued that one of the earliest insights of German feminist historiography has acted as a brake on research into women and finance. Under historical regimes of gender guardianship (*Geschlechtsvormundschaft*), women were formally denied the status of legal persons, the key precondition for undertaking any kind of business in their own right. Husbands typically enjoyed the right of disposal over property that their wives brought into the marriage. The economic disability of married women was perpetuated in the Civil Code of the new empire at the end of the nineteenth century, with particular reference to middle-class (non-labouring) households, and the responsibility of a married woman to prioritise her family and household duties over economic activity remained fixed in West German law until the 1970s. For a long time, then, a kind of knowingness about what women could not do prevailed among historians. This has begun to give way to grounded knowledge about the extent of variation over time and space in the character and application of *Geschlechtsvormundschaft* and the variety of inheritance practices in what was, after all, a highly variegated politico-legal order, and the many ways that families found to provide a degree of independence for women within marriage and after the death of their husbands.[6]

This more nuanced picture is the result not least of finding women as economic actors in history and asking how, after all, it was possible for them to act. It remains the case that at this stage in the development of the field the evidence is scattered and often anecdotal, and more suggestive than definitive. One text produced early in the century is evidence, if such were needed, of women's capacity to acquire and apply financial knowledge. This is the autobiography of Glückel von Hameln, a Jewish merchant's daughter born in Hamburg in 1646/7. In Glückel's circles, money was equally central to the business of the world and to the business of maintaining family and friendship networks. In the elaborate genealogical account that opens the book, each coupling is assessed in terms of the balance between the size of the dowry (settled on either bride or groom) and the quality of the match, each family dispute in terms of the court costs. Glückel delights in the story of her grandmother who saved her allowance and lent it out at interest in order to amass 200 Reichstaler with which to repay her son-in-law for looking after her in her old age (a gift which he honourably returned to her with a supplement of 100 Reichstaler). An important feature of the account is that as an adult woman at least Glückel could always say where the money had come from and why. Her husband traded in precious stones, and having taken an active role in the business she displays a knowledge not only of the trade itself but also of the credit instruments and forms of investment (including the primitive speculative practice of pawning inventory in anticipation of a rise in its market price) available in her day, of different currencies and of the financial implications and risks of entering into business partnerships. When her first husband died, deliberately entrusting the management of his estate and the children to her rather than appointing an administrator, she was neither surprised to find herself responsible for the repayment of substantial debts nor at a loss as to how to pay them. A sale of the remaining inventory at carefully calculated prices brought in enough to cover the debts and provide a substantial capital, most of which she lent out at interest. Her second husband's bankruptcy and the way it was managed climax her account of her maturity and old age.[7]

Glückel's affinity for money matters bespeaks a quite specific cultural and historical context. The absence of a clear distinction between financial and familial transactions (or between money and emotion as mediators of intimate relationships) was a feature of all social relations in the early modern period that retained its rationale in merchant and agrarian households well into the nineteenth century and also (in the form of the arranged marriage and the dowry) had a particular tradition and tenacity in German Jewry.[8] In terms of the forms and sources of knowledge on which she relied, too, Glückel's activity can be seen as period-specific and relatively bounded. She was socialised into the technologies and knowledges specific to her family's 'trades' and gained information through local and personal networks. Her investment activity was similarly limited to the exploitation of local opportunities for the manipulation of credit. In this respect she was not different from early modern rural or artisan women who supplemented their productive earnings by engaging in money-lending, and who could display a keen awareness of the formal and customary limits on interest that constrained their earning power.[9]

Women of the salaried middle classes were equally dependent on local networks and sources of information in their investment behaviour and probably remained so throughout the century. It is clear that unmarried women were expected to rely on the management of cash for their livelihoods beyond any direct support they could receive from family members. This was particularly true of widows, where the expectation – perhaps more often expressed than met – was that they would be able to live from the interest on a capital sum reserved by contract at marriage or fixed on them by their husband (in the form of a legacy or jointure) or their father (in the form of a dowry).[10] As a result, investment of one kind or another was central to the lives of these women. Personal credit, on both a small and a large scale, was an important source of income. In the university town of Göttingen, for example, a disproportionate number of lenders in the first half of the century were women. Widows, including the relicts of professors and officeholders disposing over large sums, were responsible for some 70 per cent of the funds lent, most of them against collateral in the form of real estate.[11] Women with money to spare also took advantage of the opportunity available in most territories of depositing capital with the city or state treasury against interest payments.

Upon learning in 1796 that the state treasury in Hanover, in which she had invested 6,000 Reichstaler, was reducing its interest rate, one Louise Barth complained of 'how hard it is to get a good return on one's money these days'.[12] This a reminder that while this kind of investment relied in the first instance on local and familiar forms of knowledge, dependence on investment income placed women in a position of being alert to new opportunities. There is evidence in Germany as elsewhere of the power of women's expanding investment activity and their demand for new kinds of financial services to drive both institutional and cultural innovation – in a kind of *tacit* contribution to economic and social modernity.[13] When and how far did they begin to participate self-consciously in financial 'modernity' by actively seeking new kinds and new sources of knowledge? When were they able to look beyond information that was case-specific and transmitted through personal networks and in the form of familiar practices ('*I know what "investing" means and want only to know what the best opportunities are within my social and geographical sphere*'), and seek to gather potentially useful information on a 'speculative', impersonal basis by inserting themselves into supra-local communication streams ('*I want to know what it means to invest [nowadays], and what kinds of opportunities there are or might be – to be found or to be made*')? The possibility of a shift of this kind is implicit in the burst of innovation in commercial practices and communications that characterised the eighteenth century, even in the backwaters of provincial Germany.[14] The evidence we have suggests that German women were relatively slow to gain access to the public and media spaces where innovation took place. Over the course of the century, however, middle-class women were able to use the opportunities provided by an increasingly information-rich environment to identify and respond to changing conditions for investment.

One place to look for widening circles of financial knowledge is the years 1718 to 1722, what might be called the 'breakthrough moment' of a modern culture of speculative investment. These witnessed the South Sea Bubble and its continental prelude, the Mississippi Scheme, through which the Scotsman John Law attempted to establish a paper-money regime in France on the basis of stock issues against a project for the settlement and exploitation of colonial territories in America. What characterised both these cases and impressed contemporaries was that the passion for buying and selling stock rapidly spread to people of all classes and both sexes – a dubious democratisation that took material form in the close association between speculative activity and public places, Exchange Alley in London and the Rue Quincampoix in Paris. The presence of both men and women in these spaces, like the independent evidence of women acting as stock traders as well as purchasers, bespeaks women's participation in information networks that equipped them with the requisite knowledge both of the market and of the product. These networks were clearly formal and supra-regional as well as informal and local, since both the South Sea and Mississippi events generated a mass of periodical and pamphlet literature.[15]

The German lands were not unaffected by the waves set off in London and Paris, but such evidence as we have so far suggests that the impact was limited. The news-sheets published in the principal German cities served as 'shop windows' for the events in foreign capitals, though the bulk of what they carried was more in the nature of gossip and sensation than useful knowledge. Of the German publications about the Mississippi project, there is one that appears to have been written for potential investors; it contains a simple but relatively detailed account of what stocks are and how they are bought and sold. Its author, Paul Jacob Marperger – a prolific populariser of economic knowledge – included in his comments an implicit critique of the provincialism of the Germans:

> To be sure, all that glitters is not gold, but on the other hand not all Columbian projects are to be rejected out of hand, even if many a one who is at home only within his own four walls cannot grasp this.[16]

Clearly, at this stage speculation was still a business for professionals in Germany. According to press reports, it was 'money men' from Hamburg (the commercial and overseas trading centre) and Leipzig (a market and banking centre) who had invested in South Sea and Mississippi shares.[17] The great bubbles found a little echo in a brief episode of the summer of 1720, when a group of Hamburg merchants began to sell stock in a new insurance company; the anxious city fathers of Hamburg brought the project to an end within six weeks. In the meanwhile, a lively speculative trade had developed. As soon as the issue was announced, trading began 'on the Exchange, [in] the Ratskeller, the Retailers' Company and other well known taprooms and coffee houses'; from six in the morning to past midnight over four consecutive days there was 'hardly any trade on the exchange except in stock'.[18] Here we also find evidence of information circulating at a supra-regional level; in creating a new kind of insurance scheme, the Hamburg traders were reported to have acted in emulation of Dutch entrepreneurs. The trading venues enumerated here, though, are the familiar loci of exchange between men of the economic and political establishment; there is little sign of the democratic free-for-all embodied in the visions of Exchange Alley and the Rue Quincampoix.

By the same token, it appears that any increase in speculative activity did not extend to women outside of very specific, largely elite circles. Of the individuals on record as trading in South Sea shares, 29 were based in the German lands (15 in Berlin, three in or near Hamburg, eight in Hanover and three in other locations), and of these, six were women.[19] As with most of the investors named, there is reason to suppose that their involvement in this speculative venture was the result of family connections that linked them to international commercial and information networks. Thus the two investors based in the city of Hamburg (one of them a woman) had English names, while the bulk of the Berlin investors, including two of the women, had French names and were probably (in one case certainly) members of the refugee Huguenot community that had been settled in Berlin since 1685. The Huguenots pioneered the development of modern financial institutions in Prussia, not least because of their continuing connections with financial centres all over Europe – including, of course,

France.[20] The relatively large contingent based in Hanover comprised members of established families who had made their careers in service to the territorial administration and/or the royal court; that is, they were particularly well placed to be aware of developments on the London Stock Exchange and likely to be interested. The South Sea investor Catharina Margarete Hinüber was one of these.[21]

A final category of female investor is represented by Countess 'Margaret Gertrud Lippe'. This was very probably Margaret Gertrud von Oeynhausen (1698–1726), daughter of George I by his mistress the Duchess of Kendal and daughter-in-law of Countess Johanna Sophie of Schaumburg-Lippe. Johanna Sophie was lady-in-waiting to the Princess of Wales, Caroline of Ansbach.

Here we have reached the nodal point in a network of communication among elite (royal) women that certainly transmitted financial news. The question of how far the participants were interested in useful knowledge, though, remains an open one. The involvement of the Princess of Wales and her associates in South Sea trading is well established. The diary of Mary Countess Cowper, lady of the bedchamber to the Princess, reveals Countess Cowper herself as a woman with intimate knowledge of the intrigues both political and financial associated with the South Sea Bubble, and at home with the jargon (at least) of stock prices and interest rates. She writes knowingly in April 1720 of Walpole's plans for making up a shortfall on South Sea income through the purchase and resale of insurances, and reports further that part of Walpole's politico-financial strategy was to buy South Sea stock in the names of both the Prince and the Princess of Wales, so that by May the Princess had a personal investment in the scheme. But Countess Cowper also takes occasion to comment on the relative innocence of the Germans: 'Bernstorff, nor Bothmar, nor none of the Germans, knew of this except the Duchess of Kendal, whom English Money and an English Title had made true to the English Ministers.'[22]

The impression of the relative innocence of the Germans in financial affairs is reinforced by the evidence of the correspondence between the Princess of Wales, Johanna Sophie Schaumburg-Lippe, and the German princess who was closest to the Mississippi scheme. This was the Duchess Elisabeth Charlotte d'Orléans, daughter of the Elector Palatine. As the mother of the Duke of Orléans, regent of France and the man principally responsible for promoting and instituting Law's financial schemes, she could hardly have been closer to the Mississippi scandal, and she observed Law's activities with interest and, initially, some enthusiasm. Moreover, her letters show that she was well aware of events in London; she reported and commented spontaneously about these matters to all of her wide circle of correspondents, and her letters to Johanna Sophie and the Princess of Wales indicate that the conversation was not a one-sided one. But the leitmotif in all of her letters is incomprehension. Thus in August 1719 she wrote to her half-sister Louise, 'For the last six days there's been nothing new here except lots of financial business, which I can't tell you about, for I do not understand it'; while 15 months later, as both London and Paris were in turmoil, she observed:

I'm willing to bet the King in England will have a great deal of trouble to bring the South Sea business to a good end. I see how it goes here with the accursed Mississippi. I have such an aversion to all this stuff that I have forbidden my people ever to speak about this or about the constitution in my presence. I understand neither the one nor the other, but they are both as abhorrent to me as a purge.[23]

Visiting London two generations later (in 1786), Sophie von la Roche displayed a similar ingenuousness about the role and function of the Bank of England. The Bank was one of the obvious attractions for an educated Anglophile tourist, and her published diary describes in considerable detail the building and the people within it, going about their various activities 'paying in bank-notes, handing out money in exchange for paper, or taking the former and giving the latter', weighing and transporting gold. But the emphasis is on the gold which materialises both the possibilities of wealth and its perils (what comes spontaneously to mind for her is the 'miserable plight of the blacks who extract it').[24] This is of interest not least because Sophie von la Roche was an entrepreneur herself; the author of extremely popular sentimental fiction and one of the first women writing in German to earn her living as an author, she also published a series of short-lived women's magazines.[25] In this sense, her own work was implicated in the development of the periodical press that was at the centre of the eighteenth century's information revolution and that certainly contributed to heightening awareness and knowledge of financial affairs. And it is accordingly unlikely that she was as indifferent to money matters as her sketch of the Bank of England implies, though her moralising ambivalence does seem more characteristic even of late-eighteenth-century Germans than of British contemporaries.[26]

As early as the 1720s, intelligencers in major cities like Hamburg carried listings of London share prices alongside those of commodity prices and exchange rates, but this was 'back-page' information for specialists.[27] By the 1780s, one of these, the *Hamburgischer Correspondent*, had achieved a circulation that was significant by international standards and gave it the character of a 'national' newspaper, and at the same time financial affairs had penetrated its reportage and advertising sections. Similarly the high-circulation monthly *Politisches Journal*, first published in 1781, featured narrative reports on new joint-stock enterprises and share issues (such as those of the new Danish trading companies) that presumed a basic understanding of the nature of stock trading and the relationship between share prices and the wider economic and political scene.[28] Women (particularly widows) of the commercial classes literally had a hand in the circulation of printed information, since they were prominent as sellers of books and news-sheets. That middle-class women were active readers too is well attested, not least by the success of Sophie von la Roche and other women writers and publishers.

Publications designed for women largely eschewed anything that might be described as financial information, focusing instead on literature, entertainment or useful knowledge – including popular science. And the extent of women's participation in the formal networks through which print information circulated – lending libraries, reading societies and the like – remains a surprisingly under-researched area. But while it seems clear that women were not encouraged to read the kind of journals that carried financial news, it seems equally clear that women and girls of the educated classes had access to such literature at home, through the subscriptions or library borrowing of their menfolk.[29]

From mid-century, then, there is evidence that women's financial knowledge, like their investment behaviour, was beginning to extend beyond the opportunities afforded by familiar local relationships and networks – even if their access to information was often mediated by male relatives or acquaintances. The still very limited evidence we have on middle-class men's stock-market activity shows wives aware of and contributing to investment decisions. Balthasar Münter, a German clergyman resident in Copenhagen who invested heavily in the Danish trading companies in 1782 and reported his rising and falling fortunes to his son in Germany, also recorded his wife's reactions to the vicissitudes of the market.[30]

A more popular innovation in the realm of financial 'products' in the second half of the century was the publicly recruiting widows' fund (a kind of proto-life insurance scheme promising survivors' pensions in perpetuity against the payment of regular contributions during the husband's lifetime), and the history of the largest of these funds provides some insight into what women knew and how they came to know it.[31] The Calenbergische Witwen-Verpflegungs-Gesellschaft was founded in Hanover in 1766–7, and invited subscribers from all over Europe; by 1781 over 5,000 married couples had joined. In principle, only married men were to be subscribers and only their widows the beneficiaries. Here, too, though, both the records of the fund and the publicity that surrounded it (and other similar foundations) show that the decision to invest was often made jointly by the husband and wife. Moreover, in spite of its founders' intentions, the Calenberg opened up a space for women's independent financial initiative, not least because of the way its operation depended on maintaining a constant flow of information. Its managers began by advertising for new subscribers in the periodical press and through printed prospectuses, and continued to keep existing subscribers informed through the publication of semi-annual reports; reprinted in the principal regional intelligencers, these *Avertissements* also provided a shop-window for prospective subscribers. A further point of contact between the fund and its members was a group of agents based in Hanover, who were responsible for corresponding with both subscribers and pensioner widows who lived outside the city. They were expected to report to their clients at least twice a year, carrying on their business by post – and this included the widows. Agents mailed the widows their pension instalments, along with the printed *Avertissements*, and the widows posted back their receipts. These agents were mainly notaries by training; although officially subcontracted to the fund, they received fees from the subscribers and widows, and over the 15 years during which the fund flourished they developed an identity closer to that of a financial adviser, priding themselves on their familiarity with each couple and each widow on their books. It is possible that the agents also visited their clients, and also that some men acted as agents in other localities on a formal or informal basis.

Certainly, word of mouth and personal recommendation played a role in spreading knowledge about the fund and who was a member. Accordingly, we find women responding and intervening independently at each stage in the development of the fund. Among the first members of the public to express an interest in the new fund in 1766 was a widow who wrote hoping to be allowed to invest in a pension for herself. And when, in 1781, the fund was threatened with collapse, pensioner widows mobilised in self-defence against the prospect of a drastic cut in their pensions. The methods they used were relatively traditional – petitions and lawsuits; as such they continued to depend on the mediation of male professionals and relatives. But there is no reason to doubt that the 568 women who appear as signatories to the documents between 1781 and 1789 – often naming one of the Calenberg agents as proxy – were sufficiently informed about the business to know what they were doing. Similarly, while there remains a very wide field for research both on the eighteenth-century scene and on the question of continuities and discontinuities in middle-class investment experiences from the 'backward' eighteenth to the bustling nineteenth century, there is every reason to be optimistic that there is more evidence of women's active engagement with sources of financial knowledge waiting to be unearthed.

Notes

1 See, for example, the exchanges between Toni Pierenkemper, Manfred Pohl and Peter Borscheid in the *Zeitschrift für Unternehmensgeschichte* 1999–2001; Hartmut Berghoff, *Moderne Unternehmensgeschichte. Eine themen- und theorieorientierte Einführung*, Paderborn: Schöningh, 2004 – with a very limited acknowledgement of women and gender issues.
2 Heidrun Homburg, 'Werbung – "eine Kunst, die gelernt sein will". Aufbrüche in eine neue Warenwelt 1750–1850', *Jahrbuch für Wirtschaftsgeschichte*, 1997, pp. 11–52; Reinhold Reith and Torsten Meyer (eds), *Luxus und Konsum. Eine historische Annäherung*, Münster: Waxmann, 2003; Michael Prinz (ed.), *Der lange Weg in den Überfluss. Anfänge und Entwicklung der Konsumgesellschaft seit der Vormoderne*, Paderborn: Schöningh, 2003. The *locus classicus* is Werner Sombart, *Luxus und Kapitalismus* (1913).
3 Coleen Dunlavy has undertaken detailed research on shareholding in German railways in international comparison, for example 'Corporate democracy: stockholder voting rights in nineteenth-century American and Prussian railroad corporations', in Lena Andersson-Skog and Olle Krantz (eds), *Institutions in the Transport and Communication Industries: State and Private Actors in the Making of Institutional Patterns, 1850–1990*, Canton, MA: Science History Publications, 1999, pp. 33–60.
4 For example, Robert Beachy, 'Profit and propriety: Sophie Henschel and gender management in the German locomotive industry', in Robert Beachy, Béatrice Craig and Alastair Owens (eds), *Women, Business and Finance in Nineteenth-Century Europe. Rethinking Separate Spheres*, Oxford and New York: Berg, 2006, pp. 67–80; Christiane Eifert, 'Deutsche Unternehmerinnen und die Rhetorik vom "weiblichen Führungsstil" nach 1945', *Zeitschrift für Unternehmensgeschichte* 50, 2005, pp. 17–35.

5 For a survey of the history of this thesis in the German historiography and critical approaches to it, see Marion Gray and Ulrike Gleixner (eds), *Gender in Transition: Discourse and Practice in German-Speaking Europe 1750–1830*, Ann Arbor, MI: University of Michigan Press, 2006.

6 See most recently Nicole Grochowina and Hendrikje Carius (eds), *Eigentumskulturen und Geschlecht in der Frühen Neuzeit* (= *Comparativ* 15/4), Leipzig: University of Leipzig, 2005; Robert Beachy, 'Women without gender: commerce, exchange codes and the erosion of German gender guardianship, 1680–1830', in David R. Green and Alastair Owens (eds), *Family Welfare: Gender, Property and Inheritance since the Seventeenth Century*, Westport, CT: Praeger, 2004, pp. 195–216.

7 *Denkwürdigkeiten der Glückel von Hameln*, trans. and ed. Alfred Feilchenfeld, 1923, reprint Bodenheim: Philo, 1999, pp. 20–9, 43, 75f, 87–9, 181, 280–2.

8 Marion Kaplan, *The Making of a Jewish Middle Class*, New York: Oxford, 1991, pp. 88f. On women in merchant families, see Daniel A. Rabuzzi, 'Women as merchants in eighteenth-century northern Germany: the case of Stralsund 1750–1830', *Central European History* 28, 1995, pp. 435–56. On the property nexus in family relations, specifically in the countryside, see David Warren Sabean, *Property, Production and Family in Neckarhausen, 1700–1870*, Cambridge: Cambridge University Press, 1990.

9 Sheilagh Ogilvie, *A Bitter Living. Women, Markets, and Social Capital in Early Modern Germany*, Oxford: Oxford University Press, 2003, pp. 241f; see also Sabean, *Property, Production, and Family in Neckarhausen*.

10 Stefan Brakensiek, *Fürstendiener – Staatsbeamte – Bürger*, Göttingen: Vandenhoeck and Ruprecht, 1999, p. 248; Silvia Möhle, *Ehekonflikte und sozialer Wandel. Göttingen 1740–1840*, Frankfurt a. M. and New York: Campus, 1997, p. 92.

11 Norbert Winnige, 'Vom Leihen und Schulden in Göttingen. Studien zum Kapitalmarkt', in Hermann Wellenreuther (ed.), *Göttingen 1690–1755: Studien zur Sozialgeschichte einer Stadt*, Göttingen: Vandenhoeck and Ruprecht, 1988, pp. 252–320. See also Möhle, *Ehekonflikte*, p. 94; Karl Heinrich Kaufhold, 'Die Wirtschaft in der frühen Neuzeit: Gewerbe, Handel und Verkehr', in Christine van den Heuvel and Manfred von Boetticher (eds), *Geschichte Niedersachsens: Politik, Wirtschaft und Gesellschaft von der Reformation bis zum Beginn des 19. Jahrhunderts*, Hanover: Hahn, 1998, pp. 351–636, especially 564–74. For international comparators, see Beverly Lemire, Ruth Pearson and Gail Campbell (eds), *Women and Credit. Researching the Past, Refiguring the Future*, Oxford and New York: Berg, 2001.

12 Louise Barth to the Treasury Committee of the Calenberg Estates, 30 March 1796, Niedersächsisches Hauptstaatsarchiv Hannover, Dep 7B, no. 385, p. 7.

13 Eve Rosenhaft, 'Did women invent life insurance? Widows and the demand for financial services in eighteenth-century Germany', in Green and Owens, *Family Welfare*, pp. 163–94; Judith Spicksley, 'Usury legislation, cash, and credit: the development of the female investor in the late Tudor and Stuart periods', *Economic History Review* 61 (2), 2007, pp. 277–301.

14 Eve Rosenhaft, 'Hands and minds: clerical workloads in the first "information society"', in Aad Blok and Greg Downey (eds), *Uncovering Labour in Information Revolutions, 1750–2000*, Cambridge and New York: Cambridge University Press, 2003, pp. 13–43.

15 For the South Sea Bubble, see Chapters 3 and 4 in this volume. For a brief outline of the Mississippi project, see Peter M. Garber, *Famous First Bubbles. The Fundamentals of Early Manias*, Cambridge, MA: MIT, 2000, pp. 91–103; the classic account in English of the popular response is Charles Mackay, *Extraordinary Popular Delusions and the Madness of Crowds*, 1841, reprint Ware: Wordsworth Editions, 1995, pp. 1–44.

16 Paul Jacob Marperger, *Kurze Remarques über den jetziger Zeit weitberuffenen Missippischen Actien-Handel in Paris* [...], Dresden: Marperger, 1720; the quota-

tion is from p. 5 of a *Fortsetzung* (supplement), bound together with the main publication.

17 *Schlesischer Nouvellen-Courier* (Breslau), 1 July 1720; *Curieuse Anmerckung über den Staat von Franckreich [...]*, Leipzig: n.p., 1720, p. 3v.

18 *Schlesischer Nouvellen-Courier* (Breslau), 29 July 1720, appendix. Cf. Friedrich Plaß, *Geschichte der Assecuranz und der hanseatischen Seeversicherungs-Börsen*, Hamburg: Friederichsen, 1902, pp. 123–38.

19 Personal communication from Ann Carlos; cf. Ann Carlos and Larry Neal, 'Women investors in early capital markets 1720–1725', *Financial History Review* 11, 2004, pp. 197–224.

20 Jürgen Wilke, 'Der Einfluß der Hugenotten auf die gewerbliche Entwicklung', in G. Bregulla (ed.), *Hugenotten in Berlin*, Berlin: Union, 1988, pp. 227–80.

21 On the Hinüber family, see Hartmut von Hinüber, '"die wahre Intention unsers allergnädigsten Königs" – Das Profil der hannoverschen Familie v. Hinüber', *Berichte aus dem Heimatland* 2007, available online: www.heimatbund-niedersachsen.de/Hinuber_Ausstellung_1_.pdf (accessed 21 December 2007).

22 *Diary of Mary Countess Cowper*, ed. Spencer Cowper, London: John Murray, 1865, pp. 144f, 158.

23 *Briefe der Herzogin Elisabeth Charlotte von Orléans aus dem Jahre 1719*, ed. W.L. Holland, Tübingen: Laupp, 1877, p. 223; *Briefe der Herzogin Elisabeth Charlotte von Orléans aus dem Jahre 1720*, ed. W.L. Holland, Tübingen: Laupp, 1879, p. 339. See also Elisabeth Charlotte d'Orléans, *Briefe an Johanna Sophie von Schaumburg-Lippe*, St. Ingbert: Röhrig, 2003, especially nos. 39, 42, 43. Cf. Dirk van der Cruysse, *Madame Palatine, Princesse européenne*, Paris: Fayard, 1988, pp. 593–8.

24 *Sophie in London 1786, being the Diary of Sophie v. la Roche*, ed. and trans. Clare Williams, London: Jonathan Cape, 1933, pp. 164f.

25 See Jeannine Blackwell, 'Sophie von La Roche', in James Hardin and Christoph Schweitzer (eds), *Dictionary of Literary Biography: The Age of Goethe*, New York: Bruccoli, Clark and Gale, 1990.

26 Heidrun Homburg, 'Fortuna und Methode. Überlegungen zu einer Kulturgeschichte von Geld und Reichtum in der zweiten Hälfte des 18. Jahrhunderts', *Vierteljahrschrift für Sozial- und Wirtschaftsgeschichte* 92, 2005, pp. 16–30.

27 See, for example, *Hamburger Relations-Courier* (Hamburg), 6 August 1720.

28 *Politisches Journal* (Altona), 7 July, 9 September, 18 October 1782. Cf. Jeremy D. Popkin, 'Political communication in the German Enlightenment: Gottlob Benedikt von Schirach's *Politische Journal*', *Eighteenth-Century Life* 20, 1996, pp. 24–41.

29 Ulrike Weckel, *Zwischen Häuslichkeit und Öffentlichkeit. Die ersten deutschen Frauenzeitschriften im späten 18. Jahrhundert und ihr Publikum*, Tübingen: Niemeyer, 1998; Moira R. Rogers, *Newtonianism for the Ladies and Other Uneducated Souls*, New York: Lang, 2003; anecdotal evidence in Dorothea Friderika Baldinger, *Versuch über meine Verstandeserziehung*, Offenbach: Weiss und Brede, 1791, reprinted in Magdalene Heuser, Ortrun Niethammer, Marion Roitzheim-Eisfeld and Petra Wulbusch (eds), *'Ich wünschte so gar gelehrt zu werden', Drei Autobiographien von Frauen des 18. Jahrhunderts*, Göttingen: Wallstein, 1994, pp. 7–24, here p. 16.

30 The correspondence is in the Danish Royal Library, Copenhagen, file NKS, 520–8°.

31 For the following, see Rosenhaft, 'Did women invent life insurance?', Rosenhaft, 'Hands and minds'; Eve Rosenhaft, 'Secrecy and publicity in the emergence of modern business culture: pension funds in Hamburg 1760–1780', in Anne Goldgar and Robert I. Frost (eds), *Institutional Culture in Early Modern Society*, Leiden: Brill, 2004, pp. 218–43.

Bibliography

Baldinger, Dorothea Friderika, *Versuch über meine Verstandeserziehung*, Offenbach: Weiss und Brede, 1791, reprinted in Heuser, M., Niethammer, O., Roitzheim-Eisfeld, M. and Wulbusch, P. (eds), *'Ich wünschte so gar gelehrt zu werden'. Drei Autobiographien von Frauen des 18. Jahrhunderts*, Göttingen: Wallstein, 1994, pp. 7–24.

Beachy, Robert, 'Profit and propriety: Sophie Henschel and gender management in the German locomotive industry', in Beachy, Robert, Craig, Béatrice and Owens, Alastair (eds), *Women, Business and Finance in Nineteenth-Century Europe. Rethinking Separate Spheres*, Oxford and New York: Berg, 2006, pp. 67–80.

Beachy, Robert, 'Women without gender: commerce, exchange codes and the erosion of German gender guardianship, 1680–1830', in Green, David R. and Owens, Alastair (eds), *Family Welfare: Gender, Property and Inheritance since the Seventeenth Century*, Westport, CT: Praeger, 2004, pp. 195–216.

Berghoff, Hartmut, *Moderne Unternehmensgeschichte. Eine themen- und theorieorientierte Einführung*, Paderborn: Schöningh, 2004.

Blackwell, Jeannine, 'Sophie von La Roche', in Hardin, James and Schweitzer, Christoph (eds), *Dictionary of Literary Biography: The Age of Goethe*, New York: Bruccoli, Clark and Gale, 1990.

Brakensiek, Stefan, *Fürstendiener – Staatsbeamte – Bürger*, Göttingen: Vandenhoeck and Ruprecht, 1999.

Carlos, Ann and Neal, Larry, 'Women investors in early capital markets 1720–1725', *Financial History Review* 11, 2004, pp. 197–224.

Cowper, Mary Countess, *Diary of Mary Countess Cowper*, ed. Spencer Cowper, London: John Murray, 1865.

Dunlavy, Coleen, 'Corporate democracy: stockholder voting rights in nineteenth-century American and Prussian railroad corporations', in Andersson-Skog, Lena and Krantz, Olle (eds), *Institutions in the Transport and Communication Industries: State and Private Actors in the Making of Institutional Patterns, 1850–1990*, Canton, MA: Science History Publications, 1999, pp. 33–60.

Eifert, Christiane, 'Deutsche Unternehmerinnen und die Rhetorik vom "weiblichen Führungsstil" nach 1945', *Zeitschrift für Unternehmensgeschichte* 50, 2005, pp. 17–35.

Garber, Peter M., *Famous First Bubbles. The Fundamentals of Early Manias*, Cambridge, MA: MIT, 2000.

Gray, Marion and Gleixner, Ulrike (eds), *Gender in Transition: Discourse and Practice in German-Speaking Europe 1750–1830*, Ann Arbor, MI: University of Michigan Press, 2006.

Grochowina, Nicole, and Carius, Hendrikje (eds), *Eigentumskulturen und Geschlecht in der Frühen Neuzeit* (= *Comparativ* 15/4), Leipzig: University of Leipzig, 2005.

Hameln, Glückel von, *Denkwürdigkeiten der Glückel von Hameln*, trans. and ed. Alfred Feilchenfeld, 1923, reprint Bodenheim: Philo, 1999.

Hinüber, Hartmut von, '"die wahre Intention unsers allergnädigsten Königs" – Das Profil der hannoverschen Familie v. Hinüber', *Berichte aus dem Heimatland* 2007, available online: www.heimatbund-niedersachsen.de/Hinuber_Ausstellung_1_.pdf (accessed 21 December 2007).

Homburg, Heidrun, 'Fortuna und Methode. Überlegungen zu einer Kulturgeschichte von Geld und Reichtum in der zweiten Hälfte des 18. Jahrhunderts', *Vierteljahrschrift für Sozial- und Wirtschaftsgeschichte* 92, 2005, pp. 16–30.

Homburg, Heidrun, 'Werbung – "eine Kunst, die gelernt sein will". Aufbrüche in eine neue Warenwelt 1750–1850', *Jahrbuch für Wirtschaftsgeschichte* 1997, pp. 11–52.

Kaplan, Marion, *The Making of a Jewish Middle Class*, New York: Oxford, 1991.

Kaufhold, Karl Heinrich, 'Die Wirtschaft in der frühen Neuzeit: Gewerbe, Handel und Verkehr', in van den Heuvel, Christine and von Boetticher, Manfred (eds), *Geschichte Niedersachsens: Politik, Wirtschaft und Gesellschaft von der Reformation bis zum Beginn des 19. Jahrhunderts*, Hanover: Hahn, 1998, pp. 351–636.

la Roche, Sophie von, *Sophie in London 1786, being the Diary of Sophie v. la Roche*, ed. and trans. Clare Williams, London: Jonathan Cape, 1933.

Lemire, Beverly, Pearson, Ruth and Campbell, Gail (eds), *Women and Credit. Researching the Past, Refiguring the Future*, Oxford and New York: Berg, 2001.

Mackay, Charles, *Extraordinary Popular Delusions and the Madness of Crowds*, 1841, reprint Ware: Wordsworth Editions, 1995.

Marperger, Paul Jacob, *Kurze Remarques über den jetizer Zeit weitberuffenen Missippischen Actien-Handel in Paris [...]*, Dresden: Marperger, 1720.

Möhle, Silvia, *Ehekonflikte und sozialer Wandel. Göttingen 1740–1840*, Frankfurt a. M. and New York: Campus, 1997.

Ogilvie, Sheilagh, *A Bitter Living. Women, Markets, and Social Capital in Early Modern Germany*, Oxford: Oxford University Press, 2003.

Orléans, Elisabeth Charlotte, Duchess of, *Briefe an Johanna Sophie von Schaumburg-Lippe*, St. Ingbert: Röhrig, 2003.

Orléans, Elisabeth Charlotte, Duchess of, *Briefe der Herzogin Elisabeth Charlotte von Orléans aus dem Jahre 1720*, ed. W.L. Holland, Tübingen: Laupp, 1879.

Orléans, Elisabeth Charlotte, Duchess of, *Briefe der Herzogin Elisabeth Charlotte von Orléans aus dem Jahre 1719*, ed. W.L. Holland, Tübingen: Laupp, 1877.

Plaß, Friedrich, *Geschichte der Assecuranz und der hanseatischen Seeversicherungs-Börsen*, Hamburg: Friederichsen, 1902, pp. 123–38.

Popkin, Jeremy D., 'Political communication in the German Enlightenment: Gottlob Benedikt von Schirach's *Politische Journal*', *Eighteenth Century Life* 20, 1996, pp. 24–41.

Prinz, Michael (ed.), *Der lange Weg in den Überfluss. Anfänge und Entwicklung der Konsumgesellschaft seit der Vormoderne*, Paderborn: Schöningh, 2003.

Rabuzzi, Daniel A., 'Women as merchants in eighteenth-century northern Germany: the case of Stralsund 1750–1830', *Central European History* 28, 1995, pp. 435–56.

Reith, Reinhold, and Meyer, Torsten (eds), *Luxus und Konsum. Eine historische Annäherung*, Münster: Waxmann, 2003.

Rogers, Moira R., *Newtonianism for the Ladies and Other Uneducated Souls*, New York: Lang, 2003.

Rosenhaft, Eve, 'Did women invent life insurance? Widows and the demand for financial services in eighteenth-century Germany', in Green, David R. and Owens, Alastair (eds), *Family Welfare: Gender, Property and Inheritance since the Seventeenth Century*, Westport, CT: Praeger, 2004, pp. 163–94.

Rosenhaft, Eve, 'Secrecy and publicity in the emergence of modern business culture: pension funds in Hamburg 1760–1780', in Goldgar, Anne and Frost, Robert I. (eds), *Institutional Culture in Early Modern Society*, Leiden: Brill, 2004, pp. 218–43.

Rosenhaft, Eve, 'Hands and minds: clerical workloads in the first "information society"', in Blok, Aad and Downey, Greg (eds), *Uncovering Labour in Information Revolutions, 1750–2000*, Cambridge and New York: Cambridge University Press, 2003, pp. 13–43.

Sabean, David Warren, *Property, Production and Family in Neckarhausen, 1700–1870*, Cambridge: Cambridge University Press, 1990.

Sombart, Werner, *Luxus und Kapitalismus* (1913), reprinted as *Liebe, Luxus und Kapitalismus. Über die Entstehung der modernen Welt aus dem Geist der Verschwendung*, Berlin: Wagenbach, 1992.

Spicksley, Judith, 'Usury legislation, cash, and credit: the development of the female investor in the late Tudor and Stuart periods', *Economic History Review* 61 (2), 2007, pp. 277–301.

van der Cruysse, Dirk, *Madame Palatine, Princesse européenne*, Paris: Fayard, 1988.

Weckel, Ulrike, *Zwischen Häuslichkeit und Öffentlichkeit. Die ersten deutschen Frauenzeitschriften im späten 18. Jahrhundert und ihr Publikum*, Tübingen: Niemeyer, 1998.

Wilke, Jürgen, 'Der Einfluß der Hugenotten auf die gewerbliche Entwicklung', in G. Bregulla (ed.), *Hugenotten in Berlin*. Berlin: Union, 1988, pp. 227–80.

Winnige, Norbert, 'Vom Leihen und Schulden in Göttingen. Studien zum Kapitalmarkt', in Wellenreuther, Hermann (ed.), *Göttingen 1690–1755: Studien zur Sozialgeschichte einer Stadt*, Göttingen: Vandenhoeck and Ruprecht, 1988, pp. 252–320.

6 Accounting for business

Financial management in the eighteenth century[1]

Christine Wiskin

In a recent article, Josephine Maltby and Janette Rutterford argued that more work was needed on 'the part played by accounting and bookkeeping in women's lives'. They acknowledged the existing canon but considered that there was room for a 'deepening understanding' of what being able to do accounts meant to women in both the past and nowadays.[2] This chapter is an attempt to widen the subject by discussing how women in business learned about money management and how to avoid (or not) the more common mistakes. In short, to consider what bookkeeping might have meant to businesswomen in past times. Following this, and in order to offer a response based on real-life examples to Maltby and Rutterford's enquiry, the accounting practices of three Georgian businesswomen will be examined. The case for the existence of independent women in business in the eighteenth-century British Isles is now well-established.[3] We know where and when women ran what sort of businesses and it is evident that women were far more commercially active, and in a wider range of trades, than has been suggested by Davidoff and Hall. Indeed Hannah Barker's claim for the centrality of businesswomen in the urban consumer boom of the late Georgian period challenges the dominance of domestic ideology argued for in *Family Fortunes*.[4]

From the later seventeenth century onwards, at least in England and Wales, the processes of bookkeeping and accounting represented a new way of looking at the world, whereby logic and reason could be used to enumerate daily transactions and predict the financial future. Reliance on divine intervention or the advice of fortune tellers became less prevalent.[5] However, deciding where we should place women in this changing intellectual world presents problems. Margaret Hunt argues for a female presence that equates to a 'mark of [their] respectability', whereas Davidoff and Hall believed accounting to be a 'quintessentially masculine skill and prerogative', while Beverly Lemire asserts that, in the home, bookkeeping became the 'paradigm of family discourse', an intellectual and emotional site shared by men and women.[6]

In this chapter, and in order to appreciate the economic climate in which women in business kept their books, there are some introductory points to be made about eighteenth-century commercial life. It was orthodoxy that success in business or trade rested on two things: good trade credit and good books. Let us begin by looking at the former, which was usually discussed by contemporary commentators in terms of the male user. This gender-based assumption reinforces the notion of women's restricted role in the economy. It takes for granted that women's use of credit was largely consumer-based, limited to household expenditure or, in the case of the female labouring poor, to combining it with all sorts of petty trading, much of it bordering on illegality.[7] Gender-based ideas about credit have also tended to conceal the presence of 'middling sort' businesswomen in retailing, where many were to be found selling the new, semi-luxury goods and services of the age. However, it would be too simplistic to discuss this as women selling to women in some sort of eighteenth-century home-shopping experience. These female shopkeepers maintained a presence in the public world of commerce, operated from fixed premises and held substantial stocks.[8] Female shopkeepers had many male customers, too, and, as Margot Finn has shown, the demand for the new consumer goods came as much from men as from women.[9] Furthermore, to understand how businesswomen were incorporated into the world of trade credit, it has to be remembered that manufacturers, producers and traders in these new items wanted to reach as wide a market as possible and would sell on credit to whomever would stock them, irrespective of their sex. Differences in the credit terms they were offered or received in these deals depended not on their gender but on their reputation for reliability, how promptly they paid and the size of their orders.[10] When it came to settling up, both sexes faced the same problem: how to pay on time while maintaining sufficient cash for other current and future commitments. What was the case in retailing was also true for businesspeople in other sectors of the economy. 'Punctual payments' kept the commercial world afloat but behind this piece of confident alliteration lay complex webs of financial management, personal relations and individual circumstances. Credit was a boon to those in business provided they used it wisely, on the one hand enabling them to buy more stock, on the other to offer credit terms to customers, in the hope of increasing turnover.[11] Sadly, dealings on credit could turn into a nightmare; there was the pitfall of trading on too small a capital, of buying more than could be paid for, or offering generous terms to customers who had little or no intention of paying their bills. Handled well, credit might lead to prosperity or even, for a very lucky few, to a fortune; disgrace, bankruptcy, even the debtors' prison awaited those businesspeople who could not control its management.

A solution to deal with this Janus-like phenomenon was advocated by contemporary commentators: it was to keep an accurate and up-to-date record of all business dealings, thereby being able to pinpoint when debts were due, to whom, and for how much. This could then be compared with potential income, the assumption being that the former would not exceed the latter on any particular date. If it were likely to, adjustments would have to be made – more deals on credit, perhaps, or greater pressure put on tardy customers. Craig Muldrew has demonstrated that 'accounts' were kept in all sorts of ways in early modern England: tally sticks, chalk marks on a wall, oral testimonies backed up by a reputation in the local community for honesty and fairness.[12] Although they were based on reckoning that did not need formal knowledge of written quantifi-cation, these were systems that worked. However, by the eighteenth century, many of these methods were deemed old-fashioned and inadequate to cope with an expanding and much more sophisticated economy, and it became a common-place that good written records were the most desirable way of knowing what was happening in one's business. The prognosis was dire if one failed to do so.[13] Given the growing ethos of quantification, some familiarity with accounts and bookkeeping seems to have been assumed among those engaged in business. It was thought to be more reliable than traditional ways of keeping tabs on things and was perceived to be indispensable when supervising clerks and workpeople.[14] Increasing literacy and the exponential growth of the book trade in the late seventeenth and eighteenth centuries meant there were plenty of self-help manuals urging their readers to accept the utility of written financial records and to take up the practice.[15] Most of the texts advocating the benefits of written financial records were directed to a male readership; occasionally an author pointed out that a businesswoman who could not do accounts was fair game for any unscrupulous person who could.[16] Possibly here was an emotional, as well as economic, worry. Early death, leaving a widow with young children, was a very real fear for businessmen and traders in this period. The grieving widow might abandon her good sense and judgement in the face of her bereavement, which would make her vulnerable to the approaches of plausible fortune hunter(s), willing to step into the shoes and bed of the late husband. All that he had worked for and the affection he had known were in danger of being requisi-tioned by an outsider because coverture would have granted the property of the remarrying widow, including all she had inherited from her first husband, to her second. This was a challenge to the foundation of the familial, economic and sexual unit the first husband had created.[17] On the other hand, as supporters of women's literacy, numeracy and bookkeeping argued, instruction in these sub-jects would provide widows, daughters and other female relatives with the wherewithal to resist such blandishments, if they needed them.

Sidney Pollard maintained that business proprietors also learned bookkeeping and commercial skills by formal training but when we consider women in busi-ness, his view seems less well-founded. The education of Georgian girls tended to be a haphazard process, dependent on their parents' inclinations and status. Some young females went to school either, if from the middle ranks, to receive a 'polite' education, tailored to meet society's expectations for them of matrimony and motherhood, or, if from the lower-middle ranks or from the deserving sec-tions of the labouring poor, to be trained for work. Instruction in schools Included simple arithmetic that, unlike mathematics, did not threaten the existing gender order, and accounts and bookkeeping were an ideal vehicle for teaching it.[18] However, formal schooling played a relatively small part in the education of most girls and young women. They might, for instance, have been taught at home, which was where Catherine Morland, the impressionable heroine of *Northanger Abbey* was tutored in accounts by her clergyman father. Girls growing up in a business household were likely to have learned, at the very least, the rudiments from family members. Many young women learned how to keep the books at work, as part of an apprenticeship or some other form of on-the-job training, or through marriage to a trades- or businessman. Instruction in accounts, whether for the household or work, or both, also seems to have been part of the socialising of girls and young women, a step on the way to the responsibilities of adulthood. Being able to cast up accounts, therefore, fulfilled both cultural and economic functions. That it was widely taught for a variety of reasons among the elite and non-elite suggests that its objectives went beyond the solely pedagogical.

Instruction in keeping accounts was one thing, proficiency was quite another. Provided the motivation was present, it was not too difficult to keep a daily note of transactions carried out and money received and spent, but turning this into a form of financial record comprehensible to both its author and any interested third party required patience and accuracy. Despite instruction by an impeccable source, the fictional Catherine Morland, for example, achieved only limited mastery of the subject.[19] There has been recent scholarly interest in women's numeracy and, as Nicola Phillips and others have shown, there were literate and numerate eighteenth-century women sufficiently adept to record their getting and spending of money. Women's personal writings have been fruitful sources about their household expenditure. Compiled for household purposes, these itemise purchases, prices, amounts, suppliers, recipients of gifts. Household diaries and accounts have also been analysed to explain consumption practices and record changes in fashion. In many instances, comments by their authors made it clear that sales and purchases were linked to personal events, reciprocity was frequently as important as monetary exchange; it was the dynamics of domestic life, as much as monetary transactions, that were being recorded.[20] For the nineteenth century, Stephen Walker argues for contemporary beliefs in women's 'unique' aptitude for doing accounts, their attention to detail and accuracy being rooted in their domesticity.[21] These examples go some way to answer Maltby and Rutterford's enquiry, although focus on domestic and household accounting still leaves unanswered questions about the place of bookkeeping in the lives of women in business. In the world of the family firm, it is evident that in the eighteenth and nineteenth centuries, wives, daughters and other female relatives still kept the books. This was unpaid work, part of their contribution to the family enterprise.[22] And this was despite Defoe's satirical comments that the newly acquired desire among the middle ranks for social mobility meant that its womenfolk now thought casting up accounts was ungenteel.[23] Other women, forced onto the labour market by circumstances, had to commodify their literacy and numeracy in order to earn a living from clerical work or bookkeeping; probably it was a very modest means of subsistence but it was one by which they might retain a modicum of respectability. The piecemeal examples of such clerical work suggest that in no way did women threaten male hegemony over these salaried occupations.[24]

So far we have established some ways in which to respond to Maltby and Rutterford. Because of its association with education and training, being able to cast up accounts was part of the rites of passage from childhood to womanhood. In the guise of personal accounting, it provided a place where women could explore the connections between their financial and emotional relationships, and where the links between women, money, and how they enumerated it, were complex and subjective, based on sentiment as much as rationality. In more mundane terms, bookkeeping skills gave women an economic justification for their existence, and might be exchanged either for bed, board and support in the family enterprise or traded for wages in the world of paid work. Women in business on their own account might well have seen bookkeeping in all or some of these ways, but there was much more to it than that because of the many advantages of well-kept books for commercial purposes. Writing down transactions, calculating debts due and owing, anticipating future income and liabilities and allowing for contingencies were all ways of keeping order and exercising discipline over the finances of the enterprise and providing information that could be used productively. Unfortunately, discussion of what this might have meant to businesswomen in the past is hampered by the paucity of sources. Account books and other written records prepared by women in business for commercial purposes in the eighteenth and early nineteenth centuries are few and far between, despite Beverly Lemire's argument that many account books, both personal and business, authored by men and women, have survived.[25] Differences in the archival experiences of scholars can be partly explained by the nature of the material. Many of the examples Lemire cites combine the mixture of financial recording and self-expression already discussed in this chapter, whereas records kept principally for commercial purposes by businesswomen in the long eighteenth century are difficult to find and, where they exist, are often incomplete. Generally, evidence of accounting for business purposes by the female entrepreneur has to be sought in records kept by others. These 'others' were both male and female, including customers, who wrote down their dealings with women shopkeepers or kept the bills they submitted and the letters they exchanged, and male suppliers from whom businesswomen bought their stock. Sometimes a businesswoman can be traced through court records, the reiteration of the circumstances that occasioned the legal dispute giving information about how she conducted her enterprise.[26]

How should today's historian assess and evaluate such material? What might it add to our understanding of the significance of accounting and bookkeeping to businesswomen in the past? In an attempt to resolve some of these issues, the business practices of three particular women are examined more closely. The primary sources used cover the spectrum of business archives: correspondence and various types of books of account, found in diverse and geographically dispersed locations. Because of this, discussion of the three women's accounting methods has had to be judged by results – success in business being believed to have resulted from good bookkeeping, the opposite leading to failure. The three subjects are Eleanor Coade (1733–1821), Charlotte Matthews (1759–1802) and Jane Tait (in business 1827–1828), who were, respectively, a manufacturer, a financier and a dressmaker. As far as their marital status was concerned, they were respectively the never-married, the previously married and the soon-to-be-married. They were able to operate as they did because, as single women, they were free from the legal restrictions imposed on wives; as 'femes sole', they could make contracts and have them enforced against them.

An outsider's opinion of the Artificial Stone Manufactory set up, owned and operated by Eleanor Coade is to be found in correspondence between Sir William Chambers and Horace Walpole.[27] Walpole believed Coade had over-charged him for the gateposts he ordered from her but she would not back down. Why else would Walpole have gone through an informal arbitration, delegating Chambers to negotiate with her agent? Aristocrats, after all, were notorious for procrastination when it came to paying to paying their bills. Coade might have been desperate for the money; clearly, she refused to be put off. She was also confident of the rightness of her case, supported by her well-kept books which she showed to both negotiators. Walpole had left the minutiae of the case to an impressed Chambers who found little to question. Her response rested on the robustness of her costing, a process whereby well-established workplace methods could be measured, recorded and calculated in objective terms.

Coade was a spinster businesswoman, whereas Charlotte Matthews was a different but much more familiar type, the entrepreneurial widow, who continued the enterprise set up by her late husband. Charlotte Marlar was 16 when she married William Matthews, a banker and merchant, in 1776, and like so many of her female contemporaries, marriage provided her with an excellent commercial education as she seems to have become William's unofficial apprentice after the knot was tied. As Mrs Matthews, she metamorphosed from a young girl into a supportive and hard-working spouse, who revelled in spending long hours in the counting house. As a business widow, she made a formidable figure with an impressive clientele for her banking and bill-broking business. We know some-thing, but not all, of her methods from ledgers at the Bank of England that record her account there from 1793 to 1799 and from the surviving part of her correspondence with the Birmingham partnership of Boulton & Watt. Boulton & Watt, however, was but one of many of Charlotte's customers and the names of major London merchant houses and traders recur in the pages of her account at the Bank of England. This clientele was remarkable – prosperous, ambitious, well-connected – and unlikely to give quarter to those they deemed weak. The ten years during which she ran this high-risk finance business on her own were extremely difficult ones: the country was at war with France, there were very poor harvests, unrest at home and economic crises, but Charlotte was still in business, financing Boulton & Watt and dealing with her other customers up to her death in 1802. All this speaks volumes about her industry and her aptitude for business that also depended on her skills in keeping accounts and managing her credit position.

The third subject is the 'about-to-be-married' Jane Tait who was a dress-maker and milliner in Liverpool – a much more typically 'feminine' business which ought, given its international customers and credit, to have been success-ful, but was not. Bankruptcy records compiled by her creditors tell a sorry tale of missed opportunities and poor credit management. In turn this suggests that she did not keep good records. Even if her books were adequate, she failed to follow up effectively the leads to which they ought to have pointed. Tait's behaviour suggests an unfocused attitude to business. Her creditors were able to quantify her liabilities, implying that she had kept some sort of tally but, for whatever reason, she failed to act upon that information.[28]

Returning to the wider question of what keeping accounts meant to women in the past, the process of achieving, at the very least, a modest proficiency in bookkeeping involved multiple objectives. It could shape girls and young women into useful adults, preparing them to take on the role of spouse and help-mate. This had many practical applications both in the home and the workplace – the benefits of a well-run and solvent household were obvious, as was the advantage of free clerical labour in the business. This was inherently a support-ing role where it was taken for granted that women acquiesced in a male-dominated society. A woman's possession of adequate skills in accounts also carried with it the hope of a modicum of protection against gold-diggers in the event of the death of the male household head, an aspiration that similarly denied agency to the socialised female. All in all, it taught girls what society expected of them.

When it came to using the knowledge gained from this training, its socialis-ing component could be further played out. Paid work doing accounts or book-keeping gave the literate and numerate woman what society expected for her – scant job security, poor pay and very limited hopes. On the other hand, the unwaged wife who acted as domestic bookkeeper was also expected to conform; she answered to her husband for household expenditure, the act of submitting the account book or books to him to check underlining her subordinate status. As Lemire has shown, tensions could arise here; each week or month the house-hold was gripped by suspense: would the wife be praised for the excellence of her records and household management or castigated for her sloppiness? If everything was in order, she could bask in her husband's approval, but the books might not balance, and even if they did, the figures might not match the cash in hand, and the scene was set for domestic dramas. The household account book could be a source of hostility and ill-feeling, but we should not cast it aside as merely being evidence of female submission because it could give women other ways of interacting with money, by articulating in words and figures much more than the dispassionate process of quantification inherent in bookkeeping. In many instances, it was in their records of domestic spending that women could revisit in positive ways relationships and life experience alongside listing pounds, shillings and pence to produce narratives that combined the objective with the highly subjective.[29]

Bearing in mind what has already been said about problems with the primary sources, it is difficult to speculate on how businesswomen might have lived out the experience of bookkeeping. Eighteenth-century commentators placed a premium on good accounting and doing so was believed to be a way of trying to make sense of their increasingly commercial world as age-old ways of doing business, based on reciprocity and community values, were being replaced by a much more hard-nosed ethos. Traditions, however, did not vanish overnight and, as Philips argues, sentiment in the form of reciprocity still had a part to play in some otherwise commercial exchanges. There was 'a degree of mutual support' in the business relations between the Durham gentry woman, Judith Baker, and two women spinners. This was, however, a very traditional type of women's work and other businesswomen who supplied Baker with the new consumer goods of the period submitted far more impersonal and objective accounts that were models of best bookkeeping practice.[30]

We would not hesitate to attribute feelings of personal satisfaction, achievement and pride to businessmen whose bookkeeping conformed to accepted norms, but the fragmented nature of the sources suggests that caution has to be used when considering businesswomen. Bookkeeping served the commercial aims of the entrepreneurial spinster or widow but this assumption leaves unanswered the question of how far the whole area of 'accounts' meant more to them than just rows of figures on a page.

Sentiments have to be deduced, if they can be deduced at all, from what is available. This involves reading between the lines in the hope that the inferences drawn will be appropriate. We have the lists of debts due and debts outstanding that were compiled by Jane Tait's male creditors from which to deduce what bookkeeping might have meant to her, and it does not seem to have been a great deal. We may, of course, be judging her too harshly; her business operated among local, national and international networks during the financial crisis and failure of many provincial banks in the 1820s, and assumptions about her accounting proficiency are, perforce, based on the reports of those to whom she owed money, hardly the most objective of observers. On the other hand, the published 'literary' output of Eleanor Coade was impressive for an eighteenth-century woman in business. She was a self-promoter, announcing new products and events in the national press, as well as producing trade cards, brochures and catalogues.[31] In the custom of the time, the text is in the third person, which produces a sense of authorial detachment. When, in the 1799 *Coade's Gallery*, she mentions individuals who helped in the success of the Manufactory, she lists the most important male designers and artists who worked for her but is silent on her own contribution. Similarly, there is very little introspection in Charlotte Matthews's correspondence with Boulton & Watt. She tells them what they want to hear – of her efforts on their financial behalf.[32]

Why such reticence? Girls were brought up to expect a life of marriage and children, where emotional attachment was focused on kin, the home and, probably, the family enterprise. Family life, particularly if tied up with business, can be full of tensions and hostility but the devil you know is usually preferable to the unfamiliar one. The situation was difficult for women without close kin. Circumstances forced them to be reliant on their own efforts, reflections on the emotional significance of what they were doing was probably a luxury few had the time to afford. Furthermore, in an economic climate of stiff competition and fears of industrial and commercial espionage, it was unwise to write down information of a personal nature in case it fell into the wrong hands.

There was also a tension between the need of the single businesswoman to keep her own books and the assumption of submission implicit in the teaching of accounts to girls and women. Instruction was predicated on the belief that accounts kept by women would, in the majority of cases, be overseen by men, whereas spinsters and widows became their own bosses, a situation with the potential to challenge the gender order. The spinster in business appeared to be relatively independent. However, she had only herself to rely on and was probably under greater pressure to make sure her accounts were well-kept and accurate. This was because she could never be certain when she would be called upon to defend her right to lines of credit as Jane Tait discovered or, as Eleanor Coade found out, to justify her prices and methods. The shortcomings in Tait's financial management suggest that sentiment and business did not go well together if they were not focused on the enterprise itself. Her forthcoming marriage seems to have meant more to her than a future in commerce, she was not channelling her emotional life into the business, and certainly not into her bookkeeping regime. On the other hand, the desire for financial stability seems to have been the rock on which the marriage of Charlotte and William Matthews was built. The discipline, which included well-kept books and scrupulous management of trade credit, that such stability demanded had been internalised by Charlotte to such an extent that her business did not fail when she alone became responsible for it. As her story shows, the influence of male figures did not die with them, lessons learned at an impressionable age were long-lasting. If it is not too fanciful, we might also speculate that the bankruptcy and death of Coade's father encouraged his daughter to follow a risk-averse strategy of order and regularity in her own business life. Her approach paid off when dealing with Walpole and his representative, for Eleanor's skill in bookkeeping enabled her to defend her position in an exchange made unequal by gender and status. Walpole's social position was unassailable and Chambers was a man 'on the up' as well as being very widely travelled and educated. Attention to detail and small print were clearly Coade's *métier* and who could blame her if she felt vindicated by the outcome. She could also be proud that the Manufactory enabled her to live independently.

Depending on her circumstances, the businesswoman widow might have been able to draw on family support or she may have had to be self-reliant; she may have had to fend for herself and her minor children but whatever her position, she too had to get it right. Assuming she had had sufficient experience of bookkeeping during her husband's lifetime, she should have been able to do so. The well trained businesswoman widow now had the chance to assert herself, either explicitly or more cautiously, drawing on both interpersonal skills that marriage fosters and sympathy for her bereaved state. It was acceptable and uncontroversial. It is tempting to assume that business life, including the niceties of well-kept books, gave succour to Charlotte Matthews during a childless marriage and widowhood. Directing her energies in that way could be read as a substitute for family life if it were not that she had many friends and a social life outside the counting house. On the other hand, she drew satisfaction from her achievements, from a job well done, as in the case of her financing of the 1797–1799 regal copper coinage.[33]

It could be argued that, by equating survival in business with proficiency in bookkeeping, leading to prosperity and happiness, is reductionism worthy of a commercially minded *Candide*. As the case studies presented here have shown, businesswomen in the long eighteenth century did not live in the best of all possible worlds nor were they in those solely of their own making. As a sex, women were expected to defer to male authority but events meant that many had to live much more independent lives. Some may have deliberately avoided matrimony, others found themselves unexpectedly single. Whether they took up business from choice or necessity, the future of their enterprises depended on their efforts and these can be judged in concrete terms of success or failure. Thus, in the end, judgement by results is what we are left with. It is far harder to pin down what the processes of bookkeeping and accounting meant to women in business on a personal level. They could certainly experience settling down to write up the books, often at the end of a long and tiring working day and in the knowledge that it would not be a good idea to put off the task until tomorrow; this called for considerable investment of time and energy. For the successful, and by extension committed, businesswoman, a job well done, achievement measured by results, probably satisfied more private yearnings.

Notes

1 An earlier version of this chapter appeared in *Accounting, Business and Financial History* 16 (2), 2006.
2 J. Maltby and J. Rutterford, 'Editorial: women, accounting and investment', *Accounting, Business and Financial History* 16 (2), 2006, pp. 133–142, especially pp. 136, 140.
3 E.C. Sanderson, *Women and Work in Eighteenth-Century Edinburgh*, Basingstoke: Macmillan, 1996; Margaret Hunt, *The Middling Sort: Commerce, Gender and the Family in England 1680–1780*, Berkeley, CA: University of California Press, 1996, ch. 5; M. Berg, 'Women's property and the Industrial Revolution', *Journal of Interdisciplinary History* 24, 1993, pp. 233–250; C. Wiskin, 'Urban businesswomen in eighteenth-century England', in R. Sweet and P. Lane (eds), *Women and Urban Life in Eighteenth-Century England 'On the Town'*, Aldershot: Ashgate, 2003, pp. 87–110; H. Barker, *The Business of Women: Female Enterprise and Urban Development in Northern England 1760–1830*, Oxford: Oxford University Press, 2006, pp. 54–71; N. Phillips, *Women in Business, 1700–1850*, Woodbridge: The Boydell Press, 2006, p. 101.
4 Barker, *The Business of Women*, pp. 9–10 and chs. 2, 3, 4.
5 L. Davidoff and C. Hall, *Family Fortunes: Men and Women of the English Middle Class 1780–1850*, London: Routledge, 1992, pp. 201–205; Hunt, *The Middling Sort*, p. 58.
6 Davidoff and Hall, *Family Fortunes*, pp. 201–205; Hunt, *The Middling Sort*, p. 89; B. Lemire, *The Business of Everyday Life: Gender, Practice and Social Politics in England, c. 1600–1900*, Manchester: Manchester University Press, 2005, p. 203.
7 P. Lane, 'Work on the margins: poor women and the informal economy of eighteenth- and nineteenth-century Leicestershire', *Midland History* 22, 1997, pp. 85–99.

8 Wiskin, 'Urban businesswomen', pp. 106–109.

9 M. Finn, 'Men's things: masculine possessions in the consumer revolution', *Social History* 25 (2), 2000, pp. 133–155.

10 C. Wiskin, 'Businesswomen and financial management: three eighteenth-century case studies', *Accounting, Business and Financial History* 16 (2), 2006, p. 43.

11 P. Earle, *The Making of the English Middle Class*, London: Methuen, 1991, pp. 115–118.

12 C. Muldrew, *The Economy of Obligation: The Culture of Credit and Social Relations in Early Modern England*, Basingstoke: Macmillan, 1998, pp. 63–64.

13 Earle, *Making of the English Middle Class*, pp. 114–115; D.A. Kent, 'Small businessmen and their credit transactions in early nineteenth-century Britain', *Business History* 36 (2), 1994, pp. 47–64.

14 S. Pollard, *The Genesis of Modern Management: A Study of the Industrial Revolution in Great Britain*, London: Edward Arnold, 1965, p. 215; Hunt, *The Middling Sort*, p. 58; Lemire, *The Business of Everyday Life*, pp. 190–192.

15 Hunt, *The Middling Sort*, p. 43.

16 D. Cressy, 'Literacy in context: meaning and measurement in early modern England', in J. Brewer and R. Porter (eds), *Consumption and the World of Goods*, London: Routledge, 1993, p. 309.

17 Barker, *The Business of Women*, pp. 142, 145–146.

18 P.C. Cohen, 'Reckoning with commerce: numeracy in eighteenth-century America', in Brewer and Porter, *Consumption and the World of Goods*, p. 322; Cressy, 'Literacy in context', p. 309.

19 J. Austen, *Northanger Abbey*, chapter 1.

20 A. Vickery, *The Gentleman's Daughter: Women's Lives in Georgian England*, London: Yale University Press, 1993, pp. 74–80, pp. 165–169; Lemire, *The Business of Everyday Life*, pp. 200–205; Phillips, *Women in Business*, pp. 102–103.

21 S.P. Walker, 'Philanthropic women and accounting. Octavia Hill and the exercise of "quiet power and sympathy"', *Accounting, Business and Financial History* 16 (2), 2006, p. 173.

22 G. Crossick and H.-G. Haupt, *The Petite Bourgeoisie in Europe 1780–1914: Enterprise, Family and Independence*, London: Routledge, 1995, pp. 96, 103.

23 Daniel Defoe quoted in I. Pinchbeck, *Women Workers and the Industrial Revolution*, London: Frank Cass, 1930, reprinted 1981, p. 283.

24 J. Brewer, *The Sinews of Power: War, Money and the English State, 1688–1783*, London: Unwin Hyman, 1989, p. 68; Pollard, *The Genesis of Modern Management*, p. 138.

25 Lemire, *The Business of Everyday Life*, p. 195.

26 Barker, *The Business of Women*, pp. 101–104; Hunt, *The Middling Sort*, pp. 140–141.

27 W.S. Lewis (ed.), *Horace Walpole's Correspondence*, Vol. 41, Part II, Miscellaneous Correspondence, Oxford: Oxford University Press, 1980, pp. 227–228.

28 Wiskin, 'Businesswomen and financial management', pp. 149–151.

29 Lemire, *The Business of Everyday Life*, pp. 206–212.

30 Phillips, *Women in Business*, pp. 117–119.

31 N. Valpy and A. Kelly, 'Advertisements for artificial stone in the Daily Advertiser', *Transactions of the English Ceramic Circle* 12 (3), 1986, pp. 206–223; *A Descriptive Catalogue of Coade's Artificial Stone Manufactory at Kings Arms Stairs, Narrow Wall ... with prices affixed*, London, 1784; *Coade's Gallery or Exhibition in Artificial Stone, Westminster Bridge Road*, London, 1799.

32 Wiskin, 'Businesswomen and financial management', pp. 156–158.

33 Wiskin, 'Businesswomen and financial management', pp. 155–159.

Bibliography

A Descriptive Catalogue of Coade's Artificial Stone Manufactory at Kings Arms Stairs, Narrow Wall ... with prices affixed, London, 1784.

Barker, Hannah, *The Business of Women: Female Enterprise and Urban Development in Northern England 1760–1830*, Oxford: Oxford University Press, 2006.

Berg, Maxine, 'Women's property and the Industrial Revolution', *Journal of Interdisciplinary History* 24, 1993, pp. 233–250.

Brewer, J., *The Sinews of Power: War, Money and the English State, 1688–1783*, London: Unwin Hyman, 1989.

Coade's Gallery or Exhibition in Artificial Stone, Westminster Bridge Road, London, 1799.

Cohen, P.C., 'Reckoning with commerce: numeracy in eighteenth-century America', in Brewer, J. and Porter, R. (eds), *Consumption and the World of Goods*, London: Routledge, 1993, pp. 320–34.

Cressy, D., 'Literacy in context: meaning and measurement in early modern England', in Brewer, J. and Porter, R. (eds), *Consumption and the World of Goods*, London: Routledge, 1993, pp. 305–19.

Crossick, G. and Haupt, H.-G., *The Petite Bourgeoisie in Europe 1780–1914: Enterprise, Family and Independence*, London: Routledge, 1995.

Davidoff, L. and Hall, C., *Family Fortunes: Men and Women of the English Middle Class 1780–1850*, London: Routledge, 1992.

Earle, P., *The Making of the English Middle Class*, London: Methuen, 1991.

Finn, M., 'Men's things: masculine possessions in the consumer revolution', *Social History* 25 (2), 2000, pp. 133–155.

Hunt, Margaret, *The Middling Sort: Commerce, Gender and the Family in England 1680–1780*, Berkeley, CA: University of California Press, 1996.

Kent, D.A., 'Small businessmen and their credit transactions in early nineteenth-century Britain', *Business History* 36 (2), 1994, pp. 47–64.

Lane, P., 'Work on the margins: poor women and the informal economy of eighteenth- and nineteenth-century Leicestershire', *Midland History* 22, 1997, pp. 85–99.

Lemire, Beverly, *The Business of Everyday Life: Gender, Practice and Social Politics in England, c.1600–1900*, Manchester: Manchester University Press, 2005.

Lewis, W.S. (ed.), *Horace Walpole's Correspondence*, Vol. 41, Oxford: Oxford University Press, 1980.

Maltby, J. and Rutterford, J., 'Editorial: women, accounting and investment', *Accounting, Business and Financial History* 16 (2), 2006, pp. 133–142.

Muldrew, C., *The Economy of Obligation: The Culture of Credit and Social Relations in Early Modern England*, Basingstoke: Macmillan, 1998.

Phillips, N., *Women in Business, 1700–1850*, Woodbridge: The Boydell Press, 2006.

Pinchbeck, I., *Women Workers and the Industrial Revolution*, London: Frank Cass, 1930, reprinted 1981.

Pollard, S., *The Genesis of Modern Management: A Study of the Industrial Revolution in Great Britain*, London: Edward Arnold, 1965.

Sanderson, Elizabeth, *Women and Work in Eighteenth-Century Edinburgh*, Basingstoke: Macmillan, 1996.

Valpy, N. and Kelly, A. 'Advertisements for artificial stone in the Daily Advertiser', *Transactions of the English Ceramic Circle* 12 (3), 1986, pp. 206–223.

Vickery, A., *The Gentleman's Daughter: Women's Lives in Georgian England*, London: Yale University Press, 1993.

Walker, S.P., 'Philanthropic women and accounting. Octavia Hill and the exercise of "quiet power and sympathy"', *Accounting, Business and Financial History* 16 (2), 2006, pp. 163–94.

Wiskin, C., 'Businesswomen and financial management: three eighteenth-century case studies', *Accounting, Business and Financial History* 16 (2), 2006, pp. 143–61.

Wiskin, C., 'Urban businesswomen in eighteenth-century England' in Sweet, R. and Lane, P. (eds), *Women and Urban Life in Eighteenth-Century England 'On the Town'*, Aldershot: Ashgate, 2003, pp. 87–110.

7 Women and wealth

The nineteenth century in Great Britain

Lucy A. Newton, Philip L. Cottrell,
Josephine Maltby and Janette Rutterford

This short chapter sets out some of the major features of the regulatory, legal and demographic framework of the period that were crucial for the investment activity of women during the nineteenth century. Its aim is to provide a context for the studies that follow which trace the effects of this regime on various kinds of women's investment behaviour in different parts of Great Britain. It concentrates on three key areas that led to increased opportunities for female investment: changes in company legislation; the Married Women's Property Acts; and changes in the types of security available. We address each of these in turn.

Company formation

Developments in legislation regulating corporate formation during the nineteenth century were vital for both businesses and investors. Piecemeal changes to the law before 1856 gradually gave potential investors some safeguards. The greatest innovation occurred in 1856, when a nominal registration process for forming limited-liability companies was introduced, allowing those with funds to invest in companies with greater safety (because their risk was limited to the amount invested) while enabling businesses, in theory, to draw upon a wider and deeper capital market than had hitherto been available. This introduction begins by exploring the background to this important development, whose impact is explored in subsequent chapters.[1]

Before 1856 business enterprises had been legally constituted in one of three ways: as private partnerships, as unincorporated companies or as corporations established by either an Act of Parliament or a royal charter. Establishing a corporation – a company that had the privilege of limited liability – was difficult and expensive to achieve before 1856. Pressure to reform company law had been developing since the late eighteenth century, and became greater with the problems arising from unincorporated companies having to obtain some of the corporation's legal capacities in a piecemeal fashion through individual private Acts.

Arguments for reform were bolstered by, on the one hand, corporate enterprises' successes in fields such as insurance and canal building and, on the other, the expanding securities market. Between 1803 and 1811 the number of quoted

securities more than doubled.[2] The legal environment for business finally began
to change with the 'Bubble' Act's repeal in 1825 (6 Geo. IV, c. 91). The process
of application for corporate status was still time-consuming and expensive, but
by 1844 there were approximately 970 unincorporated companies in existence.[3]

The repeal of the 'Bubble' Act proved to be the first in a series of gradual
changes in company law. The Banking Co-partnerships Act of 1826 (7 Geo. IV,
c. 46) permitted in England and Wales the creation of joint-stock banks – unincorporated companies with more than six partners and freely transferable shares
– outside a 65-mile radius of London (Charing Cross). The mid-1830s trade
boom witnessed the founding of railway companies, banks, mines and insurance
companies, and £20 million shares were offered by 41 companies to the public
during 1835.[4] The 1837 Companies Act gave to the Board of Trade the power of
incorporating companies, and over the ensuing 17 years 93 applications for
incorporation were approved.[5]

The widening of sources from which capital could be drawn led to issues of
share rigging and stock jobbery. Parliament became increasingly concerned with
joint-stock company fraud and established a committee in 1841 to examine the
question. It reported in 1844 and set the framework for immediate legislation –
the Act for the Registration, Incorporation and Regulation of Joint Stock Companies (7 & 8 Vict. c. 110). The Act defined a joint-stock company as 'a commercial partnership with more than 25 members or with a capital divided into
freely transferable shares'. During the 11 years that the 1844 Act was in force,
910 unlimited joint-stock companies were registered in England and Wales: in
insurance (219 companies); gas and water (211); markets and public halls (85);
shipping (46); and petty lending (41). Only 106 English and Welsh manufacturing concerns were registered, among which the largest group was 13 cotton
companies.[6]

Shareholders in such companies still shouldered the risk of unlimited liability, whereas legislation had been passed in France, Ireland, Italy and the United
States that limited the liability of company members. Concerns were therefore
growing about the protection of British investors' interests. Supporters of
limited liability argued that it would encourage middle- and working-class
investors – the 'industrious classes' – to find a productive outlet for their
savings.[7] This class was taken to include women. According to a supporter of
the new legislation, 'Women, and other, persons, not capable of actively engaging in trade, should possess safe channels of investment, which were at the
moment closed against them'.[8] On the other hand, opponents feared that limited
liability would lead to fraud, or excesses through the formation of 'bubble' companies or even gambling, 'the creation of limited companies could always speak
of the destructive whirlwind of speculation'.[9] They pointed to the extremes of
the promotional booms in the 1820s, 1830s and 1840s, and the scandalous activities of promoters, as portrayed by Dickens in *Martin Chuzzlewit* (1843).[10]

Yet, both joint-stock and limited companies were formed during the first half
of the nineteenth century, and many operated successfully. By 1800, over 100
Acts had been passed for the formation of corporate canal enterprises.[11] Railway

companies were also very large-scale operations. Following the successes of pioneering concerns, such as the Liverpool & Manchester, the promotion and construction of railways occurred in 'mania' waves from the mid-1830s to the mid-1840s and railway shares became a popular form of investment. It has been estimated that total railway share capital amounted to £126 million by 1847, much of which had been subscribed through provincial financial centres. Both Hunt and Reed have argued that 'railway mania' gave rise to a national securities market.[12] Following the legislation of 1826, bank shares became a popular form of investment for the Victorian middle classes.[13] Shares were traded on the London and newly formed provincial stock exchanges,[14] further stimulated by the development of a specialist financial press.[15] Canal, railway, insurance and banking companies provided an experience of share purchasing and ownership for middle-class investors.

All this created a favourable climate for the 1855 Limited Liability Act (18 & 19 Vict. c. 133), which allowed the creation of limited-liability companies, followed by the 1856 Joint Stock Companies Act (19 & 20 Vict. c. 47), which became part of the consolidating 1862 Joint Stock Companies Act and which introduced freedom of incorporation on the basis that there should be 'free trade in capital'. The era of modern corporate development and investment had begun. English company law had become the most liberal in Europe.[16] Shannon estimates that London registrations of limited companies between 1856 and 1883 amounted in total to 20,521 (London being the main place of registration).[17] As discussed below, the number of survivors was far fewer: less than half of this number is estimated to have survived to 1885.

Married Women Property Acts

Under English law, both spinsters and widows had the same property rights as men. Married women, however, were treated differently. English common law before 1870, under the doctrine of coverture, treated the married couple as one economic unit, and the husband controlled both his property and all the personal assets introduced by the wife before or after the wedding. 'Personal assets' included clothes, money, jewellery and investments. Real property continued to be in the wife's legal ownership during her marriage, but the husband acquired control of it. This meant that he was entitled to receive the rental income, and the wife could not dispose of her real property (sell, mortgage or rent it out) without his permission. A deserted wife could find herself completely destitute if her husband chose to remove all the property and continue to take all the income to which he was legally entitled, as with Hester Dethridge who was driven to kill her husband in Wilkie Collins' *Man and Wife*. Thus, married women's (lack of) property rights could be seen as part of their marital rather than their economic situation. The first steps to alter the situation were made in Brougham's 1857 Bill which attempted to give the same property rights to married as to single women, but this was overtaken by legislation about their rights on the breakdown of marriage. Some saw the 1857 Divorce and Matrimonial Causes Act as a substitute for these proposals, to the extent that it gave the same property rights to judicially separated or divorced women as were enjoyed by single ones.[18] It was the Married Women's Property Act 1870 (MWPA 1870) that granted all married women ownership rights – but these applied only to some types of asset that they acquired *after* marriage. These were principally inheritances and earnings from employment or skill and from some kinds of investment. The main kinds of investment earnings affected by the MWPA 1870 were those from government annuities; savings banks; public funds/stocks; fully paid shares in limited companies; industrial, provident, friendly, building and loan societies; and life insurance policies. The 1870 Act had a number of limitations. It did not give wives ownership rights over real property. It did not cover certain assets brought into the marriage – in particular savings brought into the marriage were not protected if they had not been applied to one of the above assets. It required husband and wife to make an agreement as to the ownership of any assets that were acquired later by the wife, so that a wife whose husband did not agree to her separate ownership of assets was no better off after 1870. Nevertheless, it has been argued that the MWPA 1870 had an important effect on women's investment behaviour, and in particular that it made women prefer financial investments to real property because of their enhanced rights over the former.[19] But it was not until the Married Women's Property Act 1882 that wives who married after 1 January 1883 acquired the same ownership rights as single women and men, irrespective of the date of their acquisition of property and the types of property acquired.

Female investments

We have seen how legislation concerning companies and married women increased women's investment opportunities during the nineteenth century. In this section, we consider which investments they could choose.

Women had to make investment choices both before and after limited liability was introduced. As discussed in earlier chapters, women had been active investors in the seventeenth and eighteenth centuries.[20] They had invested in the joint-stock companies before the change in company law in 1856.[21] Recent research has emphasised the collective importance of female investors to individual companies and to equity markets in general.[22] An examination of a large sample of national joint-stock companies during the first half of the nineteenth century has revealed that only 12 per cent had no female shareholders. Although they were in the minority of shareholders in any one company, the overall scope of their investments has been found to be higher than previously thought.[23]

From the beginning of the nineteenth century (and earlier) women had selected Consols (British government stocks) and stock in long-established trading concerns such as the East India Company; investments which were highly marketable while providing a regular, quarterly income.[24] Women gained some significance as shareholders in joint-stock banks and railways as the first half of the nineteenth century unfolded.[25] They tended to increase their levels of investments as these companies became more established and their record for stability and profitability more proven.[26] Some women took the opportunities presented by the new legislation but, as before, they tended to display a cautious attitude to new financial securities. Their prudence was well founded. Following the previous practice of banks and railway companies, the first limited companies tended to have shares of a large denomination on which only a fraction was called up, to create the problem of what was called 'unlimited limited liability' in the mid-1860s.[27] High levels of uncalled capital meant that those with savings could invest a small amount of money in partly paid shares that, potentially, involved a high risk and thus shareholders could assume levels of liability beyond their means. This left a shareholder without the protection on their investments that the Companies Acts had attempted to ensure.[28] Furthermore, most of the early limited-liability companies that were successfully established (about one in three of those registered) subsequently only had brief lives, of three years or so.[29]

This overall picture for England and Wales is confirmed by regional studies. In the case of 86 limited companies established in Sheffield between 1855 and 1885, females without a stated income-generating occupation supplied only 3 per cent of their aggregate paid-up capital.[30] But, although it can be argued that they were only a minority of shareholders in the new limited companies, women were present in them, and their numbers increased. As the century progressed and limited companies were perceived as a more established and less risky form of investment, with fewer and fewer companies partly paid, more women chose shares as financial assets.

Investment choices

Jefferys states that by 1885 there were 9,344 companies in the United Kingdom, with a paid-up capital of nearly £495 million.[31] Although this was still, as he points out, no more than 10 per cent of 'important business organisations', it was nevertheless a significant opportunity for investment.[32] A large proportion of British companies drew their shareholders from a small group of individuals, often including members of the same family. This was recognised in the 1907 Companies Act (consolidated in the Companies Act of 1908), which defined the private company as one required to have fewer than 50 shareholders, with restricted rights to transfer shares or debentures, and unable to promote the sale of any of its securities.

By 1914, there were nearly 63,000 limited companies in the United Kingdom but a large part of the increase was represented by private companies. Jefferys estimates that they made up 77 per cent of the total at that date.[33] Not all private companies were small businesses, but the fact that average issued share capital fell by nearly one-third between 1885 and 1915[34] suggests that many were. The consequence for women was the availability of a growing opportunity to invest in limited companies. They could choose either those that were quoted on one of a number of British stock markets or much smaller, possibly family companies where they were part of a network of investors who knew (and were often related to) one another.

Ordinary shares were originally of a high nominal value, which made them expensive investments, intended for the affluent, but as the century progressed the nominal value dropped, making them more accessible for the less affluent middle-classes.[35] The main new feature of the market in securities in the later nineteenth century was the growth in the importance of preference shares and debentures, partly driven by owners choosing to retain control over companies by holding all or the majority of ordinary shares, and partly by the demand for fixed-interest securities offering a higher yield than did government bonds. Preference shares carried a fixed dividend, entailing a lower risk and return than ordinaries: debentures were loan stock with a fixed interest rate, normally secured on the company's assets. They enjoyed a boom in popularity at the end of the nineteenth century. Studying a sample of more than 2,500 companies, Essex-Crosby finds that preference shares accounted for 12 per cent of capital in 1885 and 22 per cent in 1895, with the equivalent figure for debentures 26 and 40 per cent.[36] Women were not obliged to choose low-risk investments, but were encouraged to do so. According to a firm of company promoters, debentures were aimed at 'ladies and persons not possessed of separate sources of revenue',[37] and married women were prevented by some companies from being able to hold ordinary shares in their own names.

Conclusion

The later nineteenth century was a period in which married women were able to invest in the same way as single women and widows, after the Married Women's Property Acts of 1870 and 1882. At the same time, a wider variety of lower-risk investment assets became available – as well as government-loan stock, there were now limited-liability ordinary and preference shares and fixed-interest company debentures, offered by a widening range of public and private limited companies. The following chapters offer insights into the working of these factors in a variety of different contexts.

Notes

1 See Freeman *et al.* Chapter 8 and Newton and Cottrell, Chapter 9, this volume.
2 B. C. Hunt, *The Development of the Business Corporation in England 1800–1867*, Cambridge, MA: Harvard University Press, 1936, p. 14.
3 P. L. Cottrell, *Industrial Finance 1830–1914*, London: Methuen, 1980, p. 42; Hunt, *Development of the Business Corporation in England*, pp. 40 45
4 Cottrell, *Industrial Finance 1830–1914*, p. 76.
5 Cottrell, *Industrial Finance 1830–1914*, p. 43.
6 Cottrell, *Industrial Finance 1830–1914*, pp. 44–45.
7 Hunt, *Development of the Business Corporation in England*, pp. 118–123.
8 *Hansard*, 1854, vol. 134, 27 June: 757.
9 Cottrell, *Industrial Finance 1830–1914*, p. 41.
10 For an analysis of speculation and joint-stock companies as represented in novels and

the public debates surrounding these issues, see J. Taylor, *Creating Capitalism: Joint-Stock Enterprise in British Politics and Culture, 1800–1870*, Woodbridge: The Boydell Press, 2006, chapters 2 and 3.

11 Hunt, *Development of the Business Corporation in England*, p. 10.

12 Hunt, *Development of the Business Corporation in England*, pp. 105–107; M. C. Reed, *Railways in the Victorian Economy: Studies in Finance and Economic Growth*, Newton Abbot: David & Charles Ltd., 1968, pp. 182–183.

13 L. A. Newton, 'The birth of joint stock banking: a comparison of England and New England in the nineteenth century', *Business History Review*, forthcoming.

14 J. R. Killick and W. A. Thomas, 'The provincial Stock Exchanges, 1830–1870', *Economic History Review* 2nd series, 23, 1970, p. 96.

15 Reed, *Railways in the Victorian Economy*, pp. 179–183; W. A. Thomas, *The Provincial Stock Exchanges*, London: Frank Cass, 1973.

16 Cottrell, *Industrial Finance 1830–1914*, p. 52.

17 H. A. Shannon, 'The limited companies of 1866 and 1883', *Economic History Review* 4, 1933, p. 290.

18 Lee Holcombe, *Wives and Property*, Oxford: Martin Robertson, 1983, pp. 88–109.

19 Mary Beth Combs, 'Wives and household wealth: the impact of the 1870 British Married Women's Property Act on wealth-holding and share of household resources', *Continuity and Change* 19 (1), 2004, pp. 141–163.

20 See Editors' Introduction and Chapters 3 (Carlos *et al.*) and 4 (Laurence), this volume.

21 M. Freeman, R. Pearson and J. Taylor, '"A doe in the city": women shareholders in eighteenth- and early nineteenth-century Britain', *Accounting, Business and Financial History* 16 (2), 2006, pp. 265–291.

22 For example, see the articles collected in *Accounting, Business and Financial History* 16, 2006.

23 Freeman *et al.*, 'A doe in the city', p. 287.

24 H. V. Bowen, *The Business of Empire: The East India Company and Imperial Britain, 1756–1833*, Cambridge: Cambridge University Press, 2006, chapter 4; D. R. Green and A. Owens, 'Gentlewomanly capitalism? Spinsters, widows, and wealth holding in England and Wales, *c.*1800–1860', *Economic History Review* 56 (3), 2003, pp. 510–536.

25 Sarah Hudson, 'Attitudes to investment risk amongst West Midland canal and railway company investors 1700–1850', University of Warwick PhD thesis, 2001.

26 L. A. Newton and P. L. Cottrell, 'Female investors in the first English and Welsh commercial joint-stock banks', *Accounting, Business and Financial History* 16 (2), 2006, pp. 315–340; M. C. Reed, *Investment in Railways in Britain, 1820–1844. A Study in the Development of the Capital Market*, London: Oxford University Press, 1975; Hudson, 'Attitudes to investment risk'. But see also J. Rutterford and J. Maltby '"The nesting instinct": women and investment risk in a historical context', *Accounting History* 12 (3), 2007, pp. 305–327.

27 Cottrell, *Industrial Finance 1830–1914*, p. 58.

28 Taylor, *Creating Capitalism*, pp. 192–193.

29 H. A. Shannon, 'The first five thousand limited companies and their duration', *Economic History Review* 2, 1930–3; and Shannon, 'The limited companies of 1866 and 1883'.

30 Newton, *The Victorian Economy in Transition*, forthcoming, chapter 6.

31 J. B. Jefferys, 'Trends in business organisation in Great Britain since 1856, with special reference to the financial structure of companies, the mechanism of investment and the relations between the shareholder and the company', London University PhD thesis, 1938, vol. 1, p. 104.

32 Jefferys, 'Trends in business organisation', vol. 1, p. 105.

33 Jefferys, 'Trends in business organisation', vol. 1, p. 130.

34 Jefferys, 'Trends in business organisation', vol. 1, p. 131.
35 Jefferys, 'Trends in business organisation', vol. 1, p. 158.
36 A. Essex-Crosby, 'Joint-stock companies in England 1890–1930', University of London M.Comm. thesis, 1938, p. 31.
37 *Chadwick's Investment Circular*, 1874, p. 214.

Bibliography

Bowen, H. V., *The Business of Empire: The East India Company and Imperial Britain, 1756–1833*, Cambridge: Cambridge University Press, 2006.
Census of England and Wales 1881, London: Her Majesty's Stationery Office, 1881.
Census of England and Wales 1871, London: Her Majesty's Stationery Office, 1873.
Census of Great Britain 1851, London: Her Majesty's Stationery Office, 1852.
Combs, Mary Beth, 'Wives and household wealth: the impact of the 1870 British Married Women's Property Act on wealth-holding and share of household resources', *Continuity and Change* 19 (1), 2004, pp. 141–163.
Cottrell, P. L., *Industrial Finance 1830–1914*, London: Methuen, 1980.
Essex-Crosby, A., 'Joint-stock companies in England 1890–1930', University of London M.Comm. thesis, 1938.
Freeman, Mark, Pearson, Robin and Taylor, James, ' "A doe in the city": women shareholders in eighteenth- and early nineteenth-century Britain', *Accounting, Business and Financial History* 16 (2), 2006, pp. 265–291.
Green, D. R., and Owens, A., 'Gentlewomanly capitalism? Spinsters, widows, and wealth holding in England and Wales, c.1800–1860', *Economic History Review* 56, 2003, pp. 510–536.
Hansard, 1854, vol. 134, 27 June.
Holcombe, Lee, *Wives and Property*, Oxford: Martin Robertson, 1983.
Hoppen, K. T., *The Mid-Victorian Generation 1846–1886*, Oxford: Clarendon Press, 1998.
Hudson, Sarah, 'Attitudes to investment risk amongst West Midland canal and railway company investors 1700–1850', University of Warwick PhD thesis, 2001.
Hunt, B. C., *The Development of the Business Corporation in England 1800–1867*, Cambridge, MA: Harvard University Press, 1936.
Jefferys, James, 'Trends in business organisation in Great Britain since 1856, with special reference to the financial structure of companies, the mechanism of investment and the relations between the shareholder and the company', London University PhD thesis, 1938.
Killick, J. R., and Thomas, W. A., 'The provincial Stock Exchanges, 1830–1870', *Economic History Review* 2nd series, 23, 1970, pp. 96–111.
Newton, L. A., *The Victorian Economy in Transition*, forthcoming.
Newton, L. A., 'The birth of joint stock banking: a comparison of England and New England in the nineteenth century', *Business History Review*, forthcoming.
Newton, L. A. and Cottrell, P. L., 'Female investors in the first English and Welsh commercial joint-stock banks', *Accounting, Business and Financial History* 16 (2), 2006, pp. 315–340.
Reed, M. C., *Investment in Railways in Britain, 1820–1844. A Study in the Development of the Capital Market*, London: Oxford University Press, 1975.
Reed, M. C., *Railways in the Victorian Economy: Studies in Finance and Economic Growth*, Newton Abbot: David & Charles Ltd., 1968.
Rutterford, J. and Maltby, J., ' "The nesting instinct": women and investment risk in a historical context', *Accounting History* 12 (3), 2007, pp. 305–327.

Shannon, H. A., 'The limited companies of 1866 and 1883', *Economic History Review* 4, 1933, pp. 290–316.

Shannon, H. A., 'The first five thousand limited companies and their duration', *Economic History* 2, 1932, pp. 396–424.

Taylor, J., *Creating Capitalism: Joint-Stock Enterprise in British Politics and Culture, 1800–1870*, Woodbridge: The Boydell Press, 2006.

Thomas, W. A., *The Provincial Stock Exchanges*, London: Frank Cass, 1973.

8 Between Madam Bubble and Kitty Lorimer

Women investors in British and Irish stock companies

Mark Freeman, Robin Pearson and James Taylor

As the pilgrims came to rest on the Enchanted Ground, Mr Stand-fast, in Bunyan's *The Pilgrim's Progress* (1684), told his friends of an encounter on the road.

> 'As I was thus musing ... there was one in very pleasant attire, but old, that presented herself unto me ... [she] said if I would be ruled by her, she would make me great and happy. "For", said she, "I am the mistress of the world, and men are made happy by me." Then I asked her name, and she told me it was Madam Bubble'.[1]

The attribution of falsehood and deception as peculiarly female vices was, of course, commonplace. Restoration writers increasingly employed the term 'bubble' to indicate a deceit, or, by extension, one easily deceived and cheated.[2] There may, however, have been a more specific connection between female investors and 'bubbling' in stocks, to which Bunyan was alluding. This was the emerging prominence of noblewomen in chartered trading companies. After the Restoration, female investors become more evident, for example, in the proprietorships of the three African companies, the Royal Fishery Company and the Hudson's Bay Company founded between 1660 and 1677. The identification of corporate investment with wealthy women became impossible to avoid during the following decades when women were to be found in unprecedented numbers among the proprietors of the larger corporations. Even from the scanty data currently available, it seems that not only were female investors present in numbers at the birth of the corporate economy, but that their numbers may have grown faster than the market itself from the 1690s to the 1720s. Of the 1,268 subscribers to Bank of England stock in 1694, for instance, women comprised 12 per cent, and 17 per cent of 1,916 subscribers by 1709. Women were also found in the other major chartered companies, including 11 per cent of subscribers to the united East India Company in 1709 and 21 per cent of South Sea Company shareholders in 1723.[3]

An increasing number of women actively traded shares. Even during the bubble of 1720, women traded both in the safer investments such as Bank of England stock and in the more speculative shares such as those of the Royal

African Company.[4] By the first decade of the eighteenth century women's presence in the market, and not just that of aristocratic women, was widely acknowledged.[5] Contemporary responses varied. There was condemnation of the moral iniquity of female trading in stocks, and concern about the instability caused by women as aggressive interlopers. Such concern often took the form of satires on bubble speculation in which women played a leading role.[6] Critics also portrayed women investors as victims of speculators and jobbers.[7] The majority of commentators argued that women had no place either in the market for shares or in the joint-stock economy.[8]

Did these views change substantially between the early eighteenth and mid nineteenth centuries? Our answer remains largely speculative. In 1845, at the height of the railway mania, a *Punch* cartoon depicted a young spinster, Katherine Lorimer, signing the share register of the 'Great Didland Railway' in the company's offices. She is portrayed as a vulnerable, adventurous and, by implication, foolish victim. We have argued elsewhere that the foolish but 'knowing', and therefore culpable, victim of speculation became the dominant image of female investors by the mid-Victorian period.[9] Women, who were active and independent in the management of their financial assets, continued to be perceived as a threat to patriarchal relations in business and at home. The distance travelled over nearly two centuries from the ageing witch, Madam Bubble, mistress of iniquity, to young Kitty Lorimer, the 'doe in the city', was perhaps not so great. Most of the range of opinions about female investment in joint stocks had formed by the 1720s, and arguably what followed was merely a shift in emphasis. This chapter will argue that women investors survived and multiplied, though not without setbacks, in large segments of Britain's expanding corporate economy.

The datasets

The purpose of this chapter is to examine the volume and distribution of female investment in stock companies in Britain and Ireland between 1780 and 1850, the classic era of the first industrial revolution, and to explore some aspects of their involvement in the governance of those companies.[10] This was the time when the joint-stock sector began to grow rapidly, after a long period of slow growth since the end of the South Sea Bubble in 1720 and since the advent of restrictive legislation on unincorporated stock companies in England and Ireland. During the 1790s a boom in canal, dock, harbour and insurance promotions added to the number of companies. In the 1800s another wave of promotions drew the adverse attention of those in the judiciary who were interested in upholding the validity of the Bubble Act.[11] From the 1810s, despite the continuing legal uncertainty surrounding unincorporated companies and the lack of limited liability for their investors, a growing number of gas and water companies, joint-stock banks (from 1826), and property, shipping, manufacturing, mining, fishing and finance companies added to the size of the corporate economy.[12] Railway companies arrived in large numbers during the 1830s and

1840s. By 1840 the total capital of English joint-stock companies is estimated to have been £210 million. Just over a decade later, the total paid-up capital of British railway companies alone amounted to some £225 million.[13]

This was also the period in which, according to the historiography of separate spheres, middle-class women – those likely to have both the wealth and interest to invest in such business ventures – began to retreat into a world of domesticity and patriarchy.[14] One might expect, therefore, that these very public forms of private business enterprise were increasingly closed to women with money, unable or unwilling to attract female investors, still less benefit from their partic-ipation in company governance. The data examined in this chapter allow us to begin to answer questions about the trends in women's involvement in the joint-stock economy and, in turn, to make a modest contribution to the separate spheres debate.

Our methodology has followed certain criteria. Our principal focus has been to collect and analyse lists of the first shareholders investing in stock companies (the latter defined as those with 13 or more partners and with transferable shares) at or near the time of their foundation, that is before many shares had been transferred by sale, assignment or inheritance.[15] We have such lists for 151 companies established between 1780 and 1851. These lists have been found either in the preambles to company charters of incorporation or in the schedules attached to them, or in separately printed lists of subscribers dated from the foundation of an enterprise. For unincorporated companies, deeds of settlement (England and Ireland) or contracts of copartnery (Scotland), and, occasionally, minute books have provided lists of the first shareholders.[16] Given the propensity over time for the number of shares held by women to increase, as widows inher-ited them from their deceased husbands or daughters from their fathers, and as established businesses attracted larger numbers of female investors, our focus on lists of initial shareholders will understate the actual level of women's stock company investment at any point in time during the period 1780–1850.

Due to incomplete record survival, it is not always possible to establish when a company was founded. In some industries, acts of incorporation might be obtained after several years of business. This was most notably the case in the gas industry, where most companies began as unincorporated ventures and then sought incorporation, sometimes after a delay of a decade of more. In other sectors this was less of a problem. Canals, railways, dock, harbour, bridge and water companies were almost all established by public Acts of Parliament. By contrast, most insurance companies, joint-stock banks and miscellaneous stock companies in property development, finance and manufacturing remained unin-corporated in this period, so their private constitutional documents, such as deeds of settlement, provide the dates of their foundation.

For a number of firms we also have shareholders' lists from various dates after the company foundation. This is the case for 14 of the 151 companies with initial shareholders' lists noted above, plus another 40 companies that were either established before 1780, or for which we have not located a list of first shareholders, or for which the date of foundation is not known. Altogether, therefore, we have data on 191 companies (151+40). For 21 of these we have more than one list for different dates, so that we can follow changes in share-ownership over time, although in no case do we have an annual time series. Our data, however, allow us to say little about women's trading in stocks. Share transfer books have seldom survived for the hundreds of stock companies established between 1780 and 1850. In any case, a detailed analysis of the transactions of individual proprietors is beyond the scope of this chapter. We can, however, draw conclusions from the data about who was investing and about the scale of that investment over time and by sector, and also draw general inferences about the objectives of investment.

Finally, our focus has been on compiling new data hitherto unused by historians. The datasets described below exclude all shareholders' lists dating from before 1780 and after 1850, regardless of source, and all numbers on women's shareownership produced by other authors, regardless of their date and provenance.[17]

Two datasets have been constructed on the above principles. The first contains 229 data on women as a proportion of shareholders for 191 stock companies covering the period 1780–1851.[18] We exclude from our count of 'women's shares' shares held jointly by women and men, but we include shares held by executors on behalf of deceased women, and we count shares held jointly by more than one woman, and those held jointly by a woman and her children, as one female shareholding/shareholder. Altogether this dataset comprises 63,840 shareholders, of whom 8,011 were women. It also covers a diverse range of sectors across the joint-stock economy. As well as companies in banking, canals, railways, gas and insurance, we have 19 bridge, road and tunnel companies, 11 property companies of different types, seven shipping and five dock and harbour companies, plus a few water, fishing and manufacturing concerns. We also have sufficient data from Scottish and Irish companies – 31 and 17 companies respectively – to begin to explore differences in women's investment across the three nations.

The second dataset, which overlaps with the first and derives from the same sources, contains data on women's investment as a percentage of share capital or of subscribed shares. There are 110 observations from 80 companies. This dataset is smaller because many shareholders' lists recorded only names and not details of shareownership. Nevertheless, we can say that, together, both datasets represent the largest exploration of stock-company investment hitherto undertaken for the British Isles during the first Industrial Revolution.

Results

Figure 8.1 presents all 229 data on the percentage of women among the shareholders of 191 companies. Figure 8.2 extracts from this dataset the percentages from the 151 shareholders' lists that date from company foundations, in order to compare exactly like with like. The trend lines follow a similar path in both charts: a modest increase in the percentage of female shareholders during the 1790s, some reversal during the decade after 1815, and then around 1830 the beginnings of a growth that accelerates through the 1840s. Overall, what we see are two phases. The first, lasting until the 1820s, was marked by persistently low levels of female participation in stock companies, mostly under 15 per cent. The second, beginning after 1830, was characterised by the growth in average female shareownership to much higher levels than before. The main effect of Figure 8.2 is to remove some of the higher values seen in Figure 8.1, particularly for the period 1780–1815. In every one of the 53 new stock companies in our sample that were established before 1815, women constituted less than 15 per cent of initial subscribers to a share issue. It is possible that the late eighteenth century and the first decade of the nineteenth century marked a historic low point in women's joint-stock investments in relative terms. While women comprised 15 per cent of East India Company shareholders in 1712, by the 1750s this figure had risen to 32 per cent. Thereafter, women declined as a proportion of East India stockholders to 13 per cent in the later eighteenth century, before recovering slightly to around 17 per cent in 1818 and 1830.[19]

Figures 8.1 and 8.2 indicate that the recovery in women's participation as shareholders began around 1830 and picked up pace in the railway era. Recent research, although only examining a handful of companies, suggests that this increase continued throughout the rest of the century, stimulated by the growing surplus of single women in the population seeking to secure an income, the spread of limited liability, the removal of legal restrictions on married women's property, the decline in share denominations, and the greater availability of fully paid-up shares and of lower-risk preference shares and debentures. Women accounted for between 33 and 48 per cent of shareholders in the Ulster Bank

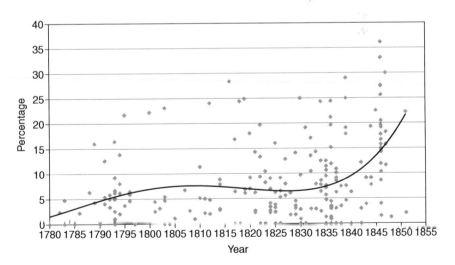

Figure 8.1 Women as a percentage of shareholders in British and Irish stock companies, 1780–1851 (sources: see text).

Note

n = 229 observations for 191 companies. Trend line is a 4th order polynomial.

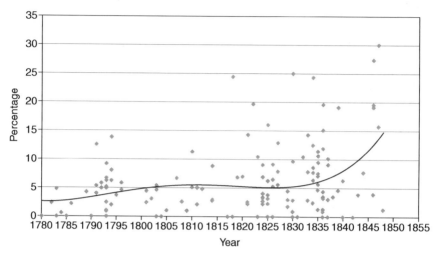

Figure 8.2 Women as a percentage of first shareholders in new joint-stock companies,
  Britain and Ireland, 1780–1850 (sources: see text).

Note

$n = 151$. Trend line is a 4th order polynomial.

between 1877 and 1914, nearly one-third of the shareholders in Martin's Bank
in 1891 and the Bank of Liverpool in 1894, and 28 per cent of the shareholders
in the Prudential Assurance Company in 1898.[20] These figures are at or beyond
the top end of the range in our dataset.

Examining pairs of shareholders' lists between different dates for individual
companies provides some insight into whether women's participation commonly
grew over time. We can calculate women as a proportion of shareholders for 21
companies with 37 pairs of data between various dates in the period 1780–1850.
Percentages declined in only six of the 37 pairs of data. For most companies at
most times the number of women grew as a proportion of shareholders, albeit at
a barely perceptible annual rate of less than half of 1 per cent (the average was
0.28 per cent). Figure 8.3, which regroups the data in Figure 8.1 by decade,
more clearly illustrates, however, that the development of women's shareownership was non-linear. The coefficients in Figure 8.3 also reveal that the range of
female per caput shareownership across the dataset widened considerably during
the canal mania of the 1790s, and during the boom of the 1820s when joint-
stock enterprises were being launched in new or different industries such as utilities, shipping and property development.[21] Thus, the low averages shown for
the 1790s and 1820s were accompanied by the biggest differences between companies in women's shareownership. As the range of investment opportunities
multiplied, some stock companies were clearly more attractive to female
investors than others. After 1830 the coefficients decline as the range of female
shareownership across the corporate economy narrowed.

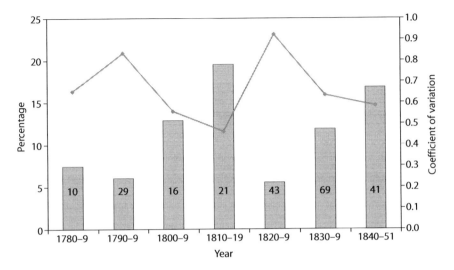

Figure 8.3 Women as a percentage of shareholders in British and Irish stock companies, by decade (sources: see text).

Note
$n = 229$ observations for 191 companies. Mean % charted in the bars, coefficients in the line. n is shown in the bars.

Figure 8.4 shows women's percentage share of share capital in 110 data for 80 companies. The average of all data in Figure 8.4 is 6.6 per cent, compared to 12.5 per cent in Figure 8.1. Thus, female proprietors were, on average, almost twice as important to their companies in terms of numbers than in terms of their shares. The trend in Figure 8.4 is similar to those in Figures 8.1 and 8.2, though rather more pronounced. The sharper increase in women's share of joint-stock capital during the 1790s and early 1800s, compared to the trend line in Figure 8.1, suggests that during this period wealthier women, or at least those making larger investments, were joining stock companies. The reverse was the case during the 1820s, when the trend in women's share of capital falls more markedly than the proportion of women among shareholders. This suggests that from this period the growing number of female shareholders were buying, on average, smaller amounts of the capital of the companies that they were investing in. This inference is supported by the data in Table 8.1 which, for a subset of 74 companies, compare the average size of women's shareholdings with the overall average shareholding by decade.[22] The ratio peaked during the 1830s, and continued to be high during the following decade, suggesting that women comprised an increasing proportion of small investors entering the equity market during the railway era.

Tables 8.2 and 8.3 show the proportion of women as shareholders and the proportion of women's share capital by sector. The presence of women was minimal in fishing, shipping, bridge, dock and insurance companies, while it

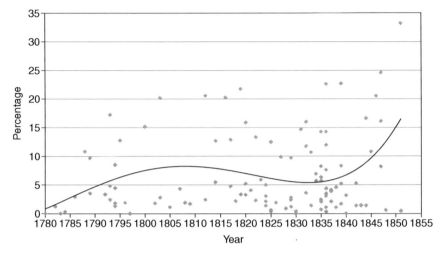

Figure 8.4 Women's share of share capital in British and Irish stock companies, 1780–1851 (sources: see text).

Note

n = 110 observations for 80 companies. Trend line is a 4th order polynomial.

Table 8.1 Ratio of average female shareholdings to overall average shareholdings, by decade and by sector

	No. of companies	*No. of observations*	*Mean of ratios*
1780–9	6	6	1.66
1790–9	9	9	1.46
1800–9	7	7	1.86
1810–19	6	8	2.31
1820–9	18	20	1.43
1830–9	31	34	2.46
1840–51	12	15	2.00
Banks	2	2	1.31
Canals	13	22	1.72
Gas	13	14	1.82
Insurance	13	16	1.82
Railways	14	16	2.69
Shipping	7	11	1.59
Other	13	18	2.28

Sources: see text.

was most visible in gas and canal companies and joint-stock banks. Altogether, just 38 of the 229 shareholders' lists (17 per cent) in Table 8.2 named no female shareholders. The coefficients, however, modify the picture. While the average insurance company had relatively few women, some companies in the sector had quite a number. There was also considerable variation in women's participation

Table 8.2 Women's per caput investment in joint-stock companies by sector, 1780–1851

	No. of companies	No. of observations	No. of women	No. of shareholders	Mean %	Coefficient variation	Correlation x time	Correlation x size
Banking	29	33	5,514	29,318	18.8	0.46	0.02	0.40
Gas	27	30	251	2,364	10.6	0.87	0.20	0.02
Canals	38	48	1,241	12,425	10.0	0.75	0.40	0.09
Railways	23	28	469	7,151	6.6	0.77	0.05	0.08
Docks, harbours	5	5	27	437	6.2	0.48	-0.28	0.09
Property	11	11	41	699	5.9	1.02	0.63	-0.21
Shipping	7	12	64	1,682	3.8	0.69	-0.13	-0.07
Insurance	21	27	264	7,480	3.5	0.96	0.29	0.16
Bridges, roads, tunnels	19	19	23	892	2.6	1.08	0.17	0.13
Other*	11	16	117	1,392	8.4	0.85	0.51	-0.02
Total	191	229	8,011	63,840	12.5	0.63	0.29	0.35
Scottish companies	31	38	2,514	16,869	14.9	0.61	0.41	0.39
Irish companies	17	22	357	4,243	8.4	0.63	0.28	0.85

Sources: see text.

Note
* Other comprises three water companies (three observations), four manufacturing companies (nine observations), three fishing companies (three observations), one finance company (one observation). An 'observation' is defined as a single list or count of shareholders at a particular date.

Table 8.3 Women's share of share capital in joint-stock companies by sector, 1780–1851

	No. of companies	No. of observations	Mean (%)
Banking	3	6	17.2
Gas	12	14	8.2
Canals	14	23	9.6
Railways	14	16	3.7
Shipping	7	11	2.9
Insurance	16	21	2.6
Other*	14	19	7.4
Total	80	110	6.6
Scottish companies	11	16	6.1
Irish companies	7	10	4.5

Sources: see text.

Note

* 'Other' comprises six property companies (six observations), three dock companies (three observations), three manufacturing companies (eight observations), one fishing company (one observation), one finance company (one observation). An 'observation' is defined as a single list or count of shareholders at a particular date. 'Mean percentages' (column 4) show the averages of women's percentage shareholdings in each sector.

in gas, bridge and property companies. None of the four cemetery companies in our dataset, for example, had women shareholders.

The correlations in Table 8.2 are not particularly insightful. The results for Scottish and Irish companies, however, are interesting. The former, comprising largely data from banks, shipping, railway and gas companies, reveal a level of female investment – 15 per cent of all shareholders – that is above the average for the dataset as whole. By contrast, women did not flock to Irish companies in large numbers, and, when they did, as the bottom row of Table 8.2 shows, there was a tendency for them to invest in the largest companies. Thus, while the Hibernian Bank had 103 women among its 533 proprietors in 1844 (19.6 per cent), and the Grand Canal had 54 women among 445 proprietors in 1842 (12.1 per cent), the majority of Irish companies in our dataset had few female shareholders or none at all.

Table 8.1 reveals that the widest gender gaps in average shareholding were to be found in railway companies and the narrowest in banks, canals and shipping. Wealthier male investors in railways appeared to have left their female counterparts behind, especially in the 1840s. A decline in the average share denominations, and the removal of limitations on the number of shares that individuals could own, may help account for the increasing differential between male and female shareholding in the railway sector, even as the base of the shareholder population expanded.[23] Low share denominations with unlimited liability became a central concern in the debate over limited liability in Britain from the 1840s through to the Overend Gurney crisis of 1866. Large nominal shares, with a substantial proportion of each share unpaid, had been regarded by some as the bedrock of the unlimited liability regime and a guarantee of 'respectable', rather than impecunious, investment. The concern about a Kitty Lorimer putting her money into the Great Didland Railway was closely related to other non-gendered concerns about small, insubstantial and uninformed investors entering the share market.[24] In the following section we discuss the identity of women investors and their role in the companies in which they owned shares.

Women's shareownership – access to shares and proprietorial rights

Many women's shares were held in family clusters – up to 50 per cent in some companies. Among the most notable examples are the five Kirwan women of Drumcondra, each holding two shares in the Hibernian Bank in 1844, while in Scotland there was the entirely female Mutter clan of Wester Melville, Lass-wade, near Edinburgh – one married woman and six spinsters – who together held 17 shares in six different Scottish banks in 1846.[25] Another variant of family shareownership was the Ross household, of Berbice Cottage, Inverness, whose members held between them five shares in the Caledonian Bank, namely John Ross, gentleman, in his own name, three shares in the names of his children, and one share held in the name of Margaret Robertson, the children's live-in nursery maid. Some wives held shares outright in their own name. Thus 'Mrs S. J. Glen, spouse of Reverend J. Glen, Portobello' owned a share in the Royal Bank of Scotland in 1846. Scots women also frequently held shares in the form of both liferents and fees, which gave them the use of the shares during their lifetime, with the fiar(s) receiving the share upon their death or at the end of a stipulated term.[26] Many women, of course, had an interest in shares over which they had no direct control or access. Husbands held shares for their wives in trust, fathers for their daughters, brothers for their sisters.[27] For married women such trusteeships could be related to a marriage contract, and the existence of such trusts for separate use helped extend the rights of *feme sole* to wives in England under equity law.[28] Shares might also be held by a third party where a woman's share had been assigned to creditors, though the records do not usually make it clear who was responsible for the assignment.[29] Women also frequently held shares belonging to others as their trustees or executors. Indeed, under English law even *feme coverts* and minors could be appointed as executors.[30] Moreover, a widow enjoyed the legal right to administer her husband's estate if he died intestate, and there are plenty of examples in our dataset of widows in both England and Scotland holding shares in this way.[31]

Thus, there were various means by which women became involved indirectly in the joint-stock economy through the mediation of others within and outside the household or the immediate family circle. The overwhelming majority of women in our dataset, however, were widows and spinsters who held shares directly in their own names. The sources listed occupations for a very small number of these and their married counterparts. The analysis of 2,586 female shareholders in 19 Scottish banks in 1846, for example, revealed only 44 women with named occupations.[32] Traditional 'female trades' – food and tobacco, dress and clothing, domestic service, and inn-keeping and hostelry – accounted for most of these, but among the women who owned Scottish bank shares there was also an engraver, a farmer, a painter and a stock maker. Female shareownership reached down through the classes to three domestic servants and the nursery maid, Margaret Robertson of Inverness, noted above. This diverse configuration of working women among Scottish bank shareholders resembled the situation at the Great Western Railway in 1837, where female proprietors included servants, small retailers, a lodging-house keeper and a cordwainer.[33]

Although we do not know of a single instance in which a woman served as a director or executive officer of a stock company, there were generally few discriminatory or even gender-specific regulations passed by British and Irish stock companies in this period. Indeed, by virtue of their shareholdings many women were eligible to stand for election as directors and governors of such companies, including the Bank of England and the South Sea Company.[34] There were some obstacles but seldom outright exclusion of women from company governance. Restricting women's rights as proprietors was not widespread. Although a tiny number, such as the Aberdeen Fire and Life Assurance Company in 1825, explicitly barred married women from owning shares, it was far more common for a woman upon marriage to be required to inform companies of her change of status and for her shares to be re-registered in her husband's name.[35] In other companies, almost certainly a minority, women were discouraged from buying shares, particularly where the board was seeking 'active' or 'eligible' investors who would promote the business. This seems to have been especially the case in shipping and insurance.[36] A few companies, such as the Salop Fire Office and the Aberdeen Fire and Life Assurance Company, denied their female shareholders any right to vote in board elections, but this was highly unusual. It was far more common to make a general constitutional provision for voting by proxy.[37] In the dataset for our larger project on corporate governance, 437 out of 514 companies (85 per cent) provided for proxy voting.[38] Of these, 65 restricted proxy voting to certain groups of shareholders, notably women, minors and all proprietors living at a distance, but this was commonly presented as a *right* of which such groups could take advantage. Of course, the proxy vote could be regarded as a device to encourage 'respectable' women to stay away from occasionally turbulent and crowded meetings in which heated words might be exchanged. Only 15 of the 437 companies, however, *compelled* women shareholders to vote by proxy. Ten of these were Scottish companies, including several banks established in the 1830s. A few Scottish companies, such as the Aberdeen Gas Light Company (1824), also barred women from acting as proxy voters for others.

Generally, however, proxy voting was offered to women, not as a compulsion, but as an alternative to voting in person, and this model became more widely accepted during the first half of the nineteenth century. The Companies Clauses Consolidation (Scotland) Act of 1845 allowed proxy voting for all shareholders as the default position for companies thereafter incorporated by Act

of Parliament.[39] Throughout the period, however, there was a widespread acceptance that women might take part in general meetings, although they were not
necessarily expected to. For the corporate governance project, we have collected
data on shareholders' attendance at general meetings from the minute books of
nearly 40 companies. There is unambiguous evidence of women attending and
voting in the meetings of several companies, for instance the Moray Firth &
London Steam Packet Company in 1824, the Preston Gas Company in 1828 and
the London & Edinburgh Shipping Company in 1818, 1835 and 1836. Elsewhere
women voted in person or by proxy, for example, at the meetings of the Leamington Priors Gas Light Company in 1842 and 1843 and the Sheffield New Gas
Company in 1842.[40] There was an incentive in the latter company for every shareholder, regardless of gender, to turn up in some shape or form, as a sixpence-per-
share fine was levied for non-attendance.[41] Such incentives were not uncommon.

In most companies at most times, however, female shareholders seldom exercised their rights, including those not discussed here, such as the right to inspect
company accounts. Women were never entirely invisible in the governance
process in most companies, but they participated in shareholders' meetings
infrequently and in small numbers. Their presence at such meetings, therefore, is
difficult to interpret as normative, although the evidence in the opposite direction is also not substantial or compelling. What can be said with some certainty
is that the great majority of stock companies placed few, if any, internal regulatory barriers in the way of female proprietors availing themselves of the same
rights as their male counterparts.

Conclusions

The above analysis points to a number of conclusions about women's participation in stock companies during this period. Women's joint-stock investments
were more widespread than previously thought. Only 36 out of 191 companies
in our dataset, fewer than one in five, had no women shareholders at some point.
The data, however, confirmed the received view that married women made up
only a tiny proportion of female shareholders. The great majority were widows
and spinsters, some of them active in business in their own right in a diverse
range of occupations that extended far down the social ladders of the employed
and self-employed.

Notwithstanding the propensity in all companies for women's shareownership to grow slowly over time with widowhood, the average proportion of
women shareholders remained low, at around 7 per cent, during the late eighteenth century, increased during the first two decades of the nineteenth century,
fell back in the 1820s, and then grew again to 17 per cent in the 1840s. The three
shareholders' lists in our dataset in which women accounted for over 30 per cent
of names – those of the Ayr Gas Company, the Bank of Scotland and the Royal
Bank of Scotland – all date from 1846–7. Even higher percentages of women
shareholders may have become more common during the second half of the
nineteenth century.

As the proportion of women investors fell during the 1790s and again during the 1820s, wealthier women appear to have entered the booming market for new promotions, for the gender gap, long entrenched in the major public stocks, between the average shareholdings of men and women, fell substantially.[42] Moreover, the rising coefficients in Figure 8.3 suggest that in both periods women became more discriminating in the companies they chose to invest in. One might reasonably speculate that their larger average investments, relative to their male counterparts, were a reflection of higher status and may have allowed these women to draw on more specialist investment advice.

This pattern, however, was reversed in the periods during which women's participation levels as shareholders rose. The coefficients of variation between companies fell and the gender gap in average shareholdings increased. The railway era, with its burgeoning financial journalism, appears to have swelled the ranks of small female investors, and wealthier women became less prominent in many stock companies. By the 1840s women shareholders were, on average, twice as important numerically to their companies than when measured by the size of their investments.

Finally, the sectoral data in Tables 8.1, 8.2 and 8.3 suggest that, as the joint-stock economy became more diverse during the course of the industrial revolution, some types of company proved more attractive to women than others. Women investors were commonly found in joint-stock banks, canals and gas companies, pointing to 'clustering' in favoured investments similar to the clustering observed by historians in certain 'women's trades' – food, retail, clothing and textiles – during the period.[43] That said, we found the highest variations in the levels of women's participation among insurance, property and bridge companies, or, to put it another way, in these industries the propensity for women to invest was least predictable.

The data examined in this chapter demonstrate not only the persistence of women investors in the joint-stock economy, but also their increasing numbers over the long term. While there was some clustering of women's investment by industry, there is no strong evidence of 'separate spheres' for male and female shareholders, still less for the idea that women were driven out of the equity markets by any new ideology that made female investment, or indeed active female participation in stock company governance, unacceptable. Thus our results generally support recent attempts to question the separate spheres concept, and the arguments for the continued visibility of women in finance and business in nineteenth-century Britain.[44] Women shareholders were certainly not 'at the heart' of the financial or business life of joint-stock companies, but they had a persistent and recognised presence in the corporate sector of the first industrial economy, one that was slowly growing in significance beyond the tired stereotypes of a Madam Bubble and a Kitty Lorimer.[45]

Notes

1 John Bunyan, *The Pilgrim's Progress*, Harmondsworth: Penguin, 1965, pp. 361–2.
2 Cf., for example, the many references to 'bubbles' and 'bubbling' in the context of

both women and money in William Wycherley, *The Country Wife: A Comedy*, London: Thomas Dring, 1675.

3 P. G. M. Dickson, *The Financial Revolution in England: A Study in the Development of Public Credit, 1688–1756*, London: Macmillan, 1967, pp. 256, 268, 282.

4 Ann M. Carlos, Karen Maguire and Larry Neal, 'Financial acumen, women speculators and the Royal African Company during the South Sea Bubble', *Accounting, Business and Financial History* 16 (2), 2006, pp. 219–43; Ann M. Carlos and Larry Neal, 'Women investors in early capital markets, 1720–1725', *Financial History Review* 11, 2004, pp. 197–224.

5 Davenant, Charles, *Reflections upon the Constitution and Management of the Trade to Africa*, London: John Morphew, 1709, p. 40.

6 Anon, *Exchange Alley: or the Stock-Jobber ... Turn'd Gentleman. A Tragi-Comical Farce*, London, 1720, preface. On this theme, see Catherine Ingrassia, 'The pleasure of business and the business of pleasure: gender, credit and the South Sea Bubble', *Studies in Eighteenth-Century Culture* 24, 1995, pp. 191–210; Susan Staves, 'Investments, votes, and "bribes": women as shareholders in the chartered national trading companies', in H. L. Smith (ed.), *Women Writers and the Early Modern Political Tradition*, Cambridge: Cambridge University Press, 1998, pp. 259–78; John Carswell, *The South Sea Bubble*, London: Cresset Press, 1960, pp. 121, 126, 144.

7 Cf. Thomas Foxton, *Jesina: or, Delusive Gold. A Pastoral, Lamenting the Misfortunes of a Young Lady of Quality, Ruined by South-Sea Stock*, London: E. Curll, 1721; Archibald Hutcheson, *Four Treatises Relating to the South-Sea Scheme and Stock*, London, 1721, preface.

8 Anon, 'A caveat against bubbling, written in the year 1732', in *Essays and Letters on Various Subjects*, London: J. Brotherton, 1739, pp. 115–23; Thomas Mortimer, *Everyman his own Broker: or, a Guide to Exchange-Alley*, second edition, London: S. Hooper, 1761, preface.

9 Mark Freeman, Robin Pearson and James Taylor, ' "A doe in the city": women shareholders in eighteenth- and early nineteenth-century Britain', *Accounting, Business and Financial History* 16 (2), 2006, pp. 265–91. We also noted, however, that this victim image could often be non-gender specific. Cf., for example, the 'deluded multitudes' of 'men, women and children' investing in railway shares, in Thomas Mulock, *Railway Revelations: Being Letters on the Subject of the Proposed Direct London and Manchester Railways*, London: George Vickers, 1845, p. 4.

10 This chapter is based on a larger research project we are conducting into the corporate governance of British stock companies, 1720–1844, supported by a grant from the Economic and Social Research Council (UK), award number RES 000 230096 (see www.corporategovernancehistory.org.uk). We are most grateful for this support.

11 Ron Harris, *Industrializing English Law: Entrepreneurship and Business Organization, 1720–1844*, Cambridge: Cambridge University Press, 2000, pp. 236–41.

12 On the legal difficulties for companies in Scotland, see Mark Freeman, Robin Pearson and James Taylor, ' "Different and better?" Scottish joint-stock companies and the law, c. 1720–1845', *English Historical Review* 122, 2007, pp. 61–81.

13 Harris, *Industrializing English Law*, pp. 194–6; Ranald C. Michie, *The Global Securities Market: A History*, Oxford: Oxford University Press, 2006, p. 92.

14 Leonore Davidoff and Catherine Hall, *Family Fortunes: Men and Women of the English Middle Class, 1780–1850*, Chicago, IL: University of Chicago Press, 1987.

15 This definition draws upon Charles Munn's distinction between unincorporated Scottish copartneries with more than 13 partners and ordinary partnerships with fewer. The larger copartneries, Munn argues, were most likely to have an elected committee to run their day-to-day affairs and thus to experience a separation of powers between managers and proprietors. Incorporated and unincorporated English stock companies can also be distinguished from small partnerships in this way. C. W. Munn, 'Scottish provincial banking companies: an assessment', *Business History* 23, 1981, pp. 19–41.

16 The full references to sources are too many to give here, but are available from the authors on request.

17 These include shareownership data on canals (S. J. Hudson, 'Attitudes to investment risk amongst West Midland canal and railway company investors, 1760–1850', University of Warwick PhD thesis, 2001; J. R. Ward, *The Finance of Canal Building in Eighteenth-Century England*, Oxford: Oxford University Press, 1974), banks (Lucy Newton and Philip L. Cottrell, 'Female investors in the first English and Welsh commercial joint-stock banks', *Accounting, Business and Financial History* 16, 2006, pp. 315–40), gas companies (J. F. Wilson, *Lighting the Town: A Study of Management in the North West Gas Industry, 1805–1880*, London, 1991), and railways (M. C. Reed, *Investment in Railways in Britain, 1820–1844: A Study in the Development of the Capital Market*, Oxford: Oxford University Press, 1975).

18 The term 'data' is used in this chapter as one observation (percentage statistic) calculated from a single list of shareholders; 229 'data' thus relates to the percentages calculated from each of the 229 lists of shareholders. A dataset is a collection of such data.

19 H. V. Bowen, *The Business of Empire: The East India Company and Imperial Britain, 1756–1833*, Cambridge: Cambridge University Press, 2006, pp. 107–8; Bruce G. Carruthers, *City of Capital: Politics and Markets in the English Financial Revolution*, Princeton, NJ: Princeton University Press, 1996, p. 158.

20 Graeme Acheson and John Turner, 'The impact of limited liability on ownership and control: Irish banking, 1877–1914', *Economic History Review* 59, 2006, pp. 320–46; Josephine Maltby and Janette Rutterford, '"She possessed her own fortune": women investors from the late nineteenth century to the early twentieth century', *Business History* 48, 2006, pp. 220–53. We are grateful to these authors for pre-publication copies of their papers.

21 All correlations are of the Pearson product moment type.

22 Table 8.1 comprises 99 data on average shareholdings for the 74 companies for which we can make this calculation.

23 Mark Freeman, Robin Pearson and James Taylor, 'The politics of business: joint stock company constitutions in Britain 1720–1844', in A. Carreras and M. Kipping (eds), *EBHA 2004: Proceedings from the 8th Annual Congress of the European Business History Association*, Barcelona, CD-Rom, 2005.

24 James Taylor, *Creating Capitalism: Joint-Stock Enterprise in British Politics and Culture, 1800–1870*, Woodbridge: Boydell, 2006, pp. 192–3.

25 Hibernian Bank, *Proprietors of Hibernian Bank Stock, 1st November 1844*, National Library of Ireland, Ir 332 H4; Anon, *A List of All the Names, Classed in Alphabetical Order, Contained in the Printed Lists of Proprietors of the Bank of Scotland, Royal Bank, and British Linen Company; and in the Returns of the other Banks in Scotland*, Edinburgh: John Johnstone, 1846.

26 Registers of Scotland, Legal Manual, 2004, online edition, chapter 39: www.ros.gov.uk/foi/legal/text/ch39.htm, accessed 18 April 2007.

27 Examples from 1846 include a share in the Edinburgh & Glasgow Bank held by 'Robert Gibson, secretary, Scottish Equitable Assurance Society, Edinburgh, as trustee for Mrs Joanna Gibson, his spouse', the eponymous R. C. Nisbet, curator in Banff, holding a share in the National Bank of Scotland 'for his daughters', and a share in the Edinburgh & Glasgow Bank held by 'Duncan Lamond, brewer, Edinburgh, as trustee for his sister, Miss Mary Lamond'. Anon, *List of all the Names*.

28 Janelle Greenberg, 'The legal status of the English woman in early eighteenth-century common law and equity', *Studies in Eighteenth-Century Culture* 4, 1975, pp. 171–81. One Scottish example was the share in the Caledonian Bank held by 'John Macdougall, Connage Cottage, and Others, trustees for Isabella Macdougall or Stevenson, under her marriage contract'. Anon, *List of all the Names*.

29 One example is the share in the Bank of Scotland held by 'the Mercantile Life Assur-

ance and Guarantee Association, assignees of the liferent interest of Mrs Helen Thomson, relict of James Thomson, W.S.' Anon, *List of all the Names*. In this case the share was possibly assigned as a further security for an annuity or a loan on a life insurance policy.

30 'All persons are capable of being executors that are capable of making wills, and many others besides; as feme-coverts, and infants'. Anon, *The Laws Respecting Women as they Regard their Natural Rights or their Connections and Conduct*, London: J. Johnson, 1777, book 2, p. 250.

31 In 84 per cent of the wills of married men in Stockport, 1800–57, the testator's wife was appointed executor or trustee. Alistair Owens, 'Property, gender and the life course: inheritance and family welfare provision in early nineteenth-century England', *Social History* 26, 2001, pp. 299–317.

32 Calculated from Anon, *List of all the Names*.

33 Freeman *et al*., ' "Doe in the city" ', p. 270.

34 Bank of England, *A List of the Names of all such Proprietors of the Bank of England who are Qualified to Vote*; South Sea Company, *A List of the Names of all such Proprietors of the Capital Stock of the Governor and Company of Merchants Trading to the South Seas ... who are Qualified to Vote ... on Tuesday, Twenty-ninth of January 1805*.

35 Aberdeen Fire and Life Assurance Company, *Contract of Copartnery, 1 November 1825* (printed D. Chalmers and Co., Aberdeen, 1826), Edinburgh University Library, Special Collections Department, FAct pamphlet file.

36 Examples include the Leeds & Yorkshire Assurance Company (1824), the London & Edinburgh Shipping Company (1809), and the Aberdeen Leith and Clyde Shipping Company (date of establishment unknown). Robin Pearson, *Insuring the Industrial Revolution: Fire Insurance in Great Britain 1700–1850*, Aldershot: Ashgate, 2004, p. 243 (for the Leeds & Yorkshire); London & Edinburgh Shipping Company, *Contract of Copartnery, 1 December 1809*, National Archives of Scotland, GD301/58/3; Aberdeen Leith and Clyde Shipping Company, *Minute Book, 1816–24*, General Meeting 4 June 1816, Aberdeen University Library, Historic Collections, Ms 3697.

37 In eighteenth-century England, in the absence of any specific reference to proxy voting in a company's constitution, the right to vote by proxy does not seem to have been recognised at common law. Samuel L. Williston, 'History of the law of business corporations', *Harvard Law Review* 2, 1888, p. 158.

38 The proxy voting data are discussed more fully in Mark Freeman, Robin Pearson and James Taylor, *Shareholder Democracies? Corporate Governance in British Business before 1850*, Chicago, IL: University of Chicago Press, forthcoming.

39 8 Vict. (1845) c. 17.

40 Leamington Priors Gas Light Company, *Resolution Book*, General meetings, 15 November 1842, 23 November 1843; Sheffield New Gas Company, *Minute Book*, General meeting 26 September 1842.

41 Sheffield New Gas Company, *Minute Book*, General meeting 31 July 1822.

42 Carruthers, *City of Capital*, p. 156; Bowen, *Business of Empire*, p. 106.

43 Hannah Barker, *The Business of Women: Female Enterprise and Urban Development in Northern England, 1760–1830*, Oxford: Oxford University Press, 2006, pp. 62–6.

44 Amy L. Erickson, 'Coverture and capitalism', *History Workshop Journal* 59, 2005, pp. 1–16; Staves, 'Investments'.

45 Barker has recently argued, using data from trade directories, that businesswomen were 'at the heart of commercial developments in northern towns'. Barker, *Business of Women*, p. 42.

Bibliography

Aberdeen Fire and Life Assurance Company, *Contract of Copartnery, 1 November 1825* (printed D. Chalmers and Co., Aberdeen, 1826): Edinburgh University Library, Special Collections Department, FAct pamphlet file.

Aberdeen Leith and Clyde Shipping Company, *Minute Book, 1816–24*, General Meeting 4 June 1816, Aberdeen University Library, Historic Collections, Ms 3697.

Acheson, Graeme and Turner, John, 'The impact of limited liability on ownership and control: Irish banking, 1877–1914', *Economic History Review* 59, 2006, pp. 320–46.

Anon, 'A caveat against bubbling, written in the year 1732', in *Essays and Letters on Various Subjects*, London: J. Brotherton, 1739, pp. 115–23.

Anon, *A List of all the Names, Classed in Alphabetical Order, Contained in the Printed Lists of Proprietors of the Bank of Scotland, Royal Bank, and British Linen Company; and in the Returns of the other Banks in Scotland*, Edinburgh: John Johnstone, 1846.

Anon, *Exchange Alley: or the Stock-Jobber … turn'd Gentleman. A Tragi-Comical Farce*, London, 1720.

Anon, *The Laws Respecting Women As they Regard their Natural Rights or their Connections and Conduct*, London: J. Johnson, 1777.

Bank of England, *A List of the Names of all such Proprietors of the Bank of England who are Qualified to Vote*, 1803, 1812, 1819, 1836.

Barker, Hannah, *The Business of Women: Female Enterprise and Urban Development in Northern England, 1760–1830*, Oxford, Oxford University Press, 2006.

Bowen, H. V., *The Business of Empire: The East India Company and Imperial Britain, 1756–1833*, Cambridge: Cambridge University Press, 2006.

Bunyan, John, *The Pilgrim's Progress*, Harmondsworth: Penguin, 1965.

Carlos, Ann M. and Neal, Larry, 'Women investors in early capital markets, 1720–1725', *Financial History Review* 11, 2004, pp. 197–224.

Carlos, Ann M., Maguire, Karen and Neal, Larry, 'Financial acumen, women speculators and the Royal African Company during the South Sea Bubble', *Accounting, Business and Financial History* 16 (2), 2006, pp. 219–43.

Carruthers, Bruce G., *City of Capital: Politics and Markets in the English Financial Revolution*, Princeton, NJ: Princeton University Press, 1996.

Carswell, John, *The South Sea Bubble*, London: Cresset Press, 1960.

Davenant, Charles, *Reflections upon the Constitution and Management of the Trade to Africa*, London: John Morphew, 1709.

Davidoff, Leonore and Hall, Catherine, *Family Fortunes: Men and Women of the English Middle Class, 1780–1850*, Chicago, IL: University of Chicago Press, 1987.

Dickson, P. G. M., *The Financial Revolution in England: A Study in the Development of Public Credit, 1688–1756*, London: Macmillan, 1967.

Erickson, Amy L., 'Coverture and capitalism', *History Workshop Journal* 59, 2005, pp. 1–16.

Foxton, Thomas, *Jesina: or, Delusive Gold. A Pastoral, Lamenting the Misfortunes of a Young Lady of Quality, Ruined by South-Sea Stock*, London: E. Curll, 1721.

Freeman, Mark, Pearson, Robin and Taylor, James, *Shareholder Democracies? Corporate Governance in British Business before 1850*, Chicago, IL: University of Chicago Press, forthcoming.

Freeman, Mark, Pearson, Robin and Taylor, James, '"Different and better?" Scottish joint-stock companies and the law, c.1720–1845', *English Historical Review* 122, 2007, pp. 61–81.

Freeman, Mark, Pearson, Robin and Taylor, James, ' "A doe in the city": women share-holders in eighteenth- and early nineteenth-century Britain', *Accounting, Business and Financial History* 16 (2), 2006, pp. 265–91.

Freeman, Mark, Pearson, Robin and Taylor, James, 'The politics of business: joint stock company constitutions in Britain 1720–1844', in Carreras, A. and Kipping, M. (eds), *EBHA 2004: Proceedings from the 8th Annual Congress of the European Business History Association*, Barcelona, CD-Rom, 2005.

Greenberg, Janelle, 'The legal status of the English woman in early eighteenth-century common law and equity', *Studies in Eighteenth-Century Culture* 4, 1975, pp. 171–81.

Harris, Ron, *Industrializing English Law: Entrepreneurship and Business Organization, 1720–1844*, Cambridge: Cambridge University Press, 2000.

Hibernian Bank, *Proprietors of Hibernian Bank Stock, 1st November 1844*, National Library of Ireland, Ir 332 H4.

Hudson, S. J., 'Attitudes to investment risk amongst West Midland canal and railway company investors, 1760–1850', University of Warwick PhD thesis, 2001.

Hutcheson, Archibald, *Four Treatises Relating to the South-Sea Scheme and Stock*, London, 1721.

Ingrassia, Catherine, 'The pleasure of business and the business of pleasure: gender, credit and the South Sea Bubble', *Studies in Eighteenth-Century Culture* 24, 1995, pp. 191–210.

Leamington Priors Gas Light Company, *Resolution Book 1834–1865*, Warwickshire County Record Office, CR 929/25.

London & Edinburgh Shipping Company, *Contract of Copartnery, 1 December 1809*, National Archives of Scotland, GD301/58/3.

Maltby, Josephine and Rutterford, Janette, ' "She possessed her own fortune": women investors from the late nineteenth century to the early twentieth century', *Business History* 48, 2006, pp. 220–53.

Michie, Ranald C., *The Global Securities Market: A History*, Oxford: Oxford University Press, 2006.

Mortimer, Thomas, *Everyman his own Broker: or, a Guide to Exchange-Alley*, 2nd edn, London: S. Hooper, 1761.

Mulock, Thomas, *Railway Revelations: Being Letters on the Subject of the Proposed Direct London and Manchester Railways*, London: George Vickers, 1845.

Munn, C. W., 'Scottish provincial banking companies: an assessment', *Business History* 23, 1981, pp. 19–41.

Newton, Lucy and Cottrell, Philip L., 'Female investors in the first English and Welsh commercial joint-stock banks', *Accounting, Business and Financial History* 16 (2), 2006, pp. 315–40.

Owens, Alistair, 'Property, gender and the life course: inheritance and family welfare provision in early nineteenth-century England', *Social History* 26, 2001, pp. 299–317.

Pearson, Robin, *Insuring the Industrial Revolution: Fire Insurance in Great Britain 1700–1850*, Aldershot: Ashgate, 2004.

Reed, M. C., *Investment in Railways in Britain, 1820–1844: A Study In the Development of the Capital Market*, Oxford: Oxford University Press, 1975.

Registers of Scotland, *Legal Manual*, 2004, online edition, chapter 39: www.ros.gov.uk/foi/legal/text/ch39.htm (accessed 18 April 2007).

Sheffield New Gas Company, *Minute Books 1818–30, 1839–44*, Sheffield Archives, GCR 1, 7.

South Sea Company, *A List of the Names of all such Proprietors of the Capital Stock of the Governor and Company of Merchants Trading to the South Seas ... who are Quali-fied to Vote ... on Tuesday, Twenty-ninth of January 1805.*

Staves, Susan, 'Investments, votes, and "bribes": women as shareholders in the chartered national trading companies', in Smith, H. L. (ed.), *Women Writers and the Early Modern Political Tradition*, Cambridge: Cambridge University Press, 1998, pp. 259–78.

Taylor, James, *Creating Capitalism: Joint-Stock Enterprise in British Politics and Culture, 1800–1870*, Woodbridge: The Boydell Press, 2006.

Ward, J. R., *The Finance of Canal Building in Eighteenth-Century England*, Oxford: Oxford University Press, 1974.

Williston, Samuel L., 'History of the law of business corporations', *Harvard Law Review* 2, 1888, pp. 149–66.

Wilson, J. F., *Lighting the Town: A Study of Management in the North West Gas Indus-try, 1805–1880*, London, 1991.

Wycherley, William, *The Country Wife: A Comedy*, London: Thomas Dring, 1675.

9   Female investors in the first English and Welsh commercial joint-stock banks[1]

Lucy A. Newton and Philip L. Cottrell

Introduction

During the mid-1850s several commentators noted the frequency of females, particularly widows and spinsters, among the shareholders of metropolitan and provincial banks.[2] The attractiveness of these institutions' shares to women, especially those who had no stated income-generating occupation, was that they offered a safe and profitable outlet for their savings.

Bank shares had become 'blue-chip' investments by the mid-1850s through joint-stock banks having become relatively stable institutions. Joint-stock banking had developed following the Banking Co-partnerships Act of 1826 (7 Geo. IV, c. 46), which permitted in England and Wales beyond a 65-mile radius of London (Charing Cross) the creation of banks with more than six partners and freely transferable shares. By the early 1840s, weaker 'corporate' banks had ceased business, whereas the Joint Stock Banking Act of 1844 checked markedly the pace of joint-stock bank formation – only 12 new 'corporate' banks were to be established during the next 13 years.[3] The number of joint-stock banks consequently stabilised at around 100 during the mid-nineteenth century. Furthermore, their market position was aided by the continuing decline of private banking.[4] As the 'corporate' banks matured, they attracted increasingly larger volumes of deposits, became more profitable and, thus, their managements were able to distribute larger dividends to shareholders.

Although joint-stock banks had become more robust by mid-century, their shares could still be risky investments. The 1826 Act had permitted joint-stock banks to be legally constituted only as *unlimited* companies. It also became the practice of bank directors to provide depositors with further security by calling up merely a fraction of the nominal value of their respective institution's shares.[5] The risks for shareholders had been even greater during the late 1820s and 1830s due to the formation of joint-stock banks being then a novel development. An element of risk remained in the mid-century since English and Welsh joint-stock banks continued to fail – a total of 22 between 1844 and 1861.[6]

This chapter considers in general terms the women who invested in joint-stock bank shares during the first half of the nineteenth century despite the risks this entailed. The discussion is based upon an analysis of the shareholders of 20 joint-stock banks established variously between 1827 and 1836, both at the time of their respective foundation (original subscriptions) and 20 years later. Our findings show that there was greater share ownership by women at this later date, demonstrating that female shareholders became more numerous as joint-stock banks developed to be more proven institutions. Women were generally more prepared to invest in shares as the associated risks decreased with the passage of time.

Early joint-stock bank promotions

This chapter examines 20 of the joint-stock banks formed under the 1826 Act's provisions. All were successful institutions in that each survived to become a constituent of a 'Big Five' clearing bank of the post-1918 era.

Seven banks in our sample were formed before 1834 (see Table 9.1), and were groundbreaking institutions. Indeed, some were founded immediately following the 1826 Act's passage. All were local unit banks (that is banks without branches), except the Huddersfield Banking Co., the management of which opened three offices soon after its promotion in 1827. The earliest joint-stock banks generally had relatively small paid-up capitals – £17,500 in the case of the Halifax Joint Stock Bank, and £20,000 in the cases of both the Bradford and Cumberland Union. The other 12 banks in our sample were established after 1834 (see Table 9.2), of which three were conversions of private houses (Coventry & Warwickshire Banking Co., Halifax & Huddersfield Union Bank, and Sheffield & Rotherham Banking Co.), one a 'district' bank (Wilts & Dorset Banking Co.), and one a metropolitan bank (London Joint Stock Bank).

Attempting to found a joint-stock bank before the early 1830s was innovative since it was an untried and untested venture. Its promoters faced suspicion from the public and fierce opposition from private bankers, with whom the bank would compete. The new joint-stock banks' managements had to struggle strenuously to consolidate their reputations and gain acceptance within local communities.[7]

Despite opposition, joint-stock bank promotions averaged four a year between 1832 and 1836. Many businessmen successfully established banks in order to meet their immediate local communities' financial demands. Joint-stock bank formations increased from August 1833, following the threat of greater regulation being lifted and clauses being introduced into the Act renewing the Bank of England's charter that widened the business they could undertake.[8] Between 1833 and 1835, joint-stock bank foundations averaged ten a year and peaked during the 'promotion mania' of 1836, when 59 joint-stock banks were established.[9]

Over the mid-1830s, founders of joint-stock banks were able to capitalise upon the pioneering institutions' successes. These included the payment in 1833 of dividends of between 6 and 10 per cent and share-price premiums ranging from 20 to 80 per cent. By 1836, dividends had reached between 6.5 and 12.5 per cent, and there were premiums of 5 to 66 per cent on bank shares.[10]

Female subscriptions to bank promotions

The extent of female participation in the capitals of joint-stock banks formed both before and after 1834 was broadly the same (see Tables 9.1 and 9.2). Overall, women numbered fewer than one in ten among the subscribers to the shares of the various banks in our sample that were established before 1834. Women in the Cumberland Union Bank comprised 13 per cent of its shareholders, whereas in the cases of the Halifax Joint Stock Bank and the Bank of Westmorland they only made up 2 per cent. The proportions of female shareholders in banks formed either before or after 1834 are broadly similar. They were even less significant in terms of the monetary value (paid-up capital) of their collective holdings, mirrored in terms of the average value of their holdings (by paid-up capital). Furthermore, the value of the average female holding was half to two-thirds the average value of all shareholdings in banks formed both before, and after, 1834.[11]

Were women reluctant or timid subscribers during the early development of joint-stock banking in England and Wales? Not necessarily. Joint-stock banking was usually taken up by local commercial and industrial groups to meet their own credit needs. Consequently, great care was taken to ensure that shares were allotted to those most likely to enhance their embryonic institution's future business. Some shares were allocated on the condition that their holder would open an account with the bank, thereby explicitly generating business for the new institution. This meant that it was unlikely that women would be sought, or welcomed, as shareholders. All in all, bank managements' share allocation decisions necessarily favoured men over women.

What were the characteristics of female investors in new joint-stock banks? Where it is possible to identify female occupations from the sources consulted, it shows the presence of female traders and manufacturers among the banks' proprietors. Their occupations reflect the typical involvement of women in business during the first half of the nineteenth century. They include participation in the hospitality sector (inn-keeping, hotel-keeping, victuallers); the clothing and footwear industries (dressmaker, milliner, draper, shoemaker, currier); retailing (bookseller); and education. A few were engaged in manufacturing (varnish and metal manufactures), reflecting the industrial character of the bank's locality. It is possible that acquiring shares in a joint-stock bank improved these female subscribers' access to credit since some bank managements subsequently gave preference to shareholders' applications for facilities.[12]

However, the vast majority of women who were initial subscribers to new joint-stock banks did not state an income-generating occupation, being, rather, 'gentlewomen', or spinsters, wives or widows. They comprised between 72 and 100 per cent of the female shareholders in 19 banks in our sample. The one exception is the Halifax Joint Stock Bank; only 64 per cent of its female shareholders did not have a stated income-generating occupation. Overall, our results correspond with Gilbert's findings regarding London joint-stock banks' shareholders, for which the largest increase between 1845 and 1855 was spinsters.[13]

Table 9.1 Subscriptions to bank shares, 1827–1833[1]

	Bradford Banking Co. 1827	Huddersfield Banking Co. 1827	Cumberland Union Banking Co. 1829	Halifax Joint Stock Bank 1829	Barnsley Banking Co. 1831	Bank of Liverpool 1831	Bank of Westmorland 1833	Average 1827–1833
Number of female shareholders as a % of all shareholders	8.70%	8.40%	12.70%	1.70%	5.30%	16.20%	2.20%	**7.90%**
Value of shares held by women as a % of the aggregate value of shares subscribed	7.90%	4.10%	6.70%	1.60%	5.30%	10.40%	1.60%	**5.40%**
Average value of women's shareholdings	£193.75	£74.90	£56.96	£87.50	£5.90	£264.01	£16.88	**£99.90**
Average value of all shareholdings	£214.57	£153.04	£108.12	£95.96	£10.42	£411.45	£61.10	**£150.66**

Sources: HSBC Group Archives (HSBCGA): Bradford Banking Co., 1827: B1 deed of settlement, 1 June 1827; Cumberland Union Banking Co., 1829: G1, deed of settlement, 1829; Huddersfield Banking Co., 1827 and 1847: H24, share register and transfer book, 1827–1890; Barnsley Banking Co., 1831 and 1851: A4, share ledger, 1832–1896; Bank of Westmorland, 1833 and 1853: C12, share ledger, 1833–1880. Lloyds TSB Group Archives (LTSBGA): Halifax Joint Stock Bank, 1829: 5354, deed of settlement, 1829. Barclays Bank Group Archives (BBGA): Bank of Liverpool, 1831: 310/152, share register.

Note
1 This sample excludes the Yorkshire Bank refounded 1843–1844.

Table 9.2 Subscriptions to bank shares, 1835–1836[1]

	Coventry & Warwickshire Banking Co. 1835	Liverpool Union Banking Co. 1835	Birmingham & Midland 1836	County of Gloucestershire Banking Co. 1836	Coventry Union Banking Co. 1836	Halifax & Huddersfield Union Banking Co. 1836	London Joint Stock Bank 1836	North & South Wales Bank 1836	Sheffield & Hallamshire Banking Co. 1836	Sheffield & Rotherham Banking Co. 1836	Swaledale & Wensleydale Banking Co. 1836	Wiltshire & Dorset Banking Co. 1836	Average 1835–1836
Number of female shareholders as a % of all shareholders	10.90	7.10	2.60	11.00	8.70	3.80	3.20	7.40	3.40	9.80	9.40	10.30	**7.30**
Value of shares held by women as a % of the aggregate value of shares subscribed	5.50	4.00	1.90	2.50	4.70	1.60	1.70	4.90	2.30	5.00	2.20	6.20	**3.50**
Average value of women's shareholdings (£)	41.88	275.00	45.00	176.92	108.70	111.67	172.70	19.57	69.20	575.78	28.57	91.30	**143.02**
Average value of all shareholdings (£)	82.41	498.00	61.82	777.94	200.48	272.85	318.70	29.56	100.80	1,172.17	123.37	144.27	**315.19**

Sources: BBGA: Swaledale & Wensleydale Banking Co., 1836 and 1856: 388/705, share register. HSBCGA: Birmingham & Midland Bank, 1836 and 1856: AA1 deed of settlement and share register; Coventry Union Banking Co., 1836: AB2, deed of settlement, 6 May 1836; London Joint Stock Bank, 1836: 592/01, share ledger, vol. 1; North & South Wales Bank, 1836: M132, Proprietors' stock ledger; Sheffield & Hallamshire Banking Co., 1836: AM48, list of share transfers. LTSBGA: County of Gloucestershire Banking Co., 1836: Book no. 1954, deed of settlement, 26 July 1836; Coventry & Warwickshire Banking Co., 1835: File no. 7013, deed of settlement, 1835; Halifax & Huddersfield Union Banking Co., 1836: File no. 5924, deed of settlement, 1 July 1836; Liverpool Union Banking Co., 1835: book no. 3544, Proprietors' ledger No. 1, 1835–1847; Wilts & Dorset Banking Co., 1836 and 1853: Book number 3177, Shareholders' register, 1835–1853. Royal Bank of Scotland Group Archives (RBSGA): Sheffield & Rotherham Banking Co., 1836 and 1863: SR/79, deed of settlement, 1 July 1836 and SR/147014000, Register of proprietors, 1863–1899.

Note
1 This sample excludes the Yorkshire Bank refounded 1843–1844.

Wives do not feature prominently in the banks' share registers, being present among the proprietors of merely five banks and, collectively, contributed very little capital. This corresponds with the very minor role of wives' investments in early English railway companies so that, for instance, only 12 appear in the 1837 list of London & Birmingham shareholders.[14] The absence of married women shareholders was due to the legal position of their assets. From the early thirteenth century until the Married Women's Property Act of 1870, English common law held that property owned by a single woman was lost, or rather transferred, to her husband upon marriage.[15] The 1870 Act prevented married women owning partly paid shares in their own names, and joint-stock banks typically issued such shares. This particular bar persisted until the 1882 Married Women's Property Act.[16] Before 1870 it was possible for married women to hold shares 'indirectly' through trusts. Their trustees were often their fathers, or their brothers or other male relatives. For example, in the case of the Huddersfield Banking Co., William Dickinson of Holmfirth held the five shares of Mrs Mary Kilner of Huddersfield in trust. However, some bank prospectuses made it clear that subscriptions from wives would not be accepted.[17]

The ways that spinsters and widows became shareholders is difficult to determine. One possibility is that they were related to males that either had established a bank or were among its first shareholders. A list of the Bank of Westmorland's initial shareholders shows that five women had the same surname as one of its directors – Harrison – but several men also shared this name.[18] Greater certainty comes with unusual surnames, so that there are stronger grounds for linking the holding of 30 shares in the Barnsley Banking Co. of Florence and Mary Cordeaux with those of Thomas Scales Cordeaux and John Cordeaux, jnr, both local linen merchants. It is also clear that the holdings of the female Rawsons arose from the conversion of their family's private house into the Halifax & Huddersfield Union Bank.

Other family connections can also be found. A feature of female subscriptions to shares of banks being founded was that of siblings acting together. Mary and Agnes Hodgson, spinsters of Liverpool, made investments of £1,775 and £1,525, respectively, in the Bank of Liverpool. Similarly, Amelia and Jane Horsfall of the Ladies Academy, Wakefield, each acquired ten shares of the Barnsley Banking Co.

Female bank shareholders

Although in most cases women did not have a major presence among the initial shareholders of joint-stock banks established over the decade following the passage of the 1826 Act, contemporary commentary points to them being more prominent at the mid-century.[19] This is confirmed when the share registers are examined for the nine banks in our sample for which they are available 20 years after their respective establishment (see Table 9.3). The data in Table 9.3 are different from those displayed in Tables 9.1 and 9.2, in that the shareholders in the latter were original subscribers whereas those in the former were holding stocks

Table 9.3 Ownership of bank shares by women, 1847–1864

	Huddersfield Banking Co. 1847	Barnsley Banking Co. 1851	Bank of Westmorland 1853	Wilts & Dorset Banking Co. 1853	London Joint Stock Bank 1856	Swaledale & Wensleydale Banking Co. 1856	Sheffield & Rotherham Banking Co. 1856	Birmingham & Midland 1859	Yorkshire Banking Co. 1864	Average
Female shareholdings as a % of all shareholdings	17.10	8.80	10.30	13.60	30.30	21.10	7.90	15.32	20.20	16.07
Value of shares held by women as a % of the aggregate value of shares subscribed	10.30	7.30	23.30	10.00	17.40	11.50	3.00	6.76	11.80	11.26
Average value of women's shareholdings (£)	10	525	121.76	199.10	379.50	188.55	139.43	591.76	461.43	290.70
Average value of all shareholdings (£)	440.06	464.71	167.92	271.70	660.00	321.44	367.86	1,482.52	663.90	537.79

Sources: Swaledale & Wensleydale Banking Co., 1836 and 1856: 388/705, share register. HSBCGA: Huddersfield Banking Co., 1827 and 1847: H24, share register and transfer book, 1827–1890; Barnsley Banking Co., 1831 and 1851: A4, share ledger, 1832–1896; Bank of Westmorland, 1833 and 1853: C12, share ledger, 1833–1880; London Joint Stock Bank, 1836: 592/01, share ledger, vol. 1; Birmingham & Midland Bank, 1836 and 1856: AA1 deed of settlement and share register; Yorkshire Banking Co. 1844 and 1864 – HSBCGA: X49, Representatives' register. LTSBGA: Wilts & Dorset Banking Co., 1836 and 1853: Book number 3177, Shareholders' register 1835–1853. RBSGA: Sheffield & Rotherham Banking Co., 1836 and 1863: SR/79, deed of settlement, 1 July 1836 and SR/147014000, Register of proprietors, 1863–1899.

in companies with dividend records. Twenty years after their establishment, these banks were proven institutions, and their share registers clearly show an increase in the participation of women. In particular, our results for the London Joint Stock Bank support *The Economist*'s observation in 1856 that a large number of shareholders in metropolitan joint-stock banks were female; in its case 30 per cent of shareholders, who collectively held 17 per cent of the capital.[20]

The size of individual female stakes in joint-stock banks had increased by mid-century. The average number of female shareholdings per bank had risen to 16 per cent of all holdings from 7–8 per cent when the institutions were promoted two decades before. The average collective stake of female shareholders by value (in terms of paid-up capital) had increased to 11 per cent from 3–5 per cent. Furthermore, the average female holding had risen to £290 from £100–£112 during the 1820s and 1830s.

Our sample of nine banks (comprising share registers dating, variously, from between 1847 and 1864) confirms contemporary observations that female shareholders in banks were significant. The occupational data for these banks' shareholders are robust, and show that the females among them were overwhelmingly those without a stated income-generating employment. The lowest proportion of such female shareholders is 97.2 per cent. A few wives again appear but the principal female holders of these institutions' capital 20 years after their respective foundations were spinsters and widows.

How had more females become bank shareholders by the mid-century, and why? There is some evidence that women inherited shares from their husbands, fathers or other male relatives; for instance, among the Barnsley Banking Co.'s proprietors, Samuel Hirst held five shares in 1831, whereas by 1851 he was no longer on the register but Hannah Hirst of the same address owned five shares.[21] Apart from inter-generational and inter-spouse transfers, there is the possibility of purchases through either some form of secondary market or the acquisition of shares when banks subsequently raised further equity capital. What motivated such purchases?

Mid-nineteenth-century investment opportunities for women

Some general 'push' and 'pull' forces can be identified to account for the increasing take-up of bank shares by women as the years passed, and joint-stock banking became firmly established.

Dividends ('pull')

The importance of dividends was mentioned in our introduction. The returns to shareholders of some of the banks in our sample during the mid-1840s and the mid-1850s are displayed in Tables 9.4 and 9.5. By 1844, the banks in our sample that were established in the 1820s would have had a dividend history of just under 20 years and by 1854 just under 30 years. Those banks established in the 1830s from our sample would have had a 10- or 20-year dividend history in 1844 and 1854, respectively.

Table 9.4 Bank shares: prices and dividends, 1844

Bank	Share price (£)	Capital paid up per share (£)	Dividend (%)
Bank of Liverpool	23 15s.	12 10s.	10
Barnsley Banking Co.	19–20	15	8
Birmingham & Midland Bank	6–15	5	8
Bradford Banking Co.	60	30	12.5
County of Gloucestershire Banking Co.	26	25	5
Coventry Union Banking Co.	'About par'	6 5s.	5
Cumberland Union Banking Co.	40	20	10
Halifax Joint Stock Bank	15	15	5
Halifax & Huddersfield Union Banking Co.	15	10	'20s. per share'
Huddersfield Banking Co.	24	10	12.5
Liverpool Union Banking Co.	11 15s.	10	8
London Joint Stock Bank	14	10	6
North & South Wales Bank	7	10	4
Sheffield & Hallamshire Banking Co.	3 10s.	4	7.5
Swaledale & Wensleydale Banking Co.		5	10

Source: *Bankers Almanac*, 1845.

In 1844, only the North & South Wales Bank was distributing a dividend of less than 5 per cent. It had been badly affected by the 1836 crisis, resulting in losses of £54,000, and dividends were not distributed during several subsequent years.[22] Conversely, the London Joint Stock Bank by 1844 was regularly paying a 6 per cent dividend.[23] In 1854 no bank in our sample was distributing a dividend of less than 5 per cent; the North & South Wales Bank was paying 6 per cent, the Bank of Westmorland as much as 18 per cent and the Cumberland Union £41 on each of its shares. Furthermore, rising dividend records were becoming established. For example, the Birmingham & Midland paid 8 per cent from 1839, 9 per cent in 1845, 10 per cent from 1846, 12 per cent in 1855, 14 per cent in 1856, 15 per cent in 1857 and 16 per cent from 1858 (until 1864, when it rose to 18 per cent).[24] In addition, some proprietors were benefiting from bonus payments.

Women with the capacity to invest (push)

The number of women holding shares and enjoying such dividends was, of course, dependent upon them having the resources to invest. Female investors came predominantly from a small but important section of society. They were primarily unmarried women or widows who had sufficient wealth and were risk averse to investing in equity. They have been recently identified in the work of Green and Owens and Rutterford and Maltby.[25] This specific female group consisted potentially of those who could invest in financial securities. Their first choice tended to be low-risk options, such as Consols or the stock of

Table 9.5 Bank shares: prices and dividends, 1854

Bank	Capital paid up per share (£)	Dividend (%)
Bank of Liverpool	£12 10s.	8 +12s 6d per share bonus for 1853–1854
Bank of Westmoreland	£10	18
Barnsley Banking Co.	£15	8
Birmingham & Midland Bank	£50	+2% bonus for 1854
Bradford Banking Co.	£15	£5 per share
County of Gloucestershire Banking Co.	£25	12.5
Coventry Union Banking Co.	£6 5s.	6
Cumberland Union Banking Co.	£30	5
Halifax Joint Stock Bank	£15	£41 per share
Halifax & Huddersfield Union Banking Co.	£10	8.5 or £20 per share
Huddersfield Banking	£10	'20s. per share'
Liverpool Union Banking Co.	£10	10
		6
London Joint Stock Bank	£10	+ bonus of 6s per share
North & South Wales Bank	£7 10s.	10
Sheffield & Hallamshire Banking Co.	£25	6
		7.5%
Swaledale & Wensleydale Banking Co.	£5	+1.5% bonus
		8
Wilts & Dorset Banking Co.	£10	+2% bonus
Yorkshire Banking Co.	£10 10s.	6
		6

Source: *Bankers Almanac*, 1855.

long-established trading and financial institutions, like the Bank of England and the East India Company. These securities were highly marketable and provided a regular, quarterly income.[26] They were therefore attractive to women who preferred low-risk investments, an understandable attitude given that most of them had considerably more restricted opportunities to generate income than men.[27] As these particular women became more accustomed to investing, and more experienced at assessing the risks, they widened the range of their investments to include bank and railway shares, especially as these securities became less risky.

Increasing the shareholding habit for women ('pull')

The preparedness of females to place their savings in securities increased, displayed by women acquiring railway shares. As with joint-stock banks, women invested in these companies as they became more mature.[28] There were particular increases over time in the number of women railway shareholders: in the cases of the Stockton & Darlington from 1823 to 1844, the Newcastle & Carlisle from 1825 to 1844 and the Great Northern of England from 1836 to 1845. Reed concluded that women became more significant shareholders a decade or so after a company had been formed, while being most numerous in concerns deemed to be established and therefore low risk. Some female investors learnt from their experiences of holding shares and invested in a number of companies.[29] Women were therefore more likely to invest in more mature and, therefore, less risky, ventures.[30]

The decline in other investment opportunities for women ('push')

The collapse of the mid-1840s 'railway mania' caused a significant change in investors' attitudes. The activity of many of the provincial stock exchanges established during the 1830s and 1840s declined significantly, with negative consequences for trading in bank shares.[31] Only ten English railway companies were distributing a dividend of more than 5 per cent during the mid-1850s and, consequently, the ordinary investor was generally only prepared to subscribe to new railway securities if they were preference shares and debentures – investments with guaranteed returns.[32] This represented a 'push' away from ordinary railway equity, while increasing the 'pull' of bank shares, particularly in the cases of gentlemen and females or, rather, the more risk-averse investor. The attractions of the only other directly competing investment outlet, insurance company shares, had also faded since only 53 of the 291 life companies projected between 1844 and 1851 were still in business in 1852/3.[33]

Pushed away from ordinary railway shares and the equity of life insurance companies, gentlemen and female rentier investors[34] during the 1850s were also faced with falling proceeds on traditional saving outlets. Land was a solid investment but returns on it were declining[35] and, likewise, Consols. Some fresh issues of Consols were made to finance Britain's participation in the Crimean War but the yield on them had fallen to 3.4 per cent by the mid-1850s.[36]

During the mid-1850s the decline of the returns on relatively 'safe' investment opportunities for rentiers was considered to constitute a 'social problem'. One solution came with the secular increase in the issue of foreign securities from the mid-1850s.[37] Another was provided by the total liberalisation of British company law between 1855 and 1862.

The liberalisation of company law ('pull')

The liberalisation of company law in 1855/6 permitted the free establishment of limited-liability companies, and was extended to banks in 1858.[38] These wholesale changes, codified in 1862, set the context for a new era in the development of British commercial banking. Banks featured prominently during the company-promotion booms of the mid-1860s and early 1870s. New limited banks were first put before the investing public in September 1861, and their promoters frequently pointed to the dividends that bank shareholders had enjoyed during the 1850s.[39] Limited liability offered a potentially safer form of investment.

Risks remained even on the shares of banks formed with limited liability. Many share denominations of the joint-stock banks formed during the 1820s and 1830s were £100 and this came to set a pattern.[40] Shares of large nominal denominations but with a high portion of uncalled capital left investors exposed to the possibility of losses.[41] The 1866 financial crisis adversely affected many shareholders through giving rise to the problem of 'unlimited limited liability', only partly resolved by the 1867 Companies Act. There was also a reluctance to reduce the denomination of bank shares due to the fear of encouraging the 'wrong' sort of investor. Furthermore, uncalled capital was often left at a high level for bank managements to draw upon it swiftly if necessary.[42] The City of Glasgow Bank failure of 1878 caused a further shock. The collapse of this unlimited bank ruined very many of its shareholders through forcing them into bankruptcy as they were called upon to meet its extensive debts. These substantial problems resulted directly in the passage of the 1879 Companies Act (42 & 43 Vict. c. 76). It introduced 'reserved liability', adopted by bank managements dividing uncalled capital equally between that which could be called up by the directors and that which could only be called upon in the event of liquidation.[43] The statute also required all limited liability banks to have properly audited accounts.

The mounting bank amalgamation movement from the 1880s led to shares in large-scale joint-stock banks becoming less risky through the growth in institutions' size and capital bases. Banks competed by extending their market presence nationwide rather than on price, the latter being subject to cartel agreements and customary practice. Furthermore, as individual banks enjoyed greater longevity, share capital was gradually called up. By 1874 shares in the Birmingham & Midland Bank were fully paid up.[44] More generally, company promoters during the late nineteenth century introduced lower share denominations and lower-risk securities, such as debentures and preference shares, as opposed to ordinary shares.[45]

Conclusion

Women of some wealth who controlled their means, predominantly spinsters and widows, participated in the developing corporate capitalism of the nineteenth century. This investing group was not large and its members appear to have been well aware of the risks involved. This is illustrated by the existence and behaviour of the female investors in the joint-stock banks identified in this study. Our evidence shows that women were prepared to invest in the shares of banking companies that had unlimited liability, whether as initial subscriptions or as purchasers of shares on the secondary market once the banks had become established. The risk of being an initial subscriber to joint-stock banks was particularly high during the 1820s and 1830s when these institutions were untried and untested. Such risks declined somewhat as corporate banks became established. Our research reveals that female shareholders became more numerous as joint-stock banks became more proven institutions. Not only had the risk on such investments reduced but also bank dividends by the mid-1840s were very attractive. Dividends provided a 'pull' factor for women to invest in bank shares, playing a part in developing a female shareholding 'habit' as the nineteenth century unfolded. The attraction of bank shares was increased by the falling returns on 'safe' investments, such as Consols, land and railway shares. More generally, the liberalisation of company law, 1855–62, which introduced limited liability, provided a potentially safer environment for women to invest.

Over the nineteenth century, an increasing volume of corporate equity became available to women who could afford to purchase it. This was an important development for the women themselves, giving them greater choice of profitable investment opportunities, but also for banks and other types of companies seeking financial backers. Women shareholders were a minority but their collective significance as 'gentlewomanly capitalism' is increasingly being appreciated by historians.

Notes

1 This chapter draws on some of the findings of a Leverhulme Trust-funded project 'The constituencies of English and Welsh joint stock banks, 1825 to c.1885'. We are grateful for the support so generously provided, and also for the very valuable assistance of the archivists who so willingly gave of their time and informed guidance: John Booker and Karen Sampson (Lloyds TSB Archives); Edwin Green and Sara Kinsey (HSBC Group Archives); Jesse Campbell and Josephine Horner (formerly Barclays Bank Archives); Fiona MacColl and Susan Snell (formerly National Westminster Bank); and Alison Turton and Philip Winterbottom (Royal Bank of Scotland (RBS)). We also wish to acknowledge fully the generous help of Professor Josephine Maltby and Professor Janette Rutterford. An extended version of this chapter by the authors can be found in *Accounting, Business and Financial History* 16 (2), 2006, pp. 315–340.

2 J. W. Gilbart, 'A ten years' retrospect of London banking', *Journal of the Statistical Society of London* 18 (4), 1855, pp. 333–344; *The Economist*, 13 March 1856, p. 290; B. L. Anderson and P. L. Cottrell, 'Another Victorian capital market: a study of banking and bank investors on Merseyside', *Economic History Review* 2nd series, 28, 1975, pp. 611–613.

3 K. S. Toft, 'A mid-nineteenth century attempt at banking control', *Revue Internationale d'Histoire de la Banque* 3, 1970, pp. 149–167.

4 M. Dawes and C. N. Ward-Perkins, *Country Banks of England and Wales. Private Provincial Banks and Bankers 1688–1953*, Vol. 1, Canterbury: CIB Publishing for the Chartered Institute of Bankers, 2000, pp. 11–12, Table 2.

5 T. Joplin, *An Examination of the Report of the Joint Stock Bank Committee*, 2nd edn, London: J. Ridgeway & Sons, 1837, pp. 2–3; J. W. Gilbart, *A Practical Treatise on Banking*, London: Effingham Wilson, 1828, pp. 54, 56–61.

6 S. E. Thomas, *The Rise and Growth of Joint Stock Banking*, I, *Britain to 1860*, London: Pitman, 1934, pp. 656–662, Appendix M.

7 Lucy A. Newton, 'The birth of joint stock banking: a comparison of England and New England in the nineteenth century', *Business History Review*, forthcoming.

8 These clauses allowed joint-stock deposit banks to operate within the metropolitan area (65-mile radius of Charing Cross) and permitted provincial joint-stock banks to draw bills on London with a value of less than £50 and a maturity shorter than six months. P. L. Cottrell and L. A. Newton, 'Banking liberalization in England and Wales, 1826–1844', in R. Sylla, R. Tilly and G. Tortella (eds), *The State, The Financial System and Economic Modernization*, Cambridge: Cambridge University Press, 1999, pp. 85–87.

9 R. C. O. Matthews, *A Study in Trade-Cycle History. Economic Fluctuation in Great Britain 1833–1842*, Cambridge: Cambridge University Press, 1954, pp. 159–164; Cottrell and Newton, 'Banking liberalization in England and Wales, 1826–1844', pp. 84, 96–102.

10 RBSGA: 574, Nottingham & Nottinghamshire Banking Co., Board of Directors Minute Books [hereafter BDM], 8 November 1833; LTSBGA: Liverpool Union Banking Co., Book No. 93, BDM, AGM, 3 January 1836; and, for the prospectus of the North Wilts Banking Co., March 1836. R. S. Sayers, *Lloyds Bank in the History of English Banking*, Oxford: Clarendon Press, 1957, p. 159 fn. 2)

11 Holdings by value, whether overall or solely those of women, were positively skewed in their distribution for all banks, the respective median values being less than those of the averages.

12 Newton, 'Birth of joint stock banking'.

13 Gilbart, 'A ten years' retrospect of London banking', p. 340.

14 M. C. Reed, *Investment in Railways in Britain, 1820–1844. A Study in the Development of the Capital Market*, London: Oxford University Press, 1975, pp. 109 fn. 2, 116.

15 J. H. Baker, *An Introduction to English Legal History*, 3rd edn, London and Boston: Butterworths, 1990, p. 552.

16 It was possible for a wife's property to be held in trust before 1882, which could protect some, or all, of her property from that of her husband, the assets in question often having been given by a father to his daughter. It was thus possible for women to own property under common law and, consequently, to have capital and income, and the ability to pass these assets to their children. Widows could also use settlements to protect resources inherited from one marriage when entering another. See L. Holcombe, *Wives and Property: Reform of the Married Women's Property Law in Nineteenth-Century England*, Oxford: Martin Robertson, 1983; R. J. Morris, 'Men, women and property', in F. M. L. Thompson (ed.), *Landowners, Capitalists and Entrepreneurs: Essays for Sir John Habakkuk*, Oxford: Clarendon Press, 1994, pp. 171–191. Others argue that trusts and settlements did little to protect a wife's property since it was common to make a husband the trustee. See S. M. Okin, 'Patriarchy and married women's property in England: questions and some current views', *Eighteenth-Century Studies* 17 (2), 1983–4, pp. 121–138; L. Davidoff and C. Hall, *Family Fortunes: Men and Women of the English Middle Class 1780–1850*, London: Routledge, 1987.

17 HSBCGA: B42/3, Bradford Banking Co., *Prospectus*, 22 March 1827, clause 8.

18 HSBCGA: C12, Bank of Westmorland, share ledger, 1833–1880.

19 Gilbart, 'A ten years' retrospect of London banking', p. 340; *Economist*, 13 March 1856, p. 290.

20 *The Economist*, 13 March 1856, p. 290.

21 HSBCGA: A4, Barnsley Banking Co., share ledger, 1832–1896.

22 W. F. Crick and J. E. Wadsworth, *A Hundred Years of Joint Stock Banking*, London: Hodder & Stoughton, 1936, 3rd edn, 1958, pp. 180–182.

23 A. D. Gayer, W. W. Rostow and A. J. Schwartz, *The Growth and Fluctuation of the British Economy 1790–1850*, Vol. 1, Oxford: Clarendon Press, 1953, pp. 448, 450.

24 A. R. Holmes and E. Green, *Midland 150 Years of Banking Business*, London: B. T. Batsford, 1986, p. 331, Appendix 4.1.

25 D. R. Green and A. Owens, 'Gentlewomanly capitalism? Spinsters, widows, and wealth holding in England and Wales, c. 1800–1860', *Economic History Review*, 56 (3), 2003, 510–536; and J. Rutterford and J. Maltby, '"The widow, the clergyman and the reckless": women investors in England, 1830–1914', *Feminist Economics* 12 (1–2), 2006, pp. 116–118.

26 Green and Owens, 'Gentlewomanly capitalism?' and H. V. Bowen, *The Business of Empire: The East India Company and Imperial Britain, 1756–1833*, Cambridge: Cambridge University Press, 2006, ch. 4.

27 Rutterford and Maltby, '"The widow, the clergyman and the reckless"', p. 129.

28 Reed, *Investment in Railways in Britain, 1820–1844*.

29 Reed, *Investment in Railways in Britain, 1820–1844*, pp. 192, 202–203, 204, 209. See also Sarah Hudson, 'Attitudes to investment risk amongst West Midland canal and railway company investors 1700–1850', University of Warwick PhD thesis, 2001.

30 Rutterford and Maltby, 'The widow, the clergyman and the reckless', p. 129.

31 For the experience of provincial share markets, see W. A. Thomas, *The Provincial Stock Exchanges*, London: Frank Cass, 1973, Ch. 2.

32 P. L. Cottrell, 'Railway finance and the crisis of 1866: contractor's bills of exchange and the finance companies', *Journal of Transport History* 2nd series, 3, 1975, p. 21.

33 J. H. Hartnoll, *A Letter to the Rt. Hon. E. Cardwell, M. P.*, London: W. S. D. Pateman, 1853, p. 6.

34 The female 'rentier' investor was an individual that looked for safe investment opportunities, as identified in the nineteenth-century discourse.

35 R. A. Ward, *A Treatise on Investments*, 2nd edn, London: Effingham Wilson, 1852, pp. 6, 61, 209.

36 P. L. Cottrell, 'Domestic finance, 1860–1914', in R. Floud and P. Johnson (eds), *The Cambridge Economic History of Modern Britain*, II, *Economic Maturity, 1860–1939*, Cambridge: Cambridge University Press, 2003, p. 257; Rutterford and Maltby, '"The widow, the clergyman and the reckless investor"', p. 129. Many investors in Consols held them in order to provide an annuity, i.e. a fixed annual income. Such investors suffered as their value declined.

37 A. H. Imlah, *Economic Elements in the Pax Britanica*, 2nd edn, New York: Russell & Russell, 1969, pp. 72–73.

38 P. L. Cottrell, *Industrial Finance 1830–1914*, London: Methuen, 1980, pp. 52–53.

39 Anderson and Cottrell, 'Another Victorian capital market', p. 604; P. L. Cottrell, 'Credit, morals and sunspots. the financial boom of the 1860s and trade cycle theory', in P. L. Cottrell and D. E. Moggridge (eds), *Money and Power*, Basingstoke: Macmillan Press, 1988, p. 46.

40 Crick and Wadsworth, *A Hundred Years of Joint-Stock Banking*, p. 86; Cottrell, *Industrial Finance*, pp. 84–86.

41 J. B. Jefferys, 'The denomination and character of shares, 1855–85', *Economic History Review* new series, 16, 1946, pp. 45–55; J. Taylor, *Creating Capitalism: Joint-Stock Enterprise in British Politics and Culture, 1800–1870*, Woodbridge: The

Boydell Press, 2006, pp. 192–193; Rutterford and Maltby, '"The widow, the clergy-man and the reckless"', pp. 122–123.
42   Rutterford and Maltby, '"The widow, the clergyman and the reckless"', p. 123; Taylor, *Creating Capitalism*, pp. 162, 174.
43   Holmes and Green, *Midland*, p. 62.
44   Crick and Wadsworth, *A Hundred Years of Joint-Stock Banking*, p. 344.
45   Rutterford and Maltby, '"The widow, the clergyman and the reckless"', p. 123.

Bibliography

Anderson, B. L. and Cottrell, P. L., 'Another Victorian capital market: a study of banking and bank investors on Merseyside', *Economic History Review* 2nd series, 28, 1975, pp. 611–613.

Baker, J. H., *An Introduction to English Legal History*, 3rd edn, London and Boston: Butterworths, 1990.

Bowen, H. V., *The Business of Empire: The East India Company and Imperial Britain, 1756–1833*, Cambridge: Cambridge University Press, 2006.

Cottrell, P. L., 'Domestic finance, 1860–1914', in Floud, R. and Johnson, P. (eds), *The Cambridge Economic History of Modern Britain*, II, *Economic Maturity, 1860–1939*, Cambridge: Cambridge University Press, 2003, pp. 253–279.

Cottrell, P. L., 'Credit, morals and sunspots: the financial boom of the 1860s and trade cycle theory', in Cottrell, P. L. and Moggridge, D. E. (eds), *Money and Power*, Basingstoke: Macmillan Press, 1988, pp. 41–71.

Cottrell, P. L. *Industrial Finance 1830–1914*, London: Methuen, 1980.

Cottrell, P. L. 'Railway finance and the crisis of 1866: contractor's bills of exchange and the finance companies', *Journal of Transport History* 2nd series, 3, 1975, pp. 20–40.

Cottrell, P. L. and Newton, L. A., 'Banking liberalization in England and Wales, 1826–1844', in Sylla, R., Tilly, R. and Tortella, G. (eds), *The State, The Financial System and Economic Modernization*, Cambridge: Cambridge University Press, 1999, pp. 75–117.

Crick, W. F. and Wadsworth, J. E., *A Hundred Years of Joint Stock Banking*, 3rd edn, London: Hodder & Stoughton, 1936, 1958.

Davidoff, L. and Hall, C., *Family Fortunes: Men and Women of the English Middle Class 1780–1850*, London: Routledge, 1987.

Dawes, M. and Ward-Perkins, C. N., *Country Banks of England and Wales. Private Provincial Banks and Bankers 1688–1953*, Vol. 1, Canterbury: CIB Publishing for the Chartered Institute of Bankers, 2000.

Economist, The.

Gayer, A. D., Rostow, W. W. and Schwartz, A. J., *The Growth and Fluctuation of the British Economy 1790–1850*, Vol. 1, Oxford: Clarendon Press, 1953.

Gilbart, J. W., 'A ten years' retrospect of London banking', *Journal of the Statistical Society of London* 18 (4), 1855, pp. 333–344.

Gilbart, J. W., *A Practical Treatise on Banking*, London: Effingham Wilson, 1828.

Green, D. R. and Owens, A., 'Gentlewomanly capitalism? Spinsters, widows, and wealth holding in England and Wales, c. 1800–1860', *Economic History Review* 56 (3), 2003, pp. 510–536.

Hartnoll, J. H., *A Letter to the Rt. Hon. E. Cardwell, M. P.*, London: W. S. D. Pateman, 1853.

Holcombe, L., *Wives and Property: Reform of the Married Women's Property Law in Nineteenth-Century England*, Oxford: Martin Robertson, 1983.

Holmes, A. R. and Green, E., *Midland 150 Years of Banking Business*, London: B. T. Batsford, 1986.

Hudson, Sarah, 'Attitudes to investment risk amongst West Midland canal and railway company investors 1700–1850', University of Warwick PhD thesis, 2001.

Imlah, A. H., *Economic Elements in the Pax Britanica*, 2nd edn, New York: Russell & Russell, 1969.

Jefferys, J. B., 'The denomination and character of shares, 1855–85', *Economic History Review* new series, 16, 1946, pp. 45–55.

Joplin, T., *An Examination of the Report of the Joint Stock Bank Committee*, 2nd edn, London: J. Ridgeway & Sons, 1837.

Matthews, R. C. O., *A Study in Trade-Cycle History. Economic Fluctuation in Great Britain 1833–1842*, Cambridge: Cambridge University Press, 1954.

Morris, R. J., 'Men, women and property', in Thompson, F. M. L. (ed.), *Landowners, Capitalists and Entrepreneurs: Essays for Sir John Habakkuk*, Oxford: Clarendon Press, 1994, pp. 171–191.

Newton, Lucy A., 'The birth of joint stock banking: a comparison of England and New England in the nineteenth century', *Business History Review*, forthcoming.

Okin, S. M., 'Patriarchy and married women's property in England: questions and some current views', *Eighteenth-Century Studies* 17 (2), 1983–4, pp. 121–138.

Reed, M. C., *Investment in Railways in Britain, 1820–1844. A Study in the Development of the Capital Market*, London: Oxford University Press, 1975.

Rutterford, J. and Maltby, J., '"The widow, the clergyman and the reckless": women investors in England, 1830–1914', *Feminist Economics* 12 (1–2), 2006, pp. 111–138.

Sayers, R. S., *Lloyds Bank in the History of English Banking*, Oxford: Clarendon Press.

Taylor, J., *Creating Capitalism: Joint-Stock Enterprise in British Politics and Culture, 1800–1870*, Woodbridge: The Boydell Press, 2006.

Thomas, S. E., *The Rise and Growth of Joint Stock Banking*, I, *Britain to 1860*, London: Pitman, 1934.

Thomas, W. A., *The Provincial Stock Exchanges*, London: Frank Cass, 1973.

Toft, K. S., 'A mid-nineteenth century attempt at banking control', *Revue Internationale d'Histoire de la Banque* 3, 1970, pp. 149–167.

Ward, R. A., *A Treatise on Investments*, 2nd edn, London: Effingham Wilson, 1852.

Barclays Bank Group Archives (BBGA), Dallimore Road, Wythenshawe, Manchester, M23 9JA.

Bank of Liverpool, 1831 – BBGA: 310/152, share register.

Swaledale & Wensleydale Banking Co., 1836 and 1856 – BBGA: 388/705, share register.

HSBC Group Archives (HSBCGA), HSBC Holdings plc, Level 36, 8 Canada Square, London, E14 5HQ.

Bank of Westmorland, 1833 and 1853 – HSBCGA: C12, share ledger, 1833–1880.

Barnsley Banking Co., 1831 and 1851 – HSBCGA: A4, share ledger, 1832–1896.

Birmingham & Midland Bank, 1836 and 1856 – HSBCGA: AA1 deed of settlement and share register.

Bradford Banking Co., 1827 – HSBCGA: B1 deed of settlement, 1 June 1827.

Coventry Union Banking Co., 1836 – HSBCGA: HSBCGA: AB2, deed of settlement, 6 May 1836.

Cumberland Union Banking Co., 1829 – HSBCGA: G1, deed of settlement, 1829.

Huddersfield Banking Co., 1827 and 1847 – HSBCGA: H24, share register and transfer book, 1827–1890.

London Joint Stock Bank, 1836 – HSBCGA: 592/01, share ledger, vol. 1.

North & South Wales Bank, 1836 – HSBCGA: M132, proprietors' stock ledger.

Sheffield & Hallamshire Banking Co., 1836 – HSBCGA: AM48, list of share transfers.

Yorkshire Banking Co. 1844 and 1864 – HSBCGA: X49, representatives' register.

Lloyds TSB Group Archives (LTSBGA), 25 Gresham Street, London, EC2V 7HN.

County of Gloucestershire Banking Co, 1836 – LTSBGA: book no. 1954, deed of settlement, 26 July 1836.

Coventry & Warwickshire Banking Co., 1835 – LTSBGA: file no. 7013, deed of settlement, 1835.

Halifax & Huddersfield Union Banking Co., 1836 – LTSBGA: file no. 5924, deed of settlement, 1 July 1836.

Halifax Joint Stock Bank, 1829 – LTSBGA: file no. 5354, deed of settlement, 1829.

Liverpool Union Banking Co., 1835 – LTSBGA: book no. 3544, proprietors' ledger no. 1, 1835–1847.

Wilts & Dorset Banking Co., 1836 and 1853 – LTSBGA: book no. 3177, shareholders' register, 1835–1853.

Royal Bank of Scotland Group Archives (RBSGA), The Royal Bank of Scotland Group plc, Regent's House, PO Box 348, 42 Islington High Street, London, N1 8XL.

Sheffield & Rotherham Banking Co., 1836 and 1863 – RBSGA: SR/79, deed of settlement, 1 July 1836 and SR/147014000, Register of proprietors, 1863–1899.

10 To do the right thing

Gender, wealth, inheritance and the London middle class[1]

David R. Green

Making provision: inheritance and the ideology of separate spheres

In the nineteenth century the notion of separate spheres, where men earned the money and women maintained the home, was a pervasive belief for the British middle class.[2] What happened, however, when men died? How did their widows sustain the family in the absence of earned income and what were the implications of this for maintaining the ideology of separate spheres? All widows, of course, faced this situation and for the working class a husband's death signalled a very real drop in household income. But for those who managed to accumulate capital over the life course, a husband's death also signalled the passage of property, usually to his widow and children. In a legal sense, this transition heralded the economic independence of a widow and, unless specified otherwise in the terms of the will, she could do with her newly acquired fortune what she wished. This situation, of course, was fraught with moral danger. Having come into money, the widow herself acquired economic power and assumed the role of the main household provider. This in itself posed problems for the ideological underpinnings of separate spheres. On the one hand the power of the wealthy widow to upset social relations became a reality, and on the other, poorly equipped to understand the ways of money, the widow either by accident or design, could leave her children penniless. In this case, inheritance became a pivotal moment in the preservation of separate spheres.

To safeguard against these threats to the gendered social order and, indeed, a man's own reputation beyond the grave, husbands frequently dictated the terms on which their widow could inherit their wealth. To do the right thing – to ensure in particular that wives, children and dependent relatives were adequately provided for after death – was a primary duty, not just for middle-class men but for anyone with money. Reputation and respectability lived on after death in the way that men, and to some extent women, made provisions for their dependants. Writing the will was therefore a responsibility that defined respectability and the failure to do so may have damned not just the beneficiaries to poverty but the testator's reputation as well. But making a will was not in itself enough. The terms of the will should conform to customary expectations of the role of lineage and this meant, as George Eliot reminded her readers in *The Mill on the Floss*, avoiding sentimentality:

> To live respected, and have the proper bearers at your funeral, was an achievement of the ends of existence that would be entirely nullified if, on the reading of your will, you sank in the opinion of your fellow-men, either by turning out to be poorer than they expected, or by leaving your money in a capricious manner, without strict regard to degrees of kin. *The right thing must always be done toward kindred. The right thing was to correct them severely, if they were other than a credit to the family, but still not to alienate from them the smallest rightful share in the family shoebuckles and other property.* (Emphasis added)[3]

But what was the 'right thing' and how were the 'shoebuckles' to be distributed? These issues are discussed here in the context of the provisions made by men for their heirs in early-nineteenth-century London. Since women formed the main beneficiaries, notably those who were left as widows, the way in which men made provision for their wives and children provides an insight into concepts of familial propriety and, perhaps more significantly for this book, helps understand the extent of female financial autonomy that arose as a result of a husband's death.

The analysis relies on a sample of men's wills proved at the Prerogative Court of Canterbury (PCC) in 1830 that were valued at less than £10,000. In that year a total of 2,661 men's and women's wills were proved in the various London probate courts, of which 2,318 were proved in the Prerogative Court of Canterbury. The remainder were proved in one of the several lower ecclesiastical courts that dealt mainly with small estates. Male testators accounted for 1,587 of these wills, or 68 per cent of the total proved in that court, and from this group a one in six systematic sample was drawn for more detailed analysis ($N=277$).[4]

As Bob Morris has recently pointed out, wills can be seen as windows on life.[5] They provide a glimpse of family relationships, friendships and social obligations at the point of death, when the domestic arrangements of the household – the balance between emotion, duty and property – were laid bare. As a legal document they entailed a settling of accounts and a set of property transactions between the living and the dead. Although not a formal contract per se, nevertheless the will had many of the attributes of a contractual relationship, particularly when executors were entrusted to make provision for beneficiaries or instructions were issued for the disposal of property long after the point of death. In their broader context, wills also hint at concepts of parental and filial duty and propriety; of social roles to be performed beyond the grave and of expectations to be performed before it. Wills therefore offer a way of unravelling and understanding a set of social relationships through the disposal of property and as such they provide a rare glimpse into the complex relationships between money, emotion and duty.

Beyond the broad similarities imposed by legal requirements, wills could and did differ considerably, particularly in relation to the ways in which assets were distributed and the conditions imposed on beneficiaries. This diversity stemmed from the testamentary freedom which characterised English law.[6] Although natural justice might have directed that men's property be passed to wives, children and relatives, there was in fact little that dictated the pattern of bequests. Other than the weak legislation relating to dower, which dealt only with the share of a husband's freehold land that could be claimed by a widow as of right, a testator was free to dispose of property however he or she wished, and this testamentary freedom underpinned the variety of wishes enshrined in the will and the diversity of conditions under which inheritance took place.[7]

De jure freedom, however, did not necessarily mean de facto freedom. Though law may have allowed testamentary freedom, custom and concepts of propriety and respectability directed otherwise. Moral considerations dictated that men should take special care to make provision for those who could not earn their own living, notably the sick, wives and children, but especially daughters. Similarly the will should also take into account filial propriety and faithful duty.[8] In return, of course, wives, sons, daughters and other relatives were expected to conform to their roles during the life of the testator. Breaches of those roles meant risking being cut off from the will – a situation which, although not common, was nevertheless not that unusual. When John Beedle left his entire estate valued at £1,000 to his wife, save for 1s each to his four children, clearly something in their behaviour had displeased him.[9] In similar fashion Joseph Pellett also cut off his four children 'due to their base conduct towards me'.[10] The terms of the will, therefore, balanced duty and emotion with reference to property and lineage. In other words, testamentary freedom was exercised in the context of customary expectations by the living as well as the dead.

Will makers and will writing

The fact that the will was primarily a document concerning the disposal of property meant that most of the population had no need to have one drawn up, either because of legal impediments to the ownership of assets, as was the case with married women without any separate settled estate and children below the age of 21, or because they fell below the threshold of property ownership. In London, persons who died with personal goods, or *bona notabilia*, valued at £10 or more (£5 elsewhere), were required to have their estates proved by an ecclesiastical court.[11] Those whose estates reached these figures but who died intestate were dealt with by administrators appointed by the probate courts. Though married women could not make a will other than for their own settled property, widows were reborn as civil actors on the death of their husband, capable of making their own decisions and distributing their estate according to their own wishes.[12]

In 1841, for the country as a whole about 13.4 per cent of adults who died either left wills or had administrators appointed to deal with their estates.[13]

Figures for London suggest that a similar proportion of the population also left estates that warranted probate.[14] In 1850, adult deaths in London amounted to 24,706 while the number of wills under £100,000 proved in the three main ecclesiastical courts for that year was 2,811, which suggests that at least 11 per cent of those who died in the city left wills. If administrations are included, this figure rises to about 13.3 per cent of those who died.[15] The very small number of estates valued above £100,000 would raise this percentage only slightly.[16] This figure corresponds very closely to that found for Leeds between 1830 and 1834 when about 13.5 per cent of those who died left a will or administration.[17]

These figures need to be set in the context of the size of the property-owning class, the group that would have been in a position to leave enough wealth to make a will or an administration necessary. Estimating the size of this group is an imprecise science. However, based on evidence from a range of taxation documents, Schwarz concludes that the upper-income group with an average income of over £200 formed only 2–3 per cent of the adult male population, while the middle-income group earning between £80 and £130 comprised between 16 and 21 per cent. The remainder consisted of the working population, although 9–10 per cent of these were shopkeepers and another 5–6 per cent self-employed artisans. If we include these two groups with the upper and middle earners, between about 32 and 40 per cent of the male population in London might have owned enough property to leave a will, with the rest of the population mainly comprising unskilled and semi-skilled workers with little or nothing of value when they died.[18] The proportion of people leaving a will in London needs to be seen in the context of the size of this property-owning group. Comparing the proportion of Londoners whose estate was probated against those who were likely to have owned property, it appears that as many as one in three of the bourgeoisie were likely to have made a will.

In terms of occupational groupings, however, and in keeping with Schwarz's view of early-nineteenth-century London that 'in any examination of the capital's bourgeoisie it is the shopkeeper who stands out', what is striking about the social make-up of male testators is the importance of dealers.[19] Table 10.1 shows the occupational breakdown both for male testators in 1830 and for occupied males recorded in the 1851 census. Two main groups stand out by virtue of their relative importance. The first include those described as 'gentlemen', although the precise meaning of this term is unclear. It was generally used to denote persons with an independent income or an income from property, although by the 1830s it had lost its traditional association with the landed elite.[20] Either way, this was clearly the wealthiest group of testators with the average value of estates more than double that of the sample as a whole.

More significant, however, are those involved in dealing, the majority of which were most likely to have been shopkeepers. Compared to their share of the working population, this group was particularly important, reflecting the fact that many retailers would have had personal property such as stock in trade and leasehold premises that could be included in a will.[21] Setting up in many branches of retailing also required significant amounts of capital: in the 1830s, for example, haberdashers required between £400 and £800, though a good business could cost in excess of £1,000.[22] When shopkeepers died they tended to leave premises, stock in trade, and debts owing, as well as the goodwill that came with an established reputation. Indeed, when valuing an estate, goodwill was sometimes included as a separate item. Though by no means as wealthy as gentlemen, or indeed those engaged in public service or the professions, retailers were on a par with manufacturers in terms of the average value of their estate. Those involved in manufacturing themselves tended to be under-represented among testators, which reflects the large number of working-class men who were likely to be enumerated in this category but who did not possess much by way of personal property.[23] Bringing up the end of the wealth hierarchy were those involved in transport and building, including a handful of bricklayers, plumbers and plasterers as well as coachmen, stable keepers and lightermen.

Wills were written and re-written to take account of changing circumstances such as marriage and the birth of children and as such the last will and testament merely represents an end point in an ongoing process of settling one's estate and disposing of one's worldly possessions. Richard Dickson recommended that married men should review their testamentary affairs on a regular basis, changing the terms according to altered circumstances.[24] However, they tended to be written or re-written relatively near to death – Figure 10.1 shows that nearly half of men's wills and 44 per cent of women's were written within a year of probate being granted (although women tended to write their wills earlier than men), with nearly one in four men making a will within three months of the grant of probate. This suggests that they frequently took the form of a final reckoning of worldly possessions.[25]

There were sound legal grounds for writing or re-writing a will close to death. For men, while marriage did not invalidate a previous will, the birth of a child did, and for women, widowhood similarly created a need for a new will. Changing emotional circumstances, such as rewarding faithful service, recognising friendly deeds and accepting personal responsibilities, could equally have prompted the writing or re-writing of a will. Henry Morrell senior, for example, wrote his will on 22 November 1828, but by the time he died in 1830 he had added three codicils. In the first, dated 2 June 1829, he made some provision for his son Henry, who he noted was of 'unsound mind and unfit to be entrusted with any property whatsoever'. The second, made on 6 November 1829, dictated that his daughter was to have the rents of one of his houses but had no power to mortgage or sell the property. As he approached death, Henry senior had clearly tired of the antics of his younger namesake and the third codicil, dated 27 December 1829, noted that, having fitted Henry junior for the Swan River 'at very great expense' and having previously provided money on several occasions, 'in justice to my other sons' no more was to be given for a period of five years. Wills, therefore, not only reflected a final reckoning but were also part of a fluid process of reconciling social relationships and as such provide a unique window into understanding how emotional understanding and personal duty meshed over time with the division of property.

Table 10.1 Occupational classification of male testators in 1830 compared to 1851 census of male occupations (Booth–Armstrong classification)

	Number leaving a will with probated value (number leaving will)**	Average probated value (£)	Median probate value (£)	1830 per cent of total wills (a)	1851 census percentage of male occupations (b)
Dealing	51 (53)	1,055.8	600	26.4	13.9
Manufacturing	46 (49)	1,016.3	450	24.4	33.3
Gentleman, esquire, independent means	43 (44)	2,572.3	1,500	21.9	1.6
Public services and professions	26 (28)	1,929.3	1,000	13.9	11.7
Transport	10	507.0	300	5.0	11.4
Building	7	760.0	600	3.5	9.8
Others*	10	1,370.0	800	5.0	18.3
Total	193 (201)	1,476.8	800	100.1	100.0
Not specified	73 (76)	1,657.3	800		

Source: (a) PROB 11 sample; See footnote 5 (b) L. D. Schwarz, London in the Age of Industrialisation, 1992, Cambridge: Cambridge University Press, appendix 3, pp. 255–58.

Notes

* Includes agriculture, fishing, breeding (4), domestic service (3), industrial service (3).
** Figures in brackets show total number leaving a will with stated occupation.

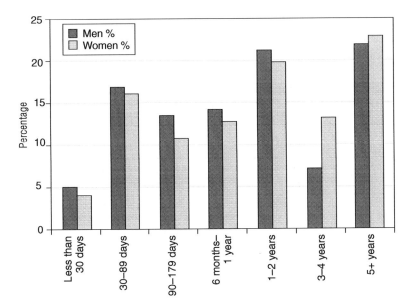

Figure 10.1 Time elapsed between making a will and the date of probate 1830 (source: see note 5).

Note
Men *N* = 277; Women *N* = 266.

Male provision for wives

Writing the will, however, was more than just a question of legal necessity. For middle-class men, making a will was viewed as both a moral imperative and a rational course of action. As Alastair Owens has noted, in writing a will men were credited with the virtues of good citizenship, family cohesion and harmony and high personal esteem.[26] Failure to make such provision, or indeed writing a will that was open to challenge, left the family vulnerable to the vicissitudes of fortune rather than the certainty of provision. As Richard Dickson observed in 1830:

> Could any man of sense who died without a will, return to this world to see his family almost beggared, his children scattered on the wide world, his business embarrassed so as to be worth nothing; how would he grieve to think that all this confusion arose from his culpable neglect of performing so simple a duty as that of making his will.[27]

Given these concerns, not surprisingly men were careful to make provision for their families. However, questions exist over the extent of women's proprietorial autonomy in men's wills. According to Owens' work on Stockport men's wills between 1800 and 1857, it is difficult to sustain the view that the evidence presents a picture of pro-prietorial independence and freedom among spouses of male property owners. Indeed ... the principal role of widows who were beneficiaries of their husband's will was to act as the custodians of the family estate.[28]

Widows often inherited property only for their natural life, or the duration of their widowhood, at the end of which any remaining property passed to children or other beneficiaries. Sometimes a widow's portion was reduced on her remar-riage, with the remaining portion being distributed to other heirs. In these situ-ations women primarily appeared to be the vehicle for the intergenerational transfer of property from fathers to their children. However, explanations for this lack of proprietorial autonomy differ. On the one hand, by imposing such conditions on the way in which widows could inherit property, it could be argued that men were merely extending patriarchal control over property and ensuring the rights of his children to a share of the family estate. On the other, conditions that limited a widow's right to possess property in her own name could be interpreted as a way of protecting her from the loss of her rights that would ensue were she to have remarried. Trusts could function in this fashion by providing women with an income but vesting actual ownership of property in the hands of appointed trustees.[29]

Evidence from the London men's wills contrasts with the experience else-where in the country. For 159 (58 per cent) of the 277 men's wills in the sample, the primary recorded relationship was between husband and wife. In most instances, the wife was the residuary legatee in the sense that she inherited most if not all of the estate and in over half these instances, as shown in Table 10.2, she was also an executor of the will. Indeed, in the majority of cases she was the sole executrix and as such would have had considerable control in the way the estate was managed.

Nevertheless, the suggestion remains that despite being named as the main beneficiary and primary executor, the terms of men's wills were such as to limit their widows' autonomy to dispose of property as they wished. They may have

Table 10.2 Executor where wife was the residual legatee[a] (*N* = 159)

	Number	*Percentage*
Wife	100	54.3
Child	15	8.2
Other relative	27	14.7
Friend	17	9.2
Not known	25	13.6
Total Executors	184	100.0

Source: See note 5.

Note

a The total number of wills in which a wife was mentioned was 167, but in eight of these it was impossible to establish if the wife was the residual legatee.

benefited from the income arising from bequests, they may have been able to make prudent use of it on their behalf and that of their children, they may have chosen to squander it, but widows were not necessarily empowered to dispose of their inheritance as they chose. In other words, they could make use of any income arising from the estate but not sell or otherwise dispose of it freely. This was an important issue since, prior to the Married Women's Property Act of 1882, if a woman married or remarried any wealth that she herself owned, with the exception of real estate and her own *paraphernalia*, became the property of her husband.[30] There were four ways that widows could avoid being placed in this potentially difficult situation, each of which could be used independently or in combination with the others. First, a husband could stipulate in his will that his wife was only entitled to use some or all of her inheritance for her natural life time or until she remarried. Second, he could establish a trust by which wealth was controlled by a set of trustees, usually his executors, who were responsible for investing it and paying out sums of money as required or thought necessary. Third, he could set up an arrangement by which any wealth inherited by a wife or daughter was for her 'separate use', irrespective of the wishes of any future husband. Finally, a woman herself on marriage or remarriage could have arranged a separate settlement that protected any property that she brought to the new household.

Disentangling which of these strategies was used and in what combinations depends on understanding the formal language used in the construction of wills. Bequests were often made for a period of time – most commonly for a person's 'natural life', or in the case of women for such time as a widow remained unmarried. Men often stipulated that women were to inherit 'absolutely' or in the case of a widow's remarriage or a daughter's marriage that their portion of the estate was to remain 'separate from their husband'. Bequests to children normally took place when they reached majority, commonly taken to be 21 years of age, although marriage was sometimes the occasion when bequests were made available. Trusts could be established by indicating in the will that the executors or other persons were to act as 'trustees' or that property was given 'upon trust' or 'in trust'. Such phrasing within wills therefore acts as a clue to the different strategies used when it came to the disposal of property after death.

Evidence from other parts of the country for the first half of the nineteenth century suggests that widows rarely inherited their husband's estates without encumbrances. According to Owens' work on Stockport, only 28 per cent of husband's bequests were made to wives 'absolutely' – where they had freedom to dispose of the estate independently.[31] In Leeds, Morris notes that the figure was even lower at about 18 per cent of men's wills.[32] Evidence from the London sample provides a contrasting story. As Table 10.3 shows, in just over half the wills where a wife was mentioned, no conditions appeared to be attached to her inheritance, leaving her free to do what she wished with her portion of the estate. In these cases, the will notes that she was granted 'absolute' control over the inheritance. In some wills, vague wishes and expectations were expressed, usually in relation to the care and provision for children, but it seemed that on

Table 10.3 Types of provision where a wife was still alive at the time of making a will

	N	Percentage	Average probate value (£)
Absolute control[a]	95	56.9	1,000
Natural life[b]	52	31.1	1,409
Till children come of age[c]	5	3.0	2,420
Reducing on remarriage[d]	15	9.0	2,847
Total	167	100.0	1,336

Source: See note 4.

Notes
a Widow had absolute access to estate without conditions.
b Widow had income from estate for rest of her natural life but no power to dispose of estate after death.
c Widow has access to whole estate during children(s) minority but at coming of age yielded part of estate.
d Widow had access to estate during her natural life but this was reduced or dispensed with upon remarriage.

most occasions widows were left to their own devices. Thomas Gill, for example, merely stated that his entire estate was to be left to Mary Ann, his wife, 'towards the maintaining of my dear family and herself – to be equally disposed between the whole of my family in the best manner she is able'.[33] Whether this situation reflected the haste with which wills were written or a real willingness to maintain the family business is difficult to determine. However, it is in stark contrast to experience elsewhere and this in itself raises the question of the extent to which London men behaved differently.

While London women appeared to be relatively free in relation to their inheritance, a husband's wishes could continue well beyond the grave and in about one-third of cases widows inherited property only for their natural life or until any children came of age. In the latter case, adult children normally inherited a part of the estate with the remainder left for the widow. In this situation, the woman had rights of use but not of disposal and she merely became the vehicle by which property was transferred to the next generation. In similar fashion, women also inherited wealth on the condition that they remained widows, and stood to lose part or all of their inheritance if they remarried. John Watkins, for example, left his pub, the Lord Nelson Tavern, to his wife, Maria, on condition that she remained a widow. In the case of her remarriage, it was to be sold and two-thirds of the profits given to his niece and her husband. The remaining one-third was to be invested in stocks and securities and the interest used for Maria's sole benefit. However, on her death the remaining assets were to be sold and divided between the other named beneficiaries.[34] Since, upon remarriage, the property left to a man's widow could potentially pass to the new husband, inserting these kinds of restrictions took account of both the widow's own security as well as those of her former husband's children or other relatives. Such conditions, therefore, cannot merely be interpreted as the desire to impose paternalistic control beyond the grave but rather should also be seen as a way of protecting a woman's material well-being, as well as that of her children, once her husband had died.

The motivations behind these different strategies of male provision are difficult to disentangle but one clear difference between those husbands that granted absolute title to their wives and those that did not was the value of the estate. As Table 10.3 shows, typically, absolute disposal tended to be associated with smaller estates worth about £1,000.[35] This figure corresponds to the value of estates left by retailers and manufacturers, noted above.

By contrast, where the wife was only given rights of use for her natural life the value of the estate tended to be larger, and where the will stipulated conditions relating to the duration of her widowhood the average value of estates was more than double. This higher-value group of estates was associated mainly, though not exclusively, with testators described as gentlemen in their will, together with professional men. This pattern matches closely Morris's finding for Leeds will makers in the same period.[36] It may have been that complexity of conditions was a function of the value of the estate, and that more assets required more careful drafting of the will. Part of the answer could also relate to the existence of real and leasehold property which tended to be associated with larger estates and which by their very nature were more difficult to divide than other forms of personal wealth.[37] In 27 out of the 47 instances when the wife was alive and where some form of real or leasehold estate was mentioned in a will, wives were given an interest in the property only for their lifetime or until remarriage, after which the terms of the will often stated that it was to be sold and the money invested or given to the remaining children or other relatives. Clearly, different levels of wealth holding were associated with different strategies of extending male control over their estates from beyond the grave.

Another common way of controlling the way property was used after a husband's death was through the formation of trusts, and here, too, the amount and composition of wealth appeared to have been important. The formation of a trust was normally indicated in the will by the appointment of trustees or a request that bequests were to be made 'upon' or 'in' trust. These arrangements could be complex, as William Read's instructions made clear. William was described as a gentleman and when he died, leaving an estate worth £1,500, he set up a trust made up of the sale of two houses and an income from the rents of two neighbouring leasehold properties. The income from the trust was to be used to support his wife and two daughters, but if his wife remarried the entire trust was to pass to the daughters alone. On reaching the age of 21, each daughter was to have one of the leasehold properties. However, even then the daughters were only to have full use, not ownership – should they die during minority or without children the will stipulated that their share should go to the surviving daughter. In the event that both died under these circumstances, the estate was to be divided equally between the testator's brother and sister. In addition, money was set aside in the trust to buy 3 per cent bank annuities to provide an income that the wife was to use for the education and maintenance of the daughters up to the age of 21.[38] Once these conditions were satisfied, any rest and residue was to go to his wife so that she could 'go into some little way of business'.[39] William's aim, therefore, was to ensure that his wife had sufficient income to educate his daughters, that his daughters would be in a position to make a favourable match, and that after this his wife could maintain herself independently.

Typically these kinds of trusts tended to be associated with larger estates, and particularly those containing freehold or leasehold estate. The average probate value of estates containing a trust was £2,205, compared to £1,249 for those without such conditions, and many of the larger estates also contained mention of real or leasehold property. Table 10.4 shows that of the 90 estates in which real or leasehold estate was mentioned, trusts were established in at least 38, comprising 41 per cent of the total. By contrast, where no real estate was mentioned, trusts were created in only 42 out of 187 wills, comprising nearly 23 per cent of cases. Real estate, and particularly freehold, was not easily divided and a trust was often a way of managing rental income for a range of beneficiaries as well as keeping the property intact, as illustrated by the complex arrangements made by William Read, noted above.

In part, the relationships between the ownership of real estate and the existence of a trust also help explain another paradox, namely that London men as a whole did not set up trusts nearly as often as their counterparts elsewhere. In Leeds, Morris estimated that 82 per cent of male wills that made provision for a widow used the mechanism of a trust to protect her property from any future husband.[40] By contrast, in London trusts protecting widows were far less common: 39 (25 per cent) out of 156 male wills in which provision was made for a widow referred to a trust. Similarly, the use of trusts in general appeared to be much lower in London than elsewhere. In Stockport for the period from 1800–1857, Owens noted the existence of trusts in 62 per cent of men's and women's wills but here some 55 per cent of testators owned real estate.[41] By contrast, Table 10.4 shows that the proportion of London men with real estate

Table 10.4 Real estate and trusts in London men's wills

	Total number of estates	Estates with real estate (%)	Number with trust	Estates with a trust (%)	Number without trust	Estates without a trust (%)
Real estate*	90	33.6	38	41.0	55	59.0
No real estate	187	66.4	42	22.8	142	77.2
Total	277	100.0	80	28.9	197	71.1

Source: See note 5

Note
* Includes any mention of freehold or leasehold.

was relatively low: only about one in three men specifically mentioned such property in their wills. Trusts were similarly less common and only about 29 per cent of London estates contained provisions for a trust. On this evidence, the reluctance of London men to set up trusts can be explained with reference to two concurrent processes: first, the frequency of small estates that was associated with the profusion of small retailers and manufacturers in the capital, and second, the relative infrequency of the ownership of real estate. The nature of the local economy and the London land market were clearly important influences in the way that men arranged for the disposal of their estates, and as such these factors also structured the economic opportunities of widows.

The relative freedom with which widows inherited from their husbands and the comparatively low incidence of trusts raise the intriguing possibility that metropolitan women were much freer than their provincial counterparts when it came to controlling their own inheritance. Although in nearly half the sample, women's interest in their husband's wealth only lasted for their lifetime or the duration of their widowhood, for the majority it seemed that inheritance came without legal strings attached. Typically, the husbands of these widows tended to be involved in retailing or manufacturing, and where this was the case it may have been that women were actively involved in running the family business already, alongside their spouses. Maintaining liquidity was likely to have been of paramount concern and the lack of conditions in men's wills regarding their widow would have helped in this respect. Though men could and did stipulate through their wills that widows only had a limited right of use over property, in most cases the absence of conditions meant that the death of a husband freed a widow to continue to maintain a business and to use her new wealth as she chose.

Conclusion: duty, business and emotion

To do the right thing when it came to inheritance involved balancing the demands of duty, the well-being of the family, the contingencies of business and the concerns of emotion. As such, inheritance practices were deeply embedded in social relationships of the family and local economic conditions and imbued with concepts of equity and equality. In this context, to share and share alike may have been superficially attractive but was not necessarily the only acceptable route to disposing of property after death. This was particularly true when it came to widows and here London men seemed to differ in their choices compared to elsewhere. What was striking in London was the extent to which husbands allowed their wives absolute freedom to use their estate as they saw fit, though when the widow died, dutiful sons and daughters who were the main carers in her own old age tended to have been favoured.[42] Those higher up the social scale, notably gentlemen and professional men, differed and tended to create trusts and impose restrictive conditions in their wills. But the majority of men, particularly those involved in trade and manufacturing, gave their heirs and notably their widows a relatively free hand to do with their estate what they wished. Possessive individualism, therefore, and outright ownership appeared to be the ultimate outcome of most men's wills.

The importance of female executors also hints at the strong ties that bound husbands and wives together in both an emotional as well as an economic sense. This testamentary freedom and legal responsibility for women reflected the nature of the family enterprise in the city. Firms tended to be relatively small, with shops and workshops often based on the household.[43] In this situation, the relationship between husband and wife, and in some cases older children, was often an economic partnership as well as an emotional one. Though a husband's death inevitably disrupted the running of the enterprise, nevertheless insofar as the business was concerned the household could in many cases continue to operate more or less successfully. This fact also helps to account for the lack of trusts, which for shopkeepers and manufacturers could have hindered the running of a business. Death of a husband, then, did not inevitably lead to death of the firm and rather than divide up the estate at the point of death, it made good sense to allow it to continue unhindered by strictly defined testamentary restrictions.

These findings raise questions about the extent to which the ideology of separate spheres continued beyond the grave. The expectations of patriarchy and the outcomes in terms of provision for widows and children need to be set in the context of the ways that family and household were embedded in the local economy. Different positions in that economy tended to be associated with variations in the way that assets were distributed at death. At that point the ideological significance of separate spheres seemed to break down, or at least its hold on gendered social relations was loosened. Understanding the ideology of separate spheres and the ways that it operated in practice, therefore, needs to be rooted in the relationships between wealth, gender and the economy in specific locations and social contexts.

Notes

1 This chapter was first delivered as a paper at the XIV International Economic History Conference, Helsinki, 21 August 2006, Session 83 'Women's Financial Decisions: Their Wealth, Their Choices, Their Activity 1700–1930'. I am grateful to participants at the session for their comments and particularly to Alastair Owens for discussing his ideas and to Craig Bailey and Michael Abate for their help in data gathering. The editors have provided valuable advice on the contents of this chapter for which I am also grateful.

2 There is an extensive literature on the concept of separate spheres. See, in particular, A. Vickery, 'Golden age to separate spheres? A review of the categories and chronology of English women's history', *Historical Journal* 36, 1993, pp. 383–414; M. L. Shanley, *Feminism, Marriage and the Law in Victorian England*, Princeton, NJ: Princeton University Press, 1989. For more recent syntheses of the literature, see K. Gleadle, *British Women in the Nineteenth Century*, Basingstoke: Palgrave, 2001 and R. Beachey, B. Craig and A. Owens (eds), *Women, Business and Finance in Nineteenth-Century Europe*, Oxford: Berg, 2006.

3 G. Eliot, *The Mill on the Floss*, 1860, available online: www.gutenberg.org/dir/etext04/mlfls10.txtl (accessed 21 June 2007).

4 The sample was drawn from the PROB 11 series of will registers in which the court clerks copied the text of the wills. Probate values drawn from the PROB 12 index to this series were attached to the sample. For a discussion of the data, see D. R. Green and A. Owens, 'Metropolitan estates of the middle class 1800–1850: probates and death duties revisited', *Historical Research* 70, 1997, pp. 294–311. Of the total number of estates 89 per cent of male estates and 93 per cent of female estates were valued at or below £10,000. Research has shown that these values provide a good estimate of the net worth of estates. For a discussion of the net worth of estates, see A. Owens, D. R. Green, C. Bailey and A. Kay, 'A measure of worth: probate valuations, personal wealth and indebtedness in England 1810–1840', *Historical Research* 79, 2006, pp. 383–403.

5 R. J. Morris, *Men, Women and Property in England 1780–1870*, Cambridge: Cambridge University Press, 2005. Strictly speaking, the will and testament were two distinct entities: the former disposed of real estate while the latter dealt with personal property, including personal effects, cash, stocks and shares, together with the value of leasehold property and annuities. The ecclesiastical courts only had jurisdiction over personal property and it was this alone that was taken into consideration when establishing the value of an estate. The ownership of land, therefore, was excluded from the valuation of estates. The term 'will', as used here, is synonymous with the will and testament as defined above.

6 As legal documents wills were required to conform to certain rules regarding their construction. As long as they were legible and the sentiments clear, they could be considered legally valid providing that they had been witnessed by at least two people. Deathbed wills, including oral instructions, could also be accepted providing they had been witnessed. However, wills were usually drawn up by a third party, primarily a solicitor, and as such reflected a formal language employed as a matter of legal convention. Over time religious sentiments receded and by the nineteenth century they were primarily couched in secular language. The Wills Act (1 Vict. c.26) formalised the rules regarding the validity of a will and required it to be in writing, signed by the testator or their designee in the presence of two or more witnesses. See Frederick Inderwicke, *The Law of Wills as Administered in the Court of Probate in England*, London: William Maxwell, 1866. See also Morris, *Men, Women and Property*, pp. 86–101.

7 Until 1833 a widow was entitled for life to a third of all her husband's lands. The Dower Act of 1833 removed that right and instead substituted the right to a jointure, or annuity, for the widow. See E. Reiss, *Rights and Duties of Englishwomen*, Manchester: Sherrat and Hughes, 1934, 26–28. According to Lee Holcombe, by that time dower right 'was so rare as to be obsolete'. See L. Holcombe, *Wives and Property*, Toronto: University of Toronto Press, 1983, p. 22.

8 See Morris, *Men, Women and Property*, pp. 97–100.

9 PROB 11 vol. 1766 fol.71 Will of John Beedle, 15 February 1830.

10 PROB 11 vol. 1770 fol.273 Will of Joseph Pellet, 19 April 1830.

11 T. Falconer, *On Probate Courts*, London: Reynell and Weight, 1850, p. 5. Those executors of estates which fell below the threshold could still seek probate but were not required by law to do so. The laws of *bona notabilia*, however, were complex and unclear even to contemporaries. See Parliamentary Papers (PP) 1833 XXII *Law of Real Property: Fourth Report (Wills)*, pp. 43–47. The best overall introduction to the legal aspects of will making on which the following relies is A. J. Camp, *Wills and their Whereabouts*, London: privately published, 1974, pp. ix–xl.

12 I have dealt with this aspect elsewhere. See D. R. Green, 'Independent women, wealth and wills in nineteenth-century London', in J. Stobart and A. Owens (eds), *Urban Fortunes: Property and Inheritance in the Town, 1700–1900*, Aldershot: Ashgate, 2000, pp. 195–222.

13 In 1841 for the country as a whole, 16,701 wills and 6,297 administrations were

submitted to the Legacy Duty Office. The total number of adult deaths (aged over 20 years) in England and Wales in 1841 was 171,234. See PP 1843 XXI *Fifth Annual Report of the Registrar General of Births, Deaths and Marriages*, pp. 422–423.

14 The evidence presented here refers solely to wills and excluded administrations, known as 'admons', concerning those who died intestate.

15 See Green and Owens, 'Metropolitan estates', p. 296.

16 According to the probate data for 1800 there were no more than 75 upper value estates, comprising a very small proportion of the total recorded for that year. W. Rubinstein's research for the period from 1809 to 1839 shows that there were 427 London estates valued at above £100,000, an average of less than 14 per annum. In terms of numbers, upper value estates comprised a very small number of the total that passed through the remit of the courts. See W. Rubinstein, 'The role of London in Britain's wealth structure, 1809–99: further evidence', in J. Stobart and A. Owens (eds), *Urban Fortunes: Property and Inheritance in the Town, 1700–1900*, Aldershot: Ashgate, 2000, p. 137.

17 Morris, *Men, Women and Property in England*, p. 79.

18 L. D. Schwarz, *London in the Age of Industrialisation*, Cambridge: Cambridge University Press, 1992, p. 57.

19 Schwarz, *London in the Age of Industrialisation*, p. 60.

20 See G. Crossick, 'From gentleman to residuum: languages of social description in Victorian Britain', in P. J. Corfield (ed.), *Language, History and Class*, Oxford: Blackwell, 1991, pp. 150–178; R. J. Morris, 'Reading the will: cash economy capitalists and urban peasants in the 1830s', in A. Kidd and D. Nicholls (eds), *The Making of the British Middle Class?*, Stroud: Sutton, 1998, p. 119.

21 A similar situation existed in Stockport for the period. See A. Owens, 'Property, will making and estate disposal in an industrial town, 1800–1857', in J. Stobart and A. Owens (eds), *Urban Fortunes: Property and Inheritance in the Town, 1700–1900*, Aldershot: Ashgate, 2000, pp. 86–88.

22 Schwarz, *London in the Age of Industrialisation*, p. 72.

23 See Owens, 'Property, will making and estate disposal', p. 88.

24 R. Dickson, *A Practical Exposition of the Law of Wills*, London: Sherwood, Gilbert and Piper, 1830, p. 12.

25 Unfortunately, dates of death were not provided with the will. The interval between a grant of probate and date of death could be several months, and therefore these figures overestimate the lapse of time between writing the will and death. In Leeds Morris suggests that half the wills between 1830 and 1834 were made within six months of a testator's death. See also Morris, *Men, Women and Property in England*, p. 91; Owen, 'Property, will making and estate disposal', pp. 91–92.

26 A. Owens, 'Property, gender and the life course: inheritance and family welfare provision in early nineteenth-century England', *Social History* 26, 2001, p. 303.

27 Cited in Owens, 'Property, gender and the life course', p. 303.

28 Owens, 'Property, gender and the life course', pp. 309–310.

29 This debate is explored more fully in M. Berg, 'Women's property and the industrial revolution', *Journal of Interdisciplinary History* 24, 1993, pp. 233–250. See also Morris, *Men, Women and Property*, pp. 101–109, 233–263; Owens, 'Property, will making and estate disposal', pp. 98–101.

30 Paraphernalia included the wife's personal clothing and ornaments. Although technically a husband owned his wife's paraphernalia, when he died he could not dispose of it. Similarly, although a husband owned his wife's real estate he could not sell it without her consent. See Reiss, *Rights and Duties*, pp. 21–26. See also B. Leigh Smith, *A Brief Summary in Plain Language of the Most Important Laws Concerning Women*, London: John Chapman, 1854.

31 Owens, 'Property, gender and the life course', p. 310. Owens' suggests that for Stockport the most common strategy was for the sale of the family firm and the distribution of the

ensuring assets through a trust. See also A. Owens, 'Inheritance and the life-cycle of family firms in the early industrial revolution', *Business History* 44, 2002, pp. 21–46.

32 Morris, *Men, Women and Property*, p. 101.

33 PROB 11 vol. 1768 fol.169 Will of Thomas Gill, 24 March 1830.

34 PROB 11 vol. 1769 fol.224 Will of John Watkins, 20 March 1830.

35 Probate valuations do not take into account the value of real estate that was passed directly to heirs. If the terms of the will directed that real estate was to be sold, the value of that property was included in the probate valuations. See Owens *et al.*, 'A measure of worth', for further discussion of probate valuations in this period.

36 See Morris, *Men, Women and Property*, p. 108.

37 The average probate value of estates in which leasehold and/or freehold property was specifically mentioned was £1,723 (N=90) compared to £1,417 (N=180) for the remainder of estates for which a probate value could be established.

38 The significance of Bank of England annuities is dealt with in D. R. Green and A. Owens, 'Gentlewomanly capitalism? Spinsters, widows and wealth holding in England and Wales, c. 1800–1860', *Economic History Review* 56, 2003, pp. 510–536.

39 PROB 11 vol. 1767 fol.117 Will of William Read, 13/02/1830.

40 Morris, *Men, Women and Property*, p. 103.

41 Owens, 'Property, will making and estate disposal', p. 93.

42 See Green, 'Independent women, wealth and wills', pp. 195–222. See also S. Goss, 'Handing down the farm: values, strategies and outcomes in inheritance practices among rural German Americans', *Journal of Family History* 21, 1996, p. 200.

43 In 1851 nearly three-quarters of London firms employed fewer than five men. See D. R. Green, 'The nineteenth-century metropolitan economy: a revisionist interpretation', *London Journal* 21, 1996, pp. 16–20.

Bibliography

Beachey, R., Craig, B. and Owens, A. (eds), *Women, Business and Finance in Nineteenth-Century Europe*, Oxford: Berg, 2006.

Berg, M., 'Women's property and the industrial revolution', *Journal of Interdisciplinary History* 24, 1993, pp. 233–250.

British Parliamentary Papers, XXI *Fifth Annual Report of the Registrar General of Births, Deaths and Marriages*, 1843.

British Parliamentary Papers, XXII *Law of Real Property: Fourth Report (Wills)*, 1833.

Camp, A. J., *Wills and their Whereabouts*, London: privately published, 1974.

Crossick, G., 'From gentleman to residuum: languages of social description in Victorian Britain', in Corfield, P. J. (ed.), *Language, History and Class*, Oxford: Blackwell, 1991, pp. 150–178.

Dickson, R., *A Practical Exposition of the Law of Wills*, London: Sherwood, Gilbert and Piper, 1830.

Eliot, G., *The Mill on the Floss*, 1860, available online: www.gutenberg.org/dir/etext04/mlfls10.txtl (accessed 21 June 2007).

Falconer, T., *On Probate Courts*, London: Reynell and Weight, 1850.

Gleadle, K., *British Women in the Nineteenth Century*, Basingstoke: Palgrave, 2001.

Goss, S., 'Handing down the farm: values, strategies and outcomes in inheritance practices among rural German Americans', *Journal of Family History* 21, 1996, pp. 192–217.

Green D. R., 'Independent women, wealth and wills in nineteenth-century London', in Stobart, J. and Owens, A. (eds), *Urban Fortunes: Property and Inheritance in the Town 1700–1900*, Aldershot: Ashgate, 2000, pp. 195–222.

Green, D. R., 'The nineteenth-century metropolitan economy: a revisionist interpretation', *London Journal* 21, 1996, pp. 9–26.

Green, D. R. and Owens, A., 'Gentlewomanly capitalism? Spinsters, widows and wealth holding in England and Wales, *c*.1800–1860', *Economic History Review* 56, 2003, pp. 510–536.

Green D. R. and Owens, A., 'Metropolitan estates of the middle class 1800–1850: probates and death duties revisited', *Historical Research* 70, 1997, pp. 294–311.

Holcombe, L., *Wives and Property*, Toronto: University of Toronto Press, 1983.

Inderwicke, F., *The Law of Wills as Administered in the Court of Probate in England*, London: William Maxwell, 1866.

Leigh Smith, B., *A Brief Summary in Plain Language of the Most Important Laws Concerning Women*, London: John Chapman, 1854.

Morris, R. J., *Men, Women and Property in England 1780–1870*, Cambridge: Cambridge University Press, 2005.

Morris, R. J., 'Reading the will: cash economy capitalists and urban peasants in the 1830s', in Kidd, A. and Nicholls, D. (eds), *The Making of the British Middle Class?*, Stroud: Sutton, 1998, pp. 113–129.

Owens, A., 'Inheritance and the life-cycle of family firms in the early industrial revolution', *Business History* 44, 2002, pp. 21–46.

Owens, A., 'Property, gender and the life course: inheritance and family welfare provision in early nineteenth-century England', *Social History* 26, 2001, pp. 299–317.

Owens, A., 'Property, will making and estate disposal in an industrial town, 1800–1857', in Stobart, J. and Owens, A. (eds), *Urban Fortunes: Property and Inheritance in the Town 1700–1900*, Aldershot: Ashgate, 2000, pp. 79–107.

Owens, A., Green, D. R., Bailey, C. and Kay, A., 'A measure of worth: probate valuations, personal wealth and indebtedness in England 1810–1840', *Historical Research* 79, 2006, pp. 383–403.

Reiss, E., *Rights and Duties of Englishwomen*, Manchester: Sherrat and Hughes, 1934.

Rubinstein, W., 'The role of London in Britain's wealth structure, 1809–99: further evidence', in Stobart, J. and Owens, A. (eds), *Urban Fortunes: Property and Inheritance in the Town, 1700–1900*, Aldershot: Ashgate, 2000, pp. 131–148.

Schwarz, L. D., *London in the Age of Industrialisation*, Cambridge: Cambridge University Press, 1992.

Shanley, M. L., *Feminism, Marriage and the Law in Victorian England*, Princeton, NJ: Princeton University Press, 1989.

Vickery, A., 'Golden age to separate spheres? A review of the categories and chronology of English women's history', *Historical Journal* 36, 1993, pp. 383–414.

11 Women and wealth in fiction in the long nineteenth century 1800–1914

Janette Rutterford and Josephine Maltby

The intersections and progressions of fictional lives that they portray are couched within a larger pattern of interaction and exchange of which capital is the protagonist.[1]

Introduction

A recurring feature of writing about the nineteenth-century novel has been the belief that the Victorian woman was 'the angel of the house ... the still point in an age of capital whose perpetual crises show no sign of waning',[2] who was morally as well as socially detached from capitalism – in accordance with the 'separate spheres' model of men's and women's roles. This is typified by Nancy Armstrong's account of the novel from the eighteenth century onwards as delineating a 'specifically female curriculum'[3] concerned with 'the household, leisure time, courtship procedures and kinship relations'.[4] She sets this in opposition to a male 'political' sphere whose concerns include class, status and money. Thus female characters who engage with money, such as the Bingley sisters in Jane Austen's *Pride and Prejudice* with their 'mercenary lust' or Blanche Ingram in Charlotte Brontë's *Jane Eyre*, who is drawn to Rochester by an 'acquisitive urge',[5] are condemned as failing to meet a norm of femininity.

There is a growing counter-argument that finds in the nineteenth-century novel an acute awareness of women's economic as well as their domestic position, and identifies women as economic actors, with all the contradictions and anxieties that this raises. It has long been recognised that Victorian novels were preoccupied with money – for instance, Reed's description of speculation as a 'familiar theme' in early-nineteenth-century fiction[6] or Poovey's conclusion that financial plots were thematically central to the Victorian novel.[7] Henry argues that this awareness has, however, been overshadowed by hostility to capitalism, so that writers have been 'blinded ... to some important dimensions of the Victorians' interactions in the financial world', one of which was the investment activity of women.[8]

The nineteenth century was, in Britain as elsewhere, a period of major change in financial behaviour, as new kinds of financial asset became available for investors. It was also a period in which women's social and economic position altered, at first slowly then with gathering speed. Their economic position changed more rapidly than did their political rights, with the Married Women's Property Acts (MWPAs) later in the century giving all women the potential, if not the means, to own and trade in financial assets. (These changes are outlined elsewhere in this volume, see Chapters 1 and 7).

The pace of economic change, for men as well as for women, created tensions and anxieties, about the speed with which money could be made and lost, the arrival of a new class of business magnates and the displacement of the traditional gentry, the loss of the countryside and the growth of the new industrial cities, as well as the destabilisation of traditional male and female roles. Searle quotes the MP Beresford Hope warning that the MWPA would turn marriage into a limited-liability company with two partners – one comment that can stand for many as an example of the anxiety that change was destabilising and subverting settled society.[9] Nunokawa reads Victorian novels as a repudiation of change: 'nothing gold can stay', with the good women of Charles Dickens's *Little Dorrit* or *Dombey and Son* representing a safe form of property that could not be alienated by the market.[10] But there is a growing recognition among critics that nineteenth-century novels do not necessarily treat women as excluded from the economic world. This chapter looks at some of the ways in which the novels of the long nineteenth century addressed these issues, by looking at their treatment of a number of themes: the 'competence' and the threats it encountered; women as managers of money in the family and as speculators; and the extent to which the notion of the 'New Woman' can be linked with a different attitude to women's finances.

The 'competence' and the dangers of poverty

Copeland's 1995 study[11] identifies the importance of money for women in numerous novels by Austen's contemporaries in the period 1790 to 1820. The ideal is a 'competence', at least sufficient to 'set the bottom line of gentility' of running one's own household with a servant:

> In contemporary women's fiction, the competence ledgers are kept meticulously neat, clean and balanced. No matter what the scenery or the philosophy, the main plot or the subplots, the sound of adding or subtraction makes its way to the surface, the clinking and clanking of arithmetic as each sum finds its way into the projected competence that fate bears in its womb for the deserving heroine.[12]

The calculation of the competence is directly linked to the 5 per cent return on government stock: the only exception he identifies is in *Pride and Prejudice*, where both Mr Collins and Mrs Bingley are unsure whether to apply 4 or 5 per cent.[13]

The competence is not always attainable. The themes of financial narratives are altered by the impact of what Copeland calls 'Gothic economics' triggered by the Napoleonic war: tax and price rises and periodic depressions that in the novels of the period are shown as resulting in bankruptcy for men and poverty or destitution for their dependent women. Women's attempts to support themselves by work – as teacher, seamstress, companion, and so on – are normally shown as hopeless and degrading.[14]

Copeland suggests that themes change in response to improvements in the economic climate: from the beginning of the nineteenth century, more of the plots he discusses deal with the woman as manager of the household budget, responsible for family welfare – but as a prudent consumer, not an investor, and drawing on money provided for her, not her own funds.[15] The novels of the early century that he discusses do not include the possibility of women earning and managing their own money.

Some of the themes identified by Copeland appear later: the precise identification of the costs of running a household, the looming threat of bankruptcy and the role of the woman as a domestic manager. But the nineteenth century also saw the introduction of new themes, to do with women's economic agency. One example of this development, we argue, is provided by Trollope, whose industrious career as a novelist began in 1847 and continued unbroken until his death in 1882.

The family and wealth

Michie emphasises the importance for Trollope of the Victorians' response to 'dramatic changes in economic practice and theory'.[16] She argues that he represents 'the economic drives and desires their culture sought to sublimate'.[17] Trollope's *The Way We Live Now*, which appeared in 1873 towards the end of his career, is plainly and famously a novel about the drastic impact of a new financial order on a settled society; but attention should also be given to Trollope's treatment of financial practice as it affects every aspect of family life in general, and marriage in particular. The discussion that follows deals also with the novels from the two series: the Barchester Chronicles about gentry and clerical life in the shires, and the political Palliser novels, for which finance is also a pervasive theme.

Inheritance, and the crucial role of primogeniture, form a key element in many of these novels.[18] Primogeniture, the favouring of the elder son over the other sons and all daughters, was a peculiarly English fascination since it 'was applied more harshly in England than elsewhere in Europe'.[19] A survey of estates carried out in 1875 revealed that one-quarter of all land in England was held by only 710 individuals.[20] This was a result of two complementary forces – primogeniture and the entail of estates. Together, their effect was not only that the eldest son inherited, but that the father was unable to sell entailed land: it had to be handed down intact to the heir unless he agreed to break the entail. This might produce conflicts of interest between father and eldest son, with the former unable to sell assets or disinherit, and the latter able to build up debts, secured on expectations. The result might be various kinds of conflict within the family. The father's position is weakened – like that of Adolphus Longestaffe in *The Way We Live Now*, vainly asking his son to break the entail so that he can raise some money. Primogeniture also led to younger sons being forced to marry money or remain single,[21] as discussed below, and a large number of upper-class daughters being made 'redundant' by the lack of a large enough marriage portion. There are numerous examples of redundant upper-class women in Trollope novels, for example, Lord George Germain's four unmarried sisters in *Is He Popenjoy?* and Sir Marmaduke Rowley's eight unmarried daughters in *He Knew He Was Right*.

Marriage was often the means – in real life and in novels – for rectifying family finances. Although Trollope's novels depict penniless women seeking riches through marriage (for example, Arabella Trefoil in *The American Senator*), it is striking that a plot often turns on a man seeking to marry money. As the narrator in *The Way We Live Now* admits: 'it is generally understood that matters will be put right by an heiress.' Marriage with a wealthy woman is the strategy for maintaining 'the proper order of things'.[22] Marriage 'often features in fiction – as indeed it functioned in aristocratic marriage – as a means of paying men's debts with women's money'.[23] The clever and homely Miss Dunstable, whose family fortune was made from patent medicine, appears in *Doctor Thorne, Framley Parsonage* and *The Last Chronicle of Barsetshire*. She is bleakly aware that she is courted for money, not for breeding or looks: she comments that her frizzy curls 'always pass muster ... when they are done up with bank-notes'.[24] Later, reflecting on her career, she talks to a friend: 'I am a sheep with two heads.' Money has turned her into 'an abortion'.[25]

One of the pervasive elements in the transfer of wealth within families was the marriage settlement, used as a means of agreeing amounts brought into a marriage by both parties and effecting or preventing redistribution of wealth. The terms of the settlement determined such issues as provision for the wife in the event of her husband's death – the widow's jointure – and for the husband if the wife died childless. The settlement also served to protect the wife's assets from the husband before the MWPAs of 1870 and 1882. There were innumerable variations that authors assumed would be understood by their readers. Collins, in his 1860 novel, *The Woman in White*, makes the heroine Laura's marriage settlement, arranged by the family solicitor, Mr Gilmore, central to the plot.

> I explained to her the object of a marriage-settlement, and then told her exactly what her prospects were – marking the distinction between the property in which she had a life-interest only, and the property which was left at her own control.[26]

The settlement also pervades Trollope's novels, almost as the consecration of marriage. Arabella, flirting warily with Lord Rufford, tells him that his sister would be more reserved than she has been: 'Her cautious nature would have trusted no man as I trusted you. Her lips, doubtless, were never unfrozen till the settlements had been signed.'[27] At the end of *Doctor Thorne*, the marriage is delayed by a complicated settlement 'and Frank himself began to make accusations that he was to be done out of his wife altogether'.[28] But matters are resolved, and Frank, who has been the penniless son of an insolvent father 'married money and became a great man'.[29]

Some of Trollope's contemporaries were critical of the importance of the role played by the marriage settlement in his novels. A recurring theme among his critics was that he took an unreasonably idealistic view of marriage: he was attacked for his 'favourite hobby of the advisableness of young people marrying without being too careful as to their future income'.[30] As a result of this, they thought, he treated 'wealth and station in themselves [as] somewhat contemptible'[31] and made the families who negotiated a settlement look like money-grubbers. This was unfair, they argued: '[T]he fact is that in his heart every man knows and feels that society has real claims which no man has a right to deny.'[32] The alternative reading of Trollope's plots was that he was not a disappointed idealist, but rather that he was prepared to admit the crucial importance of money to the Victorian family. Mrs Oliphant, writing in *Blackwood's* in 1867 took the latter view. Trollope for her was 'the only writer we know who realizes the position of a sensible and right-minded woman among the ordinary affairs of the world'.[33] But what Mrs Oliphant does not acknowledge, and what perhaps shocked the critics quoted above, is the darkness of Trollope's view – his heiress who sees herself as 'an abortion', or Lizzie Eustace and Lord Fawn coldly checking each other's wealth before marriage. Lizzie tells her companion she will have to 'look very close after the settlement', not trusting 'any lawyer to give away my property'. She announces proudly that 'He'll find out that I know how to keep what I've got in my own hands'.[34] The settlement implies a total absence of trust between husband and wife.

Women are presented by Trollope as managers of family money, but in a different way from the theme of the woman as manager of the household budget – the task at which, for instance, Agnes succeeds and Dora fails so miserably in Charles Dickens's *David Copperfield*. Where Copeland and his Victorian successors showed women as domestic managers, Trollope shows them making plans that will have enduring importance. A recurring theme for Trollope is the organisation of financially suitable marriages, as distinct from matchmaking on emotional grounds. Markwick and Koets both identify the role played by mothers in Trollope's novels in organising their sons' weddings.[35] Sisters try to make similar plans for their insolvent brothers. Charlotte Stanhope in *Barchester Towers* 'alone prevented the family from falling into utter disrepute and beggary' and explains to Bertie how he is to propose to a wealthy widow.[36] One of Miss Dunstable's female friends proposes (unsuccessfully) to her on her brother's behalf as he is inadequate to the task.[37]

Trollope does not invariably show this money management in a sinister light. For instance, Aunt Jemima in *He Knew He Was Right* relents and agrees to leave her large estate to her young nephew and niece. Miss Dunstable, once happily married, is a helpful friend. But his treatment of women and money is more ambiguous and ambivalent than is suggested by, for instance, Armstrong's claim of a 'norm of femininity'[38] that detaches women from money, or Dolin's that the woman in Victorian fiction was 'held up as a powerful icon of stable property'.[39] Trollope recognises that Victorian women, despite legal constraints, have access both to money and to decision-making about it in ways that can affect themselves and their families for good and ill. The family is not necessarily a refuge from economic pressures: Trollope's novels also depict it as a potential focus for them.

Speculation and investment

There is a growing interest in the relationship between nineteenth-century literature and the financial markets, the behaviour of investors and speculators,[40] and the extent to which, as Jonathan Rose has put it, capitalism was 'good for Victorian literature'.[41] Russell has explored the relationship between fictional characters operating in the financial world and the real-world speculations, bubbles and crashes, such as occurred in 1825, 1832, 1835, 1847, and which formed ideal literary scenarios.[42] A number of popular women authors included 'high finance' and financial crises in their novels – for instance Mrs Catherine Gore, who wrote *The Banker's Wife* in 1843 and Dinah Mary Mulock (Mrs Craik) whose *John Halifax, Gentleman* (1856) is set during the crash year of 1825.[43]

Speculation, 'a game played by all classes',[44] became linked to stock markets even before the South Sea Bubble of 1720. It was blamed on stockjobbers whose bad reputation lasted for centuries thereafter. Shadwell's satire *The Stock Jobbers* was written in 1692; Johnson's Dictionary of 1755 defined a stockjobber as 'a low wretch who gets money by buying and selling in the funds'; and Thomas Mortimer published his *The Nefarious Practice of Stockjobbing Unveiled* in 1810.[45] This gave a poor reputation to the stock market as a whole that lasted until well into the nineteenth century.

Women were implicated in stock-market speculative activity from the seventeenth century. Early female investors in companies such as the East India Company and the Bank of England were often relatively wealthy, used to gambling with their 'pin money' on games of chance. (See Carlos *et al.* and Laurence in the present volume, Chapters 3 and 4.) By the railway mania of the 1830s the growth in the number of companies in which shares could be bought was such as to bring in more women risking a much greater proportion of their wealth. What surprised contemporary observers was that the stock market did *not* exclude women, who could be found in the male environment of the City at the Bank of England regularly collecting their dividends or in company offices subscribing for shares.[46] What also shocked them was that the gentler sex could suffer as well as men in market downturns. There was continuing moral disapproval attached to the association of women with speculation. Unlike budgetary management, or even marriage-making, this was financial activity outside the safe confines of the family. It involved entry into a masculine world. A member of the Select Committee on the Married Women's Property Bill in 1868 questioned:

whether you think it would be conducive to the happiness of married life if a woman ... possessed of personal attractions, was to go out into the world and be negotiating in shares or other affairs of life with agents and people of various classes, who might not be notorious of their high notions of what is right.[47]

Stock-market activity involved an entry into a world that could not readily be dissociated from gambling. O'Connor stresses the Victorian anxiety about the close links between gambling and speculative investment.[48] In 1876, *Blackwood's* described stock-market activity as 'peeresses *playing* on their pin money' (emphasis added) and, as late as 1910, the *Financial Review of Reviews* blamed speculation on 'special social sets', with the implication that these sets were of dubious morals.[49] Women were believed to be morally vulnerable because they were 'suited to a life of speculation ... Speculation derives its food from excitement and women often feed on excitement'.[50]

Henry argues that the distinction between speculation and investment was not significant, ascribing it to 'a questionable moral logic that insists on distinctions about the amount of time we choose to leave the money in the market'.[51] This seems to be ignoring the other differences (apart from timing) that the Victorians saw between investment (for annual income or as a repository for excess savings) and speculation (for capital gain or the joy of gaming). In *The Way We Live Now*, speculative finance is exemplified by the fraudulent Melmotte: the women who are impressed by him are both, in different ways, presented as morally dubious. The louche American Mrs Hurtle has a long eulogy of him as 'a man whose hand I would kiss', and likens him to Napoleon and Washington.[52] She praises his shady railway project in similar vein: 'I wish I was a man that I might be concerned with a really great thing like that.'[53] Lady Carbury, desperate for money to support her rakish son, also hero-worships Melmotte: 'In her heart of hearts she worshipped wealth.'[54] She excuses his sharp practice as 'beneficent audacity': 'One cannot measure such men by the ordinary rule.'[55]

There is an interesting contrast between Trollope's novel and Zola's *L'Argent*, a novel whose women characters of all ages and classes cover a spectrum of views of investment. The baronne Sandorff is a passionate speculator who gambles 'like a lost soul'[56] while she conducts an affair with the promoter Saccard. The Princesse d'Orviedo is a millionairess who gives away her fortune in the course of the novel and enters a convent as a pauper – the antithesis of an investor. There is the nightmarish Mme Mechain, 'one of those wild and wretched woman gamblers whose podgy hands dabble in all sorts of squalid tasks', who prowls the Bourse with a bag full of the shares of failed companies.[57] There is a cast of women, from aristocrats to servants, who lose money on Saccard's shares. But there is also Caroline Hamelin. She too is Saccard's lover, although she recognises his moral failings. For her, 'money is the dung heap in which tomorrow's human race grew'.[58] The book ends with her expression of confidence in the potential of money, despite the range of disasters caused by the company failure: 'Why should money suffer the penalty for the dirty deeds and the crimes that it causes? Love, the creator of life, is no less soiled'.[59] As well as criticising speculation, *L'Argent* raises the possibility that women can participate fully in the market and that investment is a motor for economic growth: the English novel of the same period is far more uneasy about women's involvement in speculative investment.

Money and 'new women'

The late nineteenth and early twentieth centuries are seen as the era of the New Woman, who began to claim independence and autonomy in every aspect of her life – personally, politically and economically. Women's property rights had been enlarged by the MWPAs, and women had more freedom to earn and to go into the market to make investments. *Howard's End* shows the Schlegel sisters as confident, affluent women from the middle class. One of the tokens of their confidence is the assurance with which they buy shares in overseas companies, to the horror of their elderly Aunt:

> She learned, to her horror, that Margaret, now of age, was taking her money out of the old safe investments and putting it into Foreign Things, which always smash. Silence would have been criminal. Her own fortune was invested in Home Rails, and most ardently did she beg her niece to imitate her. 'Then we should be together, dear'.
>
> Margaret, out of politeness, invested a few hundreds in the Nottingham and Derby Railway, and, though the Foreign Things did admirably and the Nottingham and Derby declined with the steady dignity of which only Home Rails are capable, Mrs Munt never ceased to rejoice, and to say: 'I did manage that, at all events. When the smash comes poor Margaret will have a nest-egg to fall back upon'.[60]

But there is still anxiety both about the market and about women's place in it. Bennett's Anna of the Five Towns finds herself the recipient of a small fortune from her father when she reaches 21 – a portfolio made up of 'all sorts of shares, English and American [and] sundry properties in the Five Towns'.[61] She is clever and serious and determined to do well, yet she finds herself the cause of a disaster when one of her tenants hangs himself because he cannot pay the rent. Bennett does not discuss the reasons for her failure – whether they lie with her femininity or with the intractable nature of the economic system – but they cast a shadow over the prospects for women's autonomy.

Sloan comments on Gissing's 'continued moral protest against the universalizing hold of money and commodity relations' in the late nineteenth century.[62] Part of the protest takes the form of a pessimistic view of women's ability to operate in a world in which, in Ingham's words, 'Everything ... has to be paid for and comes with a price tag'.[63] The sisters of *The Odd Women* all struggle to get by on low-paid jobs: their father had foolishly believed that his £1,000 insurance policy would provide for all six of them.[64]

When one loses her job through illness, they have a crisis discussion and decide they can live another six months on 'seven and twopence a week for everything'. Alice concludes:

> with all the impressiveness of tone she could command. 'We must never intrench upon our capital – never – never! ... If we haven't a friend to look to ... then indeed we shall be glad that nothing tempted us to intrench on our capital'.[65]

And they are trapped in poverty by their inability to act independently. A practical woman friend, running her own school, suggests to one of them that they consider investing the inheritance in 'some practical enterprise'. She 'trembled deliciously' but dared not pursue the idea.[66]

In various forms, this pattern recurs in Gissing's novels – the women of the Leach family who 'had never dreamt of undertaking household management' so 'all such matters were left to a cook-housekeeper' (*The Whirlpool*), and Nancy, who has to hide her secret marriage or lose her inheritance. The treatment of the theme of women and money in the novels of the long nineteenth century is not a narrative of progress, from the heroine as helpless victim to the manager and the confident investor. Instead, the themes recur over time. Gissing's treatment of women's financial status in his 1894 *In the Year of Jubilee* is in some ways reminiscent of that outlined by Copeland at the beginning of the chapter – they are acutely aware of what is needed for financial survival, but they do not necessarily have the means to ensure it. They, too, are at the mercy of 'Gothic economics' in the form of bereavement or financial collapse.

Conclusion

The use of literature as a means of understanding history raises the question of the relationship between the two – whether a novel can be treated as a reliable transcription of what is happening, or as a text to be set among other texts (such as statistics, Parliamentary papers, newspaper reports) and given as much or as little credence as any other.[67] Another possibility again is that the novel can be added to a repertoire of other kinds of evidence, but with the proviso that, in Newton's words, it is 'always apprehended within representation' – to be set against other sources, sometimes echoing them, sometimes contradicting them.[68] Literature, it is suggested, offers another means of understanding women's economic agency, to be compared and contrasted with other kinds of evidence, sometimes endorsing and sometimes challenging them.

The discussion offered in this chapter identifies a number of themes that have also been recognised in historical writing about women and investment in the nineteenth century. Women are acknowledged to be capable of managing their own and their families' finances, and marriage is understood as an economic as well as an emotional transaction. This is consonant with, for instance, Walker's evidence of Octavia Hill and her volunteers as competent financial managers,[69] or Swan's of women as operating as independent investors.[70]

But there is also a current of anxiety and discomfort with women's financial activity, from the disasters suffered by the heroines of the early nineteenth century to the failures that 'New Women' still experience when required to deal independently with finance. What a reading of contemporary literature can add to our historical understanding is an insight into the contradiction and unease that ran alongside women's financial independence in the nineteenth century.

Notes

1 F.J. Jeffrey, 'Anthony Trollope meets Pierre Bourdieu: the conversion of capital as plot in the mid-Victorian British novel', *Victorian Literature and Culture* 31 (2), 2003, pp. 501–21.
2 J. Nunokawa, *The Afterlife of Property: Domestic Security and the Victorian Novel*, Princeton, NJ: Princeton University Press, 1994, p. 124.
3 N. Armstrong, *Desire and Domestic Fiction: A Political History of the Novel*, New York: Oxford University Press, 1987, p. 17.
4 Armstrong, *Desire and Domestic Fiction*, p. 3.
5 Armstrong, *Desire and Domestic Fiction*, p. 252.
6 J.R. Reed, 'A friend to Mammon: speculation in Victorian literature', *Victorian Studies* 27 (7), 1984, p. 184.
7 M. Poovey, 'Writing about finance in Victorian England: disclosure and secrecy in the culture of investment', *Victorian Studies* 45 (1), 2002, pp. 17–41.
8 N. Henry, '"Ladies do it?": Victorian women investors in fact and fiction', in F. O'Gorman (ed.), *Victorian Literature and Finance*, Oxford: Oxford University Press, 2007, pp. 114–15.
9 G.R. Searle, *Morality and the Market in Victorian Britain*, Oxford: Clarendon Press, 1998, p. 151.
10 Nunokawa, *The Afterlife of Property*, p. 122.
11 Edward Copeland, *Women Writing about Money: Women's Fiction in England, 1790–1820*, Cambridge: Cambridge University Press, 1995.
12 Copeland, *Women Writing about Money*, p. 23.
13 Ibid.
14 Copeland, *Women Writing about Money*, pp. 159–212.
15 Copeland, *Women Writing about Money*, p. 61, p. 87.
16 E.B. Michie, 'Buying brains: Trollope, Oliphant, and vulgar Victorian commerce', *Victorian Studies* 44 (1), 2001, pp. 77–97, 98.
17 Michie, 'Buying brains', p. 94.
18 For a more detailed discussion of this topic, see J. Rutterford and J. Maltby, '"Frank must marry money": men, women and property in Trollope's novels', *Accounting Historians Journal* 33 (2), 2006, pp. 201–31.
19 A.L. Erickson, 'Coverture and capitalism', *History Workshop Journal* 59 (1), 2005, p. 71.
20 P.M. Laurence, *Law and Custom of Primogeniture*, Cambridge: J. Hall and Son, 1878.
21 For example, of the male aristocrats born between 1840 and 1859, only 68 per cent of younger sons eventually married, compared to 86 per cent of the heirs. D. Thomas, 'Social origins of marriage partners in the British peerage in the eighteenth and nineteenth centuries', *Population Studies* 26 (1), 1972, p. 101.
22 A. Trollope, *The Way We Live Now*, first published 1875, Oxford: Oxford University Press, 1982, p. 59.

23 M. Finn, *The Character of Credit: Personal Debt in English Culture, 1740–1813*, Cambridge: Cambridge University Press, 2003, p. 49.

24 A. Trollope, *Doctor Thorne*, first published 1858, London: Penguin Books, 1991.

25 A. Trollope, *Framley Parsonage*, first published 1859–60, London: Penguin Books, 2004, p. 447.

26 W. Collins, *The Woman in White*, first published 1859, London: Collector's Library, 2006, pp. 144–5.

27 A. Trollope, *The American Senator*, first published 1876–7, Oxford: The World's Classics, 1986, p. 465.

28 Trollope, *Doctor Thorne*, p. 551.

29 Trollope, *Doctor Thorne*, p. 556.

30 D. Smalley (ed.), *Trollope: The Critical Heritage*, London: Routledge & Kegan Paul, 1969, p. 209, quoting review of *The Small House at Allington* in *Saturday Review*, May 1864.

31 Review of *Dr Thorne* in *Saturday Review*, 12 June 1858, quoted by Smalley, *Trollope*, p. 77.

32 Review of *Dr Thorne* in *Saturday Review*, 12 June 1858, quoted by Smalley, *Trollope*, p. 78.

33 Mrs Oliphant, *Blackwood's Edinburgh Magazine*, September 1867, pp. 257–80, cited in E.B. Michie, 'Buying brains', p. 82.

34 A. Trollope, *The Eustace Diamonds*, first published 1873, London: Penguin Books, 2004, pp. 124–5.

35 M. Markwick, *Trollope and Women*, London: The Hambledon Press, 1997; C.C. Koets, *Female Characters in the Works of Anthony Trollope*, Gouda: T. van Tilburg, 1932.

36 A. Trollope, *Barchester Towers*, first published 1857, London: Penguin Books, 1994, p. 64.

37 Trollope, *Framley Parsonage*, p. 297.

38 Armstrong, *Desire and Domestic Fiction*, p. 252.

39 T. Dolin, *Mistress of the House: Women of Property in the Victorian Novel*, Aldershot: Ashgate, 1997, p. 7.

40 Special issues of *Victorian Studies* 45 (1), 2002, co-edited by C. Schmitt, N. Henry and A. Arondekar on 'Victorian Investment', and a special issue of *Victorian Review* 31 (2), 2005, on 'Literature and Money' are evidence of this recent trend.

41 Cited in O'Gorman (ed.), *Victorian Literature and Finance*, p. 9.

42 N. Russell, *The Novelist and Mammon*, Oxford: Clarendon Press, 1986.

43 See also P. Delany, *Literature, Money and the Market: From Trollope to Amis*, Basingstoke: Palgrave, 2002; Henry, '"Ladies do it?"', in O'Gorman (ed.), *Victorian Literature and Finance*, pp. 111–32; N. Henry, *George Eliot and the British Empire*, Cambridge: Cambridge University Press, 2002.

44 N. Russell, *The Novelist and Mammon*, p. 19.

45 T. Shadwell, *Epsom Wells and the Volunteers: or the Stock Jobbers*, first published posthumously 1693, Boston: D.C. Heath & Co, 1930; Johnson, *Dictionary*, first published 1755, London: Penguin Classics, 2005; T. Mortimer, *The Nefarious Practice of Stockjobbing Unveiled*, London: J.M. Richardson, 1810.

46 M. Freeman, R. Pearson and J. Taylor, '"A doe in the city": women shareholders in eighteenth- and early nineteenth-century Britain', *Accounting, Business and Financial History* 16 (2), 2006, pp. 265–92; 'Dividend day', *All the Year Round*, 1893, pp. 462–5.

47 Quoted by R.J. Morris, *Men, Women and Property in England and Wales, 1780–1870*, Cambridge: Cambridge University Press, 2005, p. 403.

48 M. O'Connor, 'Imagining risk, sensationalizing speculation: a cultural history of the London Stock Exchange and financial speculation', paper presented at the Nicholson Center for British Studies Conference: 'Modernizing Politics?', University of Chicago, 21–22 May 2005.

49 Cited in J. Rutterford and J. Maltby, '"The widow, the clergyman and the reckless": women investors in England, 1830–1914', *Feminist Economics* 121 (1–2), 2006, pp. 126–7.

50 W.W. Fowler, *Twenty Years of Inside Life in Wall Street*, New York: Orange Judd Company, 1880, p. 448, cited in G. Robb, 'Women and white-collar crime: debates on gender, fraud and the corporate economy in England and America, 1850–1930', *British Journal of Criminology* 46, 2006, pp. 1058–72.

51 Henry, '"Ladies Do It?"', in O'Gorman, *Literature and Finance*, p. 120.

52 Trollope, *The Way We Live Now*, pp. 244–6.

53 Trollope, *The Way We Live Now*, p. 391.

54 Trollope, *The Way We Live Now*, p. 101.

55 Trollope, *The Way We Live Now*, p. 279.

56 E. Zola, *L'Argent*, first published 1891, Paris: Folio Classique, 1999, p. 63 (all translations authors' own).

57 Zola, *L'Argent*, p. 57.

58 Zola, *L'Argent*, p. 293.

59 Zola, *L'Argent*, p. 497.

60 E.M. Forster, *Howard's End*, first published 1910, London: Edward Arnold, 1973, pp. 11–12.

61 A. Bennett, *Anna of the Five Towns*, first published in 1902, London: Methuen, 1951, p. 41. Her mother's unadventurous portion of 'Government stock' is mockingly contrasted with her father's choice of the 'aristocracy of investments', a local colliery, railway, waterworks and brewery.

62 J. Sloan, review of Simon J. James, *Unsettled Accounts*, in *Nineteenth Century Literature* March 2005, pp. 547–50.

63 G. Gissing, *The Odd Women*, first published 1892, Oxford: Oxford University Press, 2000, p. ix.

64 Gissing, *The Odd Women*, p. 5.

65 Gissing, *The Odd Women*, pp. 19–22.

66 Gissing, *The Odd Women*, p. 29.

67 J. Brannigan, *New Historicism and Cultural Materialism*, London: St Martin's Press, 1998, p. 84.

68 J.L. Newton, '"History as Usual"? Feminism and the "New Historicism"', in H.A. Veeser (ed.), *The New Historicism*, New York: Routledge, 1989, pp. 165–6.

69 See Chapter 12.

70 See Chapter 13.

Bibliography

Armstrong, N., *Desire and Domestic Fiction: A Political History of the Novel*, New York: Oxford University Press, 1987.

Bennett, A., *Anna of the Five Towns*, first published 1902, London: Methuen, 1951.

Brannigan, J., *New Historicism and Cultural Materialism*, London: St Martin's Press, 1998.

Collins, W., *The Woman in White*, first published 1859, London: Collector's Library, 2006.

Copeland, E., *Women Writing about Money: Women's Fiction in England 1790–1820*, Cambridge: Cambridge University Press, 1995.

Delany, P., *Literature, Money and the Market: From Trollope to Amis*, Basingstoke: Palgrave, 2002.

Dolin, T., *Mistress of the House: Women of Property in the Victorian Novel*, Aldershot: Ashgate, 1997.

Erickson, A.L., 'Coverture and capitalism', *History Workshop Journal* 59 (1), 2005, pp. 1–16.

Finn, M., *The Character of Credit: Personal Debt in English Culture, 1740–1813*, Cambridge: Cambridge University Press, 2003.

Forster, E.M., *Howard's End*, first published 1910, London: Edward Arnold, 1973.

Fowler, W.W., *Twenty Years of Inside Life in Wall Street*, New York: Orange Judd Company, 1880.

Jeffrey, F.J., 'Anthony Trollope meets Pierre Bourdieu: the conversion of capital as plot in the mid-Victorian British novel', *Victorian Literature and Culture* 31 (2), 2003, pp. 501–21.

Freeman, Mark, Pearson, Robin and Taylor, James, '"A doe in the city": women shareholders in eighteenth- and early nineteenth-century Britain', *Accounting, Business and Financial History* 16 (2), 2006, pp. 265–92.

Gissing, G., *In the Year of Jubilee*, first published 1894, London: Lawrence and Bullen, 1895.

Gissing, G., *The Odd Women*, first published 1892, Oxford: Oxford University Press, 2000.

Henry, N., '"Ladies do it?": Victorian women investors in fact and fiction', in O'Gorman, F. (ed.) *Victorian Literature and Finance*, Oxford: Oxford University Press, 2007, pp. 111–32.

Henry, N., *George Eliot and the British Empire*, Cambridge: Cambridge University Press, 2002.

Johnson, S., *Dictionary*, first published 1755, London: Penguin Classics, 2005.

Koets, C.C., *Female Characters in the Works of Anthony Trollope*, Gouda: T. van Tilburg, 1932.

Laurence, P.M., *Law and Custom of Primogeniture*, Cambridge: J. Hall and Son, 1878.

Markwick, M., *Trollope and Women*, London: The Hambledon Press, 1997.

Michie, Elsie B., 'Buying brains: Trollope, Oliphant and vulgar Victorian commerce', *Victorian Studies* 44 (1), 2001, pp. 77–98.

Morris, R.J., *Men, Women and Property in England 1780–1870: A Social and Economic History of Family Strategies amongst the Leeds Middle Classes*, Cambridge: Cambridge University Press, 2005.

Mortimer, T., *The Nefarious Practice of Stockjobbing Unveiled*, London: J.M. Richardson, 1810.

Newton, J.L., 'History as usual? Feminism and the "New Historicism"', in Veeser, H.A. (ed.), *The New Historicism*, New York: Routledge, 1989, pp.152–67.

Nunokawa, J., *The Afterlife of Property: Domestic Security and the Victorian Novel*, Princeton, NJ: Princeton University Press, 1994.

O'Connor, M., 'Imagining risk, sensationalizing speculation: cultural history of the London Stock Exchange and financial speculation', paper presented at the Nicholson Center for British Studies Conference, 'Modernizing Politics?', University of Chicago, 21–22 May 2005.

O'Gorman, F., 'Introduction', in O'Gorman, F. (ed.), *Victorian Literature and Finance*, Oxford: Oxford University Press, 2007, pp. 1–16.

Poovey, M., 'Writing about finance in Victorian England: disclosure and secrecy in the culture of investment', *Victorian Studies* 45 (1), 2002, pp. 17–41.

Reed, J.R., 'A friend to Mammon: speculation in Victorian literature', *Victorian Studies* 27 (7), 1984, pp. 179–202.

Robb, G., 'Women and white-collar crime: debates on gender, fraud and the corporate economy in England and America, 1850–1930', *British Journal of Criminology* 46, 2006, pp. 1058–72.

Russell, N., *The Novelist and Mammon*, Oxford: Clarendon Press, 1986.

Rutterford, J. and Maltby, J., ' "Frank must marry money": men, women and property in Trollope's novels', *Accounting Historian's Journal* 33 (2), 2006, pp. 201–31.

Rutterford, J. and Maltby, J., ' "The widow, the clergyman and the reckless": women investors in England, 1830–1914', *Feminist Economics* 121 (1–2), 2006, pp. 111–38.

Searle, G.R., *Morality and the Market in Victorian Britain*, Oxford, Clarendon Press, 1998.

Shadwell, T., *Epsom Wells and the Volunteers: or the Stock Jobbers*, first published posthumously 1693, Boston: D.C. Heath & Co, 1930.

Sloan, J., review of Simon J. James, *Unsettled Accounts*, in *Nineteenth Century Literature* March 2005, pp. 547–50.

Smalley, D. (ed.), *Trollope: The Critical Heritage*, London: Routledge & Kegan Paul, 1969.

Thomas, D., 'Social origins of marriage partners in the British peerage in the eighteenth and nineteenth centuries', *Population Studies* 26 (1), 1972, pp. 99–111.

Trollope, A., *The American Senator*, first published 1876–7, Oxford: The World's Classics, 1986.

Trollope, A., *The Way We Live Now*, first published 1875, Oxford: Oxford University Press, 1982.

Trollope, A., *The Eustace Diamonds*, first published 1873, London: Penguin Books, 2004.

Trollope, A., *Framley Parsonage*, first published 1859–60, London: Penguin Books, 2004.

Trollope, A., *Doctor Thorne*, first published 1858, London: Penguin Books, 1991.

Trollope, A., *Barchester Towers*, first published 1857, London: Penguin Books, 1994.

Zola, E., *L'Argent*, first published 1891, Paris: Folio Classique, 1999.

12 Octavia Hill

Property manager and accountant[1]

Stephen P. Walker

Introduction

Octavia Hill (1838–1912) has been described as one the 'great social reformers' of the nineteenth century and 'a name of immense prestige in the world of philanthropy'.[2] Hill's innovative methods in housing management resulted in her being identified in 1887 as one of three women who had significantly influenced Victorian Britain.[3] She was 'the first housing reformer to reach the unskilled working classes',[4] a leading member of the open spaces movement and a co-founder of the National Trust.[5] Octavia Hill has been lauded as a heroine of the Victorian age who, released from the chains of domesticity, devoted herself to improving the lives of the poor and professionalized housing management.

Not all consider Hill's legacy in such glowing terms. Critics see her as 'a prime agent for the cultural imposition of bourgeois personal morality and middle-class family lifestyles upon the hapless London poor',[6] an autocrat who offered a localised and diversionary solution to mass overcrowding. Criticisms of Hill the disciplinarian also point to an attribute that is the focus here – she was reputedly 'one of the great organizing women of the nineteenth century'.[7] Hill's reference point for proper 'organisation' was the world of business. She held business in high esteem, adhered to commercial principles and considered that its practices were character building. Among the business skills Octavia Hill prized most was accounting. For Hill, accounting was not only a tool of financial management, it also facilitated control of her volunteer workers, and contributed to the governance and sympathetic understanding of her tenants. It is this aspect of her work that features in this chapter.

Octavia Hill's story points to the involvement of large numbers of philanthropic middle-class women in the performance of accounting and finance functions during the nineteenth century. Her case offers insights to the perceived limits of women's involvement in these activities as it took them into the public realm. Before exploring these issues and the ideals that underpinned Hill's calculative practices, it is important to establish why this eminent housing reformer came to place so much emphasis on accounting and business methods.

'Apprenticeship' in business and accounting

Octavia Hill was born in Wisbech, Cambridgeshire into a family with a strong social conscience. She was the eighth daughter and tenth child of James Hill (*c.*1800–71), merchant and banker, Owenite and campaigner for municipal reform. Her mother, Caroline Southwood Hill (1809–1902), was an educationalist.[8] Following James Hill's bankruptcy and subsequent nervous breakdown the family fractured. Caroline Hill and five of her daughters removed to Finchley. Here they were supported by friends and Dr Thomas Southwood Smith (1788–1861),[9] Caroline Hill's father. Southwood Smith was involved in social reform and his revelations on sanitary and housing conditions contributed to his grandchildren's awareness of the plight of the poor.

Financial difficulties required that the Hill girls seek employment. Octavia, aged 14, developed business and accounting skills as storekeeper and later as a manager for the 'Ladies Guild', a craft workshop where poor women were employed to make decorative glass and toy furniture.[10] In 1856 she also become part-time secretary to the women's classes at the Working Men's College, London, assuming responsibility for bookkeeping and teaching some classes in arithmetic.[11] Octavia also assumed responsibility for the domestic finances, being 'more and more regarded as the business man' of the family.[12] Prudent financial management ensured that she paid off her parent's creditors by 1861. In 1859 Hill referred to her 'life of calculation and routine and steadiness'.[13] This involved writing up the accounts on Saturdays and preparing balance sheets. She also tutored in bookkeeping and when, in 1862, the Hill sisters established a small school in Nottingham Street, London, she instilled the practice in pupils.[14]

Housing management

In the absence of state provision, the supply of housing for the Victorian working classes depended on speculative building, private investment and voluntary initiatives. These proved inadequate given rapid population growth and urbanisation. The problem of housing the poor was particularly acute in London.[15] Her grandfather's interest in accommodation schemes for the working classes together with her own observations of the living conditions of the poor directed Octavia Hill's philanthropic work towards housing.

Until their relationship fractured in 1877, Hill was deeply influenced by the author, art and social critic, John Ruskin. From 1855 she was employed by him as a copyist for his major work *Modern Painters*. In 1864 Ruskin inherited funds and a year later acquired the leases of three cottages in Paradise Place, Marylebone. Ruskin placed these houses, which were 'in a dreadful state of dirt and neglect', under Octavia Hill's management.[16] He advised that investors might be attracted to such schemes if a 5 per cent annual return could be secured.[17] In 1866 Ruskin acquired the freehold of five other houses for Hill to manage in Freshwater Place, Marylebone and in 1870 she also assumed the management of properties in Walmer Street which housed 200 poor families. Here she inaugurated an 'industrial experiment' by establishing a workroom for women and providing jobbing work for unemployed men.[18] When properties at Barrett's Court were entrusted to Hill in the early 1870s she also established a savings scheme and a working-men's club.[19] These projects reflected her strong preference for encouraging habits of industry, thrift and self-dependence among the poor.[20]

During the early 1870s Octavia Hill's work also extended to Lambeth and Whitechapel. At this time she managed 15 blocks, housing 2,000–3,000 tenants. By 1877 she boasted 'I have 3,500 tenants and £30,000 or £40,000 worth of money under my continuous charge'.[21] Two years later, she managed 20 groups of houses or 'courts', and in 1882 revealed that the value of the property under her charge had increased to £60,000.[22] From 1884 the scale of her operations was significantly increased when the Ecclesiastical Commissioners (who were responsible for the estates of the Church of England) entrusted her with the management of properties in London.

Octavia Hill's approach to accounting

On assuming the management of a 'court', Hill evicted defaulting and immoral tenants and made the property habitable. She insisted on 'extreme punctuality and diligence' in the payment of rent. Rental income was applied to the payment of rates and insurances and generating the required 5 per cent return to property owners. Any surplus was utilised for repairs and improvements to enhance the living environment of tenants.[23] Hill often suggested that, while there was never a shortage of capital to invest in properties under her management, expansion was constrained by a shortage of trained volunteer workers.[24] To alleviate this she also appropriated 5 per cent of the value of rents collected for the training of volunteer workers. One such volunteer, Augusta Maclagan, provided the following insight to the working of Hill's collection system:

> My work was to go out every Monday, directly after breakfast, armed with a bag, a book and an ink bottle slung round my neck and call on every tenant for the week's rent ... I had to go round again on Thursdays to look up any tenants who were out on Monday and pay my collection each week to the treasurer.[25]

As an increasing number of properties fell under her management, the scrutiny of books and preparation of accounts occupied more of Hill's time. In addition to the accounting involved in managing 'courts', she was also treasurer of organisations such as the Kyrle Society and the Southwark Cadet Corps. She later extended her accounting practices to the National Trust.[26]

Her correspondence reveals Hill's attention to accounting and treasuryship. In addition to frequent meetings to review accounts, she maintained constant communication with those at various sites on account-keeping and transactions processing. She was anxious that accounts be punctually and accurately written up in ink and was vigilant about periodic closing of the accounts and reconciling the books of local managers to her own central records. She was keen to ensure that cash flow was managed, transactions were properly authorised and vouched, regular audits performed, expenses incurred for legitimate purposes and appropriately allocated to operations. She was conscious that the timing of year-end transactions had an impact on the presentation of the annual accounts and that balances of unspent funds might affect future donations. She recognised the distinction between capital and revenue items but required assistance with some of the bookkeeping involved. On occasion she considered herself more prudent than the auditors.[27]

Octavia Hill's accounting practices had a number of ideological foundations. First, in accord with contemporary prescriptions,[28] she perceived regular accounting as pivotal to the achievement of order and method. The management of her properties was highly organised and the tasks performed by her volunteers were strictly defined. Procedures for the collection and accounting for rent were carefully codified. By 1879 she had arranged the printing of a supply of 'the various collecting books, rent books, order books and forms'. Attention to orderliness was also revealed by Hill's determination that the accounting system would not be disrupted by her absence through ill health, and ultimately her death.[29] Continuity in record-keeping was also to be applied by Hill's volunteers. One of them, Augusta Maclagan, recalled that 'Every worker, amateur or paid, was bound to leave her work and books in such a state that a stranger could pick up their threads with ease.'[30]

The second feature of Hill's accounting regimen was its foundation on hierarchical accountability and control. It has been observed that 'With neither "fellow workers" nor tenants could there be any doubt about who was in charge'.[31] Hill perceived that she was accountable to property owners and volunteer workers were strictly accountable to her. Given that properties were ultimately entrusted to her, Hill was adamant that 'the supervision of all and the passing of accounts rests with me'.[32] In the absence of a wage relation between Hill and most of her housing workers, the periodic presentation and scrutiny of accounts became an important instrument for reinforcing control. This was particularly the case as her capacity to maintain a personal, day-to-day involvement diminished with the expansion and spatial dispersal of housing work. Consequently the rent and tenants books of the various properties were periodically 'presented and carefully examined' at Hill's house in Marylebone Road.[33] During later years the periodic scrutiny of accounts became 'a formidable affair' for less competent volunteers.[34]

There was a decidedly militaristic tone to the manner in which Hill commanded her regiment of volunteers and held them accountable. They referred to her as 'General' and she referred to them as lieutenants or 'seconds in command'.[35] The General, of course, was in turn accountable to 'the great Commander of all things'.[36] Effective hierarchical control through accounting depended on competent bookkeeping by volunteers in the field. Hill provided formal training in the subject and expressed such disdain at deficient accounting that some volunteers withdrew their labour. Lewis relates:

In 1892, a Miss Pawl apparently broke down when put in charge of the accounts in Deptford and left suddenly … She [Hill] checked through all her workers' books with them, offering a running commentary which some, like Mary Clover, who became secretary of Girton College in 1903, found useful. Others must have found it devastating.[37]

Third, Octavia Hill's approach to accounting was conditioned by an aversion to indebtedness. The Victorians prescribed accounting as a preventative to insolvency, the consequences of which had been singularly illustrated to Hill by her father's bankruptcy. Caroline Hill noted that as household manager her daughter 'never incurred a debt, she never in her whole life borrowed a penny'.[38] Octavia her daughter associated the ill-management of money with 'a rottenness at the heart'.[39] These values were extended to her philanthropic work. Hill assured one of her donors that 'We never authorize expenditure till we have funds, I don't believe in the advisability of incurring debts'.[40] Neither did she favour the extension of credit to tenants.

Fourth, Octavia Hill was the embodiment of the notion, propagated in didactic literature, that women were uniquely suited to perform accounting functions involving the accurate processing, inscription and monitoring of myriad small transactions. Contemporaries observed her 'extraordinary mastery of detail' to the extent that she could lose sight of the bigger picture.[41] Hill assumed that if the detail was attended to, the wider success of her schemes was assured.[42] Meticulousness in accounting provided 'a power of perfection'.[43]

Relatedly, Octavia Hill pursued a vigorous assault on insufficiency of data, inaccuracy and error. In 1876 she wrote 'I … abhor and detest unbalanced uncompared books, and I feel wretched till these are absolutely proved to agree . .. or the mistakes hunted down'.[44] Conversely, she was thrilled when presented with accounts that were expertly kept.[45] Hill was censorious when volunteers failed to achieve the perfection in accounting she expected. She was most mortified on the rare occasions where she failed to live up to her own standards. In June 1888 she lost a cheque. She wrote:

> I am dreadfully ashamed of myself. I thought I had given the 5£ cheque to Miss Ironside ages ago. She says I did not, and she is most exact. That being so it must have got in with some papers some how with which it has no connection … I have not a notion where to look even … I never lost anything of the kind in my life and expect it to turn up some day in an apparently carefully sorted packet! I am so sorry to give both you and Mr Praed this trouble. (Emphasis in original.)[46]

A fifth dimension of Octavia Hill's approach to accounting was its foundation on notions of stewardship and trust. Contemporary accounting prescriptions emphasised that the presentation of accounts by an agent to a (male) principal was necessary to reveal the competent management of assets and nurture trust.[47] Hill actualised this notion through regular accounting to the proprietors of houses she managed and by external reporting to those who assigned charitable donations to her. She perceived accounting as a duty of 'faithful stewardship'.[48] Her comprehension of agency and stewardship was informed by Christian thinking. With her volunteers she assumed responsibility for the 'bits of God's earth, which He has entrusted to them'.[49] In relation to property owners she perceived herself as having a charge to keep.[50] From a more earthly perspective she also recognised that accounts were a useful vehicle for disclosing the progress of her work – how property was improved under her care.

Trust also defined her relation to the owners of the property she managed. It is worth noting that it was Hill who suggested the name National *Trust*.[51] She nurtured the trust of property owners and fulfilled her responsibilities as their steward by the quarterly or biannual submission of financial accounts and vouchers.[52] The obligation to account was emphasised by the undertaking to secure a 4–5 per cent return on investment and was essential in the many cases where the proprietor was a stranger to her.[53]

The most visible demonstration of Octavia Hill's determination to give accounts of her stewardship and reveal how she had 'fulfilled the trust' of those who committed funds to her management was the (almost) annual production of *Letters to My Fellow-Workers*. These narrative reports on progress in housing management and other aspects of Hill's work were printed and distributed privately from 1872 to 1911. While property owners received regular financial accounts, the increasing numbers who donated funds for Hill's personal disposal among the poor could scrutinise the 'balance sheets' contained in the *Letters*. She likened her increasingly dispersed supporters to 'a large company united in a common work'.[54] As the head of this 'company' Hill distributed an annual report (her *Letters*) to those who provided the resources to conduct her philanthropic activity.

A sixth characteristic of Hill's accounting was an emphasis on knowledge gathering and discipline. In accordance with her individualised approach, Hill assumed that betterment could only be achieved by focused, small-scale housing schemes where the predicaments of each family were understood and addressed. Tenants were to be 'governed' and 'ruled' in order to lift them out of poverty and pauperism.[55] To achieve this, one had to *know* the character and habits of each of them. She therefore amassed comprehensive knowledge of the 'whole circumstances' of each case.[56] It was through 'accurate and abundant knowledge' and 'continuous watchfulness' that discoveries were made as to how to assist the poor.[57] This surveillant approach was actualised through the weekly collection and recording of rent and the compilation of folio volumes in which detailed information about tenants was recorded – their number, occupation, income and a monthly history.[58] Observations and inscriptions were the basis for deciding whether the appropriate response in each case was assertive discipline or sympathetic assistance. Moreover, Hill perceived the process of monitoring rentals and information gathering as enabling because it encouraged tenants to adopt habits of regularity, economy and independence.[59]

Accounting and gendered spheres

The activities of women such as Octavia Hill in voluntary work and social reform seemingly contradicted the notion of separate spheres. Hill's performance of accounting functions and attitudes towards finance help chart the limits of her apparent departure from the private domain. Although housing management projected Hill into the public arena, her practices represent an extension of domesticity and were constrained by recognition of the limits of female influence.[60]

Hill was influenced by the concept of gendered spheres as articulated by her mentor, Ruskin. She was one of the few women who appear to have 'actually lived up' to his 'chivalric fantasies'.[61] Ruskin accepted that while women's attributes of order and caring were most obviously applicable in the home, they should also be utilised beyond it to benefit the wider community and enhance national virtue. In this way women could be elevated from mere housewives to 'queens'.[62] Indeed, Hill referred to her volunteers as *'queens* as well as *friends'*,[63] and perceived that 'national life is but an extension of family life'.[64] As her foray beyond the domestic illustrated, gendered spheres were informed, but not exclusively defined, by the public and private worlds. Hill considered that there were boundaries within the public sphere beyond which women should not venture. For example, she objected to female suffrage on the grounds that men and women have 'different gifts and different spheres' and engagement in politics would divert women from the public 'out-of-sight, silent work' of caring that emanated from the performance of homely functions.[65]

Likewise, Octavia Hill accepted a gendered division of labour in the performance of accounting functions. She considered that the veiled routine of detailed bookkeeping and accounting, particularly as it related to the home and housing, was suited to women. Finance and the performance of higher accounting functions involving deliberation and judgement, such as audit, she perceived as men's work. When she required advice on accounting, as opposed to assistance in account-keeping, Hill turned to a man.[66] One such advisor was Sydney Cockerell, a friend who worked in the City. Cockerell reviewed her accounts, and advised on accounting issues and the preparation of financial statements.[67] Together with William Shaen, her solicitor, Cockerell also advised Hill on personal investments. In May 1876 she sought their opinion on whether to sell or retain £700 of Russian Bonds. She confessed her uninformed approach to such matters, anxiety about speculation and disdain for 'meddling with things of which I know nothing'. She referred to her preference:

> to have money in things (like this house) which I control, know about, and can calculate about myself, or in other good things managed by capable people I know: or else to take the best advice I can get, obey it literally, and with a quiet mind let things take their course.[68]

Although she lauded the merits of bookkeeping to her female volunteers, Hill perceived limits to their capacity as accountants. When overwork and mental strain prompted a withdrawal from housing management in 1878, Hill arranged the audit and supervision of accounts by 'several gentlemen' who reported directly to the owners of property. She explained: 'The auditors are gentlemen accustomed to business, and the management of money. They do easily accounts which many ladies find difficult, they see clearly the safe and wise thing to do about money.'[69] Thenceforth the accounts of donations entrusted to her personal care were audited by Hill's male rather than female associates.

Thus Octavia Hill's work was essentially rooted in the 'familial and domestic'.[70] In her *Letter to My Fellow-Workers* of 1881 she stated that housing management was women's work: 'Ladies must do it, for it is detailed work; ladies must do it, for it is household work; it needs moreover, persistent patience, gentleness, hope.'[71] Hill's assumption about the gendered nature of work was illustrated in her correspondence and speeches. In October 1896 she specifically sought a 'gentleman' for the position of part-time Secretary to the National Trust. Among the traits displayed by the ideal applicant were 'accurate habits of business'.[72] In response to a suggestion that the position might be filled by a woman, Hill retorted that she had never considered that prospect. She added: 'Personally I should not be in favour of the appointment of a lady ... there is a good deal of the work which would be far better done by a man.'[73] In 1907 she advised that a 'nice motherly woman of the right character, encouraged by the owner, and backed up by a husband in good work' was a better caretaker of houses than a man because 'She deals much best with the cleaning of stairs, shewing rooms, and all the numerous household matters on which good management depends'.[74]

Conclusions

A number of studies have begun to render visible the existence of large numbers of women in nineteenth-century Britain who performed a variety of accounting functions. While women were excluded from the new profession of accountant, they were engaged in accounting as clerks, household managers, managers of businesses and as bookkeepers, especially in retailing and distribution.[75] The case of Octavia Hill indicates another hitherto-shrouded field of accounting activity performed by women – philanthropy. One authority in 1893 estimated that half a million women were substantially engaged in voluntary endeavour.[76] While men dominated the governance of most charitable organisations in Victorian Britain, women made a considerable behind-the-scenes contribution, particularly in the detailed work of day-to-day visiting, money raising and collecting. Women were also involved in financial management and accounting as treasurers or secretaries of charities and their committees.[77]

Women's engagement in accounting-related voluntary work benefited the poor through direct involvement and the impact of individuals such as Sarah Martin and Beatrice Webb (née Potter) on social policy.[78] It also contributed to the advancement of women themselves. Although rooted in contemporary domesticity, visiting the poor 'gave women a taste of power outside their own homes'.[79] For Prochaska, philanthropy was 'the leisured woman's most obvious outlet for self-expression'.[80] Women's demonstration of competence in philanthropic work was also important to their later entry to paid work in the caring professions,[81] particularly housing management where accounting featured as a significant skill.[82]

Experience in accounting gained through philanthropic work also appears to have been valuable to the women's movement. Margaret W. Nevinson (1858–1932), a leading member of the Women's Freedom League and Treasurer of the Women Writers' Suffrage League (1908), had been a volunteer rent collector in Whitechapel. Unfamiliar with accounting, she struggled to reconcile physical cash with the rent books. However, she recalled that:

> in a few months I became an expert, and learnt to count money and add up columns with the rapidity of a bank clerk. This accomplishment has been of the greatest use to me since, especially when the Suffrage movement made great demands upon women to act as treasurers used to handling large sums of money and keeping accounts.[83]

Notes

1 An extended version of this chapter can be found in S.P. Walker, 'Philanthropic women and accounting. Octavia Hill and the exercise of "quiet power and sympathy"', *Accounting, Business and Financial History* 16 (2), 2006, pp. 163–94.

2 J. Perkin, *Victorian Women*, London: John Murray, 1993, p. 216; D. Owen, *English Philanthropy 1660–1960*, Cambridge, MA: Harvard University Press, 1964, p. 387.

3 G. Darley, *Octavia Hill*, London: Constable, 1990, p. 256; N. Boyd, *Three Victorian Women who Changed their World. Josephine Butler, Octavia Hill, Florence Nightingale*, Oxford: Oxford University Press, 1982.

4 A.S. Wohl, 'Octavia Hill and the homes of the London poor', *The Journal of British Studies* 10 (2), 1971, 105–31.

5 E. Moberly Bell, *Octavia Hill. A Biography*, London: Constable & Co. Ltd, 1942, pp. 220–39.

6 J. Harris, 'Victorian values and the founders of the welfare state', *Proceedings of the British Academy* 78, 1992, pp. 165–82; P. Malpass, 'Octavia Hill, 1838–1912', in P. Barker (ed.), *Founders of the Welfare State*, London: Heinemann, 1984, pp. 31–6.

7 G.F.A. Best, *Temporal Pillars*, Cambridge: Cambridge University Press, 1964, p. 288.

8 K. Gleadle, 'Hill, Caroline Southwood (1809–1902)', *Oxford Dictionary of National Biography*, Oxford University Press, available online: www.oxforddnb.com/view/article/60328 (accessed 23 November 2004).

9 R.K. Webb, 'Smith, (Thomas) Southwood (1788–1861)', *Oxford Dictionary of National Biography*, Oxford University Press, available online: www.oxforddnb.com/view/article/25917 (accessed 23 November 2004).

10 Moberly Bell, *Octavia Hill*, p. 25.

11 Darley, *Octavia Hill*, pp. 54–7.

12 Moberly Bell, *Octavia Hill*, p. 43.

13 C.E. Maurice (ed.), *Life of Octavia Hill as Told in her Letters*, London: Macmillan and Co, 1913, p. 131.

14 Moberly Bell, *Octavia Hill*, p. 68.

15 J. Burnett, *A Social History of Housing*, London: Routledge, 1986, pp. 54–96, 140–87.

16 O. Hill, *Homes of the London Poor*, London: Macmillan and Co, 1883, p. 18.

17 Moberly Bell, *Octavia Hill*, pp. 72–7; J.N. Tarn, *Five Per Cent Philanthropy: An Account of Housing in Urban Areas Between 1840 and 1914*, Cambridge: Cambridge University Press, 1973.

18 O. Hill, 'Miss Hills report of the Walmer Street District', in Rev. W.H. Fremantle, *Pastoral Address and Report of the Charities for the Year 1870*, London: privately printed, 1870, pp. 29–38; O. Hill, *Further Account of the Walmer Street Industrial Experiment*, London: George Pulman, 1872.

19 Moberly Bell, *Octavia Hill*, pp. 132–40.

20 Hill, 'Miss Hills report', pp. 29–38; O. Hill, 'A few words to fresh workers', *Nineteenth Century* 26 (CLI), 1889, pp. 452–61.

21 Maurice, *Life of Octavia Hill ... in her Letters*, p. 348.

22 Report from the Select Committee on Artizans' and Labourers' Dwellings, *British Parliamentary Papers*, VII, 1882, 235, p. 171.

23 Darley, *Octavia Hill*, pp. 100–6.

24 O. Hill, *Letter to My Fellow-Workers, to which is Added Account of Donations Received for Work amongst the Poor*, London: privately printed, 1897, p. 5.

25 *Memorials of Augusta Maclagan, 1836–1915*, Vol. II. Unpublished manuscript in the care of Ianthe Maclagan (ianthe.maclagan@ntlworld.com), pp. 340–2.

26 Darley, *Octavia Hill*, p. 304.

27 DMisc 84/1 Letters from Octavia Hill to Miss Schuster, City of Westminster Archives Centre, 10 St Ann's Street, London; DMisc 84/2 Letters from Octavia Hill to Sir Sydney C. Cockerell, 1887–1912, City of Westminster Archives Centre, 10 St Ann's Street, London; DMisc 84/3 Letters from Octavia Hill to Sydney J. Cockerell, 1871–1912, City of Westminster Archives Centre, 10 St Ann's Street, London.

28 S.P. Walker, 'How to secure your husband's esteem. Accounting and private patriarchy in the British middle class household during the nineteenth century', *Accounting, Organisations and Society* 23 (5–6), 1998, pp. 485–514.

29 Maurice, *Life of Octavia Hill ... in her Letters*, p. 580.

30 *Memorials of Augusta Maclagan, 1836–1915*, Vol. II, p. 342.

31 D. Owen, *English Philanthropy 1660–1960*, p. 389.

32 O. Hill, *Letter Accompanying the Account of Donations Received for Work Amongst the Poor*, London: privately printed, 1874, p. 4.

33 Darley, *Octavia Hill*, p. 135.

34 Moberly Bell, *Octavia Hill*, pp. 267–8.

35 Hill, *Letter Accompanying the Account of Donations*, 1874, p. 12; E. Southwood Ouvry, *Extracts From Octavia Hill's 'Letters to Fellow-Workers' 1864–1911*, London: Adelphi Book Shop, 1933, p. 47.

36 Hill, *Letter Accompanying the Account of Donations*, 1877, p. 10.

37 J. Lewis, *Women and Social Action in Victorian and Edwardian England*, London: Edward Elgar, 1991, p. 65.

38 Darley, *Octavia Hill*, p. 59.

39 DMisc 84/2, item 94.

40 DMisc 84/1, item 2.

41 Maurice, *Life of Octavia Hill ... in her Letters*, p. 314.

42 R.H. Bremner, '"An iron scepter twined with roses": the Octavia Hill system of housing management', *Social Service Review* 39 (2), 1965, pp. 222–31.

43 Royal Commission on the Housing of the Working Classes, Vol. II, Minutes of Evidence, *British Parliamentary Papers*, XXX, 1884–5, 4402, p. 297.

44 DMisc 84/3, items 27, 28.

45 Maurice, *Life of Octavia Hill ... in her Letters*, pp. 233, 240.

46 DMisc 84/2, items 52, 55, 159.

47 Walker, 'How to secure your husband's esteem', pp. 485–514.

48 O. Hill, *Letter to My Fellow-Workers, to which is added Account of Donations Received for Work Amongst the Poor*, London: privately printed, 1893, p. 3.

49 Hill, *Letter Accompanying the Account of Donations*, 1874, p. 11.

50 O. Hill, *Letter to My Fellow-Workers, to which is added Account of Donations Received for Work amongst the Poor*, London: privately printed, 1878, p. 5.

51 J. Jenkins, 'The roots of the National Trust', *History Today* 45 (1), 1995, pp. 3–9.

52 O. Hill, *Letter Accompanying the Account of Donations*, 1872, p. 1.

53 Royal Commission on the Housing of the Working Classes, Vol. II, Minutes of Evidence, p. 307.

54 O. Hill, *Letter Accompanying the Account of Donations*, 1873, p. 9.

55 Hill, 'Miss Hills report', pp. 29–38.

56 O. Hill, *Letter Accompanying the Account of Donations*, 1876, p. 4; A.S. Wohl, 'Octavia Hill and the homes of the London poor', pp. 105–31.

57 Hill, *Letter Accompanying the Account of Donations*, 1874, p. 10.

58 *Memorials of Augusta Maclagan, 1836–1915*, Vol. II, p. 342.

59 O. Hill, *Homes of the London Poor*, London: Macmillan and Co, 1883, p. 16.

60 J. Lewis, *Women and Social Action*, pp. 31–3, 70; A. Summers, 'A home from home – women's philanthropic work in the nineteenth century', in S. Burman (ed.), *Fit Work for Women*, London: Croom Helm, 1979, pp. 33–63.

61 A. Vickery, 'Golden age to separate spheres? A review of the categories and chronology of English women's history', *Historical Journal* 36 (2), 1993, pp. 383–414.

62 J. Ruskin, *Sesame and Lilies*, first published 1865, London: Dent, 1970, pp. 71–3.

63 O. Hill, *Letter Accompanying the Account of Donations*, 1874, p. 10, emphasis in original.

64 E.S. Maurice (ed.), *Octavia Hill. Early Ideals*, London: George Allen & Unwin Ltd, 1928, pp. 225–6.

65 *Times*, 15 July 1910, p. 9.

66 Darley, *Octavia Hill*, pp. 124–5.

67 Moberly Bell, *Octavia Hill*, pp. 131–2.

68 DMisc 84/3, items 24, 32.

69 Hill, *Letter to My Fellow-Workers*, 1878, pp. 4–5.

70 Lewis, *Women and Social Action*, p. 25.

71 Ouvry, *Extracts From Octavia Hill's 'Letters to Fellow-Workers'*, p. 23.

72 DMisc 84/2, item 208.

73 DMisc 84/2, items 209, 250, 253.

74 DMisc 84/1, item 11.

75 L. Davidoff and C. Hall, 'The hidden investment: women and enterprise', in P. Sharpe (ed.), *Women's Work. The English Experience 1650–1914*, London: Arnold, 1998, pp. 239–93; L.M. Kirkham and A. Loft, 'Gender and the construction of the professional accountant', *Accounting, Organisations and Society* 18 (6), 1993, pp. 507–58; Walker, 'How to secure your husband's esteem', pp. 485–514; S.P. Walker, 'Identifying the woman behind the "railed-in desk". The proto-feminisation of bookkeeping in Britain', *Accounting, Auditing and Accountability Journal* 16 (4), 2003, pp. 606–39.

76 F.K. Prochaska, *Women and Philanthropy in Nineteenth-Century England*, Oxford: Clarendon Press, 1980, p. 224.

77 Prochaska, *Women and Philanthropy*, pp. 30–2, 44–72, 103–6.

78 G. Mogridge, *Sarah Martin, The Prison Visitor of Great Yarmouth*, London: Religious Tract Society, 1872, pp. 140–1; B. Webb, *My Apprenticeship*, London: Longmans Green and Co, 1926, pp. 230–1.

79 A. Summers, 'A home from home', pp. 33–63.

80 Prochaska, *Women and Philanthropy*, p. 5.

81 Prochaska, *Women and Philanthropy*, p. 222.

82 O. Hill, *Management of Homes for the London Poor*, London: Charity Organisation

Society, 1899, pp. 4–5; M. Brion, *Women in the Housing Service*, London: Routledge, 1995, pp. 23–42, 69–71; J.M. Upcott, *Women House Property Managers*, London: Association of Women House Property Managers, 1925, p. 36.
83 M.W. Nevinson, *Life's Fitful Fever. A Volume of Memories*, London: A. & C. Black, 1926, pp. 87–90.

Bibliography

Bell, E. Moberly, *Octavia Hill: A Biography*, London: Constable & Co. Ltd, 1942.

Best, G.F.A., *Temporal Pillars*, Cambridge: Cambridge University Press, 1964.

Boyd, N., *Three Victorian Women who Changed their World: Josephine Butler, Octavia Hill, Florence Nightingale*, Oxford: Oxford University Press, 1982.

Bremner, R.H., '"An iron scepter twined with roses": the Octavia Hill system of housing management', *Social Service Review* 39 (2), 1965, pp. 222–31.

Brion, M., *Women in the Housing Service*, London: Routledge, 1995.

Burnett, J., *A Social History of Housing*, London: Routledge, 1986.

Darley, G., *Octavia Hill*, London: Constable, 1990.

Davidoff, L. and Hall, C., 'The hidden investment: women and enterprise', in Sharpe, P. (ed.), *Women's Work. The English Experience 1650–1914*, London: Arnold, 1998, pp. 239–93.

DMisc 84/1 Letters from Octavia Hill to Miss Schuster, City of Westminster Archives Centre, 10 St Ann's Street, London.

DMisc 84/2 Letters from Octavia Hill to Sir Sydney C. Cockerell, 1887–1912, City of Westminster Archives Centre, 10 St Ann's Street, London.

DMisc 84/3 Letters from Octavia Hill to Sydney J. Cockerell, 1871–1912, City of Westminster Archives Centre, 10 St Ann's Street, London.

Gleadle, K., 'Hill, Caroline Southwood (1809–1902)', *Oxford Dictionary of National Biography*, Oxford University Press, available online: www.oxforddnb.com/view/article/60328 (accessed 23 November 2004).

Harris, J., 'Victorian values and the founders of the welfare state', *Proceedings of the British Academy* 78, 1992, pp. 165–82.

Hill, O., 'A few words to fresh workers', *Nineteenth Century* 26 (CLI), 1889, pp. 452–61.

Hill, O., 'Miss Hills report of the Walmer Street District', in Fremantle, Rev. W.H., *Pastoral Address and Report of the Charities for the Year 1870*, London: privately printed, 1870, pp. 29–38.

Hill, O., *Further Account of the Walmer Street Industrial Experiment*, London: George Pulman, 1872.

Hill, O., *Homes of the London Poor*, London: Macmillan and Co, 1883.

Hill, O., *Letter Accompanying the Account of Donations Received for Work amongst the Poor*, London: privately printed, 1872–7.

Hill, O., *Letter to My Fellow-Workers, to which is Added Account of Donations Received for Work amongst the Poor*, London: privately printed, 1878–1910.

Hill, O., *Management of Homes for the London Poor*, London: Charity Organisation Society, 1899.

Jenkins, J., 'The roots of the National Trust', *History Today* 45 (1), 1995, pp. 3–9.

Kirkham, L.M. and Loft, A., 'Gender and the construction of the professional accountant', *Accounting, Organisations and Society* 18 (6), 1993, pp. 507–58.

Lewis, J., *Women and Social Action in Victorian and Edwardian England*, London: Edward Elgar, 1991.

Malpass, P., 'Octavia Hill, 1838–1912', in Barker, P. (ed.), *Founders of the Welfare State*, London: Heinemann, 1984, pp. 31–6.

Maurice, C.E. (ed.), *Life of Octavia Hill as Told in her Letters*, London: Macmillan and Co, 1913.

Maurice, E.S. (ed.), *Octavia Hill. Early Ideals*, London: George Allen & Unwin Ltd, 1928.

Memorials of Augusta Maclagan, 1836–1915, Vol. II. Unpublished manuscript in the care of Ianthe Maclagan (ianthe.maclagan@ntlworld.com).

Mogridge, G., *Sarah Martin, The Prison Visitor of Great Yarmouth*, London: Religious Tract Society, 1872.

Nevinson, M.W., *Life's Fitful Fever. A Volume of Memories*, London: A. & C. Black, 1926.

Ouvry, E. Southwood, *Extracts From Octavia Hill's 'Letters to Fellow-Workers' 1864–1911*, London: Adelphi Book Shop, 1933.

Owen, D., *English Philanthropy 1660–1960*, Cambridge, MA: Harvard University Press, 1964.

Perkin, J., *Victorian Women*, London: John Murray, 1993.

Prochaska, F.K., *Women and Philanthropy in Nineteenth-Century England*, Oxford: Clarendon Press, 1980.

Report from the Select Committee on Artizans' and Labourers' Dwellings, *British Parliamentary Papers*, VII, 1882, 235.

Royal Commission on the Housing of the Working Classes, Vol. II, Minutes of Evidence, *British Parliamentary Papers*, XXX, 1884–5, 4402.

Ruskin, J., *Sesame and Lilies*, first published 1865, London: Dent, 1970.

Summers, A., 'A home from home – women's philanthropic work in the nineteenth century', in Burman, S. (ed.), *Fit Work for Women*, London: Croom Helm, 1979, pp. 33–63.

Tarn, J.N., *Five Per Cent Philanthropy: An Account of Housing in Urban Areas Between 1840 and 1914*, Cambridge: Cambridge University Press, 1973.

Upcott, J.M., *Women House Property Managers*, London: Association of Women House Property Managers, 1925.

Vickery, A., 'Golden age to separate spheres? A review of the categories and chronology of English women's history', *Historical Journal* 36 (2), 1993, pp. 383–414.

Walker, S.P., 'How to secure your husband's esteem. Accounting and private patriarchy in the British middle class household during the nineteenth century', *Accounting, Organisations and Society* 23 (5–6), 1998, pp. 485–514.

Walker, S.P., 'Identifying the woman behind the "railed-in desk": the proto-feminisation of bookkeeping in Britain', *Accounting, Auditing and Accountability Journal* 16 (4), 2003, pp. 606–39.

Walker, S.P., 'Philanthropic women and accounting. Octavia Hill and the exercise of "quiet power and sympathy"', *Accounting, Business and Financial History* 16 (2), 2006, pp. 163–94.

Webb, B., *My Apprenticeship*, London: Longmans Green and Co, 1926.

Webb, R.K. 'Smith, (Thomas) Southwood (1788–1861)', *Oxford Dictionary of National Biography*, Oxford University Press, available online: www.oxforddnb.com/view/article/25917 (accessed 23 November 2004).

Wohl, A.S., 'Octavia Hill and the homes of the London poor', *Journal of British Studies* 10 (2), 1971, pp. 105–31.

13 Female investors within the Scottish investment trust movement in the 1870s[1]

Claire Swan

Introduction

Recent research into the financial position of women in England points to the lack of research into the economic position of women in Scotland in the late nineteenth century.[2] Richard Rodger acknowledges the presence of women as mortgage lenders in Edinburgh and Claire Swan notes the appearance of female investors in Dundee, yet both fail to develop the importance of Scottish women as financiers.[3] However, Eleanor Gordon and Gwyneth Nair have recently attempted to analyse one section of Scottish finance in which women have played a significant role. They have discovered that some females in Glasgow held a significant degree of wealth and power. Their study demonstrates how these women infiltrated the typical male 'sphere' and were significant property owners, householders, businesswomen and, latterly, investors.[4] Their study is a pioneering investigation into the economic lives of Scottish females and calls for further studies into this area of British social and economic history.

This chapter outlines the preliminary results of a wider, but as yet incomplete, study of female investors in Scotland.[5] It considers female investment in three Dundee investment trust companies at their reconstruction in 1879 as examples of the overall trend of female participation in the Scottish investment trust movement. Using the sample of three investment trusts, I examine the numbers of female investors, the size of their investments in relation to men, and their marital status. I conclude that by 1880 there were some independent female investors, but that these were not necessarily single women. The property laws in Scotland allowed wives and widows to invest in their own names and I find that they played a significant role as investors in investment trusts. This challenges previous publications that suggest that wives had a more passive role when it came to finance.[6] This chapter also draws upon recent academic work to determine if Scottish practices were different from those in England and Wales.

Scottish investment trusts

By the 1870s, Dundee was known as the centre for handling Scottish investment.[7] At the time, Dundee was an industrial town and flourishing international port. It also had a developing financial sector, but the contribution of this activity to Dundee's economy was subtle and is a little-discussed aspect of the town's history. The First Scottish American Investment Trust (FSAIT) was created by Robert Fleming in Dundee in 1873 and was 'the first Association in Scotland for investment in American railroad bonds, carefully selected and widely distributed and where the investments would not exceed one tenth of the capital in any one security.'[8] John Guild, one of the four chairmen, reported 'while in this country you could not lend money on first-class railway debentures at over four or four and a half per cent, in America you could get seven per cent with the best security of this description.'[9] This additional yield made the United States an attractive destination for Scottish funds.

Robert Fleming, the founder of one of the most influential London banks, was known as the 'father of Scottish investment trusts'.[10] He was born in Dundee in 1845 and trained as a clerk during the period of the town's booming jute and linen industry. He was introduced to overseas investment, and in particular the American stock market, by his influential merchant employers and before long was directing their finances to return lucrative profits. His particular expertise lay in American railroad and mortgage finance which he used to create the FSAIT.[11] Following the success of this Trust, Fleming went on to establish the Second Scottish American Investment Trust (SSAIT) in 1874 and the Third Scottish American Investment Trust (TSAIT) in 1875. It is these three Trusts that make up the base of this sample.

The FSAIT issued 3,000 certificates, of which 2,960 were promptly and fully subscribed in 1873 by 494 investors. This gave the four Trustees £296,000 to invest. Similarly, the SSAIT and the TSAIT each acquired a full capital subscription of £400,000, each made up of 4,000 certificates of £100. These funds were principally invested in railroads across the Northern and Western states of America, but also in canal and coal and iron companies, and State and city bonds. The investments were carefully chosen to take advantage of favourable yields on mortgages and rate of exchange.[12]

The primary advantage of an investment trust is that it is an attractive method of diversification of funds, minimising risk by spreading investments across different types of security. For instance, a shareholder in the FSAIT with a single £100 certificate had an interest in 30 different carefully selected bonds. Not more than £7 of this capital was placed in one security, and on average not more than £3 per £100 certificate was placed in any one investment.[13] Each £100 certificate holder was entitled to one vote at business meetings or by proxy. However, although votes were extended to female investors, the votes of children and married women had to be conducted by their representatives, in other words, their guardian or husband.[14]

A second advantage of investing in an investment trust was that it provided a professionally managed financial service accessible to investors with varied financial experience and amount of funds.[15] In addition, the expertise of fund managers could be drawn upon to buy and sell securities at appropriate times for maximum financial profit.[16] Certificate holders were promised a fixed interest rate. For example, the holders of Certificates in the FSAIT were promised at least 6 per cent per annum, paid half-yearly on 1 May and 1 November each year.[17] The first Coupon of £3 per FSAIT Certificate was to be paid on 1 November 1873.[18] Once this had been paid, and all expenses cleared, the surplus profits were to be placed into a reserve fund. The reserve fund was to be used to guarantee the rate of interest, particularly in years of low, or no profit.[19] The original Trusts were only to last ten years, after which investors were to expect a full repayment of capital with the profits divided pro rata among existing Certificate holders.[20]

The FSAIT was modelled on the London-based Foreign and Colonial Investment Trust, established in 1868; however, the FSAIT and subsequent Scottish investment trusts differed from the English investment trusts in several ways. First, Scottish investment trusts did not publish lists of their investments since directors believed that they were too complex, both geographically and financially, as well as frequently changing. In fact, the directors of Scottish trusts were against publishing their investments in case they were accused of political or geographical bias and also so as not to dissuade private investors from separately buying or selling securities that were held by the trusts.[21]

A second difference was that, unlike the English trusts, Scottish trust accounts disclosed the reserve figures. Finally, and most significantly, the Scottish trusts differed from English trusts by issuing short-term (terminable) debentures, and they accepted temporary loans or deposits. For instance, they could offer terminable debentures for periods of four to 16 years.[22] Short-term debentures appealed particularly to those investors in charge of trust funds; common for women and children. They were popular for several reasons: first, they were low risk and the reserve fund guaranteed a fixed rate of interest every year. Second, the rate of interest paid was consistently higher than bank deposit rates, although below the average debenture stock rate.[23] Third, the Scottish trusts were attractive to people with limited funds available for a short period of time; say, for a child whose funds could be invested then released when they turned 21 years of age, or for a woman to be invested by her guardian until the time that she was expected to marry. Lastly, Scottish trusts did not have an administration charge, applicable under English law, for purchasing or realising the stock.[24]

Under the Joint Stock Company Act of 1879, any association operating with more than 20 members for the purpose of financial gain was made illegal.[25] This meant that the three Dundee investment trusts were required to become joint-stock companies where the shareholders had limited liability for the debts of the business. The directors strived for minimum inconvenience during reconstruction and, to this effect, each trust certificate was directly converted into one ordinary share. Every certificate-holder was thus allocated an equivalent number of shares.[26] Each Trust was reincorporated as a limited company, retained a full capital subscription and kept detailed share registers for each subsequent year thereafter. Each company had a par value of £100 per share. In 2006, using the retail price index, this was equivalent to nearly £7,000.[27] The share price and dividends of the three companies at the end of the first year after reconstruction in April 1880 are detailed in Table 13.1.

The Trustees used the reconstruction as a marketing opportunity. The legality of the new companies was emphasised; the share certificates were to be

Table 13.1 Investment trust company shares: prices and dividends for 30 April 1880 (unless otherwise stated)

ITC*	Year incorporated	Year reconstructed	Year assessed	Nominal share value £	Share type	Authorised capital £	Capital paid up (£)	Dividend (%)	No. of securities listed	Market value of investments (£)	Market value of £100 shares £ s d	Reserve fund (£)	Accumulated reserve fund to date (£)
FSAIT	1873	1879	April 1879–April 1880	100	Ord	300,000	296,700	7.5	50	425,287	143.6.9	3,895	26,093
SSAIT	1874	1879	April 1879–April 1880	100	Ord	400,000	400,000	8	60	588,715	147.3.6	2,711	37,289
TSAIT	1875	1879	April 1879–April 1880	100	Ord	400,000	400,000	7	62	554,732	138.13.8	4,479	16,714

Sources: DCA, GD/EEM/SA/1/1, First Scottish American Investment Trust Company, Limited, *Balance Sheet*, 11 May 1880; DCA, GD/EFM/SA/2/1, Second Scottish American Investment Trust Company, Limited, *Balance Sheet*, 1 May 1880; DCA, GD/EFM/SA/3/1, Third Scottish American Investment Trust Company, Limited, *Balance Sheet*, 1 July 1880.

Note
* Investment Trust Company.

registered; and the companies were to be established on a permanent, rather than a terminable, basis. The fixed rate of interest on the certificates was replaced by a dividend on the shares, and, given the trusts' previous high profits, it was expected that future annual dividends would be higher than the interest rate previously paid on the certificates.[28] One marked difference from the previous structure was that terminable debentures and deposits were to be discontinued, with these also being converted into shares.

Data and methodology

The Joint Stock Companies Act of 1879 made it law that all companies keep up-to-date registers of all financial transactions. The share registers of the three trust companies after reconstruction provide comprehensive lists of shareholders' names, addresses, marital status and, where relevant, occupation. To be able to collect consistent information of marital status is highly valuable since it was at the company's discretion whether or not they recorded this information. For example, in the later share registers of the Prudential Assurance Company, the only indication of the marital status of women was the title Miss or Mrs.[29] This, of course, does not allow for a distinction between married women and widows. In these Scottish registers, on the other hand, not only does the clerk clearly mark 'widow', but occasionally will supplement this with the widow's maiden name and full name of her late husband. This is important for understanding the nature of her shareholding. Wives, on the other hand, were clearly noted as such in the shareholding registers; they were always recorded with their maiden and married names alongside the name of their husband.[30]

The registers exist as a ledger of all share transactions, including the date shares were acquired, the number held and, if relevant, the date disposed of. In addition, some shareholder entries include notes on to whom dividends were paid and to whom the shares were transferred or bequeathed at death. These registers were regularly updated and exist as an accurate guide to the movement and retention of shares held within each company.

This study looks at the share registers of these three investment trust companies – FSAIT, SSAIT and TSAIT – from their reconstruction date in April 1879 for the period of one year.[31] No records of shareholders survive before this date of incorporation, although the registers for the three companies survive until the late 1960s.

Data have been collected for each female investor registered as a shareholder within the year from April 1879 to April 1880. Collectively, this has created a database of 598 female shareholder portfolios.[32] There are, however, limitations to this all-female database. Whereas significant conclusions can be drawn from women's holdings alone, relating to the types of women who invested, the size of their holdings and their role within Scottish foreign investment, for certain comparisons figures for men were required. In these cases, the numbers of male shareholders and the total of their holdings have been manually counted and used for some statistical analysis (see Table 13.2).

Table 13.2 Male and female investors and their shares in number and as a percentage, 1879–80*

ITC	Total no. of shares allocated	No. held by men	% held by men	No. held by women	% held by women	No. male investors	% of investors	No. female investors	% of investors
FSAIT	2,960	2,002	67.6	958	32.3	356	72.1	138	27.9
SSAIT	4,000	2,860	71.5	1,140	28.5	505	71.1	205	28.9
TSAIT	4,000	2,941	73.5	1,059	26.5	629	71.2	255	28.8
Totals	10,960	7,803	71.2	3,157	28.8	1,490	71.4	598	28.6

Sources: DCA, GD/EFM/SA/1/1, First Scottish American Investment Trust Company, Limited, *Register of Members*, vol. 1; DCA, GD/EFM/SA/2/1, Second Scottish American Investment Trust Company, Limited, *Register of Members*, vol. 1; DCA, GD/EFM/SA/3/1, Third Scottish American Investment Trust Company, Limited, *Register of Members*, vol. 1.

Note
* Where there were joint holdings these have been divided equally for the purposes of calculation.

Levels of female participation

The shareholding figures in Table 13.2 reveal that in 1879 women constituted 28.6 per cent of the investment trust shareholders, holding 28.8 per cent of the nominal value of the shares. This is a higher level of female financial participation than Lucy Newton and Philip Cottrell found to be present in the early-nineteenth-century English and Welsh commercial joint-stock banks, their study finding that women comprised an average of 7.9 per cent of the shareholders with 5.4 per cent of the stock from 1827–33, with this figure falling marginally to 7.3 per cent and 3.5 per cent respectively in 1835–6.[33] Nor is there such a large proportion of female financial activity present in the eighteenth- or nineteenth-century industrial companies referred to by Mark Freeman et al., where they find that women averaged around 10 per cent of investors in companies.[34] It does, unsurprisingly, bear a closer resemblance to surveys of shareholders later in the nineteenth century. For example, Josephine Maltby and Janette Rutterford, in a survey of three English financial companies incorporated in the last quarter of the nineteenth century, found that women represented between 28.4 per cent and 32.7 per cent of the number of shareholders, and held between 16.4 per cent and 26.5 per cent of the share capital. Similarly, Graham Acheson and John Turner, surveying investors in the Ulster Bank in 1877, found that women made up 32.5 per cent of the shareholders, holding 26.4 per cent of the share capital.[35]

Some women in my sample held shares other than their investment trust holdings, which suggests a certain degree of financial autonomy and risk. One such example in Dundee is Mary Ann Baxter, an extremely wealthy spinster who had a large and impressive portfolio of local, national and international investments and featured in the registers of the both the FSAIT and TSAIT. Her mortgage and debenture investments ranged from local Dundee Gas Commission to the Canada Permanent Loan and Savings Company. She held over £40,000 of local investment trust bonds, in addition to around £4,500 joint-stock shares. Her two shares in the FSAIT and nine shares in the TSAIT were worth a

Table 13.3 Percentage of number of different types of female investors

ITC	All women	Of whom:				
		Wives	Widows	Spinsters	Unmarried daughters	Unspecified
FSAIT	27.9	21.7	32.6	42.7	0.7	2.1
SSAIT	28.9	19.5	29.2	46.8	1.4	2.9
TSAIT	28.8	23.5	25.0	46.6	2.7	1.9
Overall	28.6	21.6	28.9	45.4	1.6	2.3

Sources: DCA, GD/EFM/SA/1/1, First Scottish American Investment Trust Company, Limited, Register of Members, vol. 1; DCA, GD/EFM/SA/2/1, Second Scottish American Investment Trust Company, Limited, Register of Members, vol. 1; DCA, GD/EFM/SA/3/1, Third Scottish American Investment Trust Company, Limited, Register of Members, vol. 1.

combined value of £1,100 in 1879 and fetched £1,630, including a half-year's dividend, at her death in 1885. This profit of £530, accumulated in only six years, amounts to roughly £39,000 today.[36]

Single women

The share registers of the three companies studied present some interesting findings about the marital status of Scottish female investors, as shown in Table 13.3. Overall, spinsters were by far the largest single group of female investors, constituting 43 per cent of the female participants in the FSAIT and almost 47 per cent in both the SSAIT and TSAIT. These figures correlate with recent English findings where spinsters were generally found to be the largest group of female investors.[37] This not only reflects single women's financial autonomy, but probably also their need for secure financial assets.

Sometimes single women's shares were provided by a male relative, as, for example, in the case of the Stratton family. William Stratton, a restaurant owner from Dundee, invested £200 worth of shares in the SSAIT and £200 worth of shares in the TSAIT for his three daughters, Helen, Marion and Prudence, and their two brothers. However, there is no evidence of similar cases. More commonly, a single woman's shares were placed in the care of a local solicitor, indicating little control by the female shareholder. This was the case with Jessie Morris, whose one share in the FSAIT was held in trust with Andrew Ogilvy, a local stockbroker. Nevertheless, it is clear that many single women were financially independent. Take the Fergusson sisters, for example. Matilda, Elizabeth and Wilhelmina each held ten shares in the FSAIT, SSAIT and TSAIT. It is likely that these shares were purchased for them by their father, since he himself was a large shareholder. However, it is indicated that the ladies had some control over their own finances as there was a mandate in each of the share registers authorising the payment of the annual dividends to be made directly into their personal bank accounts. The shares were also held in each of their own names, making it legally possible for them to sell or bequeath as they desired. In fact, Elizabeth went on to buy one more share in the SSAIT before she died in 1881 leaving her shares in the charge of her brother. Wilhelmina died in 1904 and distributed her shares between her remaining siblings and their offspring, while Matilda inherited a further nine shares from Wilhelmina's bequest. All siblings acted as executors of their father's estate on his death.

Another group of spinsters that displayed a degree of autonomy over their finances were those who were in employment.[38] Of the few women who were noted in the registers as having an occupation, most were in traditional female roles. Within the sample of 598 women, three were schoolteachers and two were at the same school in Dundee holding two and four shares respectively. They may well have exchanged information and advised each other. The sample also included two housekeepers. Interestingly, one housekeeper worked at Duncarse, the home of one of the directors involved in all three companies, Thomas Cox. She held six shares, well above the spinster average. One domestic servant had two shares, a female grocer had one share and a female baker had one share. A milliner, Janet Graham, is particularly noteworthy. She held £2,200 nominal value in shares, indicating that she was a significant businesswoman. Janet's annual income from this investment, based on the 1880 dividend, would have been a substantial £176 per year. That is equivalent to £12,289.83 today, or over £1,000 a month in relative terms.[39]

There is plenty of evidence that single women invested enough in the trusts to provide a comfortable supplementary income. One example is the Jackson sisters from Edinburgh. Margaret and Elizabeth jointly held five shares in the FSAIT, three in the SSAIT and two in the TSAIT. They both lived in the same house and the annual dividend from the £1,000 nominal-value investment would have provided a substantial annual household income amounting to £80 in 1880, equivalent to £5,476 in 2006.[40]

Women often exerted their independence and financial influence by leaving their shares to female relatives. Mary Ann Baxter, who died in 1884, had a personal estate worth nearly £300,000. Upon her death, Baxter instructed all her heritable and movable property to be sold and converted into cash. This was to be divided equally among her nephews and nieces. The money bequeathed to her nephews was to be paid in cash, but the money for her nieces was to be invested in a 'good security or securities' recommended by her trustees, with the 'exclusion of the jus mariti Right of Administration and any other legal right of the Husband or Husbands'.[41] This meant that the bequests did not become the husband's property in the event of a niece's marriage.

Some single women had large and varied investment portfolios. Eveline Ogilvy held shares and debentures in a range of public companies, mostly railroad companies in England, India, Brazil and Canada, and extensive holdings throughout the United States. She also had shares in various Scottish investment trusts, including 11 shares in the TSAIT. She had interests in Colonial Government securities in New Zealand, Queensland, Western Australia and Canada and various scattered shares in a range of enterprises, for example, the Rio de Janeiro City Improvement Company, the Eastern Telegraph Company and the Consolidated Tea and Lands Company. Her assets in investment trusts amounted to over £22,000 at her death in 1898.[42] On the surface, such an impressive and wide-ranging portfolio of investments would suggest that Ogilvy took an active role in the selection of the trusts and distribution of her finances. Yet, it is difficult to determine exactly to what extent large female shareholders controlled their own assets, or whether they were simply bought on male advice.

Although spinsters were the largest investing group, they generally held fewer shares than the typical female averages listed in Table 13.4.[43] The average nominal female holding in the FSAIT, for instance, was 6.94 shares. This was a higher mean value than that of men, who averaged 5.62 shares overall. However, single women's holdings averaged 4.96 shares, smaller than the female average overall. In the FSAIT the median holding for spinsters was three shares and the modal holding was one share. These figures are identical to the overall female median and modal holdings for the FSAIT, but drop to an

Table 13.4 Average numbers of shares held by male and female investors

ITC	Male			Female		
	Mean	*Median*	*Mode*	*Mean*	*Median*	*Mode*
FSAIT	5.62	5	1	6.94	3	1
SSAIT	7.15	5	5	5.56	3	1
TSAIT	5.85	4	1	4.15	2	1

Sources: DCA, GD/EFM/SA/1/1, First Scottish American Investment Trust Company, Limited, *Register of Members*, vol. 1; DCA, GD/EFM/SA/2/1, Second Scottish American Investment Trust Company, Limited, *Register of Members*, vol. 1; DCA, GD/EFM/SA/3/1, Third Scottish American Investment Trust Company, Limited, *Register of Members*, vol. 1.

average median holding of two in the SSAIT and one in the TSAIT, below the median and modal figures for women overall in these two trusts. The modal holding for spinsters in all three trusts was one share, indicating that spinsters had a 'tail' of small investments.[44] This looks to be typical for spinsters in low-risk financial companies; a similar result was found in England and Wales for the same period.[45]

Widows

Widows were the second most significant group in the sample in terms of numbers, comprising around 30 per cent of the female shareholders in the FSAIT and SSAIT and 25 per cent of the female shareholders in the TSAIT, as shown in Table 13.3. This is a marked difference from the findings of Maltby and Rutterford, who note that widows were consistently the least significant group in their study of English female investors during the same period.[46] Undoubtedly, though, widows held a higher proportion of the shares than single and married women, although they were perhaps largely involuntary investors, inheriting their shares as opposed to independently purchasing them. Table 13.5 lists the total nominal values of female shareholders by marital status in pounds sterling. It can be seen from the Scottish sample that, although spinsters collectively held the largest amount of stock in the SSAIT, widows overall held the largest amount of the stock of the three trusts. Ermin Edwards, widow of the deceased Allan Edwards, was by far the largest independent female shareholder in the entire sample. She inherited a huge £10,600 worth of shares in the FSAIT from her husband on his death in 1879. Similarly, she acquired £5,100 and £2,500 worth of shares in the SSAIT and TSAIT respectively, though these were bequeathed jointly to her and her two sons, Kenrick and Albert.

Wives

According to Table 13.3, wives were the least significant of the major groups in this sample in shareholding terms. This is supported by the data in Table 13.5,

Table 13.5 Total value of different types of female shareholders' holdings (£)

ITC	All women	Of whom:				
		Wives	Widows	Spinsters	Unmarried daughters	Unspecified
FSA	95,800	22,700	39,100	29,300	0	4,700
SSA	114,000	28,700	37,500	43,500	300	4,000
TSA	105,900	29,600	36,700	36,500	400	2,700
Total	315,700	81,000	113,300	109,300	700	11,400

Sources: DCA, GD/EFM/SA/1/1, First Scottish American Investment Trust Company, Limited, *Register of Members*, vol. 1; DCA, GD/EFM/SA/2/1, Second Scottish American Investment Trust Company, Limited, *Register of Members*, vol. 1; DCA, GD/EFM/SA/3/1, Third Scottish American Investment Trust Company, Limited, *Register of Members*, vol. 1.

which shows that, collectively, wives also held the least total value of stock (excluding the 'Unmarried daughters' and 'Unspecified' categories). However, wives consistently held a significant average amount of stock compared with the overall averages for women shown in Table 13.4. In the FSAIT and the SSAIT, wives typically held the same average median and modal number of shares as women did overall, with a higher average median of three shares in the TSAIT, compared with the average of two. In fact, the median holding for all shareholders collectively, both male and female, in the TSAIT was three shares; this supports the fact that wives were significant shareholders.

Isabella Martin was the largest married shareholder. She held 15 shares in the FSAIT, 31 in the SSAIT and 32 in the TSAIT. Her husband, William Martin, was also a substantial shareholder in the three companies. She, like most married women in this sample, was related to a male investor. In trust companies in England scholars have found that the wives with the largest shareholdings were usually married to directors of the company concerned.[47] What is unusual in the Scottish sample is that the wives of the four directors are not significant shareholders. In fact, only Adelaide Cox, wife of Thomas Cox, held any shares. She had ten in each of the FSAIT and TSAIT and none in the SSAIT. Although she held shares above the average nominal value of wives' holdings, this figure is insignificant in comparison to the amount that the Cox family held overall, and she held the same amount as her spinster sister-in-law, Ellen Cox.

Legal implications

This study is concerned with the investments held by women in 1879–80, prior to the Married Woman's Property (Scotland) Act 1881 (MWPAS). Before the passing of the Act, a married woman's legal status generally meant that she was subordinate to her husband. This was especially noticeable in terms of ownership and the administration of her property.[48] Of the rights and responsibilities of the husband, gained on marriage, the most important of these was the *jus mariti*.

This meant that the husband acquired the right to own all of his wife's movable estate belonging to her at the date of marriage and anything she might inherit or accrue thereafter, excluding any earnings, jewellery and clothing.[49]

To circumvent the law of the *jus mariti* it was possible to request that it be renounced in an ante-nuptial marriage contract to exclude certain clauses that could otherwise only be made dissolute by divorce.[50] Alternatively, the exclusion of the *jus mariti* could be requested when any bequest was made to the wife by a third party, as Mary Ann Baxter did with her nieces. This worked for the benefit of the woman when it came to owning or inheriting shares and other investments. However, under Common Law, an anomaly existed that meant that the husband's consent was required should the wife want to dispose (or retain) her own property as she pleased. This was known as the *jus administrationis* and was effectual where the rights of the *jus mariti* did not apply (as in the case of heritable property) or were excluded. The *jus administrationis*, therefore, disabled the wife from administering her own property without the consent of her husband.[51]

However, it would be naive to conclude that no married woman owned property until 1881.[52] In fact, before 1881 Scottish wives had greater legal rights of inheritance and legal protection over their property than their English counterparts. In marriage, the couple's movable goods were merged into one fund, albeit the husband's, but women were still eligible for a certain degree of control through the legal construction of a marriage contract to exclude the husband's *jus mariti* right.[53] Scottish female investors took advantage of this and were thus allowed to purchase or receive shares expressly 'excluding his jus mariti *and* right of administration'. It is understood that this could only be done through a marriage contract, but the fact that every married female in this sample who invested on their own did so with this clause indicates that many married women in Scotland retained a degree of equality when it came to the joint property within the marriage. Therefore, the notable presence of married shareholders in this sample is significant because Scottish wives had more flexibility than Englishwomen due to variations in the laws on property. This is evident particularly in the shareholdings of the Ulster Banks, where there are no married women present prior to the English MWPA of 1882.[54]

A Scottish widow, on the other hand, was entitled to retain a fixed proportion of the marriage estate should the husband predecease her. She was eligible for exactly half the estate should they have had no children, or one-third if otherwise. In death, the wife also retained the same degree of control, and her share of the joint property was entitled to her representatives on her behalf.[55]

By avoiding the *jus mariti* in Scotland, fathers ensured that their daughters retained their property rights when entering a marriage. Furthermore, the wife of a wealthy man could benefit greatly by retaining a substantial share of his property should they divorce or when he died.[56] Scottish women also retained the right to bequeath their shares as they wished after marriage. In short, the control that wives potentially had over their investments under Scottish law was higher than their legal entitlement suggested, and greater than was allowed to women in England. This is not to say that some women did not make joint investments with their husbands. Mary Turnbull of Edinburgh, for example, held four shares with her solicitor husband David. It would appear that they had an equal claim to these shares, although they still would have fallen under David's administration.

Conclusions and further research

By the late 1870s, investment trusts were a fairly popular option throughout Britain and many investors were attracted by the promise of a safe, yet relatively high, rate of return and the security of the buoyant reserve funds as detailed in Table 13.1. For this reason investment trusts were considered a reasonably safe option, so were these relatively popular investments for women? Larger comparative studies have yet to conclude on this issue but it is clear from this preliminary survey that some women did have portfolios that included shares in investment trusts, and appeared to have a certain degree of financial autonomy. It must be remembered, however, that the three Scottish investment trusts studied here are only a snapshot of women's shareholdings, and the suggestions and findings of this study are preliminary.

Between 1873 and 1900, 19 investment companies were established and/or reconstructed in Dundee and Edinburgh.[57] A study of all of these ventures is in progress that will increase our understanding of the investment pattern of Scottish women. For example, additional factors can be taken into account, such as the geographic location of the trusts, the types of securities in the trusts' investment portfolios, and the level of exposure to financial literature and financial promotion made available to women in Scotland at different times. What is more, some of the investment trust companies in the larger survey will allow a study of their share registers at the date of incorporation, making it possible to compare women's investment in new and existing investment trusts along the lines of Newton and Cottrell's work on early English joint-stock banks.[58] Thus, the larger survey will allow a relative assessment of marital status, gender and investors' attitude to risk in the Scottish investment trust industry. Nonetheless, some interesting suggestions can already be made from this study.

First, there were significant proportions of female shareholders involved in the three investment trust companies in the preliminary study. On average, women constituted 30 per cent of the investors, holding roughly a proportionate amount of stock. This was in line with the numbers of women investing in financial companies in England and Ulster at the time. Further research into the business correspondence of the trusts will show to what extent, if any, women had an active interest in choosing investment trust shareholdings. At this point there is no evidence to show that women held an equal proportion in the corporate decision-making of the trusts, minutes of meetings were always addressed to 'gentlemen' and it was noted that decisions had to be made on behalf of the large number of absent certificate-holders.[59] This suggests that the female investors did not play an active role in the management of their investments, but this is not to say that they did not have control of their shares. Nevertheless, such issues justify the need for more research into the area of women and finance in Scotland.

By categorising women by marital status, some interesting results have been obtained. As in England, spinsters were the largest group of female investors with a string of small shareholdings. One possible reason for the fact that they were relatively small shareholders could be that they had diversified portfolios, not unlike those women in the examples given. This would reflect their financial autonomy and also their need for secure assets. Single women had the same financial rights as men and could have made use of these to buy, sell and bequeath their shares as they wished, especially to other female relatives.

Widows, similarly, were in a good legal position to control their shareholdings. In fact, it seems, from this study, that they acquired shares on the death of their husband. It is perhaps unsurprising, then, that widows proportionately held the largest amount of shares in the sample.

It can be argued, however, that the most interesting discovery in the survey of the three investment trust companies is the position of the wives as investors. On the surface, the legal impositions that women faced prior to the MWPAS appeared to constrain them as investors. In reality, though, the opposite was true. Every wife in the sample took advantage of a marriage contract under Scottish law that allowed them full financial control and this was reflected in their shareholding values. However, it is not clear whether this marriage contract also counteracted their loss of voting rights. Nevertheless, this provides evidence that shows wives as investing separately from their husbands prior to the passage of the MWPA in Scotland.

It would, of course, be interesting to see if women did make use of their voting rights. Further research into the other investment trusts may provide evidence of women who did take an active, albeit untypical, role in the company infrastructure. A more comprehensive study incorporating the rest of the Dundee investment trust companies that were established between 1870 and 1900 is currently being undertaken and will certainly provide a more complete overview in this area of women's economic agency. One major point that has come out of this chapter is that if numbers of married women increased following the implication of the MWPAS, as they did in England and Northern Ireland, then this could significantly change the distribution of shares among women, and possibly the infrastructure of the trusts.

Overall, this small sample has offered suggestions about the role of women in the Scottish investment trust movement. This basic study, based on the marital status of female investors, opens up many other areas for the study of women's financial participation and relates to a host of wealth-holding studies currently ongoing in the UK as well as internationally.[60]

Notes

1 A version of this chapter was presented at the XIV International Economic History Congress, Helsinki 2006, where the comments offered were very much appreciated.

The author is grateful to Professor Janette Rutterford, Professor Margaret Walsh and Professor Robin Pearson for sending drafts of unpublished papers. I also want to acknowledge the generous help of Professor Rutterford, Professor Josephine Maltby and Professor James Tomlinson in the drafting of this chapter. Thanks are also owed to Richard Cullen, archivist at Dundee City Archives and Nancy Smith for help with the statistics. Any mistakes are my own.

  2 M. Freeman, R. Pearson and J. Taylor, '"A doe in the city": women shareholders in eighteenth- and nineteenth-century Britain', *Accounting, Business and Financial History* 16 (2), 2006, pp. 265–91; J. Maltby and J.M. Rutterford, '"She possessed her own fortune": women investors from the late nineteenth century to the early twentieth century', *Business History* 48, 2006, pp. 220–53; L. Newton and P.L. Cottrell, 'Female investors in the first English and Welsh commercial joint-stock banks', *Accounting, Business and Financial History* 16 (2), 2006, pp. 315–40; J.M. Rutterford and J. Maltby, '"The widow, the clergyman and the reckless": women investors in England, 1830–1914', *Feminist Economics* 12, 2006, pp. 111–38.

  3 R. Rodger, *The Transformation of Edinburgh: Land, Property and Trust in the Nineteenth Century*, Cambridge: Cambridge University Press, 2001, pp. 271–2; C.E. Swan, *Scottish Cowboys and the Dundee Investors, Dundee Investment in the Texas Panhandle, A Case Study: The Matador Land and Cattle Company*, Dundee: Abertay Historical Society, 2004, pp. 13, 22.

  4 E. Gordon and G. Nair, 'The economic role of middle class women in Victorian Glasgow', *Women's History Review* 9, 2000, pp. 791–814; they expand on this in E. Gordon and G. Nair, *Public Lives: Women, Family and Society in Victorian Britain*, New Haven, CT: Yale University Press, 2003.

  5 This chapter serves as a pilot study for the analysis of networks in the Scottish investment trust movement. Further research into this topic, with particular emphasis on the female participation in nine Dundee investment trusts at the end of the nineteenth century, will be presented in my forthcoming PhD thesis, anticipated to be completed in 2008.

  6 R.J. Morris, 'Reading wills: cash economy capitalists and urban peasants in the 1830s', in A. Kidd and D. Nicholls (eds), *The Making of the British Middle Class*, London: Alan Sutton, 1998, p. 129; G.G. Acheson and J.D. Turner, 'The impact of limited liability on ownership and control: Irish banking, 1877–1914', *Economic History Review* 59 (2), 2006, p. 15.

  7 W.T. Jackson, *The Enterprising Scot: Investors in the American West After 1873*, Edinburgh: Edinburgh University Press, 1968, p. 21.

  8 J.C. Gilbert, *A History of Investment Trusts in Dundee, 1873–1938*, London: P.S. King, 1939, p. 16.

  9 Dundee City Archives (hereafter, DCA), GD/EFM/SA/1/1, First Scottish American Investment Trust Company, *First General Meeting, Report to the Trustees*, 18 September 1873.

 10 W. Smith, *Robert Fleming*, Haddington: Whitinghame Press, 2000, pp. 2, 15–17.

 11 Smith, *Robert Fleming*, pp. 15–17.

 12 DCA, GD/EFM/SA/1/1, *Second General Meeting, Report to the Trustees*, 21 May 1874.

 13 On average, 30 different bonds at £3 each only accounts for £90 of the £100 certificate. The remainder of the funds, less expenses, were placed in a reserve fund, which is explained below.

 14 DCA, GD/EFM/SA/1/1, First Scottish American Investment Trust Company, *Prospectus*, 2 July 1873, pp. 3–4.

 15 DCA, GD/EFM/SA/1/1, First Scottish American Investment Trust Company, *Prospectus*, 2 July 1873, p. 1.

 16 Ibid.

 17 This figure of interest was estimated as an average return minus expenses and was

subject to the fluctuation of the value of American currency. It was anticipated to rise as the Trust grew, and in fact did, to 7 and 8 per cent over succeeding years. DCA, GD/EFM/SA/1/1, First Scottish American Investment Trust Company, *Prospectus*, 1873.

18 DCA, GD/EFM/SA/1/1, First Scottish American Investment Trust Company, *Prospectus*, 2 July 1873, p. 2.

19 Ibid.

20 It was recommended that a certificate holder invest his or her funds for the full period, however, it was permitted to redeem your funds at any point out of surplus income, or reserve fund, if available. However, the intention to terminate after ten years did not actually happen as the trusts were not legally entitled to survive for that long, as will be explained later in the chapter.

21 DCA, GD/EFM/SA/1/1, First Scottish American Investment Trust Company, Limited, *Memorandum of Association*, 1879.

22 DCA, GD/EFM/SA/1/1, First Scottish American Investment Trust Company, *First General Meeting, Report to the Trustees*, 18 September 1873; this was also explained for a similar company in G. Glasgow, *The Scottish Investment Trust Companies*, London: Eyre & Spottiswoode, 1932, pp. 11–15.

23 A.K. Cairncross, 'Did foreign investment pay?', *Review of Economic Studies* 3, 1935, p. 71; Gilbert, *Dundee Investment Trusts*, p. 6.

24 Gilbert, *A History of Investment Trusts*, pp. 2–3; Glasgow, *Scottish Investment Trust Companies*, p. 11.

25 N. McKendrick and J. Newlands, *A History of Foreign and Colonial*, London: F&C, 1999, p. 50; J. Rutterford, 'Learning from one's mistakes? Managing risk in the mutual fund industry, 1868–1940', European Business History Conference, Barcelona, 2004, p. 7.

26 DCA, GD/EFM/SA/1/1, First Scottish American Investment Trust Company, Limited, *First General Meeting: Report to the Trustees*, 6 March 1879.

27 Actual figure, £6,982.86, L.H. Officer, 'Purchasing power of British pounds from 1264–2006', available online: www.measuringworth.com.

28 At the time of the reconstruction, all companies were flourishing with their combined assets in excess of one-quarter of a million pounds sterling, including an 8–9 per cent reserve fund. DCA, GD/EFM/SA/1/1, First Scottish American Investment Trust Company, Limited, *First General Meeting: Report to the Trustees*, 6 March 1879.

29 Maltby and Rutterford, ' "She possessed her own fortune" ', p. 13.

30 Men were never recorded with their marital status.

31 This introduces a certain degree of complexity when determining attitudes towards investment risk since this was not the initial inception of the company, but rather their legal reconstruction date. This means that the shareholders were only allocated their shares based on previous holdings rather than buying them at this time. However, it can be surmised that since the initial subscription to the trusts were for an intended ten-year period, most of these shareholders will have already held shares before their legal incorporation. There is no way of determining if they subscribed on the first day that the companies were floated.

32 In the fuller database all men are included. These portfolios only include holdings of shares in the three investment trusts, not other investments that the women may have owned.

33 Newton and Cottrell, 'Female investors in the first English and Welsh commercial joint-stock banks', pp. 28–30.

34 This dataset covers the period 1705–1886 and includes a wide range of securities. Freeman *et al.*, ' "A doe in the city" ', p. 10.

35 Maltby and Rutterford, ' "She possessed her own fortune" ', pp. 16 and 44; Acheson and Turner, 'Irish banking', p. 15.

36 Her profit from these shares was probably more given the fact that she may have

purchased her stock before the date of incorporation and it was only converted in 1879. National Archives of Scotland (hereafter, NAS), SC45/31/35, Dundee Sheriff Court, *Testament of Mary Ann Baxter*, 10 June 1885; Officer, 'Purchasing power'.

37 Maltby and Rutterford, ' "She possessed her own fortune" ', p. 21.

38 Dundee had a large proportion of women in employment, particularly married women, who are not proportionally reflected in this sample. A search of the census could reveal valuable information about the financial status of women investors as well as their marital status and class.

39 Officer, 'Purchasing power'.

40 Officer, 'Purchasing power', taken at an 8 per cent dividend. Bear in mind that this is only a section of an investment portfolio. These women could have had an impressive portfolio providing a substantial annual income.

41 For a discussion on the significance of this, see later in the chapter. NAS, SC45/31/35, *Testament of Mary Ann Baxter*, 10 June 1885, pp. 315–16.

42 NAS, SC45/31/50, Dundee Sheriff Court, *Testament of Eveline Constance Maud Ogilvy*, 13 July 1898.

43 Maltby and Rutterford also found this in ' "She possessed her own fortune" ', pp. 22–3.

44 The ages of the spinsters in the register are not known and it is unclear whether this group included adolescent daughters. Although daughters are included as a distinct type of female investor in the tables, they were not classified as such within the share registers. Daughters were only admitted to this group where they were registered as dependent shareholders, with investments made on their behalf. Take, for instance, the daughters of William Straton: the entry in the register specifically states that he invested £200 worth of shares in the Second Scottish American and £200 worth of shares in the TSA for his three daughters, Helen, Marion and Prudence, and their two brothers. There were a few similar cases. (See my earlier comment about this in the text.)

45 Maltby and Rutterford, ' "She possessed her own fortune" ', p. 22.

46 Maltby and Rutterford, ' "She possessed her own fortune" ', p. 21.

47 Freeman *et al.*, ' "A doe in the city" ', p. 7; Maltby and Rutterford, ' "She possessed her own fortune" ', pp. 18–19.

48 A.D.M. Forte, 'Some aspects of the law of marriage in Scotland 1500–1700', in E. Craik (ed.), *Marriage and Property: Women and Marital Customs in History*, Aberdeen: Aberdeen University Press, 1991, p. 109.

49 Married women earned the right to keep their own earned income, with the exception of that earned in a business owned by the husband, with the Married Women's Property (Scotland) Act 1881. It must also be noted that this was not always to the benefit of the husband. It included all liabilities and debts, including everything contracted before the banns, previous husband's funeral expenses, and responsibilities owing to illegitimate children. W.M. Gloag and R.C. Henderson, *Introduction to the Law of Scotland*, Edinburgh: W. Green & Son, 1927, p. 521; E.M. Clive and J.M. Wilson, *The Laws of Husband and Wife in Scotland*, Edinburgh: W. Green & Son, 1974, p. 288; Forte, 'Law of marriage in Scotland', p. 110.

50 Gloag and Henderson, *Law of Scotland*, p. 521; Forte, 'Law of marriage in Scotland', p. 112.

51 Gloag and Henderson, *Law of Scotland*, p. 521.

52 Gordon and Nair, *Public Lives*, p. 161.

53 Clive and Wilson, *The Laws of Husband and Wife*, p. 286.

54 Acheson and Turner, 'Irish banking', p. 15. For information on the case in England, see Maltby and Rutterford, ' "She possessed her own fortune" ', pp. 14–15.

55 Clive and Wilson, *The Laws of Husband and Wife*, p. 286.

56 E.M. Clive, *The Laws of Husband and Wife in Scotland*, 4th edn, Edinburgh: Scottish Universities Law Institute, 1997, p. 13.

57 Jackson, *Enterprising Scot*, p. 60.
58 Newton and Cottrell, 'Female investors in the first English and Welsh commercial joint-stock banks'.
59 DCA, GD/EFM/SA/1/1, First Scottish American Investment Trust Company, Limited, *First General Meeting of Shareholders*, 11 March 1879.
60 In particular this relates to the ongoing ESRC-funded project on women investors in England and Wales, 1870–1930 (RES-000-25-1435).

Bibliography

Acheson, G.G. and Turner, J.D., 'The impact of limited liability on ownership and control: Irish Banking, 1877–1914', *Economic History Review* 59 (2), 2006, pp. 1–34.

Berg, M., 'Women's property and the Industrial Revolution', *Journal of Interdisciplinary History* 24, 1993, pp. 223–50.

Cairncross, A.K., 'Did foreign investment pay?', *Review of Economic Studies* 3, 1935, pp. 67–78.

Clive, E.M., *The Laws of Husband and Wife in Scotland*, 4th edn, Edinburgh: Scottish Universities Law Institute Ltd, 1997.

Clive, E.M. and Wilson, J.M., *The Laws of Husband and Wife in Scotland*, 1st edn, Edinburgh: W. Green & Son, 1974.

Forte, A.D.M., 'Some aspects of the law of marriage in Scotland 1500–1700', in Craik, E. (ed.), *Marriage and Property: Women and Marital Customs in History*, Aberdeen: Aberdeen University Press, 1991, pp. 104–18.

Freeman, Mark, Pearson, Robin and Taylor, James, '"A doe in the city": women shareholders in eighteenth- and early nineteenth-century Britain', *Accounting, Business and Financial History* 16 (2), 2006, pp. 265–91.

Gilbert, J.C., *A History of Investment Trusts in Dundee, 1873–1938*, London: P.S. King, 1939.

Glasgow, G., *The Scottish Investment Trust Companies*, London: Eyre & Spottiswood, 1932.

Gloag, W.M. and Henderson, R.C., *Introduction to the Law of Scotland*, Edinburgh: W. Green & Son, 1927.

Gordon, E. and Nair, G., *Public Lives: Women, Family and Society in Victorian Britain*, New Haven, CT: Yale University Press, 2003.

Gordon, E. and Nair, G., 'The economic role of middle class women in Victorian Glasgow', *Women's History Review* 9, 2000, pp. 791–814.

Green, D.R. and Owens, A., 'Gentlewomanly capitalism? Spinsters, widows, and wealth holding in England and Wales, c.1800–1860', *Economic History Review* 56, 2003, pp. 510–36.

Jackson, W.T., *The Enterprising Scot: Investors in the American West After 1873*, Edinburgh: Edinburgh University Press, 1968.

McKendrick, N. and Newlands, J., *A History of Foreign and Colonial*, London: F&C, 1999.

Maltby, J. and Rutterford, J.M., '"She possessed her own fortune": women investors from the late nineteenth century to the early twentieth century', *Business History* 48, 2006, pp. 220–53.

Morris, R.J., 'Reading wills: cash economy capitalists and urban peasants in the 1830s', in Kidd, A. and Nicholls, D. (eds), *The Making of the British Middle Class*, London: Alan Sutton, 1998, pp. 113–29.

Newton, L. and Cottrell, P.L., 'Female investors in the first English and Welsh commercial joint-stock banks', *Accounting, Business and Financial History* 16 (2), 2006, pp. 315–40.

Officer, L.H., 'Purchasing power of British pounds from 1264–2006', available online: www.measuringworth.com (accessed 22 May 2007).

Rodger, R., *The Transformation of Edinburgh: Land, Property and Trust in the Nineteenth Century*, Cambridge: Cambridge University Press, 2001.

Rutterford, J., 'Learning from one's mistakes? Managing risk in the mutual fund industry, 1868–1940', European Business History Conference, Barcelona, 2004.

Rutterford, J.M. and Maltby, J., ' "The widow, the clergyman and the reckless": women investors in England 1830–1914', *Feminist Economics* 12, 2006, pp. 111–38.

Smith, B., *Robert Fleming*, Haddington: Whitinghame Press, 2000.

Swan, C.E., *Scottish Cowboys and the Dundee Investors, Dundee Investment in the Texas Panhandle, A Case Study: The Matador Land and Cattle Company*, Dundee: Abertay Historical Society, 2004.

Dundee City Archives

GD/EFM/SA/1/1, First Scottish American Investment Trust Company, *Prospectus*, 2 July 1873; Register of Members, 1–3; Minute Book, 1; Reports to Trustees, 1873, 1874, 1879; First Report of the Shareholders, 1879; Articles of Association, 1879; Balance Sheet, 11 May 1880.

GD/EFM/SA/2/1, Second Scottish American Investment Trust Company, Register of Members, 1–3; Balance Sheet, 1 May 1880.

GD/EFM/SA/3/1, Third Scottish American Investment Trust Company, Register of Members, 1–3; Balance Sheet, 1 July 1880.

National Archives of Scotland

SC45/31/35, Dundee Sherriff Court, *Testament of Mary Ann Baxter*, 10 June 1885.

SC45/31/50, Dundee Sherriff Court, *Testament of Eveline Constance Maud Ogilvy*, 13 July 1898.

14 Women clerical staff employed in the UK-based Army Pay Department establishments, 1914–1920[1]

John Black

Introduction

This chapter explores the role of women who were temporarily employed in the UK Army Pay Department (APD) establishments during the First World War. The majority of the women recruited were employed as clerks within the army and command pay offices situated throughout the UK and Ireland. The first incumbents were, however, unpaid volunteers who, without official permission, assisted with the administration of reservist documentation, particularly in the area of separation allowances at the Army Pay Office, Woolwich from August to October 1914.[2] The first women clerks were officially recruited in November 1914 for employment at the War Office Finance Branch as its parameters expanded from two departments in 1914 to six by October 1918.[3] Women clerks were recruited as temporary civil servants and a number of seconded personnel (both male and female) from various branches of the General Post Office (GPO) filled the expansion. Temporary women clerks were first recruited to the various army pay offices within the UK from January 1915, and lady superintendents (supervisors of women clerks) one year later in January 1916. The term 'lady superintendent' was the official contemporary term used by the home civil service to describe a woman supervisor or manager. Although the lady superintendents of the APD were temporary, their status and authority equalled that of a male civilian acting paymaster (also a temporary wartime position) as well as a commissioned APD assistant paymaster to the rank of captain.

The purpose of this chapter is to outline the needs and experiences of women who were employed within the APD establishments during the First World War. Their history has been neglected, being overshadowed by that of working-class women who were employed, also on a temporary basis, in engineering and munitions industries generally, as reflected in the histories written by Marwick, Braybon and Thom.[4] Although little research has been conducted into the role of women employed in clerical functions during the First World War, more is known about women in the clerical occupations before 1914. Notable are two papers by Campbell-Kelly that focused on women who were employed on data processing at the Prudential Assurance Company and the Post Office Savings Bank (POSB).[5]

Until 1914 the state was the main employer of women involved in clerical work, and research conducted by Zimmeck focused on the expansion of clerical work for women from 1850 to 1914, mainly within the GPO and its subsidiary the POSB. In her thesis, Zimmeck identifies the concept of 'intellectual' and 'mechanical' processes of clerical tasks within the GPO and POSB.[6] This concept is important in the assessment of the organisation and management of APD establishments during the First World War. However, the notion of 'feminisation' in relation to accounting and bookkeeping[7] was not evident until after the First World War.[8] The wartime role of women staff within APD establishments during the Great War, as were their colleagues employed in the contemporary munitions industry, related more to the concept of the 'reserve army of labour'.

Traditional interpretations of war women and work during the First World War tend to focus on the positive effects on women.[9] But this experience was only temporary and fulfilled the reserve army of labour concept. The wartime experiences of women working in government or in munitions did little to change gender relations on a more permanent basis after 1918. Indeed women's position in the labour force during the 1920s reflected a similar position that existed prior to 1914, a point emphasised by Braybon.[10]

A major function of the army pay offices and the War Office Finance Branch during the Great War was that of administering separation and other allotments and allowances to dependants of Army personnel. The categories of entitlement and increasing generosity of these allowances changed dramatically between 1914 and 1919.[11] The work of Pedersen[12] is an important contribution to this comparatively unknown area of Britain and the First World War, although she does not extend her research into the mechanics of the administration of these allowances. However, Pedersen suggests that the wartime example of separation allowances administered between 1914 and 1919 may have been the embryo of the future welfare state inaugurated by Beveridge in 1942.[13]

During the course of the war, the GPO, including the POSB, seconded female permanent clerks to the War Office Finance Branch, mainly for duties associated with the supervision and welfare of women clerks who were first recruited in November 1914.[14] The accounting and gender themes are closely interlinked with military and social policy issues that arose during the First World War. Prior to 1914 women clerical workers were segregated from their male colleagues,[15] whereas the wartime APD establishments were integrated. Indeed they may have represented the first gender-integrated military establishments in the UK. This was not for any altruistic motive by the War Office; rather it was a necessity in the efficient use of available office space. The APD commandeered concert theatres (Blackheath and Shrewsbury); hotels (Preston); vacant military married quarters (Woolwich and Chatham); schools, public libraries and baths (Chatham, Nottingham and Shrewsbury); factories (Nottingham); The Royal School of Mines, London (now Imperial College);[16] and even a Freemasons' Hall (Woolwich) – the location of which was notified in Army Order 243, July 1915 – all for army pay office accommodation. From late 1916 'hutments' were

constructed on Woolwich Common[17] and on the Great Lines of the Royal Engineers Depot at Brompton Barracks, Chatham for army pay office use.[18] One
civilian acting paymaster, E. Harvey, who was employed in the hutments that
made up one-third of the estate of Army Pay Office Woolwich, described them
as follows: 'ladies fair, officers bold, splendid huts but deuced cold'.[19]

There is little evidence in the way of primary source data relating to the APD
staff and establishment staff during the Great War. There is, however, a modest 20-
page pamphlet written by the staff of the Army Pay Office Woolwich, found in the
Library of the Imperial War Museum (IWM), called *The Souvenir* (IWM,
K/87465). This publication gives glimpses of the work within one of the largest
APD establishments during the course of the war, including frequent air raid drills
from 1915. There is a two-page entry relating to the first, albeit unofficial, women
volunteers who undertook clerical duties at APO Woolwich from August to October
1914. The article, written by 'KFK' – who otherwise remains anonymous – entitled
'The boy-girls of 1914', is perhaps the only surviving reference to their existence.
However, housed within the National Archives, Kew is a contemporary file recording the history of separation allowances for the Army and Navy during the First
World War.[20] Included in this file are copies of the three official manuals for separation allowances in the Army for 1915, 1916 and 1918. There is also a contemporary
newspaper account of the Record and Army Pay Office at Nottingham.[21]

Another area of primary source data consulted was a contemporary inter-
departmental report, *The Report of the Committee on Army Pay Office Organisation 1919*, chaired by a Treasury mandarin, J. G. Griffiths. This report was, in
essence, a record of the efficiency and performance of the army pay offices
during the Great War; nevertheless little subsequent research has been undertaken into the role and performances of the Army Pay Services. The official
history, published in 1983 and written by a retired senior officer, contains little
about the women who worked in the APD establishments from 1914 to 1920.[22]

Despite this neglect, however, the employment of over 28,000 women within
the APD establishments may have been a factor in the reforms and generosity of
the allowance system as they progressed from 1915 to the end of the war in
1918. For example, Kessler-Harris[23] suggests that the influence of women may
have legitimised social welfare policies. During the course of the Great War, the
military and political authorities accepted a more liberal approach, granting entitlement to separation and other allowances. Common-law and cohabitation
status was accepted, as were multiple claims in relation to entitlement to separation allowances during the Great War only (for example, when a woman's
husband and sons were in the Army, or for a mother whose children were
fathered by different men and who were now in the Army). From January 1915,
the Command Pay Office London District, Regent Street, administered multiple
separation allowance claims. Indeed the Separation Allowances Manual was
rewritten three times from 1915 to 1918 in order to accommodate rapid changes
and the scope of claimants.[24] However, what, if any, was the influence of women
employed within the APD establishments between 1914 and 1920 on the
reforms of the allowance system is not fully known.

Women in clerical positions to 1914

Until 1914 few women were employed in the home civil service – apart from the GPO and POSB, which were then part of the civil service structure. The GPO had employed women and girls since 1861, mainly as sorters, and women were also employed within the Telegraph Department (even prior to the nationalisation of the Department in 1871), notably as manipulators or transmitters and counter clerks.[25] The reason why the GPO and its various departments employed female labour was purely a cost-minimising exercise rather than for altruistic reasons.[26]

Between 1860 and 1914, however, there was a growth in demand for clerical labour. This was met in part through the expansion of the elementary educational system after 1870 and secondary education from 1900,[27] and also by the numerous commercial and secretarial colleges that opened in provincial commercial centres in the period up to 1914.[28] There appeared to be few women graduates within the growing economy who worked in clerical positions prior to 1914, and it was not until the First World War that women graduates entered these occupations in any great numbers.[29] Women could not enter the accounting or legal professions until after 1919, although some women were temporarily employed in accountancy firms for the duration of the war.[30]

Zimmeck has contributed to the history of gender division with her study of women workers who were employed in clerical work from 1850 to 1914, particularly focusing on the GPO and POSB. It was Zimmeck who divided clerical labour functions into two broad classifications of clerical tasks, these being 'intellectual' and 'mechanical'.[31] She argued that clerical functions performed by women related to 'mechanical' clerical processes, the 'intellectual' processes being the province of men. Most, however, were employed on 'mechanical' clerical functions that, over time, were downgraded, eventually being recognised as 'women's work', as described by Zimmeck:

> Women clerks in the Savings Bank Department of the Post Office, which was organised into ledger divisions, started off 'experimentally' in a few divisions where the work was thought least taxing, and proceeded over several decades to take over one division after another from the men, until in the end they made a clean sweep and ledger work became 'women's work.... The women to gain in quantity, the men in quality'.[32]

The example of the GPO and POSB and the classification of clerical functions into 'mechanical' and 'intellectual' are important in any assessment of the organisation and structure of the APD establishments during the First World War and the employment of women clerks.

The role of the APD establishments in peace and war

The strength of the British Regular Army in 1914 was 110,000, plus a reserve (including the Regular and Special Reserve) and Territorial Force element of

40,000. The APD (commissioned officers) and Army Pay Corps (APC) (warrant officers and non-commissioned officers) totalled no more than 400 military staff of all ranks. There were 27 fixed centre army pay offices in the UK and Ireland in 1914. Most APOs employed only a small but all-male staff, numbering between 20 and 30 in strength.[33] The largest pre-1914 army pay office was at Woolwich Dockyard with a total strength of 90. (By November 1918 its strength had increased to 6,000.[34]) The Woolwich office was responsible for the personal accounts of the largest logistical corps in the Army, the Army Service Corps (ASC), as well as the two largest regiments in the Army, the Royal Field Artillery (RFA) and the Royal Horse Artillery (RHA).

The pre-1914 army pay offices within the UK still resembled a Dickensian counting house and the aforementioned changes in technology had yet to reach the offices of the Army and the APD. The relatively small size of the British Army meant that it could be administered sufficiently by what could be termed an antiquated and outdated system. Indeed, the accounts held by the APD establishments were bound in fixed leather binders that were more reminiscent of the mid nineteenth century and proved useless as the strength and casualty rate of the British Army relentlessly increased from September 1914. The major source of a paymaster's regulations was the Manual of Military Law of 1885, King's Regulations for the Army, the Royal Warrant and Separation Allowances for the Army, 1913. The frequent issues of 'Financial Instructions for the Army' from the War Office Finance Branch, and monthly Army Orders from the Secretary of State for War, supported the legal manuals for the Army. Regimental paymasters (in the rank of colonel) who commanded army pay offices prior to 1914 tended to be restricted in their ability to command by rigid rules and regulations, a point noted by the Griffiths Report when it commented that the regulations 'appeared to have afforded the Paymaster little scope for the display of initiative or powers of organization'.[35]

The paymasters were not without initiative and resourcefulness, however. For example, once the war had started and knowing the staff shortages that faced his pay office at Woolwich, the regimental paymaster, Colonel A. B. Church, accepted women on a voluntary basis without authority from the War Office.[36] The War Office Finance Branch and regimental paymasters were also extremely robust in reorganising the structure of APD establishments in order to introduce new clerical technologies, including the loose-leaf ledger system introduced in the spring of 1915. This point is further explored later.

The army pay offices were formed under the 'Dover' system in 1905,[37] and administered the accounts of all soldiers within a regimental or corps system. This system was established in the aftermath of the second Anglo-Boer War (1899–1902), where Army administration generally had been found to be wanting. The Dover system was the backdrop to the success of the army pay services during the First World War. The expansion of the Army during the Great War increased the overall duties of regimental paymasters and the functions of army pay offices. The Dover system still prevailed, although the duties involved extended well beyond the original conception of its architects in 1904.[38] The administration of separation allowance in the pre-August 1914 army was a simple bureaucratic affair because the Regular Army was a single man's army, almost a celibate organisation, a point made by Baynes. In his study of the pre-August 1914 history of the 2nd Battalion The Scottish Rifles (the Cameronians), Baynes also noted that the regimental married establishment recorded only two married and accompanied officers and these represented the two most senior officers in the battalion! Indeed, the majority of married officers and soldiers on the married establishment were unaccompanied. Thus their spouses were entitled to separation allowance. In home stations this was issued and accounted for by the soldier's regiment, whereas in overseas stations it was paid to the spouse by the respective army pay office through the Post Office.[39]

It was the administration of separation allowances and the documentation of the army pay books (AB 64) for recalled reservists that rapidly increased the bureaucracy of the army pay offices from the outbreak of war on 4 August 1914. Later, soldier allotments to next of kin expanded with the increased strength of the Army. Married soldiers were compulsorily obliged under Military Law to allot part of their basic pay to support a family, whether the marriage or family was recognised by the military or not. Soldiers were only entitled to separation allowances if they were living with their partner at the time of enlistment. Soldiers who had deserted their families and had enlisted had no entitlement to separation allowances. However, the Regimental Paymaster under the authority of Military Law could make compulsory deductions from the soldier's normal weekly pay to support his family.[40]

Most reservists were married, and at the outset in September 1914 the War Office Finance Branch made amendments in existing separation allowance rules that both reservists and those volunteering for the New Army were entitled to separation allowance on the day of enlistment. This meant that most married recruits joining the New Army were entitled to these allowances from the outset of their temporary military career, and the army pay offices were charged with administering the system throughout the Army. The government sanctioned this in order to attract voluntary recruitment into the Kitchener battalions for the New Army without resorting to conscription. Indeed, the overall duties of the wartime army pay offices increased along with the growing bureaucracy as the war progressed. By early 1915 the duties of the army pay office had dramatically changed and their workloads increased.

The deployment of women staff into the Army pay offices from 1915 to 1920

The role of the APD (including the army and command pay offices) prior to 1914 was relatively simple, the whole of the financial wing of the Army having undergone a testing time of retrenchment and reform with the temporary abandonment of the APD and APC from 1904 to 1910. The onset of total war resulted in the urgent need for industrial as well as military expansion and mobilisation. There was an urgent need for enormous administrative and clerical support, as the immediate bureaucratic expansion of the financial system of the Army caused a near-meltdown of the existing system. This necessitated the recruitment of women into all echelons of the Army's financial system.

The first women to be employed at an APD establishment were unpaid volunteers who were recruited on an unofficial basis, as occurred at the Army Pay Office Woolwich between August and October 1914. The identities of the women involved are not known, and the only record as to their existence is the article 'The boy-girls of 1914'.[41] The women concerned may have been the wives and daughters of Woolwich Garrison military officers, and the first entered the Woolwich Office during the first days of the war.[42] They assisted with the preparation of active service pay-books with red covers for reservists of the RFA, the RHA and the ASC: KFK in her article commented that the red dye of the paybooks came off on their hands.[43] Shortly after, as more women volunteered, they were put to work in the separation allowance wing which, due to the expansion of bureaucracy, relocated to empty rooms above Woolwich Town Labour Exchange that was conveniently located opposite the Post Office goods depot at Woolwich Arsenal railway station.[44] The War Office, however, did not approve and ordered their removal in late October 1914. Despite this, one week later in November 1914 the first official women clerks were recruited for duties with the War Office Finance Branch, where they were also employed in matters concerning separation allowances and the disposal of the effects of soldiers who were battle casualties.[45]

From January 1915 the War Office began to officially recruit women clerks on a temporary basis for employment in all APD establishments, including the army pay offices. The decision to recruit women clerks into the army pay offices was taken due to the increasing bureaucracy of the military system with growing numbers of military personnel being required for duties overseas in active theatres of operation. This generated necessary amounts of bureaucracy relating to records of service and entitlement of correct pay and allowances. From 1915 onwards, there were increasing numbers of women clerks employed within APD establishments in the UK measured against the decline of male clerks from 1915 to 1920. This trend can be seen in the Appendix.

The introduction and experience of the loose-leaf ledger system into the Army pay offices from 1915

The loose-leaf ledger system was introduced into the army pay offices during the spring of 1915, some months after the official recruitment of women clerks. The Griffiths Committee Report gives no information regarding the inspiration for the introduction of the system and it is unlikely this came from the women clerks or from the POSB. But the introduction of the loose-leaf ledger system possibly accelerated the numbers of women clerks needed to operate the 'mechanical' clerical function successfully. The number of women clerks recruited by July 1915 numbered only 479 (see the Appendix for a comprehensive breakdown of APD and APC staff from 1914 to 1920). Six months later in

January 1916 the number had risen to 4,556 and by July 1916 had risen to 9,304. By January 1916, with the increasing number of women clerks now employed in the army pay offices, lady superintendents were recruited to act as supervisors and welfare officers for the female staff.

The innovation of the loose-leaf ledger system, as introduced into the army pay offices, may have been the first time this system was used by the civil service. Campbell-Kelly stated that the POSB was much more resistant to change and was institutionally somewhat inward-looking. Campbell-Kelly's argument was that a major organisational change within the structure of the institution had to take place before new technology could be introduced:

> The Savings Department failed to adopt any of the new information tech-nologies of the 1880s and 1890s – typewriters, calculating machines and loose-leaf filing systems – until well into the 20th century. In part, this was because the managers were unwilling to face up to major organisational change, but it was also because there were few external pressures to mecha-nise ... In the United States office mechanisation was driven in large part by an ideology of systematic management; this ideology did not make it to Britain until after World War 1.[46]

Nevertheless, there is evidence that a systematic management organisational restructuring did occur within the War Office Finance Branch and the subordi-nate army pay offices towards the end of 1914. This came about because of the pressure of increased bureaucracy that now prevailed upon the overall Army Pay Services, as the Army size was expanding rapidly with the formation of Kitch-ener's New Army. The notion that the war begun in 1914 would be a short war, over by Christmas, had evaporated by early November 1914 with the beginnings of trench warfare and the first battle for Ypres as the war developed into total world war. At the War Office Finance Branch and the APD generally, decisions were now being made outside the pre-1914 orthodox military 'think box'. By the spring of 1915, the APD began to introduce loose-leaf ledgers and, over time, other labour-saving devices were introduced. However, the Griffiths Report only gave a short account of labour-saving devices that had been intro-duced into APD establishments by 1918, including adding and listing machines.[47]

There is evidence to show that stencil duplicators were in common use. Most records were now typed on 'Qwerty' keyboard typewriters, and it would appear from an assessment of both Admiralty and War Office files that the transition from handwritten to typewritten correspondence occurred between the last decade of the nineteenth century and the first decade of the twentieth century. Photographic evidence of APD offices during the First World War held by the Adjutant General's Corps Museum, and others held by the author, suggests that Burroughs adding machines and other labour-saving devices were being used by this time.

The introduction of the loose-leaf ledger system and accompanying clerical labour-saving devices eased the mounting accounting and bookkeeping tasks required. This included the testing of arithmetical calculations from entries posted to the ledger, as well as testing the arithmetic on other documents including applications for separation allowances. The loose-leaf system included individual files where a soldier's personal account could be stored and maintained. This personal file would include all documents relating to pay and any allowances. This had not been possible with the leather-bound ledgers that existed before 1915. The soldier's account included a master card that was also maintained in the ledger. All transactions and occurrences affecting the soldier were recorded on this master card, the Army Form N (AF N) 3085. The system allowed the army pay offices to adjust to the establishment of sections and wings (a section focusing on about 1,000 personal accounts of a unit), as was common with army pay offices administering infantry accounts. The system of loose-leaf ledgers was perhaps the most important development in the administration of the bureaucracy of the wartime army pay offices, where the personal accounts of a massive and complex army were administered, a point noted by Griffiths:

> The soldier's account is credited monthly with his pay and allowances, and debited with the charges notified through the medium of pay and mess books, the acquittance roll, the hospital return, or any other legion of forms proved to meet the exigencies of military life … An application may come for the soldier making, varying or cancelling an allotment of pay to his family. Or the Paymaster may receive from various sources of information entailing a change in the rate of separation allowance. The great problem is to secure the prompt and accurate embodiment of all these things in the ledger sheets.[48]

Girls work! Downgrading the clerical function

The routine daily maintenance of the accounts housed in the loose-leaf ledgers probably downgraded clerical duties associated with their maintenance to 'mechanical' rather than 'intellectual' processes. Zimmeck[49] identified similar observations in the pre-1914 POSB. The Griffiths Committee Report described the women clerks who administered the loose-leaf ledgers in the wartime army pay offices as compilation clerks. The compilation clerks became the engine of the army pay office and the loose-leaf system became the central decision-making system for the Regimental Paymaster commanding an army pay office, a point not missed by Griffiths:

> The compilation and disposal of these documents have become the supremely important work of the office, other operations being, in a sense, subsidiary thereto. With few exceptions every regulation that the Paymaster has to apply touches these records, every accounting document that he receives has to be collated with them, every incident in a soldier's career and every casualty in his family are reflected in them, all the Paymaster's correspondence turns on them.[50]

The 'mechanical' and 'downgrading' nature of the functions required in the daily routine of administering the ledgers by the compilers suggests that there was a shallow learning curve, therefore women and girls whose previous employment may have been as machine operatives and other unskilled factory work took on the role as compiler clerks within the army pay offices very quickly. Evidence for this relates to ongoing research focused on the Army Pay Office at Nottingham. In other army pay offices the recruitment of women workers possibly attracted women from all classes of society.[51] The Nottingham research, however, tends to demonstrate that the transfer of mechanical skills from blue collar to white blouse was quick and effective both in training and performance.[52]

Although the Griffiths Committee Report was complimentary regarding the introduction of the loose-leaf ledger system, by contrast the Committee had a poor opinion of the women clerks (compilers):

> At the outbreak the breach was partly filled by clerks with commercial experience, but the demands of other branches of the Army led to the combing out most of these and to the introduction of female labour, much of it of an inexperienced and inferior type, until 60 to 70 per cent of the staff of some offices consisted of women and girls, the majority of the remainder being men unfit for combatant service and many of them hardly fit for strenuous office work.[53]

The reason for the very unflattering comments made about women clerks who were employed in the APD establishments during the Great War may have been because most of them were working-class, and were employed as compiler clerks, coming from the same social and economic background as the contemporary munitions workers.[54]

The decision to recruit lady superintendents into UK-based APD establishments from January 1916 was due to the shortage of manpower, both military and civilian. The shortage of military paymasters from September 1914 was supplemented by the recruitment of male acting civilian paymasters who were recruited from the accounting, banking and commercial world. By the end of 1915 this source too was becoming scarce. Thus the decision was taken by the War Office Finance Branch to recruit lady superintendents who performed similar duties to military APD assistant paymasters and civilian acting paymasters. Lady superintendents were also recruited for duties in other government departments, including the Admiralty and the Ministry of Munitions. The role of lady superintendent included the supervision of subordinate women clerks that were also recruited into other government departments. Zimmeck noted that prior to 1914 women were segregated from their male colleagues at the workplace, having separate office entrances and rest areas. She also noted[55] that women were also promoted to a supervisory role to oversee women, girl and boy subordinates. Matters improved within the APD establishments during the course of the war and gender integration was a major factor in the efficiency of the War Office Finance Branch and the APD establishments during the Great War.

No personal files exist of the women staff employed at the APD establishments during the Great War. However, about 500 names of lady superintendents have been discovered through a variety of sources. The first is about 12 lady superintendents who were appointed as Members to the new Order of the British Empire (MBE) between 1917 and 1920, and details feature in the one-off publication, *Burke's Order of the British Empire*, published in 1921. Some of the names have short biographical details.

About 250 women staff employed within APD establishments and the War Office Finance Branch were, between 1918 and 1919, awarded what was known as a ' "B" List mention' in dispatches, appearing in *The Times* on 3 and 4 September 1918 and 4 June 1919. The names appearing in *The Times* were, in the press communiqués of the day, brought to the notice of the Secretary of State for War for valuable services rendered in connection with the war. The 'B' List mentions were no more than press mentions and did not equate to a mention in dispatches awarded by a commander-in-chief in the field within an Expeditionary Force operational area. Neither was a 'B' List mention a prerequisite for a higher award.[56] The basic description of a recipient of a 'B' List mention only records their name. Unfortunately for civilian staff employed within APD establishments, the establishment identity was not given. The recipient is recorded as being employed within the jurisdiction of the Financial Member of the War Office. However, the 'B' List mention list of names does identify some 250 women staff who were employed within the War Office Finance Branch and the subordinate APD establishments. Again there is no identification as to the role of the recipient, whether lady superintendent or clerk. However, the assumption can be made that most were lady superintendents.

The employment of women into APD establishments also caused problems for the appropriate military authorities that have not been recorded in history. For example, the pre-1914 army pay offices were located in existing military depots that had been constructed for an all-male population. With the deployment of women clerks, obviously sufficient toilet and other accommodation would have to be satisfactorily installed. Even in the temporary army pay offices, the accommodation requisitioned did not have the appropriate offices to satisfy women clerical workers. Gay notes that the Royal Flying Corps drawing office was located in the Royal School of Mines (an all-male institution prior to 1915) and employed 20 men and 30 women, and the Air Board was asked to cover the expense of installing lavatories for the women.[57]

Final audit: 'women, the machines that did the work'!

The mechanics of the loose-leaf accounting system allowed for pay and accounting records to be compiled together. The Griffiths Report noted that the soldier's account for pay, which included a second sheet relating to entitlement to separation and other allowances, could be attached to the original pay sheet if there was an additional entitlement. This could occur if the soldier married while in service, or with changes in the dependant category that occurred from 1915 to 1918, such as multiple claims, common-law arrangements and parental entitlement for single soldiers under 26 years of age. By this method one clerk could administer both accounts. This system was impossible when the accounts were kept in inflexible leather-bound ledgers as outlined in KFK's article.[58] For the first year, 1914–15, each account for an individual soldier itemising pay, separation allowances or other maintenance allowances, could be kept in separate binders and indeed in separate offices within different locations. Thus the loose-leaf pay and accounting system was a major factor in the successful administration of pay and allowances to an ever-expanding army during the First World War.

The Griffiths Committee observed that some 40 to 45 compilation clerks (as named by the Griffiths Committee) could administer about 20,000 accounts, and in larger army pay offices some 800 compilation clerks could effectively maintain about 350,000 accounts. The relevant entries were made in the loose-leaf accounts through casualty notifications on slips that were coloured to identify the type of entry to be made in the account. Other documents on casualty slips or through regimental routine orders or hospital admission sheets notified the soldier's account of any admissions to hospital. The APD establishments employed boy and girl clerks from the age of 14 (as did the POSB), and many of the younger girls were employed as tracers. The task of tracers was to attempt to locate a soldier's account through the booking-in and loose-leaf systems. They were mobile and would attempt to trace a soldier's record. Due to the regimental numbering system and the field commissions and transfers, soldiers accounts and documents could be transferred from one section to another, or to another army pay office. At the Army Pay Office in Shrewsbury, the Regimental Paymaster employed girls from the Priory School in the town on Saturdays and in the holidays at two shillings a day.[59]

In fact, neither the Griffiths Committee nor the War Office Finance Branch appreciated that the women clerks were the cogs that made the bureaucratic pay and financial machine of the wartime army pay office organisation run efficiently. However, two Regimental Paymasters did recognise the role of women clerical workers, and their comments appeared in *The Souvenir*. Colonel A. B. Church CMG, Regimental Paymaster at APO Woolwich, made the following point to confirm this:

> The controlling of 5 million soldier accounts and almost a similar number of those of their wives and dependants and keeping those accounts, and making continual payments in such a manner that they would not only satisfy the public, but in a way that would ensure that our gallant men at the Front should have minimum concern.[60]

His colleague Colonel Blackburn the Regimental Paymaster at nearby APO Blackheath commented that, 'Women were the machines that did the work'.[61]

The efficiency of the Army pay services generally is reflected in the fact that the proper payment of the Army in the field was not a major issue during the First World War. Most of the efficiency of the Army pay services, particularly reflected in the role of the APOs during the First World War, was due to the women staff, of whom history has previously said little. Despite a pool of clerical labour in 1914, most had 'no knowledge at all of Army Accounts – the magnitude of the work accomplished was inconceivable'.[62] The system survived and victory was achieved in the 'paper' war, for at the cessation of hostilities it was found that the books balanced, as noted by Captain J. E. Thurland APD, whose words were recorded in the final page of *The Souvenir*;

Surprises,
1 The errors found 3 years ago,
2 The excellent work done in daily checking, revision and audit
3 The accuracy of accounts when finally closed.

The volume of work and the cost of running an army pay office during the First World War can be seen from this contemporary newspaper article about the Army Pay Office Nottingham. The Nottingham pay office was formed in 1916 to control the records and accounts of the Labour Corps that was also formed in 1916.

> The Army Pay Office ... which is the centre for the payment of the whole of the members of the Labour Corps, their wives, dependents and children is another triumph of organization, employing no fewer than 4,300 clerks, of whom 1,300 are females.... These provide for the keeping of the large total of 660,000 accounts, while 25,000 postal communications are received each day.... Owing to the allowances granted by the Government to wives and dependents, all the various conditions of dependency have to be investigated ... [and] ... the weekly wage bills of the Army Pay Office in Nottingham is approximately £8,000.[63]

The women clerks, lady superintendents and other seconded women staff, mainly from the POSB, who were employed within APD establishments, as well as their male colleagues, were working with complex accounting, audit and legal systems, regulated through manuals and War Office 'Financial Instructions' that were constantly being amended. This was all part of the 'black art' of army accounting and administration that became more complicated as the war dragged on and where allowances became more generous and wider ranging. The APD women also had to cope with the alien culture of a military environment, 'Where work was carried on by both sexes under semi-military discipline the discipline though slightly irksome at times was new and possibly amusing to some.'[64] During the post-1918 era, women generally only gained certain minimal rights that had been previously denied to them. The prevailing paternalistic attitude assumed that a women's place was in the home, and where women did work it often reflected low pay and short-term contracts.[65] The women who worked in the wartime APD establishments were as temporary as the reforms of separation allowances that had expanded in breadth and scope during the Great War. The post-1918 GPO and Savings Bank Department still employed them, albeit on the same conditions that existed before 1914. Inequalities in pay structures based on gender were common in all spheres of work during most of the twentieth century, and were accepted by employer and trade unions alike.

Women aged 30 and over were enfranchised not on the same terms as male enfranchisement, and equal enfranchisement came only in 1928, ten years after the end of the Great War. Under the Sex Disqualification (Removal) Act of 1919 women were now allowed to enter the accountancy and legal professions, although few did. The same was true of the higher civil service where a few women did penetrate the higher civil service after 1920, as was the case of Hilda Martindale, who wrote an insider's view of women in the Home Civil Service in 1938. She praised women employed in 'white-bloused' government work during the First World War, most of it in a temporary capacity for the duration of the war only:

> In the War Office much responsible work was given over to women. They had to draft letters and prepare decisions that would bind the Department. They were employed on responsible accounting work in the army pay offices, in investigating disputes in connection with War Office contracts, and in coding and decoding telegrams.[66]

Many women workers did find the war a genuinely liberating experience, albeit a temporary one, including the women who were employed within the wartime APD establishments. An example of this can be seen from the 'Boy-Girl' article written in 1920, where KFK reminisced on the ten weeks spent, in the sultry summer of 1914 with a highly emotive atmosphere, at the Separation Allowance Wing temporarily housed at Woolwich labour exchange, with the bands daily playing off drafts of reservists to war with martial music as they departed from Woolwich Arsenal station:

> What days of sudden but lasting friendships, of lightning impressions, printed forever on the excited brain. Girls to whom the sight of a soldier had been something of an event, studying paysheets with sergeants and corporals, as if born to it.[67]

Appendix

Growth of the numbers and categories employed within APD establishments within the UK, 1914 to 1920 (extracts from 'The Military Effort during the Great War 1914 to 1920', section 23, 'Growth of the Royal Army Pay Department and Corps').

Table 14.1 Army Pay Department – strength at home 1914–20

	Officers, Army Pay Department	Civilian acting paymasters	Lady superintendents
1 August 1914	151	–	–
1 January 1915	165	263	–
1 July 1915	167	412	–
1 January 1916	165	516	13
1 July 1916	190	541	100
1 March 1917	207	573	148
1 August 1917	227	779	139
1 October 1917	233	785	136
1 January 1918	221	774	138
1 August 1918	254	823	140
1 December 1918	251	808	130
1 February 1919	325	812	241
1 April 1919	379	1,400	279
1 August 1919	351	1,145	252
1 December 1919	306	731	108
10 April 1920	206	326	32

Table 14.2 Army Pay Corps – strength at home 1914–20

	Army Pay Corps	Civilian writers, etc.	Male civil clerks	Female clerks
1 August 1914	585	299	–	–
1 January 1915	4,176	–	1,815	–
1 July 1915	6,368	–	2,665	479
1 January 1916	5,994	–	1,752	4,556
1 July 1916	5,667	–	1,345	9,304
1 March 1917	7,693	–	959	11,920
1 August 1917	9,851	–	1,011	14,594
1 October 1917	10,761	–	990	15,119
1 January 1918	12,226	–	990	16,081
1 August 1918	11,761	–	997	17,532
1 December 1918	18,184	–	923	18,758
1 February 1919	12,906	–	3,354	25,603
1 April 1919	8,711	–	8,896	28,472
1 August 1919	5,853	–	7,679	20,434
1 December 1919	3,096	–	6,009	11,070
10 April 1920	1,760	–	4,500	4,255

Notes

1 The author would like to acknowledge the kind assistance given by the following: Dr Christine Joy, Archivist, Manchester High School for Girls; Ms Kate Perry, Archivist, Girton College, Cambridge; Colonel J. D. Sainsbury OBE TD FSA, who directed the author to the existence of the 'B' List of mention in dispatches that were awarded to civil servants in 1918–19. The author was able to ascertain from the 'B' special mentions list the names of some 250 women staff employed within establishments under the remit of the Finance Member of the War Office, including those employed within APD establishments under the control of the War Office Finance Branch.

2 *The Souvenir*, 1920, pp. 5–6. Imperial War Museum Library (IWM) K87/465.

3 The National Archives (TNA) WO 33/11318 – *Report of the Committee on Army Pay Office Organisation*, 1919 (the Griffiths Report).

4 A. Marwick, *Women at War*, London: Fontana, 1977; G. Braybon, *Women Workers in the First World War*, London: Routledge, 1981; D. Thom, *Nice Girls and Rude Girls: Women Workers in World War I*, London: Tauris, 2000.

5 M. Campbell-Kelly, 'Large-scale data processing in the Prudential 1850–1930', *Accounting, Business and Financial History Journal* 2, 1992, pp. 120–3; M. Campbell-Kelly, 'Data processing and technological change: the Post Office Savings Bank, 1861–1930', *Technology and Culture* 39, 1998, pp. 19–22.

6 M. Zimmeck, 'Jobs for the girls: the expansion of clerical work for women, 1850–1914', in A. V. John (ed.), *Unequal Opportunities: Women's Employment in England 1800–1918*, Oxford: Basil Blackwell, 1986, pp. 159–60.

7 G. Anderson, *The White-Blouse Revolution*, Manchester: Manchester University Press, 1988; S. P. Walker, 'Identifying the women behind the "railed-in desk": the proto-feminisation of bookkeeping in Britain', *Accounting, Auditing and Accountability Journal* 16 (4), 2003, p. 3.

8 J. Black, 'War, women and accounting: female staff in the UK Army Pay Department Offices 1914–1920', *Accounting, Business and Financial History* 16 (2), 2006, pp. 195–218.

9 Marwick, *Women at War*.

10 Braybon, *Women Workers*.

11 TNA, WO 32/9316 – *History of Separation Allowances and Effects*.

12 S. Pedersen, *Family, Dependence and the Origins of the Welfare State: Britain and France 1914–1945*, Cambridge: Cambridge University Press, 1995, p. 79.

13 S. Pedersen, 'Gender, welfare and citizenship in Britain during the Great War', *American Historical Review* 95 (4), 1990, pp. 984–1006. Continuing research suggests that the scope of separation allowances during the First World War went far beyond the aspirations of Beveridge and his 1942 proposals. From 1906 to 1914 Beveridge was adviser to the government on old-age pensions and national insurance. During the First World War Beveridge was responsible for the control of manpower within the UK.

14 TNA, WO/9316, *History of Separation Allowances*.

15 Zimmeck, 'Jobs for the girls', p. 163.

16 H. Gay, *The History of Imperial College 1907–2007*, London: Imperial College Press, 2007, p. 118.

17 *The Souvenir*, 1920, p. 15.

18 J. Black, 'Supermen and superwomen: the Army Pay Services and the First World War', *Journal of the Society for Army Historical Research* 84, 2006, p. 269.

19 *The Souvenir*, 1920, p. 15.

20 TNA, WO 32/9316, *History of Separation Allowances*.

21 *Nottingham Evening Post*, 29 March 1918.

22 L. G. Hinchliffe, *'Trust and be Trusted': the Royal Army Pay Corps and its Origins*,

published privately by Corps Headquarters, RAPC Worthy Down, Winchester, 1983, p. 62.

23 A. Kessler-Harris, 'What is gender history now?', in D. Canadine (ed.), *What is History Now?* Basingstoke: Palgrave Macmillan, 2002, p. 99.

24 TNA, WO 32/9316, *History of Separation Allowances*; J. Black, 'War, women and accounting', p. 213.

25 M. Campbell-Kelly, 'Data processing and technological change', p. 2.

26 M. Campbell-Kelly, 'Data processing and technological change', pp. 20–1.

27 Manchester High School for Girls began a secretarial and commercial course in 1901 under the tutelage of Miss Violet Moore (Archives of Manchester High School for Girls).

28 George Gissing noted the rise of these secretarial colleges in his novel *The Odd Women*, first published in 1893. An example of such a secretarial college was Loreburn College, which was opened in Manchester in January 1914 and specialised in secretarial courses for both young men and women. The curriculum was, however, split along gender lines: young men could take courses related to senior and junior clerical work, but not young women. The women students had to be content with shorthand and typing courses, or typing and bookkeeping courses, although a foreign language might be available. The gender segregation in the curriculum suggests that the young men were being trained for more 'intellectual' clerical positions, whereas the women students were being specifically trained for more 'mechanical' divisions of clerical labour. (A copy of the College Prospectus of 1914 can be found in the Archives, Manchester High School for Girls.)

29 Lilian Maud Bull (1877–1943) attended Girton College from 1895 to 1898, and taught in independent and county secondary schools in Wales until 1918. From 1918 to 1923 Lilian was a junior administrative assistant at the War Office Finance Branch (Accounts 6, experimental cost accounts). She continued with secretarial work from 1923 until her death in 1943 (*Girton College Register 1869–1943*, entry for 1895, p. 91).

30 E. Jones, *Accountancy and the British Economy, 1840–1980*, London: Batsford, 1981, p. 136; K. Shackleton, 'Gender segregation in Scottish chartered accountancy: the development of male concerns about the admission of women, 1900–25', *Accounting, Business and Financial History* 9 (1), 1999, pp. 136–9. Dorothy Ashford (later Mrs Clark) attended Girton College from 1910 to 1913; she gained a teaching qualification from Cheltenham Ladies' College in 1914 and taught first at St Paul's Girls' School and then at Kirkham Grange School. From 1917 to 1919, the year of her marriage, Dorothy worked as a cashier in a chartered accountants' office in Birmingham. The first woman to be admitted to any professional accountants' body was Miss H. M. Claridge, who was admitted to the Incorporated Society of Accountants and Auditors in 1920, when her father was President. Miss E. Watts was admitted to the Institute of Chartered Accountants for England and Wales in 1924 (Jones, *Accountancy and the British Economy*, p. 136). However Miss Minnie Emily Moore, who was born in 1871, may have been the first woman graduate to enter the accounting profession. Minnie attended Girton College from 1892 to 1895, graduating with a Mathematics Tripos, 1895. Minnie became an Incorporated Accountant, being admitted as an Associate on 19 January 1922 (*Girton College Register 1869–1946*).

31 Zimmeck, 'Jobs for the girls', pp. 158–61.

32 Zimmeck, 'Jobs for the girls', p. 160.

33 TNA, WO 33/11318, the Griffiths Report, para 5.

34 *The Souvenir*, 1920, p. 3.

35 TNA, WO 33/11318, the Griffiths Report, para 5.

36 *The Souvenir*, 1920, p. 5.

37 The name 'Dover' system was derived from the Army Pay Office at Dover (responsible for the accounts of the Royal Garrison Artillery), where the pilot scheme was undertaken between 1904 and 1905.

38 J. Black, 'Administering the "Dover" system of peace and war', paper presented to the Management History Group, Queen Mary College, University of London, 19 June 2005.

39 J. Baynes, *Morale: A Study of Men and Courage*, new edn, London: Leo Cooper, 1987, p. 150.

40 J. Black, 'Supermen and superwomen', pp. 267–8. The original source for this information was the 'Poor Law Officer Manual' for 1917, p. 157. This referred to a case of a soldier of the Essex Regiment who had deserted his family and enlisted. The family were in the care of the Croydon Guardians of the Poor. The Guardians appealed to the War Office for the issue of separation allowances that were denied due to his desertion. However, the Regimental Paymaster at APO Warley made compulsory deductions from the soldier's weekly pay amounting to four shilling a week. This allowed the release of the soldier's family from the care of the Croydon Poor Law Guardians.

41 *The Souvenir*, 1920, pp. 5–6.

42 J. Black, 'War, women and accounting', pp. 197–8.

43 *The Souvenir*, 1920, p. 5.

44 Ibid.

45 TNA, WO 32/9316, *History of Separation Allowances*.

46 Campbell-Kelly, 'Data processing and technological change', p. 21.

47 TNA, WO 33/11318, the Griffiths Report, para 141.

48 TNA, WO 33/11318, the Griffiths Report, para 18.

49 Zimmeck, 'Jobs for the girls', p. 160.

50 TNA, WO 33/11318, the Griffiths Report, para 10.

51 It would appear that the majority of lady superintendents were middle class and single or widowed, although some married lady superintendents have been identified. For example, Mrs Catherine Reid Dick (née Treadwell, later Lady Reid Dick, 1890–1981). Catherine married William Reid Dick, a sculptor, on 6 August 1914, two days after the start of the First World War. Mrs Reid Dick became a superintendent at an APD establishment in London and was mentioned in dispatches in 1918 (*Times*, 3 September 1918). Her husband had enlisted into the Royal Army Medical Corps (Territorial Force) some days after his marriage and served in Egypt, transferring to the Royal Engineers as a surveyor in 1917. He became a renowned sculptor and designed the Menin Gate lions at Ypres and other war memorials, for which services he was knighted in 1935. Mrs Beryl Bradford was the widow of Captain S. B. Bradford, who died prior to 1914. Mrs Bradford was appointed MBE in 1920 for war work that included work with the Metropolitan Police as a volunteer with women patrols, 1914–15; superintendent APD, 1916–19; and Women's Controller at the Air Ministry, 1919–20. Mrs Ada Leila Gray, superintendent Army Pay Office York, was mentioned in dispatches (*Times*, 3 September 1918), and appointed MBE (*Burke's Handbook of the Order of the British Empire*, 1921, p. 223). Mrs Mary Josephine Farrant (widow from Heavitree, Exeter), senior lady superintendent, appointed MBE in 1920. Prior to 1914, Mrs Farrant had been a Home Office probation officer (*Burke's Handbook*, pp. 184–5). One lady superintendent identified from *Burke's* appeared to have been working class. Miss Nellie Hurcomb Palmer was born in Mansfield, Nottinghamshire in 1877. From 1912 to 1914 Miss Palmer was the Organising Secretary of the National Union of Suffragette Societies. From 1916 to 1920, Miss Palmer was a superintendent (technical and welfare) at the Army Pay Office Exeter and was also awarded a mention in dispatches (*Times*, 3 September 1918) and appointed MBE (*Burke's Handbook*, p. 397).

52 Again, ongoing research by the author based on the temporary army pay office established in the lace-making centre of Nottingham in 1916 suggests that the majority of women clerks recruited were from the locality and, out of 50 traced, most had previ-

ously been employed in the hosiery and lace industries as machinists. The transition from 'blue-collar' to 'white-blouse' work may have been the result of the expansion of general elementary education since the Education Act of 1870.

53 TNA, WO 33/11318, the Griffiths Report, para 3.
54 Thom, *Nice Girls*, pp. 34–5.
55 Zimmeck, 'Jobs for the girls', p. 62.
56 J. D. Sainsbury, 'The "A" and "B" lists of mentions for valuable services in connection with the war 1914–1919', *The Journal of the Orders and Medals Research Society* 17 (2), 1976, pp. 106–15.
57 Gay, *History of Imperial College*, p. 136 fn. 31.
58 *The Souvenir*, 1920, p. 5.
59 P. E. Price, *The History of Priory School 1911–1981*, Shrewsbury: privately printed, 1981, p. 36.
60 *The Souvenir*, 1920, p. 2.
61 Ibid.
62 Ibid.
63 *Nottingham Evening Post*, 29 March 1918.
64 *The Souvenir*, 1920, p. 12.
65 G. Braybon (ed.), *Evidence, History and the Great War: Historians and the Impact of 1914–18*, Oxford: Berghahn Books, 2003, pp. 216–28.
66 H. Martindale, *Women Servants of the State: A History of Women in the Civil Service*, London: George Allen & Unwin, 1938, p. 74.
67 *The Souvenir*, 1920, p. 5.

Bibliography

Anderson, G., *The White-Blouse Revolution*, Manchester: Manchester University Press, 1988.

Baynes, J., *Morale: A Study of Men and Courage*, new edn, London: Leo Cooper, 1987.

Black, J., 'War, women and accounting: female staff in the UK Army Pay Department Offices 1914–1920', *Accounting, Business and Financial History* 16 (2), 2006, pp. 195–218.

Black, J., 'Supermen and superwomen: the Army Pay Services and the First World War', *Journal of the Society for Army Historical Research* 84, 2006, pp. 260–80.

Black, J., 'Administering the "Dover" system in peace and war', paper presented to the Management History Group Meeting, Queen Mary College, University of London, June 2005.

Black, J., 'The biggest bookkeeper in Britain – the Army Pay Department 1878–1920', paper presented to the Accounting, Business and Finance History Conference, Cardiff Business School, September 1995.

Braybon, G. (ed.), *Evidence, History and the Great War: Historians and the Impact of 1914–18*, Oxford: Berghahn, 2003.

Braybon, G., *Women Workers in the First World War*, London: Routledge, 1981.

Campbell-Kelly, M., 'Data processing and technological change: the Post Office Savings Bank, 1861–1930', *Technology and Culture* 39, 1998, pp. 1–32.

Campbell-Kelly, M., 'Large-scale data processing in the Prudential 1850–1930', *Accounting, Business and Financial History* 2, 1992, pp. 117–39.

Churchill Seton, Lt Col., *Forbidden Fruit for Young Men*, 7th edn, London: James Nisbett & Co, 1909.

Gay, H., *The History of Imperial College 1907–2007*, London: Imperial College Press, 2007.

Gissing, George, *The Odd Women*, ed. Patricia Ingham, Oxford: Oxford University Press, 2000.

Hinchliffe, L. G., *'Trust and be Trusted': The Royal Army Pay Corps and its Origins*, published privately by Corps Headquarters, RAPC Worthy Down, Winchester, 1983.

Jones, E., *Accountancy and the British Economy 1840–1980*, London: Batsford, 1981.

Kessler-Harris, A., 'What is gender history now?', in Cannadine, D. (ed.), *What is History Now?* Basingstoke: Palgrave Macmillan, 2002, pp. 95–112.

Martindale, H., *Women Servants of the State: A History of Women in the Civil Service*, London: George Allen & Unwin, 1938.

Marwick, A., *Women at War*, London: Fontana, 1977.

Nottingham Evening Post, 29 March 1918.

Pedersen, S., *Family, Dependence and the Origins of the Welfare State: Britain and France 1914–1945*, Cambridge: Cambridge University Press, 1995.

Pedersen, S., 'Gender, welfare and citizenship in Britain during the Great War', *American Historical Review* 95 (4), 1990, pp. 984–1006.

Price, P. E., *The History of Priory School 1911–1981*, Shrewsbury: privately printed, 1981.

Sainsbury, J. D., 'The "A" and "B" lists of mentions for valuable services in connection with the war 1914–1919', *The Journal of the Orders and Medals Research Society* 17 (2), 1976, pp. 106–15.

Shackleton, K., 'Gender segregation in Scottish chartered accountancy: the deployment of male concerns about the admission of women, 1900–25', *Accounting, Business and Financial History* 9 (1), 1999, pp. 135–56.

Strachan, H., *The Politics of The British Army*, Oxford: Clarendon Press, 2004.

Thom, D., *Nice Girls and Rude Girls: Women Workers in World War 1*, London: Tauris, 2000.

Thompson, F., *Lark Rise to Candleford*, ed. Hannah Sambrook, Harlow: Longman, 1984.

Times, 3 September 1918.

Walker, S. P., 'Identifying the women behind the "railed-in desk": the proto-feminisation of bookkeeping in Britain', *Accounting, Auditing and Accountability Journal* 16 (4), 2003, pp. 606–39.

Zimmeck, M., 'Jobs for the girls: the expansion of clerical work for women, 1850–1914', in John, A. V. (ed.), *Unequal Opportunities: Women's Employment in England 1800–1918*, Oxford: Basil Blackwell, 1986.

Girton College Archive

Girton College Register 1869–1946 WWI Card index of undergraduates' contributions during the Great War.

Imperial War Museum Library

The Souvenir, 1920, reference K87/465.

Manchester High School for Girls Archive

Loveburn Secretarial College Prospectus 1914.

The National Archives, Kew, London:

Burke's Order of the British Empire, 1921.

Statistics of the Military Effort of the British Empire during the Great War, 1914–1920, The War Office, March 1922. Reprinted in 1999 by the Naval and Military Press, London.

WO 32/9316. *History of Separation Allowances and Effects*.

WO 33/11318. *Report of the Committee on Army Pay Office Organisation* (the Griffiths Report), 1919.

15 Women and money
The United States

Nancy Marie Robertson and Susan M. Yohn

A former colony of Britain, the United States based women's rights to property on a legal foundation drawn from English Common Law as well as equity law. Such concepts as coverture or *feme sole* were known in the American context. As the American legal system developed over time, at least two critical factors differentiated it from that of England and Wales. One was the introduction of legal ideas from elsewhere such as community property (a continental idea), and the second was that most financial and marital laws were established at the local and state not national level. Hence the history of American women's relationship to money varied from state to state and the more sophisticated analyses tend to be case studies of the situation in particular states. As noted in the general introduction, much of the work on women and money has focused on women as wage-earning workers or on the unpaid labour of women as wives and mothers.[1] In addition, in the American context, much has been written about women as consumers.[2] There is a growing literature on married women's right to own property, women's ownership of business, and the possible relationship between the two. Far less has been written about American women's engagement with other aspects of the economy, such as finance including banking, stocks, and other forms of investment.

The existing literature, as well as the two chapters that follow, raise a series of interesting questions. What was the relationship between the legal ownership of assets and the actual control of them? Was it in women's interest to be treated the same as men or was their position advanced by being treated differently? What was the relationship between the changes in women's financial position and their social and political status? Were women's financial activities, including business ownership, best understood as the consequence of their own choices or the result of social constraints?

Married Women's Property Acts

The right of American married women to own property was one of the critical legal changes of the nineteenth century. The first married women's property acts were passed in 1839 in Mississippi, 1844 in Michigan, 1845 in Massachusetts and in Texas. The laws were written into state constitutions in California (1849),

Oregon (1857) and Kansas (1859). By 1865, 29 states had some form of married women's property acts. The process was not completed nationwide until the early twentieth century. We use the umbrella term 'married women's property acts' advisedly because provisions of the laws varied from state to state and there were possible multiple incarnations within a single state. In New York, there were three versions: the original law was passed in 1848 and amended in 1849. Additional legislation was passed in 1850 and 1851 to 'eliminate the gray areas of earlier legislation'. These efforts to reform the original law culminated in the passage in 1862 of what Norma Basch identifies as one of the boldest of statutes – the New York Earnings Act – which 'gave wives the right to sue and be sued and included their wages as part of their separate estate'.[3]

Historians disagree over the causes and ultimate significance of married women's property laws and the adoption of community property laws.[4] What might be referred to as the optimistic school, as represented by Carole Shammas, asserts that these acts 'represented the most substantial change in women's legal status in 700 years of the common law'.[5] The laws contributed to changes not only in women's economic position, but also in their social and familial roles. Shammas observes that the 'late nineteenth century witnessed a more rapid increase in the divorce rate ... than at any other time in U.S. history' partially as a consequence of these laws.[6]

Other historians are more restrained in their assessment of the impact. Assessing New York's laws, Basch concludes that a key motivation was the desire of men to control the actions of other men, namely a father who wished to see a daughter's assets protected from an unscrupulous or incompetent son-in-law.[7] Suzanne Lebsock finds that in Virginia legislators sought to protect wives' money from creditors in volatile economic periods. Lebsock argues against a liberatory interpretation of the laws, writing that they were intended to *protect* women rather than make them equal. In diminishing their significance, she concurs with Mary Beard that married women's property laws 'merely transformed generally accepted equity principles into provisions of statutes'.[8] These critics find the complexity of the marketplace demanded new laws and legal options and that the 'woman question' was secondary. In addition to debating motives, some historians question the actual impact of the laws. In practice, wives could be pressured to defer to their husband's wishes. Lebsock goes so far as to suggest that, in a time of unease over social change, women may have become *more* deferential.[9] The connection between legal ownership and effective control (let alone equality) could be tenuous as women's autonomy was often elusive.

Scholars, however, agree that women at the time saw the laws as significant. Passage of married women's property acts was a priority of early women's rights advocates even before they championed suffrage. They believed that the laws could change women's economic capacity. Given the limitations we have noted, one might ask why they emphasized passage of these laws. Obviously there was a potential for financial gain, but they also believed that treating women as equal economic actors would be the basis of women's political and social power. Married women's property acts challenged the legal construct of man and wife as one. To advocates like Elizabeth Cady Stanton, the property acts redeemed a woman 'from her lost condition' and meant that she was 'no longer a legal nonentity'.[10]

In hindsight, changes in property laws ironically presented women as legal equals prior to their having the power necessary to achieve full equality. Alongside married women's property acts in many states were laws intended to protect women by requiring that women be examined separately by a notary about their wishes before signing away their property rights. In their study of legal rulings in the second half of the nineteenth century, Stacy Braukman and Michael Ross found that the courts, including the United States Supreme Court, increasingly eroded this protection. In upholding the fiction of women's equal power, the Supreme Court forwarded a 'new view [that] treated married women as equals and took them seriously as commercial actors' in cases regarding women's property rights. Braukman and Ross see the outcome as ambiguous in that it 'left propertied wives in a position that was at once less protected *and* less constrained'.[11] At the same time, the courts also maintained women's dependence when they accepted the right of a man's creditors to his wife's wages.[12] Bottom line, the US Supreme Court and many state courts favoured promoting the rights of creditors rather than protecting females or promoting their effective equality.[13]

Women's businesses

To support her belief in the impact of the new property laws, Carole Shammas points to the increase in size of women's assets over the nineteenth century; there was, she notes, 'more change in female wealthholding ... between the 1860s and 1890s than had transpired in the previous two hundred years of American history'.[14] Having gained the right to own property, however, businesswomen were often stymied by limitations on obtaining credit.[15] There were also cultural obstacles. Despite the thousands of women engaged in running businesses across the country, the reigning image of a proprietor was that of a businessman. Historians have developed a vibrant historical literature on American women as proprietors, entrepreneurs and businesswomen through case studies of individual women, specific industries and local communities.[16] Particularly useful, however, is Angel Kwolek-Folland's general survey of women's participation in business that provides a framework in which to place the vast majority of the case studies.[17] Her story is not one simple upward trend but rather one with peaks and valleys. She argues that the numbers of businesswomen increased but that women lost ground in the late nineteenth century as the economy underwent a transformation from individual proprietorships to corporate capitalism and markets shifted from local to national. Opportunities to participate in the business world increased as large corporate structures employed growing numbers of women as clerical, sales or support staff. Culturally, the image of the 'business girl' entered common parlance, but her success overshadowed the declining possibilities for women as business owners.[18]

For much of American history, businesswomen tended to start enterprises related to their domestic work, including boarding-houses, clothing and millinery, food production, laundry work, small retail stores and the beauty industry – what Edith Sparks has called the 'commerce of domesticity'.[19] An examination of the case studies of businesswomen suggests some additional trends: they operated on shoestring budgets, had access to limited credit, relied on the support of family members and other kinds of personal networks, generally remained sole proprietors, and had a relatively high failure rate. These generalizations ring true for many small businesses whether they were started by men or women. One difference was that few women sought to grow their businesses; their ambitions were checked by modest desires for a 'decent return on their risk, some value for their labors, and, if not always roses, at least bread'.[20] Whether women kept their businesses small because of their own choices or because of the constraints they faced remains open for further study. Although women had functioned as entrepreneurial capitalists, they were clearly not visible as large-scale corporate capitalists.[21] Their contribution to the development of corporate capitalism at the turn of the century would come in their role as investors.

Investment and finance

Even as state legislators debated married women's property acts in ante-bellum America, women were, in the words of Robert Wright, 'part of the cutting edge of national economic development'. As early as the colonial period they owned and speculated in government bonds and debt. Popular were investments in banks, insurance and joint-stock companies that yielded high dividends.[22] By the 1880s women's forays into the stock market were significant enough to gain the attention of leading Wall Street figures. William Fowler, a speculator himself, suggested that women's virtues – hope, patience, fortitude, excitement, fancy – were all associated with speculation.[23] Fowler's contemporary, trader Henry Clews was less favourable in his assessment of women's investing abilities. Wall Street, he argued, should be off-limits to women. They did not have the 'nature' for speculation. They ran the risk of being 'fleeced'. He warned them not to speculate because they were 'impulsive' and 'impressionable'. He concluded that 'it is probably only in the matrimonial line that women can become successful speculators'.[24] These comments were not trivial nor made in passing, but represented serious social constraints upon women's ability to participate in the investment world. The prescriptive literature of the time advised women to turn over management of their financial portfolios to trusted male advisors. To date there have been no studies building on Robert Wright's work for the later period in America. What women did or did not do, we do not know.

Money has often been seen as something related only to the business sector. An analysis of women and money suggests the need to look also at the 'non-profit' or 'voluntary' sector. Wright points out that women's benevolent associations of the early nation were engaged in the financial markets, investing in equities to support their reform activities.[25] In examining the history of women and money, one must look at the role played by women's voluntary associations in training women to raise, manage, dispense and invest money.[26] By the late nineteenth century, women's organizations advocating issues ranging from suffrage to Protestant missions raised millions of dollars and were a potent economic force. Women presented these undertakings as being for social or moral good rather than as a sign of their economic or political acumen. While the small proprietor may not have 'grown' her business, the female leaders of these reform organizations essentially operated international businesses where they bought and sold property, invested in equities and employed thousands. Observers at the time described these women's voluntary efforts as paralleling those of their male family members engaged in the corporate sector. J. P. Morgan credited Grace Dodge, head of several national reform organizations, as having 'the finest business brain in the United States, not excepting that of any man'. While Dodge's male family members exerted their efforts in commerce and mining, Dodge found her calling, as one biographer put it, as a 'merchant of dreams'.[27]

Historians such as Alan Trachtenberg and Alfred Chandler have analysed the rise of a national integrated corporate order in the early twentieth century.[28] This trend was replicated among voluntary associations, with the difference being that in this sector it was women who had built the large systematic organizations. The association of reform work with notions like 'voluntary' or 'non-profit' has blinded many historians to the large amounts of money involved. Male leaders at the time were not so near-sighted. In the 1920s, they increasingly identified female-controlled organizations as the targets for what were essentially hostile takeovers.[29] At the end of the day, women in both voluntary and for-profit organizations were in comparable positions, relegated to a limited number of jobs, in bureaucracies where they faced what we would come to call 'glass ceilings'. Women were incorporated into male-dominated organizations where they exercised little authority over the financial decisions made. Paradoxically, this decrease in women's power came as they owned more wealth, but management and control of that wealth was administered (and controlled) by financial professionals.[30]

Notes

1 Among the many works on wage-earning women in the United States, one of the most comprehensive remains Alice Kessler-Harris, *Out to Work: A History of Wage Earning Women in the United States*, New York: Oxford University Press, 1982; see also Ava Baron (ed.), *Work Engendered: Toward a New History of American Labor*, Ithaca, NY: Cornell University Press, 1991.
2 Susan Porter Benson, *Counter Cultures: Saleswomen, Managers, and Customers in American Department Stores, 1890–1940*, Urbana, IL: University of Illinois Press, 1986; Elaine S. Abelson, *When Ladies Go A-Thieving*, New York: Oxford University Press, 1989; and Kathy Lee Peiss, *Cheap Amusements: Working Women and Leisure in Turn-of-the-Century New York*, Philadelphia, PA: Temple University Press, 1986.
3 Norma Basch, *In the Eyes of the Law: Women, Marriage, and Property in*

Nineteenth-Century New York, Ithaca, NY: Cornell University Press, 1982, p. 28. A woman's right to her earnings was more controversial than her rights to retain property (that she held prior to marriage). This stemmed from the beliefs both that there was a unity of interests in the marriage and that a man was the head of the household. Therefore money that a woman earned during marriage was 'rightfully' the man's to control. Additionally, many at the time believed that a man was entitled to his wife's time and services (and any resulting wages).

4 A brief discussion of community property laws can be found in Carole Shammas, 'Re-assessing the Married Women's Property Acts', *Journal of Women's History* 6 (1), 1994, pp. 9, 11, and Stacy Lorraine Braukman and Michael A. Ross, 'Married women's property and male coercion: United States' courts and the privy examination, 1864–1887', *Journal of Women's History* 12 (2), 2000, p. 60.

5 Shammas, 'Re-assessing the Married Women's Property Acts', p. 9.

6 Shammas, 'Re-assessing the Married Women's Property Acts', p. 26. Family law, like financial laws, varied from state to state.

7 Basch, *In the Eyes of the Law*.

8 Mary Beard quoted in Suzanne Lebsock, *The Free Women of Petersburg: Status and Culture in a Southern Town, 1784–1860*, New York: W.W. Norton, 1984, p. 84.

9 Lebsock, *The Free Women of Petersburg*, p. 86.

10 From Elizabeth Cady Stanton's address to the Legislature of the State of New York (1854); see Elizabeth Cady Stanton, Susan B. Anthony and Matilda Joslyn Gage (eds), *History of Woman Suffrage*, Vol. 1, *1848–1861*, New York: Fowler & Wells, 1881, pp. 600–601.

11 Braukman and Ross, 'Married women's property and male coercion', p. 75 (emphasis added).

12 Braukman and Ross, 'Married women's property and male coercion', pp. 71–72, 74. The Supreme Court ruled in these cases because they entailed citizens of one state suing those of another. Although the decisions were not binding on states, state courts accepted them as legal precedent to overturn laws protecting women.

13 As suggested above, there was a fair amount of variation among states; for one example of extreme differences in a single region (the South), see Suzanne D. Lebsock, 'Radical reconstruction and the property rights of Southern women', *Journal of Southern History* 43 (2), 1977, pp. 195–216.

14 Shammas, 'Re-assessing the Married Women's Property Acts', p. 21.

15 Access to credit became an issue for the women's rights movement of the late twentieth century and was finally achieved with the passage in 1974 of the Equal Credit Opportunity Act.

16 Lynn Hudson, *The Making of 'Mammy Pleasant': A Black Entrepreneur in Nineteenth-Century San Francisco*, Urbana, IL: University of Illinois Press, 2002; Wendy Gamber, *The Female Economy: The Millinery and Dressmaking Trades, 1860–1930*, Urbana, IL: University of Illinois Press, 1997; Kathy Lee Peiss, *Hope in a Jar: The Making of America's Beauty Culture*, New York: Metropolitan Books, 1998; Edith Sparks, *Capital Intentions: Female Proprietors in San Francisco, 1850–1920*, Chapel Hill, NC: University of North Carolina Press, 2006.

17 Angel Kwolek-Folland, *Incorporating Women: A History of Women and Business in the United States*, New York: Twayne Publishers, 1998.

18 See Angel Kwolek-Folland, *Engendering Business: Men and Women in the Corporate Office, 1870–1930*, Baltimore, MD: Johns Hopkins Press, 1994, for a discussion of the growing presence and importance of women in corporate offices in the United States and the rise of the image of the 'business girl'.

19 Sparks, *Capital Intentions*, also calls it 'commercial domesticity'.

20 Kwolek-Folland, *Incorporating Women*, p. 216. See Edith Sparks on the decline in women's proprietorships from 1880 to 1920.

21 For a general discussion of women's 'invisibility' in the business history literature

and the obstacles they faced, see Mary Yeager, 'Will there ever be a feminist business history', in Mary Yeager (ed.), *Women in Business*, 3 vols, Cheltenham: Edward Elgar, 1999, vol. 1, pp. xi–xciii.

22 Robert Wright, 'Women and finance in the early national U.S.', *Essays in History* 42, 2000, available online: http://etext.lib.virginia.edu/journals/EH/EH42/EH42.html (accessed 29 July 2008), para 31.

23 William Worthington Fowler, *Twenty Years of Inside Life in Wall Street*, New York: Orange Judd Co., 1880.

24 Henry Clews, *Twenty-Eight Years in Wall Street*, New York: J.S. Ogilvie Publishing Co., 1887, pp. 443–445.

25 Wright, 'Women and finance in the early national U.S.', para 38.

26 For more on this subject, see Anne Boylan, *The Origins of Women's Activism: New York and Boston, 1797–1840*, Chapel Hill, NC: University of North Carolina Press, 2002; Lori Ginzberg, *Women and the Work of Benevolence: Morality, Politics, and Class in the Nineteenth-Century United States*, New Haven, CT: Yale University Press, 1990; Susan Yohn, 'Let Christian women set the example in their own gifts: the "business" of Protestant women's organizations', in Margaret Bendroth and Virginia Brereton (eds), *Women and Twentieth Century Protestantism*, Urbana, IL: University of Illinois Press, 2002, pp. 213–235.

27 Abbie Graham, *Grace Dodge: Merchant of Dreams*, New York: Women's Press, 1926, p. 328.

28 Alan Trachtenberg, *The Incorporation of America: Culture and Society in the Gilded Age*, New York: Hill & Wang, 1982; Alfred Chandler, *Strategy and Structure: Chapters in the History of the Industrial Enterprise*, Cambridge, MA: MIT Press, 1962.

29 See Susan Yohn, 'Let Christian women set the example', pp. 221–225.

30 Some of this increased wealth came from women's earnings but substantial amounts came from inheritances.

Bibliography

Abelson, Elaine S., *When Ladies Go A-Thieving*, New York: Oxford University Press, 1989.

Baron, Ava (ed.), *Work Engendered: Toward a New History of American Labor*, Ithaca, NY: Cornell University Press, 1991.

Basch, Norma, *In the Eyes of the Law: Women, Marriage, and Property in Nineteenth-Century New York*, Ithaca, NY: Cornell University Press, 1982.

Benson, Susan Porter, *Counter Cultures: Saleswomen, Managers, and Customers in American Department Stores, 1890–1940*, Urbana, IL: University of Illinois Press, 1986.

Boylan, Anne, *The Origins of Women's Activism: New York and Boston, 1797–1840*, Chapel Hill, NC: University of North Carolina Press, 2002.

Braukman, Stacey Lorraine and Ross, Michael A., 'Married women's property and male coercion: United States' courts and the privy examination, 1864–1887', *Journal of Women's History* 12 (2), 2000, pp. 57–80.

Chandler, Alfred, *Strategy and Structure: Chapters in the History of the Industrial Enterprise*, Cambridge, MA: MIT Press, 1962.

Clews, Henry, *Twenty-Eight Years in Wall Street*, New York: J.S. Ogilvie Publishing Co., 1887.

Fowler, Willliam Worthington, *Twenty Years of Inside Life in Wall Street*, New York: Orange Judd Co., 1880.

Gamber, Wendy, *The Female Economy: The Millinery and Dressmaking Trades, 1860–1930*, Urbana, IL: University of Illinois Press, 1997.

Ginzberg, Lori, *Women and the Work of Benevolence: Morality, Politics, and Class in the Nineteenth-Century United States*, New Haven, CT: Yale University Press, 1990.

Graham, Abbie, *Grace Dodge: Merchant of Dreams*, New York: Women's Press, 1926.

Hudson, Lynn, *The Making of 'Mammy Pleasant': A Black Entrepreneur in Nineteenth-Century San Francisco*, Urbana, IL: University of Illinois Press, 2002.

Kessler-Harris, Alice, *Out to Work: A History of Wage Earning Women in the United States*, New York: Oxford University Press, 1982.

Kwolek-Folland, Angel, *Engendering Business: Men and Women in the Corporate Office, 1870–1930*, Baltimore, MD: Johns Hopkins Press, 1994.

Kwolek-Folland, Angel, *Incorporating Women: A History of Women and Business in the United States*, New York: Twayne Publishers, 1998.

Lebsock, Suzanne, *The Free Women of Petersburg: Status and Culture in a Southern Town, 1784–1860*, New York: W.W. Norton, 1984.

Lebsock, Suzanne, 'Radical reconstruction and the property rights of Southern women', *Journal of Southern History* 43 (2), 1977, pp. 195–216.

Peiss, Kathy Lee, *Cheap Amusements: Working Women and Leisure in Turn-of-the-Century New York*, Philadelphia, PA: Temple University Press, 1986.

Peiss, Kathy Lee, *Hope in a Jar: The Making of America's Beauty Culture*, New York: Metropolitan Books, 1998.

Shammas, Carole, 'Re-assessing the Married Women's Property Acts', *Journal of Women's History* 6 (1), 1994, pp. 9–30.

Sparks, Edith, *Capital Intentions: Female Proprietors in San Francisco, 1850–1920*, Chapel Hill, NC: University of North Carolina Press, 2006.

Stanton, Elizabeth Cady, Anthony, Susan B. and Gage, Matilda Joslyn (eds), *History of Woman Suffrage*, Vol. 1, *1848–1861*, New York: Fowler & Wells, 1881.

Trachtenberg, Alan, *The Incorporation of America: Culture and Society in the Gilded Age*, New York: Hill & Wang, 1982.

Wright, Robert, 'Women and finance in the early national U.S.', *Essays in History* 42, 2000, available online: http://etext.lib.virginia.edu/journals/EH/EH42/EH42.html (accessed 29 July 2008).

Yeager, Mary (ed.), *Women in Business*, 3 vols, Cheltenham: Edward Elgar, 1999.

Yohn, Susan, 'Let Christian women set the example in their own gifts: the "business" of Protestant women's organizations', in Bendroth, Margaret and Brereton, Virginia (eds), *Women and Twentieth Century Protestantism*, Urbana, IL: University of Illinois Press, 2002, pp. 213–235.

16 'Men seem to take delight in cheating women'

Legal challenges faced by businesswomen in the United States, 1880–1920

Susan M. Yohn

On 28 June 1911, readers of the *New York Times* were greeted by the headline 'Nellie Bly Fighting for Financial Life ... Lost $1,400,000 by Forgery'. What followed were the tribulations of steel-barrel manufacturer, Elizabeth C. Seaman (known also as the 'girl' reporter, Nellie Bly), one more story in her three-year legal ordeal to save the company originally built by her husband Robert that she had made into a profitable and thriving concern. About the fraud perpetrated against Seaman, the *Times* concluded: 'That's An Incident In A Business Where Men Are As Kind To A Successful Woman as Wolves Are To Rabbits'.[1] Two weeks later, the *New York Evening Journal*, the newspaper that had formerly employed Nellie Bly, reiterated this point when it declared about her business problems, 'Men That Wouldn't Cheat Each Other ... Seem to Take Delight in Cheating Women'.[2] These particular headlines pointed the finger at a business milieu in which the women were marked as prey; here men were to women as wolves to rabbits. Seaman's drama was not exceptional but one in a series of sensational trials which showcased the vulnerabilities of women who dared to enter and compete successfully in the business world and financial markets. Likewise, neither the courts nor the legal system were helpful to women's money-making efforts; the justice they sought proved elusive.

Nineteenth-century American women faced numerous obstacles to their money-making ambitions. Legal reforms enabling women to control their own money were relatively new, yet credit was hard to come by. Social mores discouraged women from pursuing money-making activities even as a growing number of women opened their own businesses. These entrepreneurial efforts proved to be a favourite form of investment activity for American women. Few of them, however, were able to translate their investment into businesses worthy of note.[3] So disdainful of women's efforts were the editors of *Fortune* magazine that, in 1935, they could not name even 100 women who had made businesses that the editors could refer to as 'brilliant successes'. They wrote of the history of women in business, 'Carnegies are lacking ... success stories are few and faint'.[4] For businesswomen, 'success' was defined more modestly, marked, for example, by the ability to draw an income better than the meagre wages a woman might earn as an employee, by the number of years she was able to sustain her enterprise, or by turning enough of a profit that she could buy real estate. Given the lesson of courtroom trials endured by those businesswomen who had made themselves 'brilliant', the vast majority of female entrepreneurs probably deemed it prudent to keep a low profile, do a modest business and stay on the good side of creditors and the law.

To examine how the legal challenges faced by businesswomen could determine the course of their careers and limit their economic opportunity, this chapter focuses on three highly publicized trials that involved contemporaneous businesswomen in late-nineteenth- and early-twentieth-century New York City: financier and real-estate mogul Hetty Green's challenge to her aunt's will; cosmetic manufacturer Harriet Hubbard Ayer's insanity trial; and the bankruptcy trial of iron-goods manufacturer Elizabeth Cochran Seaman. In each case, these women found their abilities, ambitions, achievements and their fitness called into question. As the title suggests, many Americans recognized at the time that these were events where gender was deployed by the women involved, as well as by the men who participated, observed and also reported on the cases. Moreover, the courtroom served as a stage from which larger social lessons about appropriate gender roles could be imparted. As Norma Basch has pointed out in her work on the Married Women's Property Acts in New York State, the adjudication process did not favour women. Women were largely excluded from the legal profession, unable to act as advocates for one another. They faced a 'judiciary that was essentially a conservative all-male elite eager to preserve the status quo'.[5] More pointedly, as Mary Yeager writes, 'the law, like business, was a gendered instrument, used for different purposes by men and women to achieve different ends'. She argues that

> as laws came to be applied, they reinforced and legitimized inequalities of power and status between men and women.... They gave men easier access to and title of property; they reinforced men's domination over the family and over family businesses; they defined the rules of the economic game, including patterns of competition and combination, acquisition and merger.[6]

In the courtroom and at the trials described here, men asserted a hegemonic claim, while the women in question sought justice or a return of that which they believed was being stolen from them. For a larger public, these trials, 'like rituals, [functioned] as a way for the public to confront chaotic, painful, and contradictory social issues' about the appropriate role for women in the larger economy.[7]

Harriet Hubbard Ayer

Harriet Hubbard Ayer's story is especially dramatic. After her marriage to manufacturer Herbert Ayer failed, Harriet built a successful cosmetics business, the Recamier Manufacturing Company, only to have her principal financial backer, James Seymour, challenge her business decisions. Initially he tried to wrest control from her by contesting her patents in court. When he lost this first case, he convinced Ayer's former husband to have her committed to an insane asylum in 1893. What followed was an emotional series of confrontations in court where Ayer argued for her liberty. A year later she was free but she was unable to reclaim her business. She spent the rest of her life lecturing and writing beauty columns for the newspaper, *New York World*.[8]

Reporting on her committal to Granger's sanatorium in Bronxville, the *New York Times* summed up the whole of Harriet Hubbard Ayer's adult life in just one short paragraph:

> Herbert C. Ayer was formerly a rich iron merchant in Chicago. His wife secured a divorce from him, naming an actress as co-respondent. Mrs. Ayer then came to this city and started in the business of manufacturing and selling toilet articles. The custody of her two children was first given to Mrs. Ayer, but Mr. Ayer afterward secured the control of the children himself. The case was an exceedingly sensational one at the time. Mrs. Ayer had much trouble with her partners in business, which resulted in a number of law suits.[9]

Harriet Ayer's life was lived in the public eye. When her demise came, when her former husband, Herbert, and principal investor, Seymour, finally succeeded in quite literally 'capturing' her, the doctors were reporting that she heard voices, she cried constantly, she 'declared that she wanted to die' and she 'was in acute misery'. Having been committed on 9 February 1893, one month later a jury declared her insane, appraised her property and directed that a guardian be appointed for her. Called to testify on her own behalf, Ayer was reported to have been dressed in black, covered in a veil and able only to say 'no' when asked if she knew why she was in court.[10]

The 'experts' in this case were in agreement. Dr Granger, at whose institution Ayer found herself, testified that her case was grave, that she was 'probably incurable' and that her chances for recovery 'were very small, but her case was not hopeless'. Given that he also admitted that, while under his care, Ayer had only spoken to answer his questions and then as briefly as possible, his diagnosis was based on very little. He could not confirm that she was an alcoholic as her family claimed because she had never asked for stimulants of this sort. Asserting that he had known Mrs Ayer for six years, Dr George Hammond followed Dr Granger and was emphatic that she had grown increasingly melancholy. To his mind, she had become unquestionably insane. He was also sure that he knew the causes. While there were 'many', he stressed that 'over-attention to business was doubtless one'.

Ayer's insanity trial followed at least five years of relentless pressure from Seymour, who acted in concert with his son, Allen, and daughter-in-law, Hattie (Ayer's older daughter) and Harriet's ex-husband, to take the business from her.

The *Times* called these 'sensational' trials and indeed they were. Ayer's character was attacked; she was accused of being a morphine addict and alcoholic, a negligent mother and was said to be unfit to run her business. How and when her troubles began exactly and who instigated them is open to some question, but Ayer had sued Seymour in 1889 for trying to wrest control of her business, claiming that he had stolen documents from her apartment. Even then, the charges exchanged in court were salacious. She claimed that Seymour and her son-in-law had conspired to take control of company stock by both defrauding and poisoning her. Foreshadowing events to come, she also claimed that they were trying to 'destroy her health and reason, and to have her considered insane'.[11]

Ayer won this round, but newspaper accounts could not have helped her image. The stories had everyone keeping their 'cool' (this was the word used) except Ayer herself, as Seymour and her family argued that they simply wanted to help Ayer overcome 'the dreadful habit which makes everybody hate her', that is, her supposed alcoholism. In round two, Seymour persuaded a French woman to sue Ayer, charging that the formula upon which the Recamier preparations were based had been stolen from her by Ayer. Again, Ayer won. The victory was short-lived, however, as that case was followed by an attempt by Herbert in 1891 to take custody of her youngest daughter, Margaret. Reeling from these battles, Ayer was said to have been left both financially and physically spent. The final blow was Herbert's signature on the order that led to her committal.

Because the records do not remain, it is impossible to know exactly how Ayer built and conducted her business. By all indications, her line of cosmetic products was very successful. The speculation was that she had earned between $10,000 and $15,000 a year as a designer, and $12,000 annually in salary from Recamier. Calculated in 2005 dollars she was earning approximately $252,000 annually as she entered into her fight with Seymour and her ex-husband.[12] Her transition from designer and decorator, and saleswoman of antiques at New York's Sypher & Company, to beauty-product manufacturer, appears to have been seamless. She continued selling antiques for a period as she built her cosmetics business, with Seymour as her principal backer, but was able to repay her $50,000 debt to him by 1888.[13]

Much of Ayer's success was attributed to her advertisements, called a 'system of bold advertising conducted on a scale seldom equalled', which she authored and which touted testamentary statements by famous users of her products.[14] By the late 1880s her line had grown to include balm, freckle and mouth lotion, soap and powder, all in addition to her original skin cream,[15] Biographers credit Ayer for her innovative promotional strategies, seen as setting the precedent for the advertising campaigns of the twentieth century, but what draws the most attention is the final chapter of Ayer's life. Released from the sanatorium after 14 months, Ayer lectured widely on the evils of involuntary confinement and then, until her death at 54 in 1903, wrote a health and beauty column for the *New York World*. These columns became the basis of a popular beauty book she published in 1899, *Harriet Hubbard Ayer's Book: A Complete and Authentic Treatise on the Laws of Health and Beauty.*

Ayer's resurrection from her committal and her success as a writer and beauty advocate is noteworthy. However, the six years of her undoing as a businesswoman are critical, for they point directly to the challenges that entrepreneurial women faced at the time, especially those who dared to build a major firm. Ayer may well have been 'insane', though not in the ways that her family claimed. Determined to make her own way after separating from and divorcing Herbert in the early 1880s, she conceived of and produced a new line of products, and then built up the business by developing additional products. If the speculations about her salary were correct, in the period between 1886 when she began and 1893 when forced to give up her business, her personal income from Recamier Manufacturing, in 2005 dollars, was well over one million dollars.

Certainly Ayer would have qualified as one of the handful of 'brilliant successes' *Fortune* magazine was seeking. A successful capitalist at a time when this was not expected of women, she related to a reporter in 1887 some of the challenges she faced:

> When I first announced my intention to go into business my friends were very much concerned – everybody predicted sure failure, and did everything in the world to persuade me to take a position as governess or companion, or some other such position as is usually sought by women who have to support themselves, but having two daughters to educate I felt that I would be unable to do them justice on any salary that I could earn and determined to branch right out into business (like a man,) and the results prove that my judgment was correct – my success has been unprecedented. I have had a hard fight, and am now victorious.[16]

Given what followed, we know that her 'victory' was a temporary one. Ayer's 'success' was dependent on the support of her backer, James Seymour. Furthermore, like most working women, Ayer also relied on support (in her case emotional rather than financial) from her family. When these were withdrawn, she could not sustain her business. When Seymour moved in to claim his stake and her daughters turned against her, Ayer was undermined. That her family moved to incarcerate her seems extreme, yet it was not uncommon in this period for women to be committed under these circumstances.[17]

Although news accounts of Ayer's insanity trial mention her earlier legal confrontations with James Seymour, her major creditor remained in the background in the final round. At the end, Ayer's former husband, Herbert, claimed that he had taken this action to protect her daughters' interests.[18] However, other sources suggest that by the late 1880s and early 1890s Seymour's growing financial troubles may explain his growing interest in Ayer's cosmetic business and his attempts to take it over. When the New York agents of the R. G. Dun & Co. credit agency first reported on Seymour in 1882, he was listed as being in stocks and mining and to have moved from Chicago to New York in 1880. He was believed to be worth 'a good deal of money', made from investments in mining, but his actual wealth could not be determined. The Chicago office of R. G. Dun & Co. reported Seymour and his son Allen to be worth half a million dollars and deemed them 'a safe house with whom to do business'.[19]

By 1885 Seymour and son were largely out of business in Chicago. The 1886 update confirmed that

> They have three large bank accounts and apparently are more than easy in all money matters and are not borrowers. The main partner J.M. Seymour is the principal capitalist and claims to be worth a million dollars personally and this is believed to be true although it is very difficult to obtain a definite confirmation of a broker's statement. They are looked upon as shrewd money making people and are considered pretty sharp in their transactions.

This success, however, was short-lived. The 1887 entry in the R. G. Dun & Co. records show that judgments were 'found against them'. By 1888, the firm was said to be 'dissolved, there will be no succession'. By 1889, the agent could find no office, 'the firm is not in existence and we do not know where any of the partners are to be found now'.[20]

We can only speculate about Seymour's interest in Harriet Ayer's business. Perhaps they had known each other or moved in the same Chicago society circles. Seymour dealt in mining stocks and Ayer's husband Herbert was the son of a wealthy iron dealer; their business interests might well have crossed. Harriet and Seymour both moved to New York in the early 1880s; here they might have renewed an acquaintance.[21] Ayer may have approached Seymour with her idea for Recamier cosmetics at the height of his own financial power, when he was flush with money to invest. The marriage of her daughter Hattie to his son Allen probably further cemented the business alliance. When his other stocks declined and other assets dwindled, his investment in her booming business may have taken on greater significance.

Here, then, is the set up for a classic confrontation and business takeover. Seymour, a powerful investor seeks to assert his managerial will and know-how over the interests of the founding director, Harriet Ayer. But in this case issues of gender come into play, as Ayer's physical and mental health, and her family obligations, were used to question the validity of her business judgements, indeed, the integrity of the whole enterprise (i.e. the charge made that she 'stole' the formula while in France). Daughter Margaret Ayer's biography of her mother focuses on the doubts Harriet felt about the enterprise, saying that 'she was living, she knew, a strange kind of life   Perhaps she wasn't meant to be happy. Perhaps she had been too ambitious'. Her ambivalence, suggests Margaret, had business consequences. When she made her agreement with Seymour for the initial $50,000, she neglected to draw up a contract that made official what she believed to be their agreement. Upon repayment, Seymour would return his stock and recognize her control. Says Margaret, 'she was always clever at making money, never very good at the details of keeping it'. Ayer neglected to make the agreement legal even though she knew that Seymour had a reputation on Wall Street for 'sharp dealing'.[22]

She had dared to think 'like a man' (her words) when she entered business, but Ayer remained largely enmeshed in and could not think beyond traditional gender roles. Marilyn Perry argues that in the final years of her life Ayer grew more interested in feminism as she came into contact with women of different social classes, but 'her attitude that wives needed beauty to keep husbands and that working women needed physical appeal to move ahead in the workplace kept her within traditional attitudes of her time'.[23] Even as she fought to hold on to her business, she could not reconcile the conflicts she must have felt about her failed marriage and her troubled relationships with her daughters to see the charges she faced as primarily an attack on her economic autonomy. Even as she appeared for a time in the 1880s to be a self-supporting independent woman, her insanity trial in 1893 was a reminder to spectators of the power men held over women, be they doctors, former husbands, creditors, lawyers or guardians. Ayer regained her freedom the following year, her ambitions limited to that of beauty consultant and writer, not entrepreneur; her new employer one of the newspapers that had formerly advertised Recamier products.

Elizabeth Cochran Seaman

Before she became an entrepreneur, Elizabeth Cochran established her reputation as the popular journalist, Nellie Bly, stunt girl reporter who made her career by masquerading as a hysteric, sex slave, exploited worker to reveal the lives of marginalized women to the newspaper-reading public. Like Ayer, she understood the power of the news as an agent of publicity and, like Ayer, Bly would also find herself an object of the publicity generated by the news.[24] Widely hailed for her stories about the 'common man', her most famous reportorial exploit came in 1889 when she challenged the 80-day round-the-world record of Jules Verne's fictional Phineas Fogg. In 1895 she added marriage to an ageing New York industrialist, Robert Seaman, to her list of feats.[25]

By the time of her husband's death in 1904, Bly had taken over running Robert Seaman's Iron Clad Manufacturing Company, held 25 patents in her own name and claimed that she had increased its sales to $1 million a year, with an annual profit of $200,000. Also important was the system of social welfare that she instituted for the company's 1,500 workers. Seaman's special contribution to the growth of this already established business was to open a subsidiary, the American Steel Barrel Company, the first plant in the US to manufacture steel barrels. Even though in a completely different business from Ayer, Seaman was equally concerned with publicity. She attached her public name – Nellie Bly – to the company's products and proudly proclaimed on advertisements that she was 'the only woman in the world personally managing industries of such a magnitude'.[26] Seaman revelled in the Nellie Bly remade as businesswoman. An article in 1906 stated her worth at about $5 million and had her producing 500 or more steel barrels daily.[27] This businesswoman also had a heart: she had installed a gymnasium for her employees, she sponsored entertainments for them on Saturday evenings and she schemed to build a model town around her factories. When the company issued its financial statement in 1906, all was well.[28]

By 1911 she was bankrupt. Seaman would later admit that she had never taken any interest in the finances of the company and this would prove to be her undoing. The company was in trouble as it was most profitable. Seaman confronted a variety of problems – challenges from other companies that she claimed were manufacturing containers based on her patents, a 1907 recession which led to a downturn in real-estate values and the tightening of credit, and evidence that trusted employees, among them her manager and cashier, were stealing from her. Even before Robert's death there were forewarnings that managing a business of this size was not a simple endeavour. The Seamans had been concerned as early as 1899 about the manner in which business was being conducted and had moved to install a new general manager at Iron Clad.[29] This manager, Edward Gilman, would prove no better than his predecessor. Seaman would learn after his death, in 1910, that he had stolen hundreds of thousands of dollars from the company. In addition, the chief cashier, Charles Caccia, was discovered to have cashed cheques at Brooklyn banks under Seaman's forged name. As the scheme began to unravel, creditors descended on Seaman, demanding payment for outstanding debts. She soon learned, much to her surprise and distress, that there had been what she called a 'conspiracy to loot the Iron Clad' by employees of her finance department.[30]

She had only herself to blame, she said, for 'not having learned banking methods and commercial accounting when I first went to Iron Clad', and her lack of interest in the financial matters had allowed Gilman, Caccia and other employees to take advantage.[31] What followed was a veritable maelstrom as various creditors pursued her, serving her summonses, with others 'filing petitions of involuntary bankruptcy' to protect their interests. As the frenzy ensued, Seaman sought to separate the American Steel operations from those of Iron Clad, claiming they were two separate companies, hoping to preserve some part of her investment and to keep American Steel operating and profitable. What is striking is how surprised and disappointed she was that so many would want to see her fail. She reminded her audience that many companies had been robbed by dishonest employees; in this Iron Clad was not exceptional. Why, when a company was otherwise productive, should it be crippled by the demands of creditors? She chafed at the restrictions that were placed upon her by the courts arbitrating these many claims; because of these her company could not produce to capacity. She had to cancel orders because she could not ship barrels.[32] Bankruptcy proceedings might ensure that her creditors would see some of their money, but they impeded productivity and profitability. Seaman was relegated to watching her companies further undermined.

Seaman's disappointment or 'hurt' turned to anger as events unfolded.[33] She was furious, for example, that banks had cashed cheques with her forged signature, especially those cheques where the written amounts had clearly been altered. Iron Clad was put into receivership and, as the case dragged on, Seaman did battle with everyone. She refused to recognize Appleton Clark, the receiver. She sued him and destroyed company property. She appeared irrational or 'mad'. Women in business, she would conclude, were not 'treated according to that code by which men deal with one another'. Particularly harsh in her assessment of lawyers, she said that 'her finances are free-picking for every law firm that can get its clutches on her'. Worse yet, nobody seemed to care that a wrong was being done; 'to stir any group of men to resentment against it' she added, 'is very, very hard'. She had not been a 'suffragette' previously (as a journalist she had written stories poking fun at suffrage activists) but given these experiences, she proclaimed herself to be one. Without the ballot, Seaman asserted, she had an 'orphan-like struggle all the time'.[34]

Seaman refused to recognize the legitimacy of the actions against her. Jean Lutes argues that as a reporter Bly's popularity had been built on her refusal to accept the growing class of professional 'experts' emerging in the late nineteenth century – whether this be in the courtroom, classroom or hospital. They shared a language that marginalized and excluded those who did not share a similar training or set of connections. As she battled to save her companies, Seaman adopted the same 'straight-shooting style she had presented in her reporting', fashioning herself the outsider bent on exposing, in this case, the malfeasance of the legal and banking professions.[35] She refused to cooperate with the receiver appointed by the court. When she attempted to have him removed, the court soundly chastised her. Called to testify, her answers were evasive at best. So egregious was the fraud perpetrated against Seaman that even *New York Times* editorial writers questioned the receiver who '[professed] an inability to repair a machine which Mrs. Seaman, as soon as she can force her way to it, promptly starts running as well as ever'. The court, they argued, would be 'judicious' in moving to clear up the impression that 'the "woman in the case" is not getting fair treatment, to say nothing of consideration, and that she has excuse, if not reason, for declaring herself a victim of a large, elaborate, and continuing conspiracy'.[36]

This dizzying state of affairs lasted four years, during which Seaman fought with judges, receivers, bankers and lawyers. Every interaction was fraught with tension, so sure was she that she was being robbed. Indeed, her good friend and employer, publisher Arthur Brisbane, did his part to underscore her predicament. 'REMEMBER THAT MEN USUALLY CHEAT WOMEN WHEN THEY GET THE CHANCE', screamed one of his stories about her case.[37] Privately, he reiterated this same message to Seaman, agreeing that she had been robbed, 'I have no doubt whatever that men have robbed you – as they usually rob women in business and out of business – whenever they get the chance'.[38] By 1914 this chapter of Seaman's life was over. She had lost Iron Clad but was once again president of American Steel Barrel.[39] In total she had lost over one million dollars.[40] Most unfair was that Iron Clad's cashier, Charles Caccia, the man whose actions had precipitated her undoing, was never convicted. Having eluded prosecution for several years, his trial ended in a hung jury with the court deciding not to retry him.

Harriet Ayer, whose path must have crossed Seaman's in the mid-1890s when they worked at the *World*, would never speak about the legal judgments against her as a function of gender. Elizabeth Seaman, however, did. Central to the presentation of her case in the court of public opinion was Seaman's insistence that women were especially vulnerable to fraud. They had neither the experience, the skills, nor the support necessary to successfully represent their interests in a court of law. Responding to a citation that she was in contempt of court, Seaman said:

> While I do not seek any consideration on the ground of sex, however, I may say that I have been under a physical and mental strain for something like two years that would have broken down many a strong man. To be forced to look helplessly on at the destruction of property one has spent the best years of one's life in building up, that experience following months of wearing anxiety due to the events that precipitated the catastrophe, is not conducive to suavity of deportment.[41]

Had Ayer not been so beleaguered by the time of her insanity trial, she might well have made a similar statement. Both women had spent over ten years investing time and energy building businesses and in their late 40s (Ayer was 49 when committed and Seaman was 45 when her legal battles began) they confronted situations where their authority was challenged, undermined and their businesses essentially stolen from them. Seaman fought harder and longer, perhaps because, unlike Ayer, she did not have to deal with the disapproval of her family. Like Ayer, Seaman turned to reporting. They remained in the public eye as salaried employees, not as manufacturers or producers.[42] As reporters, what power and influence they wielded was largely social or cultural but not economic.

Hetty Green

By contrast, when financier and investor Hetty Howland Green died in 1916, at the age of 82, she was the wealthiest woman in the world, leaving an estate worth some $100 million. Starting with an inheritance of several millions from her wealthy whaling and seafaring Rhode Island family, she had invested in government bonds, railroad stock and real estate. Her strategy was to sell when others were buying and buy when others were selling, and she kept a fair amount of her money in cash which allowed her to make loans when credit was otherwise tight. One imagines her reading the newspaper accounts of Ayer's and Seaman's battles, perhaps sympathizing with their troubles, but also frustrated at the faith they had placed in these men who had stolen from them.[43] Her legal battle in the 1860s to secure what she viewed as her rightful inheritance from her aunt, and the subsequent claims made on her wealth, led Green to conclude that lawyers especially were 'schemers' and 'buzzards', never to be trusted.[44] She accused these 'schemers' of trying to get her money. She hated them for robbing her of some part of her inheritance from her father. She regularly challenged the integrity of various lawyers whom she encountered in the course of her business. While Seaman and Ayer finally gave up, packed up their ambitions, ceded control of their businesses and retreated to jobs considered more appropriate for women, Green refused to be done in by the legal frictions she encountered. For this she earned the reputation as the 'Witch of Wall Street'. Her investment skills, her 'genius'– though one nineteenth-century observer called it a 'terrible genius'[45] – with money, would be obscured by accounts that presented her as penny-pinching and mean spirited.[46]

Green's contentious relationship with lawyers started in 1865 when her father died and she learned that by the terms of his will she was entitled only to one-ninth of his $6 million estate outright. The rest was to be held in trust with Green to receive the income annually, the estate administered by trustees.[47] To Green, who later recounted that she had early in her life developed an interest and aptitude for business, these constraints were upsetting. Six weeks later, her aunt, Sylvia Howland, died, leaving an estate worth some $2 million. Again, Green was to receive the income with the principal to be divided among other relatives after her death. Particularly upset by this turn of events, Green sued, claiming that there was another will that made her the outright primary benefi-ciary. This second will, which she produced, would become the centre of a highly charged case – the Howland Will Case – which was eventually decided against her on a technicality. However, her actions in this case would forever brand her as avaricious and ruthless. Public interest in the case was piqued, says writer Louis Menand, by the 'spectacle of the female heir to one of the greatest fortunes in the country fighting to gain control of every last penny'.[48]

Green built her $100 million fortune from the $1 million she inherited out-right and the annual payments that would come for the rest of her life, but as she grew older it must have galled her even more that she had not gained access to the whole of her father's and aunt's estates. Reportedly she expressed sympathy for women who had been denied access to or robbed of inheritances.[49] When asked at age 70 if she was not weary of all the litigation that she had undertaken, she agreed that it was tiring and that she had contended with 'persecution all of my life'. 'My whole life,' she argued, 'has been a struggle against heavy odds. I have been more abused and misrepresented than any woman alive.' Fully aware of the stereotypes that dogged businesswomen, she continued, 'periodical attempts have been made to declare me crazy, and for forty years I have had to fight every inch of my way'.[50]

A brilliant investor, it is worth considering what Green might have done with an $8 million dollar inheritance outright, versus the $1 million plus annual pay-ments that she did receive. Menand calls her 'one of the greatest individual prac-titioners of the art of finance capitalism who ever lived' and compares her wealth to that of J. P. Morgan who was worth $80 million when he died (though Green's wealth pales when compared to John D. Rockefeller's $900 million worth in 1916).[51] Undaunted by the public attention focused on her, and the mostly unflattering news accounts of her life and actions, she decided early on that she was exceptional. She came to feel that she was destined to be a female Ishmael – an 'outcast', portrayed as 'heartless' because people did not care to know the 'real' Green.[52] Her comments about women as money-makers echoed every popular stereotype that existed at the time. She faulted women for not being methodical enough, for impulsively investing in enterprises about which they knew little, as well as being too emotional and easily diverted. While agreeing with her male contemporaries that women could not succeed at business, she was not completely willing to agree that these were essential faults or part of women's nature per se. She preferred to lay the blame on their lack of training. Even so, her judgement was harsh – women preferred to spend rather than save and 'as long as women won't save we're not likely to have many women millionaires in this country', she concluded.[53]

Imagine Hetty Green sitting in her small apartment across the river from Manhattan in Hoboken, New Jersey, dressed in the plain old black dress for which critics disparaged her (after all, they argued, a woman with her wealth should not be dressed in rags), reading newspaper stories of first Ayer's and then, later, Seaman's legal problems. One supposes that she would have been sympathetic to Ayer's plight, recognizing her family's attempt to steal from her, to alienate her from the business she built, though she was probably also frustrated by Ayer's refusal to fight the insanity charges. About Seaman, she would have been more critical, particularly when she read Seaman's statement that she had taken no interest in the financial end of Iron Clad. However, she would have admired Seaman's fight to retain control. Like Green, Seaman showed no respect while in court. Her charges that the court was against her, her refusal to answer questions, the contempt she showed for the process, would have satisfied Green. Green had spoken out of turn while in court, had insisted on crossexamining witnesses in the cases that stemmed from the suits she brought, and generally challenged the authority of lawyers and judges.

In each of these examples, these women's court appearances were a literal representation of the trials that they faced as businesswomen. In the courtroom they engaged in a form of public theatre, exposing the authorities who would rob them of their autonomy or limit their capacity to do business and to make money. Newspaper-reading Americans could see clearly the obstacles that entrepreneurial women of the time confronted. They watched the unfolding conflict between the 'individual autonomy of women and the social authority of men' that marked the period.[54] They also saw that women rarely won their cases outright. At best, the process was a draw, more often their claims were denied. For Ayer and Seaman, losing meant the demise of thriving and profitable businesses. Green persevered, but to do so she made choices that rendered her an outcast, she became forever, the 'Witch of Wall Street'.

Notes

1 *New York Times*, 28 June 1911, p. 7.
2 *New York Evening Journal*, 11 July 1911.

3 The best general history of women in business in the United States is A. Kwolek-Folland's *Incorporating Women: A History of Women and Business in the United States*, New York: Palgrave, 2002. W. Gamber's *Female Economy: The Millinery and Dressmaking Trades, 1860–1930*, Urbana, IL: University of Illinois Press, 1997, provides a detailed analysis of the problems confronting businesswomen in a particular industry, while E. Sparks' *Capital Intentions: Female Proprietors in San Francisco, 1850–1920*, Chapel Hill, NC: University of North Carolina Press, 2006, provides a detailed analysis of the fortunes of businesswomen in one American city during the period covered in this chapter. For a discussion of the ideas and attitudes about women entrepreneurs see S. Yohn, 'Crippled capitalists: the inscription of economic dependence and the challenge of female entrepreneurship in nineteenth-century America', *Feminist Economics* 12 (1–2), 2006, pp. 85–109.

4 Quoted by M. Yeager, 'Will there ever be a feminist business history', in Mary Yeager (ed.), *Women in Business*, 3 vols, Cheltenham: Edward Elgar, 1999, vol. 1, p. 3.

5 N. Basch, *In the Eyes of the Law: Women, Marriage and Property in Nineteenth-Century New York*, Ithaca, NY: Cornell University Press, 1982, p. 208.

6 M. Yeager, 'Introduction', in Yeager, *Women in Business*, vol. 1, p. xxxiii.

7 I am indebted here to L. Winner for her ideas about the intersection of theatre, rituals and trials. See Winner, 'Democratic acts: theater of public trials', *Theater Topics* 15 (2), 2005, p. 151.

8 The most complete, though undocumented, biography of Ayer is that written by her younger daughter M. Ayer, *The Three Lives of Harriet Hubbard Ayer*, Philadelphia, PA: Lippincott, 1957. Other biographical sketches consulted for this chapter include, 'Ayer, Harriet Hubbard', *The National Cyclopedia of National Biography*, vol. 43, pp. 452–453, and M. E. Perry, 'Ayer, Harriet Hubbard', *American National Biography*, vol. 1, pp. 790–791; and B. Weisberger, 'Ayer, Harriet Hubbard', *Notable American Women: A Biographical Dictionary*, Cambridge, MA: Belknap Press, 1971, vol. 1, pp. 72–74.

9 'The courts: questioning Mrs. Ayer's sanity. A commission appointed to inquire as to her mental condition', *New York Times*, 28 February 1893, p. 9, col. 1.

10 'Found Mrs. Ayer insane: decision of a jury after hearing evidence. Testimony that while her chances for recovery are small, her case is not hopeless – no signs of alcoholism or the morphine habit – she could not testify', *New York Times*, 11 March 1893, p. 8, col. 3.

11 'Mrs. Ayer's queer story: she says she was drugged by Mr. Seymour. Stock in the Recamier company in dispute – Judge Dale presented with many affidavits', *New York Times*, 21 May 1889, p. 4, col. 1.

12 'Mrs. Ayer in an asylum; the latest development in a remarkable career. Taken to a Bronxville sanitarium on an order from Judge M'Adam – now her former husband asks for a commission to pass on her mental condition', *New York Times*, 28 February 1911, p. 1.

13 *New York Times*, 28 February 1911, p. 1.

14 The statement about her 'bold system' is from the *New York Times*, ibid. See also the work of Melanie Gustafson who has extensively researched Ayer's advertising innovations and her paper, 'The business of beauty: Harriet Hubbard Ayer's New York career in face creams, health tonics and advice to women and men', presented June 2006 at the 27th Conference on New York State History, Columbia University.

15 Biographical information drawn from *National Cyclopedia of American Biography*, and Perry, *American National Biography*.

16 'Mrs. James Brown Potter: A practical business woman expresses an opinion – what Mrs. Harriet Hubbard Ayer thinks of this charming actress and society belle', *New York Times*, 4 December 1887, p. 5, col. 3.

17 For a discussion of women incarcerated because their families wanted access to their

money, see J. L. Geller and M. Harris (eds), *Women of the Asylum: Voices from Behind the Walls, 1840–1945*, New York: Anchor Books, 1994.

18 See 'Mrs. Ayer: her divorced husband tells why he had her placed in an asylum', *New York Times*, 3 March 1893, p. 6, col. 6.

19 For entries on James M. Seymour, see R. G. Dun & Co., New York, vol. 424, p. 819, Cambridge, MA: R. G. Dun & Co. Collection, Baker Library, Harvard Business School.

20 Ibid., p. 900 a/4.

21 The *Cyclopedia of American Biography* entry on Harriet Ayer claims that their business relationship began when Seymour commissioned her to furnish his yacht. He wanted a duplicate of that owned by the Prince of Wales, *Cyclopedia of American Biography*, p. 452.

22 Ayer, *The Three Lives of Harriet Hubbard Ayer*, pp. 150–152.

23 Perry, *American National Biography*, vol. 1, p. 791.

24 For the observation of Bly as both an agent and object of publicity and how 'girl' reporters used this in their reporting, see J. M. Lutes, 'Into the madhouse with Nellie Bly: girl stunt reporting in late nineteenth-century America', *American Quarterly* 54 (2), 2002, pp. 217–253.

25 This chapter relies heavily on B. Kroeger's biography, *Nellie Bly: Daredevil, Reporter, Feminist*, New York: Times Books, 1994, the most scholarly and complete of Bly biographies. Additional biographical information can be found in I. Ross, *Charmers and Cranks*, New York: Harper & Row Publishers, 1965, see chapter 'Nellie Bly', pp. 196–216, and B. Weisberger, 'Seaman, Elizabeth Cochrane', *Notable American Women: A Biographical Dictionary*, Cambridge, MA: Belknap Press, 1971, pp. 253–255. Kroeger's biography provides a critical antidote to the judgements rendered by Ross and Weisberger. Ross claims that Seaman's business demise came because she was overly ambitious (p. 215) and Weisberger notes that the Iron Clad chapter of her life was 'anticlimactic' by contrast to her years as a reporter (p. 254).

26 Kroeger, *Nellie Bly: Daredevil*, p. 309.

27 From a *Pittsburg Gazette-Time* article, 5 May 1906, cited by Kroeger.

28 Kroeger, *Nellie Bly: Daredevil*, p. 310.

29 Kroeger, *Nellie Bly: Daredevil*, p. 299.

30 Kroeger, *Nellie Bly: Daredevil*, p. 327.

31 Kroeger, *Nellie Bly: Daredevil*, p. 329 – Quoted from 'How I was robbed of two million dollars', *Fair Play*, 20 January 1912, p. 28.

32 Kroeger, *Nellie Bly: Daredevil*, pp. 333–335.

33 Kroeger, *Nellie Bly: Daredevil*, 334. See *Brooklyn Daily Eagle*, 21 June 1911, p. 2, col. 2.

34 *New York Times*, 28 June 1911, p. 7. See also Kroeger, *Nellie Bly: Daredevil*, p. 339.

35 Lutes, 'Into the madhouse', pp. 225–227.

36 'Topics of the Times: appearances of evil to be avoided', *New York Times*, 10 July 1911, p. 6.

37 *New York Evening Journal*, 7 July 1911, editorial page, col. 1. See also Kroeger, *Nellie Bly: Daredevil*, p. 47.

38 Quoted by Kroeger, *Nellie Bly: Daredevil*, p. 362, from letter by Brisbane to Bly, 13 June 1912, in Brisbane Family Papers.

39 American Steel was not a going or viable concern after the bankruptcy trials. When Bly died in 1922 the company had operated in debt for many years. See Kroeger, *Nellie Bly: Daredevil*, p. 506.

40 'Say Nellie Bly was $1,680,000 fraud victim', *New York Evening Journal*, 11 March 1913, p. 1, col. 2.

41 '"Nellie Bly" explains: that worry and ill-health have affected her deportment in the courts', *New York Times*, 17 March 1912, p. 17.

42 In subsequent chapters of their lives, both women recommitted themselves to traditional gender roles. Ayer stressed a woman's health and beauty as playing an integral role in maintaining happy marriages, while Seaman argued strenuously against married women working outside the home when they had children unless they were in dire financial need.

43 In her biographical entry about Nellie Bly, I. Ross, *Charmers and Cranks*, p. 213, claims that Hetty Green and Nellie Bly were friends, saying 'Among her friends was Hetty Green, who had little use for human contacts but who found in Nellie a responsive spark, an understanding of the intense drive that made both women such strong individualists'. Ross's entry is not footnoted, hence where the evidence for this claim can be found is not clear.

44 L. M. Hodges, 'The richest woman in America: Mrs. Hetty Green as she is seen in her home and in the business world', *Ladies Home Journal* 17, June 1900, pp. 3–4. She is quoted as using the term 'legal buzzards' in 'Mrs. Green is sarcastic: she remarks about lawyer Stayton's attentiveness to her', *New York Times*, 18 May 1898, p. 12, col. 1.

45 This was a description offered by a contemporary of hers, financier Henry Clews in his 1882 book, *Twenty-Eight Years in Wall Street*, New York: J. S. Ogilvie Publishing Co.

46 There are a number of different generations of biographies about Green. The most sensational of these is by B. Sparkes and S. T. Moore, *Hetty Green, A Woman Who Loved Money*, Garden City, NY: Doubleday, Doran & Co., 1930. This was reprinted in 1935 with the new title, *The Witch of Wall Street: Hetty Green*. More recent and more balanced ones include, J. Coryell, 'Hetty Green', in *Encyclopedia of American Business History and Biography, Business and Finance, to 1913*, New York: Bruccoli Clark Layman, 1990, pp. 233–238; C. Slack, *Hetty: The Genius and Madness of America's First Female Tycoon*, New York: HarperCollins, 2004.

47 As late as 1894, Green had still not come to terms with this set up. She sued the trustees for an accounting of the estate saying that there were irregularities. See 'Mrs. Green a plaintiff: trustees of her father's estate charged with irregularities. accused of spending $1,300,000,' *New York Times*, 23 December 1894, p. 3, col. 4.

48 L. Menand, 'Dept. of avarice: she had to have it: the heiress, the fortune and the forgery', *The New Yorker*, 23 and 30 April 2001, p. 66.

49 She also got herself in trouble by doing so. Green was sympathetic to the case of Mary Irene Hoyt who, in the 1880s, fought a six-year suit contesting her father's will. The Jesse Hoyt Will case made headlines for years. Just before his death Hoyt had rewritten his will stipulating that his daughter would inherit $1,250,000 to be held in trust. The income would constitute the allowance on which she was expected to live. Upon her death the money would be distributed to his nieces and nephews. The reason for Hoyt's action was said to be Mary Irene's 'infirmities' and trial testimony included details about her committal to insane asylums. Hoyt later settled out of court. While engaged in one of her own lawsuits, Green revived memories of this case when she invoked Mary Irene's name to damn a group of lawyers she referred to as 'set of buzzards'. Hoyt, who did not appreciate Green's support, sued Green for slander, claiming that she had 'been leading a quiet life, like any other sane and respectable person', and that she did not appreciate having public interest in her earlier suit revived. See 'Mrs. Hetty Green sued: Miss Mary Irene Hoyt charges her with slander', *New York Times*, 6 June 1895, p. 8.

50 'Seventy years rest lightly on Mrs. Hetty Green: Tuesday fortnight the richest woman in America will be threescore and ten – her optimistic outlook upon life – foundation and growth of her great fortune', *New York Times*, 5 November 1905, pt. 3, p. 3.

51 Menand, 'Dept. of Avarice', p. 70.

52 For more information on Hetty Green's attitudes towards women as money-makers, see S. Yohn, 'Crippled capitalists', p. 90.

53 'Why women don't get rich: Mrs. Hetty Green says it is because they try the wrong way', *Brooklyn Daily Eagle*, 1 July 1901. See also H. Green, 'Why women are not money makers', *Harper's Bazaar*, 10 March 1900, vol. 33, p. 201.

54 See N. Basch, *Framing American Divorce: From the Revolutionary Generation to the Victorians*, Berkeley, CA: University of California Press, 1999, particularly chapter 6, 'Divorce stories', p. 185. She argues that larger social tensions about the social freedom of women and the conjugal responsibilities of married men were exposed and opened to public discussion in the newspaper coverage of divorce trials. These stories were largely sympathetic to women and ultimately subversive of an older, more conservative ideal of marriage. Newspaper coverage of Ayer's, Seaman's and Green's cases ranged from neutral to largely sympathetic but, most importantly, provided yet another platform from which they pleaded their case. For Ayer and Seaman particularly, the newspaper was one more vehicle by which they could gain justice. However, in the case of businesswomen, the take-away lesson for readers of these stories was not inspiring. In other words, the stories underscored the perception, best expressed by Brisbane, that women were often cheated.

Bibliography

'Ayer, Harriet Hubbard', *The National Cyclopedia of National Biography*, New York: J. T. White, 1969, vol. 43, pp. 452–453.

Ayer, Margaret, *The Three Lives of Harriet Hubbard Ayer*, Philadelphia, PA: Lippincott, 1957.

Basch, Norma, *Framing American Divorce: From the Revolutionary Generation to the Victorians*, Berkeley, CA: University of California Press, 1999.

Basch, Norma, *In the Eyes of the Law: Women, Marriage and Property in Nineteenth-Century New York*, Ithaca, NY: Cornell University Press, 1982.

Brooklyn Daily Eagle.

Clews, Henry, *Twenty-Eight Years in Wall Street*, New York: J. S. Ogilvie Publishing Co., 1882.

Coryell, Janet, 'Hetty Green', *Encyclopedia of American Business History and Biography, Business and Finance, to 1913*, New York: Bruccoli Clark Layman, 1990, pp. 233–238.

Gamber, Wendy, *Female Economy: The Millinery and Dressmaking Trades, 1860–1930*, Urbana, IL: University of Illinois Press, 1997.

Geller, Jeffrey L. and Harris, Maxine (eds), *Women of the Asylum: Voices from Behind the Walls, 1840–1945*, New York: Anchor Books, 1994.

Green, Hetty, 'Why women are not money makers', *Harper's Bazaar*, 10 March 1900, vol. 33, p. 201.

Gustafson, Melanie, 'The business of beauty: Harriet Hubbard Ayer's New York career in face creams, health tonics and advice to women and men', paper presented at the 27th Conference on New York State History, Columbia University, June 2006.

Harper's Bazaar.

Hodges, Leigh, 'The richest woman in America: Mrs. Hetty Green as she is seen in her home and in the business world', *Ladies Home Journal* 17, June 1900, pp. 3–4.

Kroeger, Brooke, *Nellie Bly: Daredevil, Reporter, Feminist*, New York: Times Books: 1994.

Kwolek-Folland, Angel, *Incorporating Women: A History of Women and Business in the United States*, New York: Palgrave, 2002.

Lutes, Jean Marie, 'Into the madhouse with Nellie Bly: girl stunt reporting in late nineteenth-century America', *American Quarterly* 54 (2), 2002, pp. 217–253.

Menand, Louis, 'Dept. of avarice: she had to have it: the heiress, the fortune and the forgery', *The New Yorker*, 23 and 30 April 2001, p. 66.

New York Evening Journal.

New York Times.

New Yorker.

Perry, Marilyn E., 'Ayer, Harriet Hubbard', *American National Biography*, vol. 1, pp. 790–791.

Pittsburg Gazette-Time.

R. G. Dun & Co., New York, vol. 424, p. 819, Cambridge, MA: R. G. Dun & Co. Collection, Baker Library, Harvard Business School.

Ross, Ishbel, *Charmers and Cranks*, New York: Harper & Row Publishers, 1965.

Slack, Charles, *Hetty: The Genius and Madness of America's First Female Tycoon*, New York: HarperCollins, 2004.

Sparkes, Boyden and Moore, Samuel Taylor, *Hetty Green, A Woman Who Loved Money*, Garden City, NY: Doubleday, Doran & Co., 1930.

Sparks, Edith, *Capital Intentions: Female Proprietors in San Francisco, 1850–1920*, Chapel Hill, NC: University of North Carolina Press, 2006.

Weisberger, Bernard, *Notable American Women: A Biographical Dictionary*, Cambridge, MA: Belknap Press, 1971.

Winner, Lucy, 'Democratic acts: theater of public trials', *Theater Topics* 15 (2), 2005, pp. 149–169.

Yeager, Mary (ed.), *Women in Business*, 3 vols, Cheltenham: Edward Elgar, 1999.

Yohn, Susan, 'Crippled capitalists: the inscription of economic dependence and the challenge of female entrepreneurship in nineteenth-century America', *Feminist Economics* 12 (1–2), 2006, pp. 85–109.

17 'The principles of sound banking and financial *noblesse oblige*'

Women's departments in US banks at the turn of the twentieth century

Nancy Marie Robertson

Beginning in the late nineteenth century, a small number of financial institutions in the United States – the Fifth Avenue Bank of New York; the First National Bank of Chicago; the American Security and Trust Company in Washington, DC; as well as banks in cities like Rochester, New Haven and Spokane – started 'women's departments'.[1] They catered to the middle and wealthy classes by offering separate spaces for women to escape from the hustle and bustle of the busy street or jostling by busy men in the main banking rooms. The Garfield National Bank in New York informed 'ladies' that the rooms meant that 'they do not have to come in contact with the general customers and business of the bank'.[2] The rooms included divans and upholstered chairs, writing tables, flowers and (when available) telephones. A flyer for the Fifth Avenue Bank in New York described 'a comfortable and completely appointed reception room, warmed in chilly days by an open fire and attended by a maid who has had twenty years' experience in this one department'.[3] The homey spaces sounded (and looked) like parlours, sometimes quite luxurious. Women were invited to conduct their business in a leisurely manner or to meet acquaintances there. It is clear from the locations of banks and the description of the departments that the invitation was for a particular class of women, namely ladies of leisure.[4]

Banks were not alone in this effort to open commercial public spaces to ladies. Department stores had waged a long campaign to bring women with disposable incomes through their doors by including features like waiting rooms and tea parlours. There were separate lines at some post offices, ladies' rooms in stockbrokerages, and 'rest rooms' in insurance offices. 'Ladies' compartments' were increasingly commonplace on late-nineteenth-century railroads.[5]

Banks offered women more than their own space, as bank officials offered to help women balance their bank accounts and determine budgets.[6] In most cases, the employees who met these needs were men – apparently the preferred person was the 'courtly gentleman who had a way with the ladies'.[7] While there was some awareness that a growing number of women had access to money (the banks, along with a larger literature, urged men of means to give allowances to their wives), there is little evidence that these departments were seen as paying ventures.[8] The financial and general press stressed the inconvenience to male bankers of handling the accounts. There were constant jokes about women's inability to handle money, especially cheques, and a sense, in the subsequent reminiscences of one banker, that banks 'often classed women's accounts as a "nuisance" '.[9]

Given the domestic imagery associated with women's departments, it is tempting to see them simply as a reproduction of 'separate spheres'. When women appeared in the male public realm of business, every effort would be made to recast the physical space as private and an extension of the home. An examination of women's departments, however, suggests ways in which the boundary between the public world of finance and the private world of home was, in actuality, quite blurred. Whatever their decor, the spaces were part of a commercial world. The potential for women's departments to challenge the metaphor of separate spheres is further realized by an analysis of a second wave of women's departments.

In 1915, one of the first banks representing this trend, the Columbia Trust Company of New York, appointed Virginia D. H. Furman as 'Manager' of its new women's department.[10] By the early 1920s, female-run women's departments had taken off. In an address to the Financial Advertisers' Association, Anne Seward, a pioneer in the departments, announced that in New York City 'at present time there is scarcely a bank of note above the "Macy and Ditson" line of Thirty-fourth street which does not have a women's department managed by a woman'.[11] Women's departments were observed throughout the country, although commentators noted regional variations with the Midwest being more supportive than the East, while the South was the most resistant.[12]

For almost two decades, women's departments were one of the few areas in banks where women were hired in an executive capacity. The number of women who held these positions was minimal – perhaps no more than several hundred at the most. Despite the limited number of women's departments, the press coverage was impressive.[13] Not surprisingly women's magazines like *The Independent Woman* (the publication of the National Federation of Business and Professional Women's Clubs) and *Ladies' Home Journal* covered the ' "Bank within a Bank" for Women', but so did house publications and industry periodicals: *The Chase, The Coast Banker, The New York Commercial, The Burroughs Clearing House* and *Financial Age*, among others, ran countless articles.[14] As might be expected, some of the latter coverage was negative. Writers queried whether women could handle money or business, employing 'nature' to make their case; one sceptic noted 'woman's lack of that cumulative experience which is the inheritance of every man or boy who enters the office or factory'.[15] Others pointed to their lack of 'permanence' in the work force.[16] Why, after all, should banks train women who would only leave to get married?

Even the more positive articles raised questions about whether the departments were viable: would female customers come to women bankers or would they choose men?[17] For everyone who argued that women preferred men (either for semi-flirtatious reasons or because men supposedly had better business skills), the supporters of women's departments argued that women customers preferred female professionals. The reasons given as to why a woman might choose to go to another woman were various. One of the most frequently offered was that a woman understood other women better than a man could. Anne Seward of the Empire Trust Company said of women and their 'financial perplexities', that they

> prefer to tell a woman about it. Women love to talk and women take a long time, as a rule to tell their story. Men are too busy or interrupt. And it is often the patient audience that does the most good.[18]

Banks' hiring decisions, however, went beyond the presumed rapport between a female banker and an individual female customer. Banking officials knew (or quickly came to realize) that the women who staffed women's departments were connected to a network of female voluntary associations. When the Columbia Trust Company elected Virginia Furman as Assistant Secretary, the first female officer in a New York City trust company, the Women's City Club of New York and the New York State Suffrage Party pulled their accounts out of other banks to bring to Furman's department.[19] That the women involved in women's departments were active in a range of voluntary organizations increased their banks' chances of winning the accounts. As women's organizations were stressing the need to be more efficient and businesslike, promotional literature for women's departments emphasized the services that they would provide to the treasurers of those groups to manage and grow their financial assets. 'The old order changeth' declared Cora Tatham of the Young Women's Christian Association,

> And this change has a distinct bearing on the attitude of women toward the securing of funds for the maintenance of charitable and philanthropic work. It is a far cry from the day of the ice cream and strawberry festival to the adoption of scientific methods in money raising.[20]

Banks capitalized on women's social connections when selecting women for women's departments. What exactly qualified a woman to be selected was the topic of many articles. Some, like Mina Bruère, started out as a private secretary to a bank president and worked their way up. Others had been active in First World War efforts – either administering relief efforts or fundraising. Mary Vail Andress, billed as the 'first woman to become an official at the main office of one of the large downtown banks', had overseen Red Cross work in France during the First World War and was the first woman to receive the 'Distinguished Service Medal'. Other women had played critical roles in the campaigns to raise money for war bonds – some 65 per cent of American war funds during the First World War were raised through voluntary efforts. Of course, as Anne Seward admitted, 'pull' helped; a notable number of female bankers had male family members who were also bankers.[21]

But however a woman acquired her position, the issue remained: what was the head of a women's department to do? The answer begins to suggest ways in which female bank officers helped to define the role of the financial profes-sional in the twentieth-century United States. The woman banker, wrote Eliza-beth Barry of the United States National Bank in Portland, Oregon, was a 'friend and advisor, social worker, banker and economist, all in one'.[22] As her words suggest, female bankers emphasized a personal touch. Their speeches and writings were full of terms like 'service' and 'missionary' efforts.[23] Their 'services' ranged from locating a customer's purse that had been left at the opera to advising women on budgets, from promoting well-being in the office to offering financial advice.[24] These tasks required a range of skills. Helen Knox, of the Chase National, described the need to have learned both the 'principles of sound banking *and* financial "noblesse oblige"'.[25] Businesses, especially those in what would come to be thought of as the service sector, increasingly provided personal assistance in an impersonal world. Women's ability to combine financial expertise and service represented a valuable combination.

The supporters of women bankers offered one other reason why they appealed to women customers: the belief that the bankers themselves had to learn the information and, therefore, their customers would not see themselves as comparatively stupid. Customers 'mind, perhaps, appearing slow or dull before men, and they know that the woman manager has also had to make a study of this work', observed one banker. '[With] what incredulous eyes I saw ... a woman akin to myself, a mere human being – perhaps a humane being – one whose own mother might have congenital difficulty adding nine and seven', wrote one customer of her encounter with a woman banker.[26] This formulation took women's supposed 'lack of that cumulative experience which is the inheri-tance of every man or boy' and turned it into an asset.

We make a profound error, however, if we see women's departments in banks as benefiting only women and not the banks – if we think of their signific-ance as being for the historians of women but not business historians. Women bankers and their supporters argued that women's departments made financial sense to banks. In a 1924 survey, Paul Hardesty of the Union Trust Company concluded that a higher percentage of women's accounts (32 per cent) were profitable than men's (23 per cent).[27] A critical service that women bankers pro-vided was to advise women, especially widows, on investments. Women's ownership of stocks was increasing as was concern about that ownership. Writing in the *Ladies' Home Journal* in 1931, Catharine Oglesby graphically conveyed the magnitude of the situation when she wrote that if current trends continued, 'in 2025 the entire wealth of America will be in the hands of women'.[28] Emilie H. Burcham of the Old National Bank and Union Trust Company of Spokane thought her department justified itself,

> Because of the friends it has won for the Bank and Trust Company, for the habit of thrift it has helped to establish, for the money it has saved from unwise investment, and for the hundreds of small services it has been able to render women.[29]

The discussion of 'unwise' investment reveals that banks faced competition – from legitimate and illegitimate businesses – for investment funds. Grace Stoermer, of the Bank of Italy, repeated Andrew Mellon's observation in 1929 that $790,000,000 worth of fraudulent stocks had been sold to women the previous year.[30] 'Service', then, was a term that covered potentially profitable business endeavours at the same time that it encouraged female customers to expect a certain relationship at their banks.

It is clear that, if women's accounts had once been deemed a 'nuisance', that was no longer the case. Given the success of women's departments, it is striking that by the mid-1930s, many, if not most, had been eliminated. In 1929, the Association of Bank Women (ABW) reported a membership of 350 women who were bank officers, of whom 44 were managers of women's departments. By 1935, membership had dropped to 208, of whom 30 were managers of women's departments. By 1942, ABW members who had once seen the departments as gateways for female customers and professionals worried that they had come to represent 'segregation'.[31] Additionally, the economic devastation of the Great Depression wreaked havoc on departments as fewer people had money to save, women were often fired and replaced by men, and banks closed. But problems for women and the departments predated the 1930s.

Some women had always opposed women's departments, cautioning that women might find themselves trapped in them. Even women who had advocated for women's departments had developed a strategy to promote some interaction between men and women in banks. Anne Seward approvingly spoke of places where the manager of the women's department also served male customers and male bankers could serve women for the customers' convenience.[32] It is tempting to conclude that once women's departments had succeeded in winning the profitable accounts of women, male bankers came to see serving female customers as good business. Opportunistically utilizing a language of equality, they sought to ease female professionals out of the picture. Some argued that changing social conditions (particularly the 1920 ratification of the Nineteenth Amendment to the US Constitution giving the vote to American women) meant that 'no special consideration' for female customers was necessary. In the mid-1920s, the National Bank of Commerce in St Louis responded to requests for a women's department by saying, 'We feel that so many women like yourself have entered the business world with such success that it is no longer necessary to treat them as a separate entity in business relationships'.[33]

Women bankers had walked a tightrope – as women, they were supposed to have a unique bond with *female* customers, but as financial professionals, they were to be distinguished from their female customers. Again and again as women bankers argued for a shared experience with their customers, they also laid claim to the skills which they had acquired that separated them. Katherine Buckeley expressed alarm in 1922 that newspaper accounts suggested 'that the way into the Women's Department of today was through the presidency of the local Woman's Club'. She and her sister bankers preferred to emphasize the knowledge of banking and long training necessary for female bankers to be successful (whether or not they themselves had had such experience prior to assuming their positions).[34] In a 1935 series on women in business, *Fortune* magazine vividly presented how difficult it could be to negotiate the relationship between financial professional and customer:

> The women of Los Angeles complained that Grace [Stoermer] was bossy and that they didn't come in to be talked of as though they were feeble-minded and why should they be herded off by themselves anyway as though they didn't know how to write a check?[35]

In learning 'to talk like a man' *and* teaching their customers how to function in the economic world, women bankers had undermined the rationale for their positions.[36]

The challenges that women faced were not simply found in women's departments. The historical literature on women's voluntary associations points out that during the 1920s, increasing emphasis was placed on coeducation and there was a shying away from – even attack upon – sex-segregated organizations and spaces. While the trend was by no means complete or unchallenged, many men and women alike promoted a heterosocial culture where men and women should be treated equally. Among the women bankers themselves, the pioneers were retiring or dying and they were seemingly unable to recruit or train the next generation. And, by the 1930s, many men believed women professionals were no longer necessary and, amid financial turmoil, the departments became a luxury rather than a necessity.

If we were to stop here, we would simply have a compensatory history – identifying an example of early female financial professionals. Their experiences have, however, the potential to shift our analysis of the economic transformation at the end of the nineteenth century. The rise of corporate capitalism saw changes in the kinds of work open to women. But the changes went beyond those of individual women. Banking, like other financial industries, was increasingly conducted in bureaucratic organizations. But even as bureaucracies were large and impersonal, there was a rising importance placed on ideas like 'personality' and 'service'. In his study of banking, Richard Germain has noted that it was precisely at this time that male bankers adopted (were forced to adopt) a more service-oriented approach to customers to offset the growing impersonal nature of the interaction.[37]

In examining women's impact on these processes, we can profit from the historical and sociological literature on women's support for the establishment of the European and US welfare states. Scholars such as Seth Koven, Sonya Michel, Robin Muncy and Theda Skocpol have demonstrated how a full understanding of political history necessitates examining the history of women and vice versa.[38] Even when women lacked full political citizenship, it was their activism in the voluntary sector that provided a critical bridge between an ostensibly 'private' world of women's culture and the major changes in a 'public' world of politics. In the process, they, in Paula Baker's words, 'domesticated' politics.[39] The ostensibly gender-neutral language of expertise and professionalism had served to undercut female bankers' position. But 'service', in all its meanings, worked to 'domesticate' business for men as well as women.

Notes

1 Brief scholarly accounts of women's departments include: W. H. Chafe, *The American Woman: Her Changing Social, Economic, and Political Roles, 1920–1970*, New York: Oxford University Press, 1972, pp. 90–1; S. Alpern, 'Women in banking: the early years', in L. Schweikart (ed.), *Banking and Finance, 1913–1989*, New York: Facts on File, 1990, pp. 468–71; S. Alpern, 'In the beginning: a history of women in management', in E. A. Fagenson (ed.), *Women in Management: Trends, Issues, and Challenges in Managerial Diversity*, vol. 4, *Women and Work*, Newbury Park, CA: Sage Publications, Inc., 1993, pp. 19–51; A. Kwolek-Folland, *Engendering Business: Men and Women in the Corporate Office, 1870–1930*, Baltimore, MD: Johns Hopkins University Press, 1994, pp. 103–5, 150–1, 171–3; R. N. Germain, *Dollars through the Doors: A Pre-1930 History of Bank Marketing in America*, Westport, CT: Greenwood Press, 1996, ch. 5, 'Gender Segregation', pp. 77–96; A. Kwolek-Folland, *Incorporating Women: A History of Women and Business in the United States*, New York: Twayne Publishers, 1998, pp. 108–10; and E. Sparks, *Capital Intentions: Female Proprietors in San Francisco, 1850–1920*, Chapel Hill, NC: University of North Carolina Press, 2006, esp. pp. 94, 97–8, 170–2. For an indication of the variety of banks that offered services, see Germain, *Dollars through the Doors*, esp. Tables 5.1 and 5.2.

2 Typescript for undated booklet (issued prior to 1909), JP Morgan Chase Archives (hereafter JPMC).

3 Quoted in the 'Story of the Fifth Avenue Bank Service', 1932, Bank of New York Archives (hereafter BONY).

4 Although this chapter focuses upon women's involvement in banks and trust companies, there is a complementary story to tell of women's activities in the savings and loan industry; see D. L. Mason, *From Buildings and Loans to Bail-Outs: A History of the American Savings and Loan Industry, 1831–1995*, New York: Cambridge University Press, 2004, pp. 29–32, 62–3, 273. He notes that working women's association with the home, as well as morality and thrift, meant that savings and loans were often seen as part of their sphere. Also useful in this context is the work on African-American women's involvement in mutual aid societies; see E. Barkley-Brown, 'Womanist consciousness: Maggie Lena Walker and the Independent Order of St. Luke' in V. L. Ruiz and E. C. Dubois (eds), *Unequal Sisters: A Multi-Cultural Reader in U.S. Women's History*, New York: Routledge, 1994, pp. 268–83.

5 On department stores, see W. R. Leach, 'Transformations in a culture of consumption: women and department stores, 1890–1925', *Journal of American History* 71, 1984, pp. 319–42, esp. 329; for post offices and brokerage firms, see L. L. Levinson, *Wall Street: A Pictorial History*, New York: Ziff-Davis, 1961, pp. 122, 200; and for railroads, A. G. Richter, *Home on the Rails: Women, the Railroad, and the Rise of Public Domesticity*, Chapel Hill, NC: University of North Carolina Press, 2005, esp. ch. 4. For an insightful analysis of architectural patterns for customers in commercial buildings, see Kwolek-Folland, *Engendering Business*, pp. 103–6.

6 *Bank Notes for Women*, Rochester, New York: Alliance Bank, 1905, p. 9 (JPMC).

7 See Germain, *Dollars through the Doors*, pp. 88–9; the quotation is from an informant describing the male banker for a Washington, DC bank's women's department. The department was one that continued into the 1950s, but apparently held onto the nineteenth-century patterns.

8 On allowances, see J. G. Cannon, *Bank Accounts for Women*, New York: Putnam, 1888, pp. 5–7 (BONY).

9 For 'humorous' stories about cheques and accounts, see C. K. Hood, 'The trials of bankers who received deposits from women', *Business Woman's Journal* 3, January–February 1891, p. 16 and 'A bank woman's department', *The Coast Banker* 12, January 1914, p. 462. For the quotation about nuisance accounts, A. P. Kenny, 'Women and banking', *Association News Bulletin* 9, 9 March 1928, p. 37.

10 'Woman gets bank office: Columbia Trust elects Miss Virginia Furman as Assistant Secretary', *New York Times*, 18 July 1919, p. 7.

11 Anne Seward's address to the Financial Advertisers' Association reported in 'Women bankers give distinctive service', (probably the *Springfield Republican*, c.1926; clipping located in the Sophia Smith Collection). 'Macy' and 'Ditson' were New York department stores, although the comment is also clearly a play on the phrase 'Mason/Dixon line'.

12 For comments on the East and 'West' (meaning the American Midwest), see A. Seward, *The Women's Department*, New York: Banker's Publishing Company, 1924, pp. 14–15; for an indication of less activity in the South, see pp. 114–20.

13 Based on census figures, Angel Kwolek-Folland estimates the number of women employed by banks in 1910 as approximately 22,000 and in 1930 as 158,700. The number of women identified as bankers and bank officials in 1910 was 325 (or 1.5 per cent), while in 1930 the comparable number had risen to 5,927 (or 3.7 per cent), Kwolek-Folland, *Engendering Business*, pp. 5–6.

14 The phrase is from P. E. Ritchey, 'The "Bank within a Bank" for Women', *The Burroughs Clearing House*, 8, June 1924, p. 12.

15 M. C. McCarroll, 'Women in business', *The New York Commercial*, 2 April 1926, p. 3.

16 J. L. Blauss, 'Speaking of women as bankers', *Bankers Home Magazine* 17, September 1923, p. 1; 'If we call the roll of the 39 women Assistant Cashiers reported in 1913, a matter of 10 years, the silences are amazing. The names drop out of the bank directories like the leaves in an October wind' (located in the Schlesinger Library on the History of Women in America's microfilmed records for the Bureau of Vocational Information (hereafter BVI)).

17 E. Wallace, 'Pioneering in Wall Street', *Century Magazine*, August 1927, pp. 411–19 and L. L. Clarke, 'Women and the banking field', *The Independent Woman*, July 1927, pp. 8, 32.

18 Seward, *The Women's Department*, pp. 76–7. For a recent example of similar language, see T. L. Duffy, 'Women feel they're better suited to trust work than men!!', *Trusts and Estates*, August 1977, pp. 530–1.

19 G. N. Gildersleeve, *Women in Banking: A History of the National Association of Bank Women*, Washington, DC: Public Affairs Press, 1959, pp. 1–2.

20 C. L. Tatham, 'Women in finance', *Association Monthly* 14, January 1920, p. 14.

21 For Mina Bruère, see records at JPMC. As Sara Alpern and others have observed, 'private secretary' was more of an executive training position than it is now; see Alpern, 'In the beginning', pp. 32–3. For information on Andress's war efforts, see 'Mary V. Andress, banker, 86, dies', *New York Times*, 17 May 1964, p. 87. Julie Russel, of the Union Trust Company of Detroit, had also been active in France during the War; 'Girl holds novel position with Trust Co.' (BVI).

On 'pull', see Seward, *The Women's Department*, p. 104; see also M. V. Andress, *Banking as a Career for Women*, New York: The Chase National Bank, 1928, p. 7 (JPMC). The female bankers discussed here who had male family members who were also in banking include Bruère, whose brother was president of the largest savings company in the country, as well as Virginia Furman and Helen Knox, whose fathers were bankers. It is not clear whether this trend for female bankers was different than that for male bankers.

22 E. Barry, 'Where women bankers excel', *The Coast Banker* 36, May 1926, p. 541.

23 Alice Fairbrother of Chase National said 'service' was 'the chief feature of a woman's department'; quoted in 'The Chase Bank leads again', *The Chase*, November 1924, p. 329 (JPMC).

24 Women bankers were equated with service, which could entail many kinds of activities: as a concierge (Seward, *The Women's Department*, pp. 60–2); providing corporate welfare for other women within the Bank ('Girl holds novel position with Trust Co.'); and aid to customers on budgets – often referred to as 'home economics' (E. Wallace, 'Banking Careers', *The Independent Woman*, November 1927, p. 14). There is a growing literature on the importance of service, corporate welfare and personnel work; see Kwolek-Folland, *Engendering Business*, pp. 138–9 and A. Tone, *The Business of Benevolence: Industrial Paternalism in Progressive America*, Ithaca, NY: Cornell University Press, 1997, esp. ch. 7.

25 Quoted in 'Miss Knox', *The Chase*, August 1927, p. 324 (emphasis added) (JPMC).

26 Comment from a woman banker from Seward, *The Women's Department*, p. 89; quotation from a customer, A. O'Hagan, 'Jean Arnot Reid, who makes banking easy', *Woman's Journal*, October 1920, p. 20.

27 P. L. Hardesty, 'Are women better savers than men?' *Bankers Monthly* 41, May 1924, pp. 9–10, quoted in Germain, *Dollars through the Doors*, p. 93.

28 C. Oglesby, 'Women in banking', *Ladies' Home Journal*, March 1931, p. 26.

29 'Woman banker heads new kind of department', *The Coast Banker* 36, January 1926, p. 101.

30 G. S. Stoermer, 'How women best serve banks', *The Coast Banker* 43, 20 November 1929, p. 430.

31 E. L. Maddison, 'Women to bank upon', *The Coast Banker* 43, 20 October 1929, p. 344 and the 'Association of Bank Women: 1935 list of members' (BVI). The concern can be found in a 1942 survey included in Association of Bank Women, *Women in Banking: 25th Anniversary Edition*, n.p., Association of Bank Women, 1946, p. 48. Women who were active in and strong supporters of women's departments had founded the ABW in 1921.

32 Seward, *The Women's Department*, pp. 33–4. Clara Porter, who had participated in early planning meetings for the ABW, withdrew apparently over the issue. She had proudly stated there was not a women's department in her bank because 'we believe there is no sex in business'; quoted in 'Women in the banking field', *American Business & National Acceptance Journal*, 20 August 1920, p. 33 (BVI). See also Alpern, 'Women in banking', p. 469.

33 Quoted in 'Why a Women's Department', *Financial Age*, 9 November 1924 (BVI). One of the earliest analyses of the phenomenon is E. B. Freedman, 'Separatism as strategy: female institution building and American feminism, 1870–1930', *Feminist Studies* 5, 1979, pp. 512–29.

34 Seward, *The Women's Department*, pp. 70–2; K. Buckeley, 'A follow-up letter', *BVI News-Bulletin*, 1 December 1922, p. 5.

35 'Women in Business', *Fortune*, 12 September 1935, p. 88.

36 The metaphor is Sarah Deutsch's; see her 'Learning to talk more like a man: Boston women's class-bridging organizations, 1870–1940', *American Historical Review* 97, 1992, pp. 379–404.

37 See Germain, *Dollars through the Doors*, pp. 38–9, he identifies a long history of complaints about poor service from male employees.

38 The literature is extensive, but useful pieces include: S. Koven and S. Michel, 'Womanly duties: maternalist politics and the origins of the welfare states in France, Germany, Great Britain, and the United States, 1880–1920', *American Historical Review* 95, 1990, pp. 1076–108; T. Skocpol, *Protecting Soldiers and Mothers: The Political Origins of Social Policy in the United States*, Cambridge, MA: Harvard University Press, 1992; R. Muncy, *Creating a Female Dominion in American Reform*,

1890–1935, New York: Oxford University Press, 1991; and N. M. Robertson, 'Kindness or justice: women's associations and the politics of race and history', in W. W. Powell and E. S. Clemens (eds), *Private Action and the Public Good*, New Haven, CT: Yale University Press, 1998, pp. 193–205.

39 See her 'The domestication of politics: women and American political society, 1780–1920' *American Historical Review* 89, 1984, pp. 620–47.

Bibliography

Alpern, S., 'In the beginning: a history of women in management', in Fagenson, E. A. (ed.), *Women in Management: Trends, Issues, and Challenges in Managerial Diversity*, vol. 4, *Women and Work*, Newbury Park, CA: Sage Publications, Inc., 1993, pp. 19–51.

Alpern, S., 'Women in banking: the early years', in Schweikart, L. (ed.), *Banking and Finance, 1913–1989*, New York: Facts on File, 1990, pp. 468–71.

Association of Bank Women, *Women in Banking: 25th Anniversary Edition*, Association of Bank Women, 1946.

Baker, P., 'The domestication of politics: women and American political society, 1780–1920', *American Historical Review* 89, 1984, pp. 620–47.

Barkley-Brown, E., 'Womanist consciousness: Maggie Lena Walker and the Independent Order of St. Luke', in Ruiz, V. L. and Dubois, E. C. (eds), *Unequal Sisters: A Multi-Cultural Reader in U.S. Women's History*, New York: Routledge, 1994, pp. 268–83.

Chafe, W. H., *The American Woman: Her Changing Social, Economic, and Political Roles, 1920–1970*, New York: Oxford University Press, 1972.

Deutsch, S., 'Learning to talk more like a man: Boston women's class-bridging organizations, 1870–1940', *American Historical Review* 97, 1992, pp. 379–404.

Duffy, T. L., 'Women feel they're better suited to trust work than men!!', *Trusts and Estates*, August 1977, pp. 530–1.

Freedman, E. B., 'Separatism as strategy: female institution building and American feminism, 1870–1930', *Feminist Studies* 5, 1979, pp. 512–29.

Germain, R. N., *Dollars through the Doors: a Pre-1930 History of Bank Marketing in America*, Westport, CT: Greenwood Press, 1996.

Gildersleeve, G. N., *Women in Banking: A History of the National Association of Bank Women*, Washington, DC: Public Affairs Press, 1959.

Koven, S. and Michel, S., 'Womanly duties: maternalist politics and the origins of the welfare states in France, Germany, Great Britain, and the United States, 1880–1920', *American Historical Review* 95, 1990, pp. 1076–108.

Kwolek-Folland, A., *Incorporating Women: A History of Women and Business in the United States*, New York: Twayne Publishers, 1998.

Kwolek-Folland, A., *Engendering Business: Men and Women in the Corporate Office, 1870–1930*, Baltimore, MD: Johns Hopkins University Press, 1994.

Leach, W. R., 'Transformations in a culture of consumption: women and department stores, 1890–1925', *Journal of American History* 71, 1984, pp. 319–42.

Levinson, L. L., *Wall Street: A Pictorial History*, New York: Ziff-Davis, 1961.

Mason, D. L., *From Buildings and Loans to Bail-Outs: A History of the American Savings and Loan Industry, 1831–1995*, New York: Cambridge University Press, 2004.

Muncy, R., *Creating a Female Dominion in American Reform, 1890–1935*, New York: Oxford University Press, 1991.

Richter, A. G., *Home on the Rails: Women, the Railroad, and the Rise of Public Domesticity*, Chapel Hill, NC: University of North Carolina Press, 2005.

Robertson, N. M., 'Kindness or justice: women's associations and the politics of race and history', in Powell, W. W. and Clemens, E. S. (eds), *Private Action and the Public Good*, New Haven, CT: Yale University Press, 1998, pp. 193–205.

Seward, A., *The Women's Department*, New York: The Banker's Publishing Company, 1924.

Skocpol, T., *Protecting Soldiers and Mothers: The Political Origins of Social Policy in the United States*, Cambridge, MA: Harvard University Press, 1992.

Sparks, E., *Capital Intentions: Female Proprietors in San Francisco, 1850–1920*, Chapel Hill, NC: University of North Carolina Press, 2006.

Tone, A., *The Business of Benevolence: Industrial Paternalism in Progressive America*, Ithaca, NY: Cornell University Press, 1997.

18 Women, money and the financial revolution

A gender perspective on the development of the Swedish financial system, c.1860–1920[1]

Tom Petersson

In the late nineteenth and early twentieth century Sweden experienced an intense industrial spurt that brought the levels of general economic progress and welfare much closer to those of the more developed countries in Western Europe. An important part of the industrialization process, which thus transformed Sweden from one of Europe's poorest economies to one of its richest, was the parallel development of a modernized financial system. The internationally recognized Swedish financial historian, Lars Sandberg, has stated that an important reason for the successful transformation of the Swedish economy was the financial liberalization and growth from the 1860s. A large number of private banks were established, the institutional and organizational boundaries between private and public financial intermediaries were made clear and, most importantly, a wide range of new financial services were introduced to the general public.[2]

Studies on the development of the financial system in this period have continued to be an essential part of research in Swedish economic history and have flourished in recent years. In thorough and substantial empirical studies, several contemporary researchers, especially Anders Ögren, have taken on the task of testing Sandberg's statements regarding the positive role of the financial system for general economic growth. There is a general consensus that the financial system to a high degree supported the industrialization process and spurred general economic development. The industrial revolution was thus supported by a financial revolution.[3]

However, there is one perspective that has often been overlooked in previous studies of the Swedish financial system: the *gender* perspective. Given the fact that there exists a wide range of studies on women capitalists and businesswomen in general, this lack of perspective is perhaps even more striking. Contemporary research has, for example, concluded that women, especially widows and unmarried younger women, were very active as small-scale entrepreneurs within commerce and traditional crafts in cities all around the country. In the late nineteenth century approximately one-third of all urban retailers in Sweden were women.[4] Also, the much larger industrial companies, which have been considered one of the hallmarks of the Swedish industrial revolution, to some extent depended on the contributions of women capitalists. Studies have shown that women, especially those belonging to the founder families, in many cases supplied these companies with venture capital. But they could also make use of their personal networks in order to enhance the development of the companies; that is, women made use of both their financial and social capital.[5]

The aim of this chapter is to place a gender perspective on the development of the Swedish financial system in the late nineteenth and early twentieth centuries. The analysis will briefly include the general economic development of the Swedish economy and the institutional arrangements regarding women's legal rights and their potential to act as independent economic agents. One underlying issue, which will be addressed throughout this chapter, is the question of women's subordination or empowerment within the new and modernized financial system that developed from the 1860s onwards.

The Swedish industrial and financial revolution

Up until the late nineteenth century Sweden was a relatively undeveloped and poor country on the northern periphery of Europe. To paraphrase Alexander Gerschenkron and his grand scheme on national industrial and economic development, Sweden, like the other Scandinavian countries, was a 'moderately backward' economy. In such economies, capital and entrepreneurship were considered to be scarce production factors. Banks, together with active government measures, could, however, compensate for the lack of private initiatives and scarcity of resource within other sectors of the economy. The large German universal banks have often been regarded as probably the best example of how banks aid the successful industrial transformation of an economy.[6]

Sweden's road to industrialization accelerated from the 1870s. In fact, from a European perspective the Scandinavian countries are all cases of successful industrialization and economic growth from the latter part of the nineteenth century (Table 18.1). Swedish industrial development has been ascribed both to

Table 18.1 Growth rates of real GDP per head of population in Sweden, Denmark, Finland, Norway, UK, Germany and France, 1820–1913 (annual average compound growth rates)

	Sweden	Denmark	Finland	Norway	UK	Germany	France
1820–70	0.1	0.9	0.8	0.7	1.2	0.7	0.8
1870–1913	2.0	1.6	1.4	1.3	1.0	1.6	1.5

Source: A. Maddison, *Dynamic Forces in Capitalist Development. A Long-Run Comparative View*, Oxford: Oxford University Press, 1991, p. 49.

Note
Data for Sweden 1870–1913 are from O. Krantz 'Svensk ekonomisk tillväxt under 1900-talet', *Ekonomisk Debatt* 28, 2000, p. 9.

external and internal (domestic) forces. Some scholars have stressed the performance of the export sector and open economy forces; industrialization was, according to this perspective, by and large a response to foreign demand, especially from the most industrialized and developed countries such as Britain, Belgium and France.[7] Others have stressed the importance of internal factors for the successful transformation. Evolving domestic demand and efficient markets have been considered to be important explanations for the country's capability to respond to external influences and demands.[8]

Turning now to the development of the Swedish financial system, it was in an embryonic stage up to the mid nineteenth century. The severe economic crisis in the late 1810s had wiped out the few existing financial organizations that were open to the public (the so-called discount houses). Naturally, the public's confidence in banks and financial intermediaries in general, as well as its willingness to hand over its money to such organizations, also diminished. The informal credit market, dominated by local merchants and moneylenders, continued to be the main source for capital for several decades. Early-nineteenth-century credit markets thus had a very strongly local and fragmented, and therefore limited, character. By 1850 Sweden had only eight commercial banks and 90 savings banks, all of which were strictly concentrated in small, local credit markets. Cooperation between banks in different regions, which could have transferred capital from regions with a surplus of capital to regions with large investment needs, was very rare. In addition, the National Bank of Sweden had a monopoly on conducting banking business in the three largest cities, thus effectively keeping private initiatives down. And the National Bank was more interested in the distribution of subsidized loans, preferably to large landowners, than in contributing to the build-up of a nationwide, modernized financial system.[9] In summary, up to the mid nineteenth century there was a constant lack of money for large-scale investments and the possibilities for the private banks to play a part in the capital-intensive industrial transformation was very limited.

But in the 1860s something happened that could be called the start of a Swedish financial revolution. In their extensive work on financial revolutions throughout the world Peter Rousseau and Richard Sylla have listed five key components that constitute the existence of a 'good' financial system, i.e. a financial system that supports and drives general economic growth and development. These components are: (1) sound public finance and public debt management; (2) stable monetary arrangements; (3) a variety of banks, some with domestic and some with international orientations; (4) a central bank to stabilize domestic finances and manage international financial relations; and (5) well-functioning securities markets.[10]

Several studies indicate that there actually was a financial revolution in Sweden and that the financial system had a strongly positive effect on general economic growth. One study of the relationship between financial markets and economic growth between 1834 and 1991 concludes that this relationship was mutually beneficial during the whole period and that, in the period from 1890 to 1930, financial growth preceded economic growth. Other studies have confirmed that Sweden was a case of finance-led economic growth. In a recent study Anders Ögren concludes that the Swedish financial system in the nineteenth century did indeed develop in the way that would be expected in the case of a financial revolution. The supply of liquidity played a major role in the possibility of allocating resources, and thus the part of the financial revolution that facilitated monetization also encouraged economic growth.[11]

Together with a considerable number of studies of local and regional credit markets, and especially of financial networks and the interaction between different kinds of financial organizations, there is quite a lot of empirical evidence supporting the idea of a financial revolution in Sweden and that the financial system did drive general economic growth.[12] The exact timing of the financial revolution, however, remains somewhat unclear. If we look at some aggregate statistics reflecting the financial revolution, for example the growth of the banks' business in relation to GDP, the 1860s was indeed a period of remarkable expansion (see Table 18.2). But on the other hand, it was not until the late nineteenth century that the financial system became truly inclusive, in the sense that almost every inhabitant had the possibility of using the services offered by the banks. And it was at this point that the long-lasting and in many ways highly effective bank–industry networks within Swedish business were established.

The legal framework

Before exploring women's role in the financial markets in more detail, we must consider the legal framework. In practically all economies extensive legal frameworks and institutional arrangements have surrounded financial activities,

Table 18.2 Various financial measures in percentage of GDP and the organizational development of the Swedish banking system, 1860–1910

	1860	*1870*	*1880*	*1890*	*1900*	*1910*
Money supply (M2)	13	19	36	50	62	78
Commercial bank assets	10	20	37	45	62	79
Savings bank assets	4	7	12	21	22	28
Commercial bank deposits	2	8	19	24	35	46
Savings bank deposits	3	6	11	19	20	25
Commercial bank lending	5	11	21	31	46	65
Savings bank lending	3	6	9	17	17	23
No. of commercial banks	30	36	44	43	67	80
No. of commercial bank offices	50	136	205	190	269	625
No. of savings banks	155	251	347	380	391	441
No. of savings bank offices	n.a.	n.a.	921	909	748	854

Source: A. Ögren, 'Financial revolution, commercial banking, liquidity and economic growth in Sweden, 1834–1913', paper presented at the Sixth European Historical Economics Society Conference in Istanbul, 9–10 September 2005, and T. Petersson, *Framväxten av ett lokalt banksystem*, Uppsala Studies in Economic History 56, Department of Economic History, Uppsala University, 2001, pp. 71–5.

including matters such as indebtedness and the granting of credits. The legal system in Sweden, as well as in other parts of Western Europe, was to a great extent built around the concept of the household, since men and women worked together in what generally has been called 'the family economy'.[13]

One of the most important aspects of individual independence in economic and financial transactions is the issue of property rights or ownership. In the nineteenth century the Swedish Code of 1734 was in force in all its parts. The Code has been recognized as being in accord with the societal needs of the pre-capitalist economy, i.e. the basic need to guarantee household production. Hence, the concept of ownership in the Code was a *collective* one, and in general the master of the household had the right to dispose of the property belonging to the household. Also, according to the Code of 1734, women and children were placed under the father's, brother's or husband's legal guardianship. The only women with full legal rights in economic matters were the widows.[14]

But in the nineteenth century legislation was thoroughly reformed, and the Code was broken up into its components. Many of the reforms constituted the first steps towards legal equality between men and women. The right of inheritance was cognatic, but still not equal. Among the nobility and the peasants in the countryside, sons inherited twice as much as daughters, while the inheritance rights among burghers and clergymen in towns were equal. In 1845, daughters, regardless of their parents' economic or social status, were granted the right to inherit an equal share of their families' estates. Between 1846 and 1864 women's rights to conduct commerce were greatly extended. From 1858 to 1884 unmarried women were gradually released from their legal incapacity. The age of majority of unmarried women in 1884 was thus 21 years, the same as for unmarried men. Another change in the legal system took place in 1874. Now it was possible even for married women to control their own property, which could be withdrawn from the husband's disposal either in premarital settlements or through a division of the joint property of husband and wife. Under the same provisions, a married woman also had the right to dispose of her own income. However, it was not until 1921 that married women had the same economic and legal rights as their husbands. From this point on, men and women in Sweden were equals in the formal, legal sense. But for spouses this was only the case provided that they were married *after* 1921.[15]

However, in spite of the numerous changes towards equality between the sexes, it is not true that men and women had the same opportunities to act as independent economic agents. Women in general, and wives and adolescent women in particular, at least up to 1921, were in this respect subordinated, both in relation to men in general and within the socio-economic system as a whole.

Women and the growth of institutional savings

One of the most important features of an effective financial system is its ability to collect and redistribute the savings of 'ordinary people', i.e. the bulk of the population. In this sense the Swedish financial organizations, especially the savings banks and the commercial banks, were very successful. From the 1860s, a long period of growth in the deposits collected by these banks occurred. Playing the role of *market makers* on local savings markets, the savings banks had a quantitative advantage in relation to the commercial banks up to the late 1860s. Another explanation for the success of the savings banks was their philanthropic and non-profit character, which in turn attracted new socio-economic categories of savers and increased their trust in the savings banks.

Beginning with Stockholm's Enskilda Bank, commercial banks from the 1860s also began to get interested in exploiting local and regional deposit markets as a way of funding their lending activities. In 1868, the total deposits in the commercial banks surpassed those in the savings banks for the first time. The savings banks never managed to catch up with the commercial banks. By 1920 the public's deposits in the commercial banks were almost three times larger than those in the savings banks (see Table 18.3). It is also important to emphasize that it was the savings banks and the commercial banks that totally dominated the institutional deposit market in Sweden. Together they accounted for around 90 per cent of the Swedish market from the 1850s onwards. It was not until the inter-war years that other financial organizations, especially insurance companies, managed to establish themselves as credible savings alternatives to the savings banks and commercial banks.[16]

A number of investigations have been carried out on the socio-economic structure of depositors in the savings banks, both in the cities and in the countryside. Approximately one-third of all depositors in the savings banks were children under the age of 16. As it was the parents who opened accounts in their names, these children naturally often belonged to the middle and upper classes. Approximately 50 per cent of the adult depositors were women. A very large share, often between 70 and 75 per cent, of the women depositors was young (16–25 years of age) and unmarried. One must also stress the importance of young, unmarried female servants as a category of depositor in the Swedish savings banks, often making up more than half of the woman depositors.[17]

And as mentioned, the commercial banks also soon realized the advantage of offering financial services, at least the possibility of saving, to a broad layer of the public. Their strategy of engaging in the local deposit markets was intentionally aimed directly at some of the savings banks' traditional customers, especially the wealthier private persons, among them widows. For example, in Stockholm's Enskilda Bank, 40–50 per cent of the individual deposit accounts were held by women in the late nineteenth century.[18] Considering the socio-economic structure of the depositors in the Swedish banks, it is thus possible to consider the financial system as being truly *inclusive*, i.e. a financial system that was open to all socio-economic categories of the population.

It is also obvious that the savings behaviour of women depositors differed considerably from their male counterparts. Women in general saved much more than men in the same socio-economic category, both in absolute and relative terms. The balances of women's savings accounts were often 20–30 per cent

Table 18.3 The growth of deposits in the savings banks and the commercial banks, 1860–1920 (at 1860 constant prices)

Year	Total deposits, millions of SEK		No. of accounts, thousands		Average balance, SEK	
	Savings banks	Commercial banks	Savings banks	Commercial banks	Savings banks	Commercial banks
1860	27	18	188	n.a.	145	n/a
1880	159	268	753	128	177	1,416 (151)*
1900	466	824	1,201	446	334	1,608 (478)*
1920	614	1,598	2,270	2,752	270	798 (427)*

Source: Statistics of Swedish Commercial Banks; K. Lilja, *Marknad och hushåll*, Uppsala Studies in Economic History 71, Department of Economic History, Uppsala University, 2004, p. 33 and T. Petersson, T., *Framväxten av ett lokalt banksystem*, Uppsala Studies in Economic History 56, Department of Economic History, Uppsala University, 2001, p. 73.

Note
* Average balance on savings accounts.

higher than men's. The most diligent savers were young, unmarried women in their twenties, who saved more than twice as much as men of the same age and marital status. Perhaps even more important, women depositors, at least in the savings banks, saved continuously and on a long-term basis. This meant that once their savings had been deposited in the savings bank, the capital could be transformed into productive investments. There is also a lot of evidence suggesting that, once the young female depositors got married, the savings within the family/household were transferred to the husband's accounts. For the ages 55 and above, an age when many women had became widows, the average female depositor once again saved considerably more than male depositors of the same age.[19] From the banks' point of view, the female savers must have been considered the ultimate customers: they were loyal, saved large amounts on a long-term basis and very seldom, if at all, made any demands to gain influence (for example, regarding how the banks were managed and who was granted credits) in correlation to their actual importance to the banks.

What was the reason for women's propensity to use the new financial organizations and their decisions to leave their money in the hands of savings and commercial banks? Research does not, so far, offer a satisfactory answer. Obviously some of the deposits made by women were more or less non-voluntary, since it was common for employers to open an account in their employees' names and to transfer part of their salaries to these accounts. But there must also be other explanations. Perhaps the older, informal financial system was considered less attractive due to its lack of transparency and stability. In any case, an important explanation as to why the Swedish financial system was able to show a steady growth for more than half a decade and to contribute to the financing of the industrial revolution was its ability to attract women's financial savings.

Women as bondholders and shareholders

Another important factor in the formation of a new financial system in Sweden was the national market for bond issuing. As early as the 1830s a number of regional mortgage institutions had issued bonds to finance the restructuring and modernization of the agricultural sector. But the volume of issued bonds was very modest up to the 1870s. Then new categories of borrowers, particularly the state, local municipalities and railway companies, started to issue bonds on a much larger scale than before. By the turn of the century, as the industrial revolution gained momentum, private industrial companies took over as the largest category among the bond issuers (see Table 18.4).

Who then bought the bonds? Up to the 1870s a large majority of the issued bonds were sold on foreign markets, especially in Hamburg, London and Paris. After that, and up to the early twentieth century, domestic buyers absorbed approximately half of the bonds issued by Swedish borrowers. It is thus obvious that the inflow of foreign capital was exceptionally important for the financing of the Swedish industrial revolution. Among the domestic buyers, financial

Table 18.4 Swedish bond loans distributed by borrower, 1835–1916

Years	Mortgage institutions (%)	State (%)	Municipality (%)	Railway (%)	Industry (%)	Others (%)	Total, millions of SEK
1835–49	100	0	0	0	0	0	34
1850–9	77	22	0	0	0	1	101
1860–9	53	35	8	1	3	0	265
1870–9	47	26	5	15	6	1	669
1880–9	36	39	14	4	5	2	761
1890–9	19	18	13	25	24	1	500
1900–9	11	21	24	7	34	3	1,048
1910–16	18	35	14	4	29	0	2,040

Source: T. Petersson, *Framväxten av ett lokalt banksystem*, p. 147.

organizations, especially savings banks and insurance companies, invested heavily in bonds, not least due to new legislation that more or less forced them to invest in such 'safe' financial instruments. In the 1920s the savings banks and the insurance companies together held around 70 per cent of the bonds sold on the Swedish market.[20]

Studies of households' and private persons' investments in bonds are very rare. Daniel Waldenström has, however, carried out a study on the structure of bond customers at by far the largest private banker in Sweden, the banking firm C.G. Cervin from 1881 to 1930. The speciality of C.G. Cervin was to intermediate in bond issuing, and it had its clientele primarily in the largest cities, i.e. Stockholm, Göteborg and Malmö. Waldenström's study, based on more than 1,200 observations, divides the bond customers into two categories: institutions (banks, companies, insurance companies, etc.) who bought bonds for their own accounts, and households that invested their capital in long-term bonds. The trend towards increased institutional bondholding in the C.G. Cervin firm was clear. In 1881 40 per cent of the bonds intermediated by C.G. Cervin were sold to institutions, and in 1930 the quota had risen to almost 70 per cent. Waldenström's results thus confirm the general trend within the Swedish bond market.[21]

The gender distribution of the bond customers can also be studied. The proportion of women among the household clients rose from 20 per cent in 1881 and the mid-1890s to approximately 40 per cent in the 1910s and 1921, then finally to 60 per cent in 1930. Women in general invested smaller amounts than did men, so women's share of the total household investments was lower than for their number. But one must also bear in mind that among the household clients of the C.G. Cervin firm we find a number of Sweden's largest and, at the time, most successful industrial entrepreneurs, such as James Dickson in Göteborg, who in 1894–7 invested more than one million SEK in bonds issued by industrial companies. Dickson's investment alone corresponded to one-third of all the industrial bonds intermediated by the C.G. Cervin firm in these years. There does not seem to be any significant difference regarding the investment behaviour of women and men respectively. Women invested in approximately the same type of bonds as men did. The only noteworthy difference that can be observed is in 1920–1, when women preferred to invest more heavily in bonds issued by industrial companies, while men preferred bonds issued by financial organizations (see Table 18.5). There is thus no support in this source material for the hypothesis that women in general were more risk-averse than men in their investment behaviour.[22]

The joint-stock company, and the related concept of limited liability, was yet another financial innovation that appeared in the latter half of the nineteenth century. From the 1890s onwards, there was a sharp rise in the establishment of joint-stock companies in Sweden, especially within industry and trading.[23] Unfortunately, as in the case of the bond market, empirical studies into the individual investors in shares are very rare. A few case studies of industrial companies have shown that women owned considerable numbers of the shares, but did not engage actively in the management or on the boards of these companies.[24] When it comes to the financial sector, there are some findings concerning the so-called Enskilda banks, i.e. commercial banks based on the principle of personal responsibility. A rather rudimentary study of the ownership in eight such banks came to the conclusion that between 25 and 43 per cent of the shareholders were women. And since women shareholders in general did own almost as much as their male counterparts, women owned between 23 and 36 per cent of all the shares in these banks.[25]

Was the new financial system mutually beneficial?

We have concluded that the Swedish financial system from the 1860s onwards gradually became more inclusive as it offered its services to a wider range of the population. It is also apparent that woman depositors contributed a substantial part of total savings within the institutional financial system and that the banks, both savings and commercial, depended on women's savings for the financing of their lending activities. Considering this dependency, one might have expected there to be a corresponding increase in the number of women borrowers. This, however, was not the case. Only a very small proportion of the total credit volumes in both savings and commercial banks were granted to women. Based on a large number of investigations on the subject of the commercial banks' lending and financing activities, combined with data from the governmental Banking Inspection, there is no empirical evidence of women being borrowers in the commercial banks to any measurable extent. Also, the savings banks granted only a very small share of their loans to women. Data from a number of savings banks, both in cities and in the countryside, show that approximately 2–4 per cent of annual new loans were granted to women. Widows were, not surprisingly, the predominant category of woman borrowers. The savings banks also demanded better collateral from the women borrowers. Women could not, unlike male borrowers, depend on their good name and their personal networks. Signature loans were thus not an option for

Table 18.5 Women investors at the C.G. Cervin banking firm, 1881–1930

Year	Total no. of household investors (%)	Total household investments (%)	Distribution of bond investments, women and (men) respectively (%)			
			Railway	Industry	Municipal	Financial
1881	20	12	78 (79)	10 (13)	12 (8)	0 (0)
1894–7	18	7	33 (23)	66 (69)	1 (8)	0 (0)
1909–11	42	25	41 (33)	51 (52)	8 (15)	0 (0)
1920–1	39	14	0 (0)	100 (100)	0 (0)	0 (0)
1928–30	61	40	0 (0)	78 (45)	0 (0)	22 (55)

Source: List of bondholders, the archives of the C.G. Cervin banking firm, National Archives, Stockholm.

Note
In 1921, the C.G. Cervin firm only intermediated bond loans issued by industrial companies/borrowers.

women. Instead, woman had to possess some kind of real estate that could be used as collateral.[26]

Neither were women able, or allowed, to advance in the organizational hierarchies of the banks. Up until the late 1920s, we do not find a single female board member or executive in the Swedish commercial banks. As in other Swedish companies, ownership, even of a substantial nature, was not a guarantee for gaining influence and the possibility to execute the power of ownership. Women shareholders were thus by and large reduced to taking the position of silent partners. Women did, however, become more visible in financial organizations in one particular aspect: as employees. Initially, women bank employees mainly worked in the 'back office', as cash controllers, bookkeepers and checking clerks, and thus did not usually have direct contact with the customers. Gradually, however, the number of female cashiers rose, as it became more accepted to have women in direct contact with customers (see Table 18.6). It is also notable that Stockholm's Enskilda Bank, the first commercial bank to really specialize in attracting women depositors, was also the bank that had the largest proportion of female employees. As early as in the 1890s, one-third of its employees were women.

Conclusion

The Swedish financial system underwent a remarkable period of growth, renewal and innovation in the late nineteenth and early twentieth centuries. A large number of relatively new financial organizations, especially savings banks and commercial banks, were established, the institutional setting was redefined and adjusted to new demands and standards, and a wide set of financial services were offered to the greater public. The financial system was thus both effective and inclusive, and perhaps most important of all, it contributed largely to the successful Swedish industrial revolution.

In explaining the success of the financial system, previous research has, among other things, stressed the importance of the high level of literacy as one reason why the Swedish population in general so swiftly accepted the new financial organizations and the new way of saving and investing. The commercial banks' ability to create liquidity and thus to contribute to the creation of credit and the changes in the institutional setting, thereby promoting the establishment of more commercial banks, is another important explanation put forward by recent research. Perhaps one can add an argument concerning the role of women and their financial capital.

This chapter has tried to show that women as a collective category did play an important role within the new institutionalized financial system. Women had a high propensity to use the new financial organizations and to leave their savings in the hands of savings and commercial banks. They were, from the banks' point of view, probably the ideal customers. They saved on a long-term basis with relatively large sums of money and did not demand influence, or even credit, in return. Also, in the emerging markets for bonds and company shares,

Table 18.6 Gender distribution of executives, middle managers and employees in Swedish commercial banks 1891, 1916 and 1927

	1891			1916			1927		
	N	Men (%)	Women (%)	N	Men (%)	Women (%)	N	Men (%)	Women (%)
Executives	41	100	0	45	100	0	155	100	0
Branch managers	31	97	3	241	98	2	244	98	2
Middle managers	248	98	2	867	98	2	967	98	2
Cash controllers	35	63	37	143	52	48	189	49	51
Cashiers	173	84	16	573	53	47	986	49	51
Bookkeepers	349	80	20	1,128	68	32	1,168	63	37
Checking clerks	31	6	94	132	37	63	267	9	91
Others	91	92	8	561	84	16	2,121	84	16
Total	999	85	15	3,690	76	24	6,097	73	27
No. of banks	43	–	–	61	–	–	27	–	–

Source: Svensk Bankmatrikel 1891, 1916 and 1927.

Note
Middle managers = accountants. chief of cashiers departments, ombudsman and controllers.

both key elements in the financing of the industrial revolution, women capitalists made substantial contributions.

Did the new financial system mean that women's position as independent economic agents was strengthened or weakened? Despite the institutional changes towards equality between the sexes, there is no doubt that woman capitalists in general continued to face severe problems in exercising their economic power. For example, woman shareholders, mostly because of strong traditions regarding what a woman could and could not do, had to delegate their authority as shareholders and capitalists to men. There is thus not much evidence of women increasing their formal influence as the financial system became more institutionalized. Instead a majority of the women capitalists continued to be the silent partners of the financial system, loyally and continuously delivering their savings and investments to the new financial organizations.

Notes

1 I would like to thank Mats Larsson, Kristina Lilja, Hilda Hellgren, Anders Sjölander, Lars Fälting and Lynn Karlsson. I have also benefited greatly from Anders Ögren's extensive research on Swedish financial history. I am very grateful to Daniel Waldenström, who provided me with data on the C.G. Cervin banking firm, and to Johanna Rosén, who let me use data on employees and managers in Swedish banks.

2 L. Sandberg, 'Banking and economic growth in Sweden before World War I', *Journal of Economic History* 38, 1978, pp. 650–80 and L. Sandberg, 'The case of the impoverished sophisticate: human capital and Swedish economic growth before World War I', *Journal of Economic History* 39, 1979, pp. 225–41.

3 A. Ögren, *Empirical Studies in Money, Credit and Banking: The Swedish Credit Market in Transition, 1834–1913*, Stockholm: Stockholm School of Economics, 2003; A. Ögren, 'Financial revolution, commercial banking, liquidity and economic growth in Sweden, 1834–1913', paper presented at the Sixth European Historical Economics Society Conference in Istanbul, 9–10 September 2005 and A. Ögren, 'Free or central banking? Liquidity and financial deepening in Sweden, 1834–1913', *Explorations in Economic History* 43, 2006, pp. 64–93. See also H. Lindgren and H. Sjögren, 'Banking systems as "ideal types" and as political economy: the Swedish case, 1820–1914', in D. Forsyth and D. Verdier (eds), *The Origins of National Financial Systems. Alexander Gerschenkron Reconsidered*, London and New York: Routledge, 2003, and O. Broberg, *Konsten att skapa pengar. Aktiebolagens genombrott och finansiell modernisering kring sekelskiftet 1900*, Göteborg University, Department of Economic History, 2006.

4 T. Ericsson, 'Limited opportunities? Female retailing in nineteenth-century Sweden', in R. Beachy, B. Craig and A. Owens (eds), *Rethinking Separate Spheres. Women, Business and Finance in Nineteenth-Century Europe*, London and New York: Berg Publishers, 2006, p. 144.

5 A. Göransson, 'Gender and property rights: capital, kin and owner influence in nineteenth and twentieth-century Sweden', *Business History* 33, 1993, pp. 11–32 and K. Norlander, 'Women capitalists and the industrialization of Sweden', *Umeå Papers in Economic History* 12, 1994, Umeå University.

6 A. Gerschenkron, *Economic Backwardness in Historical Perspective. A Book of Essays*, Cambridge: Cambridge University Press, 1965; R. Cameron, *Banking in the Early Stages of Industrialization*, New York: Oxford University Press, 1967 and D. Ziegler, 'The influence of banking on the rise and expansion of industrial capitalism in Germany', in A. Teichova, G. Kurgan-van Hentenryk and D. Ziegler (eds),

Banking, Trade and Industry. Europe, America and Asia from the Thirteenth to the Twentieth Century, Cambridge: Cambridge University Press, 1997.

7 R. Cameron, *A Concise Economic History of the World*, New York: Oxford University Press, 1997, pp. 252–5; B. Gustafsson, 'The Industrial Revolution in Sweden', in M. Teich and R. Porter (eds), *The Industrial Revolution in national context: Europe and the USA*, Cambridge: Cambridge University Press, 1996.

8 J. Ljungberg and L. Schön, 'Domestic markets and international integration. Paths to industrialization in the Nordic countries', paper presented at the Biannual *Swedish Economic History Meeting*, 19–21 October 2001, Gothenburg. See also E. Hansen, *European Economic History. From Mercantilism to Maastricht and Beyond*, Copenhagen: Copenhagen Business School Press, 2001.

9 B. Andersson, 'Early history of banking in Gothenburg. Discount house operations 1783–1818', *Scandinavian Economic History Review* 31, 1983, pp. 49–67, and I. Nygren, 'Transformation of bank structures in the industrial period: the case of Sweden 1820–1913', *Journal of European Economic History* 11, 1983, pp. 575–603.

10 P. Rousseau and R. Sylla, 'Financial systems, economic growth and globalization', *NBER Working Paper 8323*, 2001, pp. 2–3. See also P. Rousseau and R. Sylla, 'Financial revolutions and economic growth', *Explorations in Economic History* 43, 2006, pp. 1–12.

11 Ögren, 'Free or central banking?'. See also P. Hansson and L. Jonung, 'Finance and economic growth: the case of Sweden 1834–1991', *Research in Economics* 51, 1997, pp. 275–301 and P. Rousseau and P. Wachtel, 'Financial intermediation and economic performance: historical evidence from five industrialized countries', *Journal of Money, Credit and Banking* 30, 1998, pp. 657–78.

12 See for example T. Petersson, 'Framväxten av ett lokalt banksystem', *Uppsala Studies in Economic History* 56, Uppsala University, Department of Economic History, 2001; H. Hellgren, 'Fasta förbindelser', *Uppsala Studies in Economic History* 66, Uppsala University, Department of Economic History, 2003, and K. Lilja, 'Marknad och hushåll', *Uppsala Studies in Economic History* 71, Uppsala University, Department of Economic History, 2004.

13 See L. Tilly and J. Scott, *Women, Work and Family*, New York: Holt, Rinehart & Winston, 1978.

14 G. Qvist, 'Policy towards women and the women's struggle in Sweden', *Scandinavian Journal of History* 5, 1980, pp. 51–74, and Norlander, 'Women capitalists'.

15 Qvist, 'Policy towards women'; Göransson, 'Gender and property rights', and M. Ågren, 'Fadern, systern och brodern', *Historisk Tidskrift* 119, 1999, pp. 683–708.

16 M. Larsson, 'Aktörer, marknader och regleringar', *Uppsala Papers in Financial History* 1, Uppsala University, 1993, and Petersson, 'Framväxten av ett lokalt banksystem', p. 71.

17 T. Petersson, 'The silent partners: women, capital and the development of the financial system in nineteenth-century Sweden', in Beachy *et al.*, *Rethinking Separate Spheres*. The savings banks considered depositors older than 16 years of age to be adult, although up to 1884 the formal full age was 21 years for men and 25 years for women.

18 Petersson, 'The silent partners'.

19 Petersson, 'The silent partners', and A. Perlinge, *Sockenbankirerna*, Stockholm University, Department of Ethnology, 2006, pp. 110–11.

20 H. Sjögren (ed.), *Obligationsmarknaden*, Stockholm: SNS Förlag, 1993, pp. 62–82, and Petersson, 'Framväxten av ett lokal banksystem', pp. 146–7.

21 D. Waldenström, 'Early bondholding in Stockholm 1881–1930', *Research Report no. 8*, Stockholm: Stockholm School of Economics, 1998, p. 27.

22 List of bondholders, D IV:1–4, Archives of C.G. Cervin, National Archives, Stockholm. Women's occupations were generally not stated in the source material from C.G. Cervin so it is not possible to make an exact socio-economic classification of the

women bondholders. There is, however, no doubt that a large majority of them belonged to the middle and upper classes.

23 Broberg, *Konsten att skapa pengar*, p. 85.
24 See for example Norlander, 'Women capitalists'.
25 Petersson, 'The silent partners'.
26 Petersson, 'The silent partners'; Perlinge, *Sockenbankirerna*, p. 193.

Bibliography

Ågren, M., 'Fadern, systern och brodern', *Historisk Tidskrift*, 119, 1999, pp. 683–708.

Andersson, B., 'Early history of banking in Gothenburg. Discount house operations 1783–1818', *Scandinavian Economic History Review* 31, 1983, pp. 49–67.

Broberg, O., *Konsten att skapa pengar. Aktiebolagens genombrott och finansiell modernisering kring sekelskiftet 1900*, Göteborg University, Department of Economic History, 2006.

Cameron, R., *A Concise Economic History of the World*, New York: Oxford University Press, 1997.

Cameron, R., *Banking in the Early Stages of Industrialization. A study in Comparative Economic History*, New York: Oxford University Press, 1967.

Ericsson, T., 'Limited opportunities? Female retailing in nineteenth-century Sweden', in Beachy, R., Craig, B. and Owens, A. (eds), *Rethinking Separate Spheres. Women, Business and Finance in Nineteenth-Century Europe*, London and New York: Berg Publishers, 2006, pp. 139–51.

Gerschenkron, A., *Economic Backwardness in Historical Perspective. A Book of Essays*, Cambridge: Cambridge University Press, 1965.

Göransson, A., 'Gender and property rights: capital, kin and owner influence in nineteenth and twentieth-century Sweden', *Business History* 35, 1993, pp. 11–32.

Gustafsson, B. 'The industrial revolution in Sweden', in Teich, M. and Porter, R. (eds), *The Industrial Revolution in National Context: Europe and the USA*, Cambridge: Cambridge University Press, 1996, pp. 201–25.

Hansen, E., *European Economic History. From Mercantilism to Maastricht and Beyond*, Copenhagen: Copenhagen Business School Press, 2001.

Hansson, P. and Jonung, L., 'Finance and economic growth: the case of Sweden 1834–1991', *Research in Economics* 51, 1997, pp. 275–301.

Hellgren, H., 'Fasta förbindelser', *Uppsala Studies in Economic History* 66, Department of Economic History, Uppsala University, 2003.

Karlsson, M. and Petersson, T., 'Banking or philanthropy? The development and characteristics of the nineteenth century Scandinavian savings banks', *Nordic Historical Review* 2, 2006, pp. 167–92.

Krantz, O., 'Svensk ekonomisk tillväxt under 1900-talet – en problematisk historia', *Ekonomisk Debatt* 28, 2000, pp. 7–15.

Larsson, M., 'Aktörer, marknader och regleringar', *Uppsala Papers in Financial History, no. 1*, Uppsala University, 1993.

Lilja, K., 'Marknad och hushåll', *Uppsala Studies in Economic History* 71, Department of Economic History, Uppsala University, 2004.

Lindgren, H. and Sjögren, H., 'Banking systems as "ideal types" and as political economy: the Swedish case, 1820–1914', in Forsyth, D. and Verdier, D. (eds), *The Origins of National Financial Systems. Alexander Gerschenkron Reconsidered*, London and New York: Routledge, 2003, pp. 126–43.

Ljungberg, J. and Schön, L., 'Domestic markets and international integration. Paths to industrialization in the Nordic countries', paper presented at the Biannual Swedish Economic History Meeting, 19–21 October 2001, Gothenburg.

Maddison, A., *Dynamic Forces in Capitalist Development. A Long-Run Comparative View*, Oxford: Oxford University Press, 1991.

Norlander, K., 'Women capitalists and the industrialization of Sweden', *Umeå Papers in Economic History* 12, 1994, Umeå University.

Nygren, I., 'Transformation of bank structures in the industrial period: the case of Sweden 1820–1913', *Journal of European Economic History* 11, 1983, pp. 575–603.

Ögren, A., 'Free or central banking? Liquidity and financial deepening in Sweden, 1834–1913', *Explorations in Economic History* 43, 2006, pp. 64–93.

Ögren, A., 'Financial revolution, commercial banking, liquidity and economic growth in Sweden, 1834–1913', paper presented at the Sixth European Historical Economics Society Conference in Istanbul, September 9–10, 2005.

Ögren, A., *Empirical Studies in Money, Credit and Banking: The Swedish Credit Market in Transition, 1834–1913*, Stockholm: Stockholm School of Economics, 2003.

Perlinge, A., *Sockenbankirerna*, Stockholm University, Department of Ethnology, 2005.

Petersson, T., 'The silent partners: women, capital and the development of the financial system in nineteenth-century Sweden', in Beachy, R., Craig, B. and Owens, A. (eds), *Rethinking Separate Spheres. Women, Business and Finance in Nineteenth-century Europe*, London and New York: Berg Publishers, 2006, pp. 36–51.

Petersson, T., 'Framväxten av ett lokalt banksystem', *Uppsala Studies in Economic History* 56, Uppsala University, Department of Economic History, 2001.

Qvist, G., 'Policy towards women and the women's struggle in Sweden', *Scandinavian Journal of History* 5, 1980, pp. 51–74.

Rousseau, P. and Sylla, R., 'Financial revolutions and economic growth', *Explorations in Economic History* 43, 2006, pp. 1–12.

Rousseau, P. and Sylla, R., 'Financial systems, economic growth and globalization', *NBER Working Paper 8323*, 2001.

Rousseau, P. and Wachtel, P., 'Financial intermediation and economic performance: historical evidence from five industrialized countries', *Journal of Money, Credit and Banking* 30, 1998, pp. 657–78.

Sandberg, L., 'The case of the impoverished sophisticate: human capital and Swedish economic growth before World War I', *Journal of Economic History* 39, 1979, pp. 225–41.

Sandberg, L., 'Banking and economic growth in Sweden before World War I', *Journal of Economic History* 38, 1978, pp. 650–80.

Sjögren, H. (ed.), *Obligationsmarknaden*, Stockholm: SNS Förlag, 1993.

Svensk Bankmatrikel [Register of board members, directors and employees in Swedish banks], 1891, 1916 and 1927, Stockholm.

Tilly, L. and Scott, J., *Women, Work and Family*, New York: Holt, Rinehart & Winston, 1978.

Waldenström, D., 'Early bondholding in Stockholm 1881–1930', *Research Report no. 8*, Stockholm: Stockholm School of Economics, 1998.

Ziegler, D., 'The influence of banking on the rise and expansion of industrial capitalism in Germany', in Teichova, A., Kurgan-van Hentenryk, G. and Ziegler, D. (eds), *Banking, Trade and Industry. Europe, America and Asia from the Thirteenth to the Twentieth Century*, Cambridge: Cambridge University Press, 1997, pp. 131–56.

19 Women's wealth and finance in nineteenth-century Milan

Stefania Licini

In 1865, the introduction of a new civil code in the Italian Kingdom consolidated women's dependence on men. Wives needed their husband's authorization both to handle their own property autonomously and to allow them to trade. Women on the whole were hindered from practising liberal professions and they had no free access to secondary schooling.[1] However, as an equitable inheritance system was in force and sons and daughters had the same rights to their parents' property,[2] women's proprietorship was neither occasional nor trifling at the time. This is why the chapter aims to provide evidence about the economic position of women in nineteenth-century Italy, especially concerning the amount and kind of financial assets they held.

The share of wealth retained by women is the first question highlighted, then attention turns to the structure of female patrimonies. Both men's and women's estates are analysed and details on wealth composition are given. Finally, the research focuses on the loans made by women in order to reveal their role in the credit market.

The research is based on fiscal sources, estate and income tax returns. More precisely, all the papers recorded at the Registry Office of Milan in the period 1862–1900[3] are taken into account, along with a list of taxpayers published by the Ministry of Finance in 1872.[4] Milan, a large northern Italian city, was at that time second only to Naples in demographic size and first in terms of economic development. By the 1880s, the early phase of industrialization was already complete there: many textile industries (silk and cotton) had settled in the surrounding areas and, inside the town, in addition to a few mechanical factories established during the 1840s, chemical works, paper works and ceramic manufactures were starting up.[5] As early as 1881, during the first national industrial exhibition, people had begun to refer to Milan as the 'economic capital' of Italy. However, Milan, up to the end of the nineteenth century, suffered from the lack of an institutionalized financial system: only savings and cooperative banks were located there, besides one joint-stock bank and the local branch of the National Bank. Before 1894, when a big investment bank, the Banca commerciale italiana, was established in the city, there was in Milan chiefly a network of private bankers, entrepreneurs, friends and relations that granted the credit required by trade and industry.[6] As many scholars have pointed out,[7] wealthy women could

play a significant role in such a context and hence they merit special consideration in order to assess, first, who and how many they were.

Wealthy women

Among the 39,122 decedents with positive wealth recorded at the Registrar's
Office of Milan in the second half of the nineteenth century, there were 15,499
women: they held almost 500 million lire, 23 per cent of the total amount of the
estates.[8] In Milan, two out of five individuals with positive wealth at death were
women, although, being poorer than men, they owned less than one-quarter of
the urban fortunes (Table 19.1). The average and median values of the estates,
respectively 72,026 and 6,924 lire for men, 32,006 and 4,305 lire for women,[9]
confirm the expected, unequal distribution of wealth between the sexes.

Results are similar if we take another standard indicator such as percentiles.
Men, being 60 per cent of the total population with positive wealth, accounted
for 84.4 per cent of the top first percentile and 77.3 per cent of the top tenth.
Symmetrically, women accounted for 15.6 and 22.7 per cent, regaining some
position only in the bottom fiftieth (43.6 per cent) (Table 19.2). The female top
first percentile and top tenth accounted, respectively, for 0.4 and 5.7 per cent of
women with positive wealth at death, compared to 1.4 and 12.8 per cent of men
included in the male top first and tenth percentile. The female fiftieth bottom
percentile made up the majority (54.4 per cent) of women, while men owning
assets valued less than the median value were only 47.1 per cent (Table 19.3).

From another point of view, less than 1 per cent of women (0.79 per cent)
held estate valued at more than 500,000 lire, while affluent men owning at least

Table 19.1 Decedents with positive wealth at death, by sex, Milan, 1862–1900

	Cases	Wealth (lire)	Cases (%)	Wealth (%)
Women	15,499	496,056,374	39.6	22.6
Men	23,620	1,701,250,285	60.4	77.4
Not known	3	–	0.0	0.0
All	39,122	2,197,306,659	100.0	100.0

Sources: ARSM, database, 1862–1900.

Table 19.2 Top and bottom percentiles, by sex. Total population with positive wealth,
Milan, 1862–1900

	Top first (%)	Top tenth (%)	Bottom fiftieth (%)
Men	84.4	77.3	56.4
Women	15.6	22.7	43.6
All	100.0	100.0	100.0

Source: ARSM, database, 1862–1900.

Table 19.3 Female and male population with positive wealth: percentile shares Milan, 1862–1900

	Top first (%)	*Top tenth (%)*	*Bottom fiftieth share (%)*
Men	1.4	12.8	47.1
Women	0.4	5.7	54.4

Source: ARSM, database, 1862–1900.

500,000 lire at death were nearly 2.69 per cent of the male population. In contrast, 87 per cent of women, compared with 77 per cent of men, owned property worth less than 50,000 lire (Table 19.4). Moreover, it must be stressed that men greatly prevailed in the highest echelons of wealth: no woman, but 18 men, owned more than 5 million lire at death and just 6 women, compared with 44 men, had fortunes assessed at more than 3 million lire. The great majority (83.7 per cent) of millionaire individuals were men (Table 19.5). In short, in Milan, as in various other European and American areas, 'women tended to be skewed more towards the lower end of the ownership spectrum',[10] although a number of them sometimes possessed very large fortune and female wealth, on the whole, was 'by no means insubstantial'.[11]

The second topic under consideration is the composition of male and female wealth. In order to analyse this in detail, the assets men and women held at death in 1871 and 1881 have been considered, as census figures regarding nineteenth-century Italy are available only for these two years. They are essential in order to link probate data with civil status and job position of the decedents, so such a choice is unavoidable.[12] Nevertheless, is worthwhile assessing how far these sample years are representative.

Both the proportion of women and their share of wealth in 1871 and 1881 (Table 19.6) are consistent with the data regarding the entire period 1862–1900, although, on the whole, the average value and the degree of concentration of the

Table 19.4 Distribution of the estates, by sex and rank of wealth, Milan, 1862–1900

Rank (thousand lire)	Women		Men	
	No.	%	No.	%
>500	122	0.8	621	2.6
>100<500	906	5.8	2,737	11.6
>50>100	953	6.1	1,992	8.4
>10<50	3,601	23.2	5,227	22.1
>1<10	5,545	35.8	7,273	30.8
<1	4,372	28.2	5,770	24.4
Total	15,499	100.0	23,620	100.0

Source: ARSM, database, 1862–1900.

Table 19.5 Distribution of large estates, by sex, Milan, 1862–1900

Rank (thousand lire)	Women		Men		All	
	%	No.	%	No.	%	No.
>1,000	16.3	47	83.7	242	100.0	289
>3,000	12.0	6	88.0	44	100.0	50
>5,000	0.0	0	100.0	18	100.0	18

Source: ARSM, database, 1862–1900.

Table 19.6 Decedents with positive wealth, by sex, Milan, 1871–81

	Cases	Wealth (lire)	Cases (%)	Wealth (%)
Men	933	91,812,496	58.7	77.4
Women	657	26,791,711	41.3	22.6
All	1,590	118,604,207	100.0	100.0

Source: ARSM, database, 1871–81.

estates are slightly higher. In fact, in 1871 and 1881, the top first percentile of the population accounted for 37.6 per cent of wealth compared with 32.8 per cent calculated for the period 1862–1900; moreover, the mean value of the estates worth more than 500,000 lire is particularly high. However, being aware of such discrepancies, as well as of the fact that the standard deviation of the value of the estate is particularly broad in 1871,[13] these two sample years can be reasonably accepted and utilized.

Wealth composition

A comprehensive glance at the composition of the estates first reveals that in women's fortunes, the share of real estate was lower, amounting to 48.9 per cent compared with 59.8 per cent of men (Table 19.7). The long-standing Italian dowry tradition helps explain such figures. According to the Italian civil code, enacted in 1865, daughters and sons, 'without any prejudice of age or sex', were equitably entitled to their parents' inheritance.[14] However, the legal obligation concerned only the so-called '*legittima*': a share of inheritance amounting, at the time, to 50 per cent of the decedents' assets. Customarily, female offspring were left only what the law required, while males received also the 'disposal' portion; moreover, widespread inheritance practices favoured sons in the transmission of land, buildings and industrial concerns, so that daughters were left mostly personal property. Also, it must be pointed out that in Milan, as in many other European areas, only very rich individuals could invest in real estate and, as women were hindered from undertaking profitable activities, it was very difficult, if not impossible, for them to purchase land and buildings by themselves during their lifetimes.

Table 19.7 Wealth composition, by sex, Milan, 1871–81

	Men (%)	Women (%)
Real property	59.8	48.9
Financial assets	31.1	45.1
Other	9.2	6.0
Total	100.0	100.0

Source: ARSM, database, 1871–81.

Nevertheless, the circumstance of having no male competitor for the family fortune could drive large landed properties into women's hands and this is likely to have happened in a number of cases, given the value of the female real estate totalling more than 10 million lire.[15] It is also plausible that houses and allotments of land were bequeathed to daughters when the parents were entrepreneurs and their purpose was to comply with the inheritance law while preserving untouched the family business. Whatever the circumstances were, evidence from Milan further emphasizes that landowning, in nineteenth-century Europe, was not only a men's affair.[16]

Focusing now on personal property, the first thing worthy of note is the high share of financial assets held by women: on the whole it accounted for 30 per cent, while women's global share of wealth, as reported above, was 23 per cent. From another point of view, just one-third of men's estate was put into financial assets compared with 45.1 per cent of women's estate (see Table 19.7).

In detail, women held more than half of the personal loans in the sample,[17] 42.2 per cent of bonds, 39.5 per cent of government securities and 23.9 per cent of private loans, that is, loans given to any person who was outside the decedent's family or business relations.[18] Men, instead, owned the absolute majority (98.5 per cent) of partnership shares and commercial loans (95.9 per cent) along with the bulk (87.5 per cent) of stocks (Table 19.8). Not surprisingly, female wealth was not correlated to personally run economic activities. Besides, a large part (31 per cent) was invested in government securities, thus apparently confirming the hypothesis that while men held proactive capital, suitable for seeking 'higher returns and higher risk of entrepreneurial activity',[19] women sought 'lower gains and risks'.[20] This assumption seems to be reinforced by the percentage of bonds and stocks held, respectively, by men (4.1 and 13.5) and women (6.9 and 4.5), the latter clearly shrinking from shareholding (Table 19.9). However, further specifications could at least partially disprove such evidence.

Wealth holding was at the time much more connected with inheritance than income. The assets that single individuals owned at death were often simply the results of investments or acquisitions made by parents and other ancestors, although, occasionally, large fortunes had been accumulated during the course of life, especially by 'first industrialists' and other entrepreneurs. The occupational status provided by census data, available for 560 women and 796 men[21] confirms this situation.

Table 19.8 Financial assets, by sex, Milan, 1871–81

	Men (%)	Women (%)	All (%)
Bank deposits	75.2	24.8	100.0
Personal loans	42.8	57.2	100.0
Private loans	76.1	23.9	100.0
Commercial loans	95.9	4.1	100.0
Government securities	60.5	39.5	100.0
Bonds	57.8	42.2	100.0
Stocks	87.5	12.5	100.0
Partnerships	98.5	1.5	100.0
Total	70.0	30.0	100.0

Source: ARSM, database,1871–81.

Table 19.9 Financial assets composition, by sex, Milan, 1871–81

	Men (%)	Women (%)
Bank deposits	4.3	3.4
Personal loans	7.8	24.2
Private loans	28.4	28.7
Commercial loans	12.3	1.2
Government securities	20.2	30.8
Bonds	4.1	6.9
Stocks	13.5	4.5
Partnerships	9.4	0.3
Total	100.0	100.0

Source: ARSM, database,1871–81.

Heirs and heiresses

One woman out of three from this sample was in employment, the others declared themselves 'possidenti' (landowners), 'benestanti' (well-off) and 'agiati/e' (annuitants) and held, on the whole, more than 95 per cent of female wealth. Some 22.5 per cent of men did not work and they owned more than half of the male wealth (Table 19.10).

The data must be treated with caution as, at the time, many people proclaimed themselves to be men – or women – of property, simply to give themselves a more respectable standing, all the more in the case of women who were expected not to work unless it was absolutely necessary. However, the figures, in addition to exposing the different position of men and women, definitely stress the significance of bequests as a source of male, and especially female, wealth. Evidence provided by the top first percentile further corroborates the assumption, revealing that only one out of three of the richest men were engaged

Table 19.10 Decedents by occupational status and sex, Milan, 1871–81

	Women		Men	
	Cases (%)	*Wealth (%)*	*Cases (%)*	*Wealth (%)*
Rentiers	68.2	96.5	22.5	61.5
Others	31.8	3.5	77.5	38.5
All	100.0	100.0	100.0	100.0

Source: ARSM, database, 1871–81.

Table 19.11 Top first and tenth percentiles by occupational status and sex. Total population with positive wealth, Milan, 1871–81

	Men			Women		
	Rentier	*Others*	*Total*	*Rentier*	*Others*	*Total*
Top first	8	4	12	6	0	6
	67%	33%	100%	100%	0%	100%
Top tenth	66	54	120	36	1	37
	55%	45%	100%	97%	3%	100%

Source: ARSM, database,1871–81.

in some economic activity,[22] while no woman was. In the top tenth percentile, men employed in trade, manufacturing and the professions increase to 45 per cent, but only one woman (out of 37) declared herself not a 'rentier' (Table 19.11). She was a needleworker who had inherited some plots of land just a few months before dying).[23]

Bearing in mind that both men and women belonging to the top tenth percentile, due to the high rate of wealth concentration of the time, held a very large share of the urban fortunes (respectively 77.1 and 75.2 per cent), it is worthwhile turning attention to the composition of their estates. The aim is also to compare it with that of the estates owned by the population under the median, who were mostly employed in professions, shopkeeping, arts and crafts and a variety of salaried jobs.[24]

Real property was of overwhelming importance in the estates of both very rich men and women, although the figures differ by ten percentage points (63.8 and 33.9 per cent, respectively). In the bottom fiftieth percentile, the share of real property was scarce on the whole, but, again, it was greater in the male estates. Symmetrically, financial assets, always noticeable in the female patrimonies, increase along with the decrease in the level of wealth (Table 19.12). A closer look at the single patrimonial items shows that government securities were predominant in rich women's estates (32.5), while stocks and partnership shares, totalling 28.6 per cent, were prevalent in men's (Table 19.13). As women's large fortunes were inherited, the data once more denotes that mostly resources not necessary to the economic activity of the family were bequeathed to daughters, with the aim of granting them a safe and secure income. Sons, on the other hand, were directly involved in business. From a different point of view, the contribution of women to financing state expenditures, which has been highlighted with regard to other European areas, is definitely corroborated by data concerning Milan.[25]

In fact, although the distance between the female and male share of public debt certificates narrows in the bottom fiftieth percentile, women still held a more conspicuous portion of government securities. In contrast, commercial loans, stocks and partnership shares still remain higher in the male hereditaments, albeit very low, just what was required by the management of small enterprises, shops or craft studios. On the whole, among the poorer part of the population, equities and debentures drop, while the value of bank deposits, both

Table 19.12 Top tenth and bottom fiftieth percentiles: wealth composition by sex. Total population with positive wealth, Milan, 1871–81

	Women		Men	
	Top tenth (%)	Bottom fiftieth (%)	Top tenth (%)	Bottom fiftieth (%)
Real property	53.9	9.4	63.8	17.6
Financial assets	40.3	57.1	28.9	41.1
Other	5.8	33.5	7.3	41.3
Total	100.0	100.0	100.0	100.0

Source: ARSM, database 1871–81.

Table 19.13 Top tenth and bottom fiftieth percentiles, financial assets by sex. Total population with positive wealth, Milan, 1871–81

	Women		Men	
	Top tenth (%)	Bottom fiftieth (%)	Top tenth (%)	Bottom fiftieth (%)
Bank deposits	2.4	15.4	2.9	14.9
Personal loans	23.0	29.9	8.5	7.3
Private loans	27.5	22.0	25.0	35.6
Commercial loans	1.0	0.6	12.7	12.2
Government securities	32.5	29.3	18.0	22.2
Bonds	8.1	0.8	4.3	2.1
Stocks	5.2	1.9	16.0	3.7
Partnerships	0.3	0.1	12.6	2.0
Total	100.0	100.0	100.0	100.0

Source: ARSM, database,1871–81

for men and women, rises considerably (Table 19.3). It is likely that, at the lowest echelon of the wealth structure, people of either sex mostly attempted to secure their earnings and savings in this way.

A feature common to the high and low ranks of wealth that is worth highlighting is the structure of female and male loans. Both in the top tenth and bottom fiftieth percentiles, commercial credits were irrelevant in women's portfolios, while they varied between 22 and 27 per cent in the men's. Personal loans, that is, the dowry, undivided inheritance and sums of money lent to relatives for whatever reason, were mainly connected with women, instead. Private loans, finally, were almost equally distributed between the sexes, although their share decreases among the poorer female population in favour of loans given to family members (Table 19.14). On the whole, liquidity provided by both men and women to various borrowers against mortgage or a simple IOU (*credito chirografo*) accounted for more than half of the loans item in the top male and female tenth percentile (Table 19.14).

Lending was a safe investment in nineteenth-century Milan and the return, given the current interest rate assessed at around 5 per cent, was good. Wealthy men, in particular entrepreneurs, often put their surplus liquidity in loans and not infrequently the fathers' portfolio was bequeathed to daughters, along with bond and government securities. However, another point worth considering is the total amount of loans women held. If personal loans are added to private ones, it appears that 53 per cent of female financial assets, compared with 49 per cent of men's, were tied up in loans (Table 19.9). This phenomenon merits further examination.

The credit market: an equal opportunities arena?

That women played an important role as money lenders in industrializing areas of Europe has been recently highlighted by many scholars.[26] In Milan, the evidence provided above corroborates such an assumption and additional proof can be found in another fiscal source available in Italy: the Ricchezza Mobile, an income tax put into effect in 1866.

The tax was organized into three categories, A, B and C. The first aimed to be a charge on the 'revenue from capital' (the returns of lending activities); the

Table 19.14 Men's and women's loans

	Top tenth		Bottom fiftieth		All estates	
	Men (%)	Women (%)	Men (%)	Women (%)	Men (%)	Women (%)
Personal	18.5	43.8	13.3	56.4	16.0	44.7
Private	54.1	54.2	64.5	42.6	58.5	53.0
Commercial	27.4	2.0	22.2	1.0	25.5	2.3
Total	100.0	100.0	100.0	100.0	100.0	100.0

second, the 'mixed revenue from labour and capital' (entrepreneurial activities); and the last, the 'revenue from labour' (professional activities).[27] Unsurprisingly, given the legal context, no women except for three teachers and two midwives, were included in the list of 500 professionals recorded in category C. Women increased to 7.1 per cent among the taxpayers of category B – shopkeepers, craftsmen/women, heads of small workshops, etc. – but their revenues accounted only for 3 per cent of the total declared income.[28] In contrast, in category A, women played an important part.

According to the category A tax rolls, published by the Ministry of Finance in 1872 and reporting the name of every person taxed for a yearly income worth more than 1,000 lire, women accounted for 37.4 per cent of the taxpayers and owned 38.6 per cent of the overall declared income (Table 19.15). As the interest rate was at the time around 5 per cent, the return of 1.7 million lire a year means women lent at least 35 million lire, a truly high amount considering that, in Milan, the share capital of a large joint-stock company was on average worth nearly 30 million lire.[29] Besides, avoidance and evasion must be taken into account, as private loans were often made without mortgage, simply against an IOU. It should also be considered that the List reports only incomes totalling more than 1,000 lire, thus excluding, for example, the great quantity of modest dowries most women 'lent' to their husbands. On the whole, it is evident that women's capital was significant in the local supply of liquidity and this fact becomes even more relevant considering the paucity of the urban financial system previously described.

Moreover, it is worth noting that a number of women (19) were among the 51 individuals who could be considered 'professional lenders', as they were listed in the category A tax rolls with an income over 10,000 lire and the capital they lent was assessed at around 50 million lire. The percentage of women was more or less the same among the taxpayers with an income assessed over 20,000 lire (five out of 14) and further increases (up to 50 per cent) among the very rich lenders (income in excess of 30,000 lire) (Table 19.16). A considerable amount of capital was in women's hands, but this does not mean that they actually controlled the credit activity. In fact, according to the law, women, upon marriage, would remain owners of their property, but would lose the right to administer it. In the Kingdom of Italy, the legal institution of 'marital authorization' was

Table 19.15 Taxpayers, category A, by sex, Milan, 1872

	Number	%	Income (lire)	%
Men	1,001	58.3	2,509,677	56.3
Women	642	37.4	1,721,719	38.6
Both	75	4.3	226,800	5.1
All	1,718	100.0	4,458,196	100.0

Source: Ministero delle Finanze, Direzione generale delle imposte dirette, *Elenco dei contribuenti*, pp. 5–11.

Table 19.16 Taxpayers, category A, by sex. Income >10,000, Milan, 1872.

Income	Men		Women		All	
Rank (lire)	No.	%	No.	%	No.	%
>10,000	32	63	19	37	51	100
>20,000	14	74	5	26	19	100
>30,000	3	50	3	50	6	100

Source: Ministero delle Finanze, Direzione generale delle imposte dirette, *Elenco dei contribuenti* pp. 5–11.

Table 19.17 Female wealth composition, by civil status, Milan, 1871–81

	Widows (%)	Married (%)	Spinsters (%)
Real property	50.1	44.7	49.1
Financial assets	39.4	47.3	46.2
Other	10.5	8.0	4.7
Total	100.0	100.0	100.0

Source: ARSM, database, 1871–81.

effective from 1865 to 1919 and married women needed their husbands' approval both to handle their own resources autonomously and enter in trade.[30]

Personal information would be useful in order to verify whether civil status did matter in shaping the female role in the credit market, but the tax rolls did not provide it, nor did the census for the year 1872. To overcome this obstacle, the estates that spinsters, widows and married women held at death, in the sample years 1871–81, have been taken into account.

Looking at wealth composition on the whole, no substantial difference emerges in the structure of female fortunes, apart from the slightly lower share of real property married women held (Table 19.17).[31] On the contrary, focusing on the financial assets, the amount of government securities owned by spinsters (47.7 per cent) stands out, as well as the quantity of personal loans (44.1 per cent) married women made (Table 19.18). On one hand, the relevance of the dowry is reaffirmed; on the other, the role played by inheritance strategies is further underlined. unmarried daughters were left mainly safe public certificates, which upon marriage were converted into a loan to the husband, the dowry. Spinsters' share of loans was unsurprisingly very low (35 per cent) compared with widows' and married women's. The last-named lent mainly to family members and other relatives, while widows, who probably had more freedom to act, also provided liquid capital to people outside the family network (Table 19.19).

Table 19.18 Female financial assets, by civil status, Milan, 1871–81

	Widows (%)	Married (%)	Spinsters (%)
Bank deposits	5.0	3.5	14.7
Personal loans	28.8	44.1	2.8
Private loans	31.3	10.9	30.0
Commercial loans	0.6	1.3	2.5
Government securities	23.4	31.6	47.7
Bonds	4.9	2.4	0.7
Stocks	5.3	6.2	1.6
Partnerships	0.7	0.0	0.0
Total	100.0	100.0	100.0

Source: ARSM, database, 1871–81.

Table 19.19 Female loans composition, by civil status, Milan, 1871–81

	Widows (%)	Married (%)	Spinsters (%)
Personal loans	47.4	78.4	8.0
Private loans	51.6	19.3	85.0
Commercial loans	1.0	2.3	7.0
Total	100.0	100.0	100.0
Loans as percentage of financial assets	60.7	56.3	35.3

Source: ARSM, database, 1871–81.

The identity of the people who borrowed from women, and why, is the final topic to deal with, to further describe the role of female financial resources in an industrializing area like Milan.

The loans portfolio of four (out of five) top wealthy female lenders (income in excess of 20,000 lire) is, fortunately, recorded in every detail on the act of succession registered in their name. This allows us to identify the borrowers and, in a few cases, the use they made of the money they received. It should, however, first be stressed that taking into account these four women, located at the top of the income echelon, we are dealing with persons whose credits at death amounted on the whole to 4.35 million lire (Table 19.20). This means that they were not only very rich but also quite influential from a social point of view. So, notwithstanding the sample is numerically poor, it could be considered significant and, overall, a good starting point for further reflection and enquiry.

Conclusion

Focusing on the four very wealthy female lenders under examination (Table 19.20), it is worthwhile pointing out, first, that they were all independent women: three widows and one divorced. So the case of Milan further confirms that it was principally *femmes sole* who could act autonomously and play a role in the European financial markets of the nineteenth century.[32] Second, it is important to underline that they all belonged to the bourgeois elite of the town. Since noblewomen were mostly left real property, they had more difficulty in disposing of liquidity, all the more so because at the time the Italian aristocracy had to face serious economic problems.[33]

Looking in detail at the 'loans portfolio' of the four female 'great lenders', it must be noted that in the case of Adele Antonelli, it was simply the result of her father's strategies. She was the only daughter of a prominent merchant of the city and she died very young. The property she held at death, which included government securities, stocks and bonds, together with a number of safe loans made to aristocrats and landowners,[34] was typical of the well-balanced portfolio constituted by entrepreneurs in order to diversify risks.

The composition of Carolina Angiolini's fortune was quite similar. It must be emphasized, however, that such a various and secure patrimony was not the mere outcome of an inheritance process. Carolina, in fact, achieved most of her property by herself, using her own personal 'substance', as stated in the will. She had inherited some allotments of land and a certain amount of movables from a bourgeois landowner; she then personally bought some land and a certain number of buildings in a semi-central area of Milan. She participated directly in the restructuring of these buildings and purchased a number of stocks and bonds; in addition she gave loans for a global value of 1.5 million lire. A number of loans, amounting to nearly 300,000 lire, were made to the aristocratic elite of Milan, the rest to entrepreneurs and enterprises involved, unsurprisingly, in the construction industry.[35]

As a widow, Carolina Angiolini was free to act and so she did, all the more so because neither her husband – a well-known art collector – nor her two sons were interested in economic or financial activities. On the contrary, it is likely she was endowed with a certain entrepreneurial talent that she decided to direct

Table 19.20 Female 'great lenders', income >20,000 lire, Milan, 1872

Last name	First name	Income (lire)	Estate at death (lire)
Angiolini	Carolina	44,751	3,147,000
Vonwiller	Sofia	35,525	1,979,773
Antonelli	Adele	32,394	1,331,654
Besana	sisters	29,035	not known
Mennet	Sofia	23,622	1,574,176

Sources: ARSM Database, 1862–1900; Ministero delle Finanze, Direzione generale delle imposte dirette, *Elenco dei contribuenti* p. 5. ASM, Successioni, 198/3, 182/20, 133/26, 135/15.

towards the business of the time: building speculation,[36] although such a risky investment was accompanied by the safer purchase of securities and credits.

Quite different was the position of the remaining two, elderly widows Sofia Mennet and Sofia Vonwiller, both belonging to a religious (Protestant) and linguistic (German) minority as well as to entrepreneurial dynasties. They were clearly bound by their familial ties, to the point that the majority of their property had been lent, respectively, to a son and to a brother. In particular, the former gave 1.2 million lire to her son Federico Mylius, when the Genoa branch of the Milan-based banking house he had inherited from his father opened. The latter simply renounced her share of inheritance, formally giving her brother a loan worth 800,000 lire.[37] Though these women were both daughters of entrepreneurs engaged in trade and manufacture, their behaviour was not at all similar. The former, Sofia Mennet, utilized the wealth bequeathed to her in order to benefit her new family by lending money to her son; the latter, Sofia Vonwiller, left her property at the disposal of the original family firm. The entrepreneurial dynasty to which Sofia Vonwiller belonged was still active; consequently her fortune was simply a resource for the enterprise. In the other case, instead, Sofia Mennet was free to make a choice and she undertook the risk of granting a loan to her son. This is enough to strengthen the thesis that in order to understand the economic activity of women 'the main place to look is the family',[38] all the more so because, as seen above, nearly one-quarter of the financial assets held by women were in the hands of family members.

Summing up, women were far from being a 'unitary entity', but a number of them, although they prioritized family needs, certainly actively supported the credit market and the economy in general. As many scholars have pointed out, women usually preferred to stay 'hidden from public eyes',[39] lending their money to individuals or companies directly engaged in trade, service or manufacture, but along this way the contribution they provided was significant and deserves to be fully assessed and appreciated.

Notes

1 For an overview of women's legal position in nineteenth-century Italy, in addition to *Codice civile del Regno d'Italia*, Firenze: E. Sonzogno, 1865, see M. Bellomo, *La condizione giuridica della donna in Italia. Vicende antiche e moderne*, Turin: Eri, 1970; M. Fioravanzo, 'Sull'autorizzazione Maritale. Ricerche sulla condizione giuridica femminile nell'Italia Unita', *Clio* 4, 1994, pp. 641–725; C. Saraceno, 'Women, family, and the law, 1750–1942', *Journal of Family History* 15, 1990, pp. 427–42; E. Sarogni, *La Donna Italiana. Il Lungo Cammino Verso i Diritti, 1861–1994*, Parma: Pratiche, 1995; P. Ungari, *Storia del diritto di famiglia in Italia*, Bologna: Il Mulino, 1974; D. Vincenzi Amato, 'La famiglia e il diritto', in P. Melograni (ed.), *La famiglia italiana dall'ottocento ad oggi*, Bari: Laterza, 1988, pp. 629–700; G. Vismara, *Il Diritto di famiglia in Italia dalla Riforma ai Codici. Appunti*, Milan: Giuffrè, 1978; A. M. Galoppini, *Il lungo viaggio verso la parità. I diritti civili politici delle donne dall'unità ad oggi*, Bologna: Il Mulino, 1980.
2 *Codice civile* and P. Ungari, *Storia del diritto*, pp. 50–68.
3 In the new Kingdom of Italy (1861), on 21 April 1862, the Registry law was enacted.

Following the French example, it obliged any person who had inherited an estate to declare it and give an estimate of its worth. Both real and personal estate had to be listed and the form (declaration) submitted to the Registrar's Office nearest to the deceased's residence. For an exhaustive description of this fiscal source in the Italian context, see A. M. Banti, 'Una fonte per lo studio delle élites ottocentesche: le dichiarazioni di successione dell'Ufficio del registro', *Rassegna degli archivi di stato* 1, 1983, pp. 83–118; and S. Licini, *Guida ai patrimoni milanesi. Le dichiarazioni di successione ottocentesche*, Soveria Mannelli: Rubettino, 1999. Further references can also be found in 'Legge generale sul Registro', 21 April 1862, in *Raccolta ufficiale delle leggie dei decreti del Regno d'Italia*, Torino: Stamperia reale, 1861–1946.

4 In 1866, an income tax, Ricchezza Mobile, was introduced in Italy and lists of the major taxpayers were published by the Ministry of Finance for 1872, 1874, 1889, 1922, 1924, 1928, 1929, 1933 and 1960. This study takes account of the publication in 1873 (1872 tax returns), because it is the only one that also considered income generated by money-lending activity. See Ministero delle Finanze, Direzione generale delle imposte dirette, *Elenco dei contribuenti all'imposta sulla ricchezza mobile aventi un reddito imponibile complessivo superiore alle 1,000 lire, desunti dai ruoli principali del 1872*. Firenze: Stamperia reale, 1873, vol. 1.

5 For information about the industrial and economic development of this Italian region and its chief town, refer to E. Dalmasso, *Milano capitale economica d'Italia*, Milano: Franco Angeli, 1972; V. Hunecke, *Classe operaia e rivoluzione industriale a Milano, 1859–1892*, Bologna: Il Mulino, 1982; B. Caizzi, *L'economia lombarda durante la Restaurazione, 1815–1859*, Milano: Banca commerciale italiana, 1972; F. Della Peruta, *Milano. Lavoro e fabbrica, 1814–1915*, Milano: Franco Angeli, 1987; S. Zaninelli (ed.), *Un sistema manifatturiero aperto al mercato, dal Settecento all'Unità politica*, Milano: Il Polifilo, 1988; S. Zaninelli and P. Cafaro (eds), *Alla guida della prima industrializzazione italiana. Dall'unità politica alla fine dell'Ottocento*, Milano: Il Polifilo, 1990.

6 See P. Cafaro, 'Finanziamento e ruolo della banca', in S. Zaninelli and P. Cafaro (eds), *Alla guida della prima industrializzazione italiana*, Milan: Il Polifilo, 1990–1, and S. Licini, 'Banca e credito a Milano, nella prima fase dell'industrializzazione (1840–1880)', in E. Decleva (ed.), *Antonio Allievi: dalle 'scienze civili' alla pratica del credito*, Rome and Bari: Laterza, 1997, pp. 527–59.

7 See especially R. C. Beachy, B. Craig and A. Owens, 'Introduction', and T. Petersson, 'The silent partners: women, capital and the development of the financial system in Nineteenth-century Sweden', both in R. C. Beachy, B. Craig and A. Owens (eds), *Women, Business and Finance in Nineteenth-Century Europe*, Oxford: Berg, 2006, pp. 1–19 and pp. 36–51, respectively. See also M. E. Wiesner, *Women and Gender in Early Modern Europe*, Cambridge: Cambridge University Press, 1993.

8 The calculations are made on a database, constructed by utilizing all the documents recorded at the Registrar Office of Milan between 1862 and 1900 and available on the website www.uni-unibe.it, which includes name, surname, date of death and gross amount of the estate of each decedent (henceforth ARSM, database, 1862–1900). The original papers are deposited at the State Archive of Milan, fondo Successioni (hereafter, ASM, Successioni).

9 Calculations on ARSM, database 1862–1900.

10 D. R. Green, 'Independent women, wealth and wills in nineteenth-century London', in J. Stobart and A. Owens (eds), *Urban Fortunes. Property and Inheritance in the Town, 1700–1900*, Aldershot: Ashgate, 2000, p. 221.

11 D. R. Green, and A. Owens 'Metropolitan estates of the middle-class, 1800–50: probates and death duties revisited,' *Historical Research* 70, 1997, p. 310.

12 Another database has been constructed (hereafter, ARSM, database, 1871–81), taking into consideration every item of the assets each decedent declared. Civil status and job position have been linked, when available.

13 Only in 1871 and 1889 was the value of the standard deviation more than 400,000 lire. See ARSM, database, 1862–1900.

14 *Codice civile*, art.38. On inheritance laws and dowry system in Italy, see also I. Fazio, 'Valori economici.e. valori simbolici: il declino della dote nell'Italia dell'Ottocento', *Quaderni Storici* 27, 1992, pp. 291–311; and I. Fazio, 'Le ricchezze e le donne: verso una ri-problematizzazione', *Quaderni Storici* 34, 1999, pp. 539–50.

15 More precisely, the value of female real property was 13,043,292 lire and the men's was 54,066,364. See ARSM, database, 1871–81.

16 Female landowning is particularly emphasized by A. Mitson, 'An exchange of letters: estate management and Lady Yarborough', *Women's History Review* 7 (4), 1998, pp. 547–63; M. Malatesta, *Le aristocrazie terriere nell'Europa contemporanea*, Bari: Laterza, 1999; I. Chabot, 'Risorse e diritti patrimoniali', in A. Groppi (ed.), *Il lavoro delle donne*, Bari: Laterza, 1996, pp. 47–69; B. A. Crosswhite, 'Women and land: aristocratic ownership of property in early modern England', *New York University Law Review* 77 (4), 2002, pp. 1119–56. The share of real property held by women was demonstrated some years ago by M. Berg, 'Women's property and the industrial revolution', *Journal of Interdisciplinary History* 24 (2), 1993, pp. 223–50.

17 Dowry or portions of unclaimed inheritance as well as other credits given to close relatives have been included in this category.

18 Under the item 'loans', Registrar officials entered any sum of money that the deceased had lent to any person or body. The name of the borrower (person or company) was always reported on the papers, so that it is possible to identify which kind of loan it was.

19 R. J. Morris, 'Men, women and property: the reform of the Married Women's Property Act 1870', in F. M. L. Thompson (ed.), *Landowners, Capitalists and Entrepreneurs: Essays for Sir John Habbakuk*, Oxford, Clarendon Press, 1994, p. 179.

20 Ibid.

21 See Historical Town Archives, Milan, Registers of death 1871 and 1881.

22 There were two merchants, one manufacturer and one professional accountant. ARSM, database, 1871–1881.

23 This was the case of Caterina Baroggi, see ASM, Successioni, *ad vocem*.

24 Further details on this topic can be found in S. Licini, 'Women's wealth in nineteenth-century: some evidence from the probate records of Milan, Italy (1862–1900)', *Women's History Magazine* 53, 2006, in particular pp. 14–15.

25 On this topic, refer in particular to D. R. Green and A. Owens, 'Gentlewomanly capitalism? Spinsters, widows and wealth holding in England and Wales, c. 1800–1860', *Economic History Review* 56, 2003, pp. 510–36. See also Licini, 'Women's wealth'.

26 Refer in particular to M. Wiesner, *Women and Gender in Early Modern Europe*, Cambridge: Cambridge University Press, 1993 and T. Petersson, 'The silent partners', in R. C. Beachy, B. Craig and A. Owens (eds), *Women, Business and Finance in Nineteenth-Century Europe*, Oxford: Berg, 2006.

27 Ministero della Finanze, Direzione generale delle imposte dirette, *Elenco dei contribuenti all'imposta sulla ricchezza mobile*, pp. 4–5. Further considerations on this Italian fiscal source in P. Frascani, *Finanza, economia ed intervento pubblico dall'Unificazione agli anni trenta*, Bologna: Il Mulino, 1982.

28 S. Licini, 'Donne e affari a Milano nell'Ottocento', *Annali di storia d'impresa* 18, 2007, pp. 53–73.

29 See, on the topic, S. Licini, 'Finanza e industria a Milano nel triennio 1870–73: azionisti.e. nuove imprese', *Rivista di storia economica*, n.s., XI (2), 1994, pp. 213–52.

30 On the topic see in particular C. Saraceno, 'Le donne nella famiglia: una complesssa ricostruzione giuridica, 1750–1942', in M. Barbagli and D. Kertzer (eds), *Storia della famiglia italiana, 1750–1950*, Bologna: Il Mulino, 1992, pp. 103–27.

31 Due to the fact that in the sample years 1871–81 a widow and a spinster died who were great landowners' only heiresses. Licini, 'Women's wealth'.

32 See, for example, the evidence provided by A. Owens, 'Making some provision for the contingencies to which their sex is particularly liable: women and investment in early nineteenth century England', in Beachy, Craig and Owens, *Women, Business and Finance* and D. R. Green, 'Independent women', in J. Stobart and A. Owens (eds), *Urban Fortunes: Property and Inheritance in the Town, 1700–1900*, Aldershot: Ashgate, 2000.

33 S. Licini, 'Women as investors: some evidence from the case of Milan, Italy (1860–1890)', paper presented at the Sixth European Social Science History Conference, Amsterdam, 22–25 March 2006.

34 ASM Successioni, *ad vocem*.

35 ASM Successioni, *ad vocem*.

36 Details about the buildings speculation in nineteenth century Milan, can be found in G. Bigatti, 'Spazi urbani.e. industria a Milano nei decenni centrali dell'ottocento', *Società e storia* 52, 1991, pp. 363–91, and M. Tiepolo, 'La proprietà immobiliare nel quartiere dell'ex Lazzaretto a Milano dal 1882 al 1892', in *Storia urbana* 39, 1987, pp. 163–84.

37 ASM Succesioni, *ad vocem*.

38 M. R. Hunt, *The Middling Sort. Commerce, Gender and the Family in England, 1680–1780*, Berkeley, CA: University of California Press, 1996, p. 146

39 Beachy *et al.*, *Women, Business and Finance*, 'Introduction'.

Bibliography

Banti, A. M., 'Una fonte per lo studio delle élites ottocentesche: le dichiarazioni di successione dell'Ufficio del registro', *Rassegna degli archivi di stato* 1, 1983, pp. 83–118.

Beachy, R. C., Craig, B. and Owens, A., 'Introduction', in Beachy, R. C., Craig, B. and Owens, A. (eds), *Women, Business and Finance in Nineteenth-Century Europe*, Oxford: Berg, 2006, pp. 1–19.

Bellomo, M., *La condizione giuridica della donna in Italia: vicende antiche e moderne*, Turin: Eri, 1970.

Berg, M., 'Women's property and the industrial revolution', *Journal of Interdisciplinary History* 24 (2), pp. 223–50.

Bigatti, G., 'Spazi urbani.e. industria a Milano nei decenni centrali dell'ottocento', *Società e storia* 52, 1991, pp. 363–91.

Cafaro, P., 'Finanziamento e ruolo della banca', in Zaninelli, S. and Cafaro, P. (eds), *Alla guida della prima industrializzazione italiana. Dall'unità politica alla fine dell'Ottocento*, Milan: Il Polifilo, 1990–1, pp. 159–259.

Caizzi, B., *L'economia lombarda durante la Restaurazione: 1814–1859*, Milan: Banca commerciale italiana, 1972.

Chabot, I., 'Risorse e diritti patrimoniali', in Groppi, A. (ed.), *Il lavoro delle donne*, Bari: Laterza, 1996, pp. 47–69.

Codice civile del Regno d'Italia, 2nd edn, Firenze: E. Sonzogno, 1865.

Crosswhite, B. A., 'Women and land: aristocratic ownership of property in early modern England', *New York University Law Review* 77 (4), 2002, pp. 1119–56.

Dalmasso, E., *Milano capitale economica d'Italia*, Milano: Franco Angeli, 1972.

Della Peruta, F., *Milano. Lavoro e fabbrica, 1814–1915*, Milano: Franco Angeli, 1987.

Fazio, I., 'Le ricchezze e le donne: verso una ri-problematizzazione', *Quaderni Storici* 34, 1999, pp. 539–50.

Fazio, I., 'Valori economici.e. valori simbolici: il declino della dote nell' Italia dell'Ottocento', *Quaderni Storici* 27, 1992, pp. 291–311.

Fioravanzo, M., 'Sull'autorizzazione maritale. Ricerche sulla condizione giuridica femminile nell'Italia Unita', *Clio. Rivista trimestrale di studi storici* 4, 1994, pp. 641–725.

Frascani, P., *Finanza, economia ed intervento pubblico dall'Unificazione agli anni trenta*, Bologna: Il Mulino, 1982.

Galoppini, A. M., *Il lungo viaggio verso la parità. I diritti civili.e. politici delle donne dall'unità ad oggi*, Bologna: Il Mulino, 1980.

Green, D. R., 'Independent women, wealth and wills in nineteenth-century London', in Stobart, J. and Owens, A. (eds), *Urban Fortunes: Property and Inheritance in the Town, 1700–1900*, Aldershot: Ashgate, 2000, pp. 186–221.

Green, D. R. and Owens, A., 'Gentlewomanly capitalism? Spinsters, widows and wealth holding in England and Wales, c.1800–1860', *Economic History Review* 56, 2003, pp. 510–36.

Green, D. R. and Owens, A., 'Metropolitan estates of the middle-class, 1800–50: Probates and death duties revisited', *Historical Research* 70, 1997, pp. 294–311.

Hunecke, V., *Classe operaia e rivoluzione industriale a Milano, 1859–1892*, Bologna: Il Mulino, 1982.

Hunt, M. R., *The Middling Sort. Commerce, Gender and the Family in England, 1680–1780*, Berkeley, CA: University of California Press, 1996.

'Legge generale sul registro', 21 April 1862, in *Raccolta ufficiale delle leggi.e. dei decreti del Regno d'Italia*, Turin: Stamperia reale, 1861–1946.

Licini, S., 'Donne e affari a Milano nell'Ottocento', *Annali di storia d'impresa*, 18, 2007, pp. 53–73.

Licini, S., 'Women as investors: some evidence from the case of Milan, Italy (1860–1890)', paper presented at the Sixth European Social Science History Conference, Amsterdam, 22–25 March 2006.

Licini, S., 'Women's wealth in nineteenth-century: some evidence from the probate records of Milan, Italy (1862–1900)', *Women's History Magazine* 53, 2006, pp. 13–21.

Licini, S., *Guida ai patrimoni milanesi. Le dichiarazioni di successione ottocentesche*, Soveria Mannelli: Rubbettino, 1999.

Licini, S., 'Banca e credito a Milano, nella prima fase dell'industrializzazione (1840–1880)', in Decleva, E. (ed.), *Antonio Allievi: dalle 'scienze civili' alla pratica del credito*, Rome and Bari: Laterza, 1997, pp. 527–59.

Licini, S., 'Finanza e industria a Milano nel triennio 1870–73: azionisti.e. nuove imprese', *Rivista di storia economica*, n.s., XI (2), 1994, pp. 213–52.

Malatesta, M., *Le aristocrazie terriere nell'Europa contemporanea*, Bari: Laterza, 1999.

Ministero delle Finanze, Direzione generale delle imposte dirette, *Elenco dei contribuenti all'imposta sulla ricchezza mobile aventi un reddito imponibile complessivo superiore alle 1.000 lire, desunti dai ruoli principali del 1872*, Firenze: Stamperia reale, 1873, vol. 1.

Mitson, A., 'An exchange of letters: estate management and Lady Yarborough', *Women's History Review* 7 (4), 1998, pp. 547–63.

Morris, R. J., 'Men, women and property: the reform of the Married Women's Property Act, 1870', in Thompson, F. M. L. (ed.), *Landowners, Capitalists and Entrepreneurs: Essays for Sir John Habbakuk*, Oxford: Clarendon Press, 1994, pp. 171–91.

Owens, A., 'Making some provision for the contingencies to which their sex is particularly liable: women and investment in early nineteenth century England', in Beachy, R. C., Craig, B. and Owens, A. (eds), *Women, Business and Finance in Nineteenth-Century Europe*, Oxford: Berg, 2006, pp. 20–35.

Petersson, T. 'The silent partners: women, capital and the development of the financial system in nineteenth-century Sweden', in Beachy, R. C., Craig, B. and Owens, A. (eds), *Women, Business and Finance in Nineteenth-Century Europe*, Oxford: Berg, 2006, pp. 36–51.

Saraceno, C., 'Le donne nella famiglia: una complessa ricostruzione giuridica, 1750–1942', in Barbagli, M. and Kertzer, D. (eds), *Storia della famiglia italiana, 1750–1950*, Bologna: Il Mulino, 1992, pp. 103–27.

Saraceno, C., 'Women, family, and the law, 1750–1942', *Journal of Family History* 15, 1990, pp. 427–42.

Sarogni, E., *La Donna Italiana: Il Lungo Cammino Verso i Diritti, 1861–1994*, Parma: Pratiche, 1995.

Stobart, J. and Owens, A. (eds), *Urban Fortunes. Property and Inheritance in the Town, 1700–1900*, Aldershot: Ashgate, 2000.

Tiepolo, M., 'La proprietà immobiliare nel quartiere dell'ex Lazzaretto a Milano dal 1882 al 1892', *Storia urbana* 39, 1987, pp. 163–84.

Ungari, P., *Storia del diritto di famiglia in Italia*, Bologna: Il Mulino, 1974.

Vincenzi Amato, D., 'La famiglia e il diritto' in Melograni, P. (ed.), *La famiglia italiana dall'Ottocento a oggi*, Bari: Laterza, 1988, pp. 629–700.

Vismara, G., *Il Diritto di famiglia in Italia dalla Riforma ai Codici. Appunti*, Milan: Giuffrè, 1978.

Wiesner, M. E., *Women and Gender in Early Modern Europe*, Cambridge: Cambridge University Press, 1993.

Zaninelli, S. and Cafaro, P. (eds), *Alla guida della prima industrializzazione italiana. Dall'unità politica alla fine dell'Ottocento*, Milan: Il Polifilo, 1990.

Zaninelli, S. (ed.), *Un sistema manifatturiero aperto al mercato, dal Settecento all'Unità politica*, Milan: Il Polifilo, 1988.

20 The transformation from 'thrifty accountant' to 'independent investor'?

The changing relationship of Japanese women and finance under the influence of globalization[1]

Naoko Komori

Introduction

Japan is witnessing the increasing involvement of women in investment and financial activities. The issue of finance is a key concern among Japanese women: a recent survey reported that 'finance and money' is the primary interest of women in Japan, pushing 'health' into second place.[2]

The growth in investment activity among women highlights how the relationship between women and finance in Japan has changed. Women in Japan have historically had a strong association with bookkeeping and accounting at home, and they have had control over the domestic economy since the pre-modern era.[3] Household accounting practice has been a significant tool in household management: it has enabled women to manage and control the behaviour of their husbands and has been the backbone of their authority within the household at key points in Japanese history. This strong association between women and domestic accounting has been closely linked to the government-defined social role of the household: to accumulate savings that can be used to fund investment in industry. However, under the influence of globalization, government policy with regard to the social role of the household has changed. The recent strengthening of the relationship between women and investment has been driven by policy changes that have encouraged them to make the transition from accountant to investor.

The changes that Japan is currently experiencing in the relationship between women and accounting and finance provide a number of interesting perspectives from which to develop the historical study of gender issues in accounting and finance. First, the experience of Japanese women as financial managers and accountants in the domestic arena may illuminate a history that in the past has all too often been ignored in favour of concentration on women's experiences in the public arena. Recent decades have seen a growing awareness in gender research in accounting in the West of the importance of shifting the research

focus onto the experiences of women in the private arena.[4] Using new materials
such as personal records, these studies have shed valuable light on the hidden
economic activities of women outside the accounting profession.[5] In particular,
Japan provides an interesting research site since women have continued their
accounting practice in the domestic arena at the same time as they have started
to enter the public arena. Monitoring their accounting practice in the two different spheres will help us to understand how women's relationship with accounting in the domestic arena has been affected by their changing role in the public
arena.

Second, the study of Japanese women's experiences will supply evidence
from a non-Anglo-Saxon context. Although gender research in accounting has
made significant progress, this area of research is still dominated by the experiences of women in Anglo-Saxon countries and their perspectives. There has
been a call for research that looks beyond the comfort zone of the Anglo-Saxon
countries and reveals accounting in action in unfamiliar, non-Anglo-Saxon settings.[6] Study of the Japanese context would be a profitable way of responding to
this call.

Third, such a study will illuminate women's role and position in the world of
investments. Although many studies have revealed the relationship between
gender and accounting, the close examination of the role of women investors has
only just begun.[7] By examining the changing nature of Japanese women's financial activity, the process by which women have made the transition from
accountants to investors may be mapped.

With these aims in mind, this chapter seeks to understand the driving forces
behind women's changing relationship with accounting and finance, and what
the resultant changes signify. It does so by locating the increasing involvement
of women with investment activities within the historical development of the
relationship between women and accounting in Japan. First, the chapter examines the relationship currently developing between Japanese women and investment agencies. The following section gives an overview of the changing
relationship between women and accounting in different periods in Japanese
history. These include: pre-modern times; the periods of modernization, industrialization and the inter-war period; the post-war period and the era of globalization currently taking place. Each section explores the changes in the role and
position of women in accounting and finance and how these have influenced
women's lives. The chapter concludes by considering the forces driving their
increasing involvement in investment activities.

Women and investment: the experience of women in Japan

The relationship between women and investment activity has become stronger in
Japan in recent years. A number of securities companies, in conjunction with the
Tokyo Stock Exchange, now hold investment seminars for women to promote
their understanding of investment. A number of large department stores and cosmetics companies have held women-only investor relationship (IR) seminars.[8] In

these seminars, the lectures on how to build up an investment portfolio follow make-up lessons and wine-tasting sessions. Women investors are beginning to feature in the mass media. An increasing number of books and articles have been published that talk about the significance of investments for women and encourage their involvement.[9] The increasing involvement of women in investment activities signifies that the traditional role of women in the household and their relationship with household accounting are undergoing profound change.

The current trend is being driven by the interaction between women's demand for investment activities and the supply from banks and business corporations eager to offer them such opportunities.

Japanese women are showing a keen interest in investing in property as well as in stocks and other financial products. The first women-only IR seminar held in March 2006 by Resona Bank, one of the major banks in Japan, attracted applications from some 500 women for 180 seats.[10] Their growing interest in investment activities reflects their demand for independence from their traditional role in the household. This is also evident in women's increasing awareness of their entitlement to a share of the household assets. According to a study conducted by the Institute for Research on Household Economics, approximately 46 per cent of women interviewed in 2000 felt it was important to protect their entitlement to joint assets; this figure had increased to 80 per cent by 2006.[11] The growing awareness among women of their entitlement to property ownership signifies a change in the gender roles that have historically sustained the integrity of the Japanese household; old attitudes are dissolving, with household members becoming more individual-oriented.

Since the end of the 1990s, as interest among women has grown, companies, banks and securities companies have been intensifying their efforts to attract more women investors, in order to increase diversity among independent investors. These companies are paying particular attention to female investors, whom they consider more careful and serious, qualities conducive to long-term investment relationships.[12]

Thus, as women demand greater access to investment opportunities and Japanese companies seek to attract more female investors, this mutually supportive cycle means that the involvement of women in finance may be expected to strengthen. The fact that this process has been led by the demand from women raises the question of what has aroused women's interest in investment issues. What is their role within the household, how has this role been constructed and what makes them seek independence from it? We now turn to the past to seek answers to these questions.

The historical development of women's role in financial management and their accounting practices

'Okami-san' (female proprietor): women's role as financial managers in the pre-modern era

We first examine the pre-modern period before the Meiji Restoration in 1868; this includes ancient and medieval times (*chusei*) as well as the *Tokugawa Shogiunate* Era (*kinsei*), the period when Japan prepared for the coming of modernization under the Tokugawa Regime (1603–1867).

In ancient and medieval times (until the middle of the fourteenth century), farmers, fishermen and merchants made up 80 per cent of the population in Japan. The household as a social unit, based upon the husband and wife partnership, did not prevail until the tenth century.[13] Many of the ancient agricultural villages were organized along communal lines with the community determining issues such as exchanges of work and marriage alliances for its members.[14] In these villages, where the economy ran on a non-monetary basis, women had control over rice. In a context where rice functioned as a form of currency, 'control over rice meant control over the domestic economy'.[15]

The woman's role as the manager of the domestic economy was further strengthened in medieval times when the household started to prevail as a social unit. In medieval times, the household (*ie*) came increasingly to replace the community, establishing itself as the unit that determined the social role of individuals. Women were allocated the job of managing the finances of the household and their role was closely linked to the nature of the *ie*.

Under the Tokugawa Regime (established in 1600), the country isolated itself from foreign trade and set up a social structure that would later enable it to resist the unwanted elements in the tide of Westernization that swept the country at the end of the nineteenth century. Alongside the drive towards modernization, Tokugawa society retained the pre-modern characteristic of being strictly divided into different classes, and there were clear differences between the ruling samurai class and the other classes in terms of the position of women.

In the samurai class, which enjoyed the most privileged position in Tokugawa society, women were kept out of the public sphere, which was dominated by men. Instead, they remained in the back room of the house (*oku*) and had no involvement with economic activities. On the other hand, women in the commoner's class, which was unaffected by Confucian ideology, enjoyed a more significant role. Women in the merchant class, in particular, occupied important positions as bookkeepers[16] and financial managers, running the business in the absence of their husbands.[17]

Mine (1771–1828), the only daughter of a merchant in Wakayama in Western Japan, married a man who at 21 succeeded to the household business. It was her job to record the flow of goods through the shop, bookkeeping and cross-checking the accounts.[18] She also supported her husband by welcoming visitors and keeping a detailed record of the gifts they were given (type and volume).

Women household heads did not just play a supporting role to their male counterparts; they often took centre stage if the male household head died or was incapable. Juhou (1590–1676), the mother of Takatoshi Mitsui, the first master of a prominent merchant family that developed itself into one of the biggest *zaibatsu* families in Japan, actively engaged in the family business, while her husband devoted his time to reading poetry, playing cards and art. Her talents for business and client management were widely recognized; subsequent generations of the Mitsui family paid great respect to Juhou, calling her the founder of the Mitsui business.[19]

In merchant families of the Tokugawa era, women were called *Okami-san*, which means female proprietor, and not *Oku-san*, which literally signifies wives who stay in the back room of the house (where samurais' wives were located). Bookkeeping and accounting work was a central task for the women in merchant households.

Growing awareness of identity among women and state control: modernization, industrialization and the inter-war period (from the Meiji Period (1868) to the beginning of the Showa Period (early twentieth century))

However, women in the commoner's class began to lose the power they had had in the traditional household (*ie*) in the modern period. The modern period began with the defeat of the Tokugawa Regime in the middle of the nineteenth century and the establishment of the Meiji government in 1868. After isolating itself for more than two centuries, the country opened up commercial and diplomatic contacts with Western countries. Under the national goal of 'catching up with the West', the Meiji government made a series of social, economic and political reforms to transform Japan from an agrarian to an industrial economy. One such reform was the construction of the family–state structure. The traditional Japanese household (*ie*) eventually came to be replaced by the patriarchal family system instituted by the Meiji government. In this family–state structure, the role of women was to serve their men and to maintain the continuity of the Japanese patriarchal family system. The role defined for women by the Meiji government led to a change in the role of household accounting, and consequently to a decline in the power and position of women in the household in the commoner's class.[20] The state stressed that it was important for women to manage their household accounting in such a way as to accumulate savings that could then be used to fund the new industries and develop military power. The government also introduced informal bookkeeping into the formal education programme for women. Thus, accounting was employed by the state as an instrument to construct the knowledge that helped to establish social gender roles and the position of women in society.[21]

The significance of household accounting was also recognized by some of the women themselves. Mrs Motoko Hani, Japan's first woman journalist, played a leading role in the modernization of Japanese households by establishing the women's magazine *Fujin no Tomo* (The Women's Friend), and publishing the first household accounting book in Japan. Since its establishment, *Fujin no Tomo* has played an important role in supporting women's household accounting work.[22]

The position determined for women by the state was challenged during the process of modernization and industrialization. From the last decade of the nineteenth century, the government set up initiatives to make the country an industrially advanced nation and to build up its military power to enable it to defend its independence. The demand for workers helped to increase the opportunities available to women to engage in work beyond the household. As their activities outside the home expanded, some women in Japan's urban centres started to question their position and their identity, which encouraged the growth of the feminist movement in Japan.

It was the war regime that resolved the conflict between the role and position advocated for women by the state and women's own growing awareness of their feminine identity.[23] The Japanese government not only controlled the entire economy but also initiated a number of policies to strengthen national unity and accumulate capital to support military and industrial development. Savings goals were set by the government for Japanese citizens: they were ordered to save 23 billion yen in 1941. The state also redefined the role of women as 'mothers of the nation', encouraging women to serve their country by helping to amass the savings necessary for military and industrial investment.

Women proactively responded to the role given them by the government to a degree unique in Japanese history. A number of women's groups were set up, the initiative coming from women themselves rather than from the government, coming together to share ideas and give mutual support with household accounting practice.[24] They particularly emphasized that cooperation among neighbours was a way of enhancing community spirit. *Fujin no Tomo* encouraged this community spirit by urging its readers to share their household accounting problems with their neighbours:

> After paying rent, tax, compulsory savings, and sending some money to my mother, 33 yen remains in my hand. I cannot spend this on clothing, furniture or entertainment. I have an extra income of 14 or 15 yen which I earn once or twice a year. For food, I spend 2 sen [1 yen equals 100 sen] in the morning, 3 sen on lunch, and 4 sen for dinner. I spend 24 sen 5 days a month in order to enjoy eating beef and pork. My husband's pocket money is 3 yen and 82 sen. This amount seems large, but this is actually used for my children's stationery and snacks for guests. When some money remains, we go somewhere with the children.[25]

It must be noted that these actions by the publishers of women's magazines, like women's efforts to encourage national unity, were not the result of state intervention. Women were seeking an independent feminine identity and a sense of social purpose, which they found by embracing the 'mother of the nation' role advocated by the state and by contributing to national savings through their household accounting practice.

Becoming an independent investor: post-war and the influence of globalization

The war regime set down the basis of the social structure that operated in post-war Japan. After Japan's defeat in the Second World War, the Allied Forces embarked on the drastic reform of Japanese society, with the aim of rebuilding Japan as a democratic country. Society was reconstructed in such a way as to revitalize its economy and industry: in the so-called 'Corporate Society', business enterprises would play the central role.[26] Japanese companies and the government constructed the post-war Japanese family as a site for the reproduction of the human resources that corporations need and to generate savings for corporate investment. The government took the initiative by supporting a savings promotion movement. In 1952, the Central Council for Savings Information (CCSI) was established with the support of the Japanese government. CCSI organized study groups and sent officers to different districts in Japan to spread the idea of lifestyle planning and to emphasize the importance of saving through prudent household accounting practice.

Housewives became a widespread phenomenon in the Corporate Society. This development came to Japan relatively late compared to the Western industrialized nations, where a large proportion of women were already housewives in the nineteenth century.[27] However, housewives in Japan were expected to play an important social role; they were initially expected to support corporate activities from within the household, bringing up the next generation of corporate warriors and accumulating the savings necessary for corporate investment. They proactively responded to this call through the practice of household accounting. The nature of their household accounting practice was and remains unique; it is characterized by detail and cooperation, taking in lifestyle choices, family values and broader social issues such as the environment. Some women in Japan have used accounting at home to foster shared values and family unity by holding family conferences to design long-term investment plans. Household accounting information has not only assisted women to educate their children about monetary values; it has also helped to raise the awareness of family members of wider social policies by highlighting non-consumable expenditure such as tax, social insurance, health and housing. In addition, by enabling families to calculate their CO_2 emissions from their expenditure on fossil fuels, household accounting has made consumers more environmentally aware.[28] The household accounting practice of generations of Japanese women has made a vital contribution to the country's national savings and corporate activities.

However, some women have more recently begun to use accounting for a different purpose. In the 1970s, housewives established a number of consumer groups, such as *Shufu Rengo Kai* (The Japan Housewives' Association). These associations have acted collectively to challenge powerful corporate/government institutions and have exerted political influence over political activities. Household accounting records gathered from association members have provided significant evidence to legitimize their actions.[29]

Post-war change has also brought new opportunities for women to engage in accounting work in the public arena. With the introduction after the Second World War of the US model of auditing and corporate financial disclosure, accountants began to organize and establish their profession. For those women seeking to escape from their traditional role and lead an independent life, the accounting profession has offered a good career. In 2002, women comprised 19.2 per cent of the candidates for the CPA examination. This highlights the dramatic increase in the number of women in the accounting profession since the early 1980s, when the figure was 3 per cent. The increase in the number of women seeking entry into the profession is expected to continue, as more women are driven by their wish to realize their independent identity.[30]

Following the globalization of the last two decades, women in Japan are increasingly taking up investment activities. Under the aim of establishing an internationally attractive financial market, Japan's Financial Service Agency set up a programme they called 'Moving towards a financial service nation' to reform the financial system. In this programme, the emphasis in household finance has shifted from savings to investment and asset management, with the aim of revitalizing the economy by mobilizing the huge savings currently frozen in banks offering close to zero interest rates. In 2001, The Central Council for Financial Information (CCFI) was established, replacing the CCSI. The CCFI is playing a major role in the disseminating of financial and economic information, running a wide range of activities in schools and local communities to promote sensible financial and life planning.

Women's increasing involvement in investment activities is also related to the growing globalization of the capital market and the influence this has had on the ownership structure of Japanese corporations. Foreign investors have grown significantly; by 2005 they were some of the biggest traders in the Japanese securities market.[31] Through their repeated criticism of the group-oriented nature of Japanese corporate management, these foreign investors have helped to promote transparency among Japanese corporate management, leading to a reduction in mutual shareholdings among Japanese banks and business corporations. Currently, a number of government policies are being redirected towards individual investors, and business corporations have also been at pains to improve their relations with individual investors. In this context, women investors are expected to have a significant effect on the business corporations' shift from group-oriented financing in a development that could further enhance the transparency and diversity of corporate management. Increasingly, investment companies are launching products designed specially for female investors; the latest ethical investment funds encourage women to invest in companies that promote women to managerial positions and sell women's goods and services.[32]

Simultaneously, women themselves are showing increasing interest in becoming investors. This is one outcome of the greater freedom Japanese women have to choose their own lifestyle. In contrast to the past, when the only option open to women was to be a 'good mother and wife', a growing number of women are marrying later, or choosing not to marry at all; the percentage of unmarried women has continued to rise, while the average marriage age is now 27-plus, compared to 24 in 1990.[33] The general tendency is for these unmarried women to live with their parents, a phenomenon that is affecting the housing market. At the same time, women in Japan are increasingly seeking independence from their traditional household role; the divorce rate has climbed steadily from 0.5 per cent in 1970 to 2.4 per cent in 2003.[34] These figures suggest that the gender roles embedded in the Corporate Society and the traditional life patterns (particularly of women) that have sustained it are dissolving. In spite of the changing expectations and perceptions of women, however, corporations still offer few opportunities for women to progress their careers. Less than 10 per cent of women are promoted to managerial positions, the lowest figure in any industrialized country.[35] Although employment among women is increasing steadily, many are still positioned as only 'irregular' employees (i.e. temporary, part-time or casual workers). Against this background, more women are realizing that, in order to have the freedom to live as they wish, they must first secure economic independence; and that skilful asset investment and management should form part of their life plan.

Conclusion

Maltby and Rutterford (2006) identified two ways in which women are involved in economic activities: as accountants and as investors. This historical review of the experience of Japanese women in accounting and finance has revealed that women in Japan are currently making the transition from the first role to the second.

The growth in their involvement with investment activities has been led by an increasing demand among women for independence from the household, and for freedom from the role and position that has been defined for them by the state since the modern period. Examination of the historical relationship between Japanese women and accounting demonstrates that their demand for independence has developed gradually throughout Japanese history; their role in household accounting has had a significant impact on women's lives, and in the post-war period, it helped to shape their sense of independent feminine identity. In a social context where the opportunities for women to enter the public arena are still limited, investment activities have the potential to help them achieve the economic independence they need to realize this identity.

At the same time, globalization has significantly helped to strengthen their relationship with the investment market. With the globalization of business and capital markets, Japanese business and society have had to restructure themselves: Japanese business corporations have been pressured to change their traditional behaviours, while the state has redefined the role of the household. The repositioning of Japanese corporate business in the global economy and the impact this has had on society have been key factors in raising the profile of female investors.

The Japanese experience suggests that the relationship between women and investment in the country is crucially affected by the interactive relationship between women's social role and position, and the position of the Japanese corporations in the global economy. It would certainly be worth monitoring whether their investment activities have as significant an impact on these women's lives and identities as accounting has done throughout Japanese history.

Notes

1 I would like to express my thanks to Professor Kimiko Kimoto, Ryoko Okazaki and Masaya Ono from the Bank of Japan and Koko Chiba from *Fujin no Tomo* for offering me much valuable information. This project was supported financially by The Daiwa Anglo-Japanese Foundation and the Japan Foundation. Both are gratefully acknowledged.

2 Nikko Cordial Co., '*Josei ni yutaka na jinsei no tameno toshi wo gotean suru kikakubusho wo shinsetsu* (Attracting women to investment)', 2005, available online: www.nikko.co.jp/news/2005/pdf/050310.pdf (accessed 5 June 2006).

3 N. Komori, 'The "hidden" history of accounting in Japan: an historical examination of the relationship between Japanese women and accounting', *Accounting History* 12 (3), 2007, pp. 329–358.

4 See for example, S. Walker, 'Identifying women behind the railed in desk', *Accounting, Auditing and Accountability Journal* 16 (4), 2003, pp. 606–639; S. Walker and S. Llewellyn, 'Accounting at home: some interdisciplinary perspectives', *Accounting, Auditing and Accountability Journal* 13 (4), 2000, pp. 425–449. Also, see L. Kirkham and A. Loft, 'The lady and the accounts: missing from accounting history?', *Accounting Historians Journal* 28, June 2001, pp. 66–80: G. Carnegie and S. Walker, 'Household accounting in Australia: a microhistorical study', *Accounting, Auditing and Accountability Journal* 20 (2), 2007, pp. 210–236.

5 Stephen Walker, 'Octavia Hill: property manager and accountant', Chapter 12 in this volume.

6 See, for example, M. Annisette, 'People and period untouched by accounting history: an ancient Yoruba practice', *Accounting History* 11 (4), 2006, pp. 399–417.

7 J. Maltby and J. Rutterford, 'Editorial: women, accounting and investment', *Accounting, Business and Financial History* 16 (2), 2006, pp. 133–142.

8 *Nikkei Financial Newspaper*, 'Shiseido and Kosei – developing women investors', 9 November 2004; *Nikkei Marketing Journal*, 'Kosei – holding women-only IR seminars with make-up lessons', 7 September 2004, p. 27.

9 For example, the *Mainichi Economist Journal* published a special issue on female investors in March 2006, highlighting their experiences of and perspectives on investment.

10 *The Japan Times*, 'Banks target women's purse strings amid growing interest in investment', May 23 2006, available online: http://search.japantimes.co.jp/print/nb20060523a4.html (accessed 2 June 2006).

11 M. Mihune, '*Josei no kinyu shisan to jutaku shoyu* (Women's ownership of financial assets and property)', in *Kakei Keizai Kenkyusho* (Institute for Research on Household Economics), *Research Report no. 3: Josei no Lifecourse to Jutaku shoyu* (Women's Lifecourse and Property), Tokyo: Institute for Research on Household Economics, 2006, p. 76.

12 K. Kawabuchi, '*Josei kabunushi kakutoku no torikumi* (Activities to attract women investors)', *Kigyo Kaikei* (Corporate Accounting) 57 (6), 2005, pp. 70–71.

13 K. Inuma, '*Goke no chikara-sono seiristu to yakuwari wo megutte* (Power of *goke*: its establishment and role)', in S. Minegishi (ed.), *Chusei wo kangaeru kazoku to josei* (The Study of Family and Women in Medieval Japan), Tokyo: Yoshikawa Kobunkan, 1992, p. 164.

14 C. Ueno, 'Position of Japanese women reconsidered', *Current Anthropology* 28 (4), August–October 1987, S77–78.

15 C. Ueno, 'Position of Japanese women reconsidered', S77–78.

16 M. Maxon, 'Women in family business', in J. Lebra, J. Paulson and E. Powers (eds), *Women in Changing Japan*, Boulder, CO: Western Press, 1976, pp. 89–106.

17 R. Hayashi, '*Machia josei to kagyo* (Women and household business)', in H. Wakita, R. Hayashi, and K. Nagahara (eds), *Nihon Josei Shi* (Women's History in Japan), Tokyo: Yoshikawa Koubunnkan, 1987, pp. 155–159.

18 R. Hayashi, '*Machia josei to kagyo*', pp. 157–158.

19 R. Hayashi, '*Machia josei to kagyo*', pp. 156–157.

20 N. Komori, 'The "hidden" history of accounting in Japan'.

21 N. Komori, 'The "hidden" history of accounting in Japan'.

22 *Fujin no Tomo*, '*Itsukara demo Kakei Jouzu* (Good Household Economy)', Tokyo: Dainihon Insatsu, 2006, p. 33.

23 For a discussion on how household accounting helped to strengthen women's motivation to support the war regime, and helped to accommodate the interests of the state and those of women, see N. Komori, 'The "hidden" history of accounting in Japan'.

24 N. Komori, 'The "hidden" history of accounting in Japan'.

25 *Fujin no Tomo*, '*Kakeibo ga kataru seikatsushi* (The Life History of 90 Years of Household Bookkeeping)', *Fujin no Tomo* 87 (4), 1993, p. 58.

26 K. Kimoto, *Kazoku, Gender, Kigyoushakai* (Family, Gender, Corporate Society), Kyoto: Minerva Shobou, 1995; K. Kimoto, '*Kigyou shakai ron karano approach* (Approach from corporate society perspective)', in K. Ishihara (ed.), *Kazoku to Shokugyo: Kyougou to Chousei* (Family and Work: Competition and Control), Tokyo: Minerva Shobou, 2002, pp. 62–86.

27 K. Tanaka, 'Work, education and the family', in K. Fujiwara-Fanselow and A. Kameda (eds), *Japanese Women: New Feminist Perspectives on the Past, Present and Future*, New York: The Feminist Press, 1995, p. 305.

28 For examples of household accounting practice in post-war Japan, and how this practice and people's experiences have changed, see N. Komori and C. Humphrey, 'From an envelope to a dream note and a computer: the award-winning experiences of post-war Japanese household accounting practices', *Accounting, Auditing and Accountability Journal* 13 (4), 2000, pp. 456–470.

29 N. Komori, 'The "hidden" history of accounting in Japan'.

30 N. Komori, 'Choosing to be *kyapi kyapi* or *gati gati*: the real-life experiences of women in the accounting profession in Japan', Interdisciplinary Perspectives on Accounting (IPA) conference, Cardiff, July 2006.

31 Tokyo Stock Exchange, 'The survey result on the stock distribution and ownership structure in 2006', Tokyo: Tokyo Stock Exchange, 2006.

32 *Financial Times*, 'Japanese funds tap into women power', 1 June 2006.

33 National Council for Women's Education, *Danjo Kyoudo Sanka Toukei Data Book 2003* (Statistical Data Book on Gender Equality in Japan), Tokyo: Shinyosha, 2003, pp. 22–25.

34 A. Nagai, 'Women's lifecourse and property', in *Kakei Keizai Kenkyusho* (Institute for Research on Household Economics), *Research Report no. 3: Josei no Lifecourse to Jutaku shoyu* (Women's lifecourse and property), Tokyo: Institute for Research on Household Economics, 2006, pp. 56–64.

35 National Council for Women's Education, *Danjo Kyoudo Sanka Toukei Data Book 2003*, p. 38.

Bibliography

Annisette, M., 'People and period untouched by accounting history: an ancient Yoruba practice', *Accounting History* 11 (4), 2006, pp. 399–417.

Carnegie, G. and Walker, S. 'Household accounting in Australia: a microhistorical study', *Accounting, Auditing and Accountability Journal* 20 (2), 2007, pp. 210–236.

Financial Times, 'Japanese funds tap into women power', 1 June 2006.

Fujin no Tomo, '*Itsukara demo Kakei Jouzu* (Good Household Economy)', Tokyo: Dainihon Insatsu, 2006.

Fujin no Tomo, '*Kakeibo ga kataru seikatsushi* (The Life History of 90 Years of Household Bookkeeping)', *Fujin no Tomo* 87 (4), 1993, pp. 51–82.

Hayashi, R., '*Machia josei to kagyo* (Women and household business)', in Wakita, H., Hayashi, R. and Nagahara, K. (eds), *Nihon Josei Shi* (Women's History in Japan), Tokyo: Yoshikawa Koubunnkan, 1987, pp. 155–159.

Inuma, K., '*Goke no chikara-sono seiritsu to yakuwari wo megutte* (Power of *goke*: its establishment and role)', in Minegishi, S. (ed.) *Chusei wo kangaeru kazoku to josei* (The Study of Family and Women in Medieval Japan), Tokyo: Yoshikawa Kobunkan, 1992, pp. 152–178.

Japan Times, 'Banks target women's purse strings amid growing interest in investment', 23 May 2006, available online: http://search.japantimes.co.jp/print/nb20060523a4.html (accessed 2 June 2006).

Kawabuchi, K. '*Josei kabunushi kakutoku no torikumi* (Activities to attract women investors)', *Kigyo Kaikei* (Corporate Accounting) 57 (6), 2005, pp. 70–71.

Kimoto, K., '*Kigyou shakai ron karano approach* (Approach from corporate society perspective)', in Ishihara, K. (ed.), *Kazoku to Shokugyo: Kyougou to Chousei* (Family and Work: Competition and Control), Tokyo: Minerva Shobou, 2002, pp. 62–86.

Kimoto, K., *Kazoku, Gender, Kigyoushakai* (Family, Gender, Corporate Society), Kyoto: Minerva Shobou, 1995.

Kirkham, L. and Loft, A., 'The lady and the accounts: missing from accounting history?', *Accounting Historians Journal* 28, June 2001, pp. 66–80.

Komori, N., 'The "hidden" history of accounting in Japan: an historical examination of the relationship between Japanese women and accounting', *Accounting History* 12 (3), 2007, pp. 329–358.

Komori, N., 'Choosing to be *kyapi kyapi* or *gati gati*: The real-life experiences of women in the accounting profession in Japan', Interdisciplinary Perspectives on Accounting (IPA) conference, Cardiff, July 2006.

Komori, N. and Humphrey, C., 'From an envelope to a dream note and a computer: the award-winning experiences of post-war Japanese household accounting practices', *Accounting, Auditing and Accountability Journal* 13 (4), 2000, pp. 450–474.

Maltby, J. and Rutterford, J., 'Editorial: women, accounting and investment' *Accounting, Business and Financial History* 16 (2), 2006, pp. 133–142.

Maxon, M., 'Women in family business', in Lebra, J., Paulson, J. and E. Powers (eds), *Women in Changing Japan*, Boulder, CO: Western Press, 1976, pp. 89–106.

Mihune, M. '*Josei no kinyu shisan to jutaku shoyu* (Women's ownership of financial assets and property)', in *Kakei Keizai Kenkyusho* (Institute for Research on Household Economics), *Research Report no. 3: Josei no Lifecourse to Jutaku shoyu* (Women's Lifecourse and Property), Tokyo: Institute for Research on Household Economics, 2006, pp. 71–89.

Nagai, A., 'Women's lifecourse and property', *Kakei Keizai Kenkyusho* (Institute for

Research on Household Economics), *Research Report no. 3: Josei no Lifecourse to Jutaku shoyu* (Women's Lifecourse and Property), Tokyo: Institute for Research on Household Economics, 2006, pp. 56–64.

National Council for Women's Education, *Danjo Kyoudo Sanka Toukei Data Book 2003* (Statistical data book on gender equality in Japan), Tokyo: Shinyosha.

Nikkei Financial Newspaper, 'Shiseido and Kosei – Developing Women Investors', 9 November 2004.

Nikkei Marketing Journal, 'Kosei holding women-only IR seminars with make-up lessons', 7 September 2004, p. 27.

Nikko Cordial Co., '*Josei ni yutaka na jinsei no tameno toshi wo gotean suru kikakubusho wo shinsetsu* (Attracting women to investment)', 2005, available online: www.nikko.co.jp/news/2005/pdf/050310.pdf (accessed 5 June 2006).

Tanaka, K., 'Work, education and the family', in Fujiwara-Fanselow, K. and Kameda, A. (eds), *Japanese Women: New Feminist Perspectives on the Past, Present and Future*, New York: The Feminist Press, 1995, pp. 295–308.

Tokyo Stock Exchange, 'The survey result on the stock distribution and ownership structure in 2006', Tokyo: Tokyo Stock Exchange, 2006.

Ueno, C., 'Position of Japanese women reconsidered', *Current Anthropology* 28 (4), August–October 1987, Supplement pp. S74–84.

Walker, S., 'Identifying women behind the railed in desk', *Accounting, Auditing and Accountability Journal*, 16 (4), 2003, pp. 606–639.

Walker, S. and Llewellyn, S., 'Accounting at home: some interdisciplinary perspectives', *Accounting, Auditing and Accountability Journal*, 13 (4), 2000, pp. 425–449.

Index

Made in the USA
San Bernardino, CA
08 December 2017